Patent Management and Valuation

T0295746

Professor Thoma provides a wonderful entrance into the strategic and geographic elements of patent valuation. His well-researched book offers a more complex, theoretical model that would help a range of legal and management audiences to more fully ground their future patent valuation.

—Kali Murray, Marquette University, USA

Research on patent valuation has become increasingly important in academic and policy circles in the last few decades. In part, this is the outcome of the wide consensus that innovation is a crucial ingredient for growth at various levels. On the other hand, there has also been an overcoming of growth models unilaterally focused on technological-oriented approaches. This book presents novel and original research on patent value determinants, which are intrinsic or extrinsic to the innovator's business model.

Grid Thoma has undertaken a long study on the strategic factors affecting patent valuation, bringing extensive quantitative evidences across various geographical and institutional contexts. Beforehand the valuation of the patent real options is appraised when the innovator can postpone the additional investment required for the patent's successful exploitation. Then, he analyses what other complementary IP strategies are combined with patenting that in turn directly affect the value of patents. Moreover, the book scrutinizes the so called 'strategic patenting' hypothesis according to which innovators obtain patents for other reasons beyond gaining IP protection.

A second order of strategic factors affecting the value of patents resides at the outset of the invention process. These are constituted by knowledge spillovers, which are typically mediated by the local geographical context where the invention process takes place. The analysis shows that the contribution of knowledge spillovers from business and nonbusiness organizations to the value of the patented R&D constitutes a relevant aspect for an innovator's decision making.

This thoughtful, cutting-edge research book is vital reading for researchers, academics, and policy decision makers in the area of in market valuation, management of technology, innovation management, and economic geography.

Grid Thoma is assistant professor with tenure of economics and management at University of Camerino, Italy.

Routledge Studies in Technology, Work and Organizations

Edited by David Preece, University of Teeside, UK.

For a full list of titles in this series, please visit www.routledge.com

3   Managing Complex Projects
    Networks, knowledge and innovation
    Neil Alderman, Chris Ivory, Ian McLoughlin, and Roger Vaughan

4   Information and Communication Technologies in rural society
    Being rural in a digital age
    Grete Rusten and Sarah Skerratt

5   Software and Organizations
    The biography of the enterprise-wide system or how SAP conquered
    the world
    Neil Pollock and Robin Williams

6   Technological Communities and Networks
    Triggers and Drivers for Innovation
    Dimitris Assimakopoulos

7   Health Technology Development and Use
    From Practice-Bound Imagination to Evolving Impacts
    Sampsa Hyysalo

8   Nanotechnology and Sustainable Development
    Claire Auplat

9   Challenging the Innovation Paradigm
    *Edited by Karl-Erik Sveiby, Pernilla Gripenberg and
    Beata Segercrantz*

10 Innovation Management in Robot Society
    Kristian Wasen

11 Patent Management and Valuation
    The Strategic and Geographical Dimension
    Edited by Grid Thoma

Patent Management and Valuation

The Strategic and Geographical Dimension

Edited by Grid Thoma

Routledge
Taylor & Francis Group

NEW YORK AND LONDON

First published 2017
by Routledge
711 Third Avenue, New York, NY 10017

and by Routledge
2 Park Square, Milton Park, Abingdon, Oxon OX14 4RN

First issued in paperback 2018

Routledge is an imprint of the Taylor & Francis Group, an informa business

Library of Congress Cataloging-in-Publication Data
Names: Thoma, Grid, editor.
Title: Patent management and valuation : the strategic and geographical dimension / edited by Grid Thoma.
Description: New York : Routledge, 2016. | Series: Routledge studies in technology, work and organizations ; 11 | Includes bibliographical references and index.
Identifiers: LCCN 2016003283 | ISBN 9781138926424 (cloth : alk. paper) | ISBN 9781315683287 (ebook)
Subjects: LCSH: Patents—Economic aspects. | Patents—Valuation. | Diffusion of innovations. | Technological innovations. | New products.
Classification: LCC T211 .P376 2016 | DDC 608—dc23
LC record available at http://lccn.loc.gov/2016003283

ISBN 13: 978-1-138-33993-4 (pbk)
ISBN 13: 978-1-138-92642-4 (hbk)

Typeset in Sabon
by Apex CoVantage, LLC

I dedicate this book to my parents and my brother.

Contents

List of Tables and Figures   ix
Preface   xi
Acknowledgments   xvii
List of Contributors   xix

PART I
The Valuation of Patent Assets   1

1 The Market Value of Patents and R&D   3
   GRID THOMA

2 The Composite Value Index of Patent Indicators   42
   GRID THOMA

PART II
The Strategic Dimension of Patent Valuation   61

3 Combined IP Strategies and the Valuation of
   Patent Premium   63
   GRID THOMA

4 Patent Valuation of a General Purpose Technology:
   An Analysis of Financial Patents and Business Methods   99
   GRID THOMA, BRONWYN H. HALL, AND SALVATORE TORRISI

5 Commercialization Strategies of a General
   Purpose Technology   151
   GRID THOMA

PART III
The Geographic Dimension of Patent Valuation 179

6 The Determinants of the Localization of
Knowledge Spillovers 181
GRID THOMA

7 Inventor Location and the Globalization of R&D 215
GRID THOMA AND DIETMAR HARHOFF

8 The Value of Chinese Patenting 252
GRID THOMA

Conclusion: Patent Valuation from
the Decision Maker's Perspective 280
GRID THOMA

Index 285

Tables and Figures

Tables

1.1	Descriptive Statistics	29
1.2	Market Value Regressions: Dependent Variable = Log Tobin's Q	31
2.1	Patent Asset Value: Log Linear Regression with Patent Indicators	50
2.2	Descriptive Statistics and Correlation Table of the Patent Indicators	54
2.3	Factor Loadings of the Principal Component Analysis with Maximum Likelihood	55
2.4	Patent Asset Value: Log Linear Regression with Patent Indices	56
3.1	Descriptive Statistics	78
3.2	Pairwise Correlations	80
3.3	Patent Premium Value: Log Linear Regression Results	81
3.4	Probability of Trademark Renewal: Probit Marginal Effects	88
4.1	Financial Patents by the Country and Sector of the Patentee	114
4.2	Top Financial Patentees and Their Patent Portfolio Composition	118
4.3	Comparing Financial to all Other Patents	120
4.4	Probability of Decision, Grant, and Opposition Conditional on Grant 1978–2005. Financial Patents vs. a 1 Percent Sample of Other Patents	126
4.5	Probability of Decision, Grant, and Opposition Conditional on Grant 1978–2005. Financial Patents Only	128
5.1	Main Components of LonWorks Technology and Patenting Strategy Followed by Echelon	159
6.1	Citation Probability—European panel 1990–2009	195
6.2	Citation Probability of Inventor-Added Citations— European Panel 1990–2009	198

6.3   The Determinants of the Country Border Effect   200
6.4   Citation Probability of Inventor-Added Citations—North
       American Panel 1990–2009   202
7.1   Coverage of the Sample: Top R&D Performers in
       Europe and United States   218
7.2   Distribution of Inventors by Patentee and Inventor
       Country   224
7.3   Distribution of Inventors by Patentee and Inventor
       Country—Top European and US R&D Performers   227
7.4   Share of Foreign Inventors by Technological Class and
       Patentee Country   229
7.5   Descriptive Statistics   233
7.6   Correlation of Inventor Counts and R&D Expenditures   234
7.7   R&D Accounting Regressions Based on Inventor Counts   236
7.8   Market value Regressions Based on Inventor Counts   241
7.9   Productivity Regressions Based on Inventor Counts   244
7.10 GMM Productivity Regressions Based on Inventor
       Counts   246
8.1   Descriptive Statistics by Groups of Patents   262
8.2   Probability of Granting Decision   267
8.3   Probability of Supplementary Search Report   268
8.4   Probability of Opposition Conditional on Grant   269
8.5   Probability of Renewal Conditional on Grant   271

Figures

1.1   Intangible Assets as Percentage of Total Fixed
       Assets over Time for the European Firms   4
3.1   Absolute Impact of Patent Indicators on Patent
       Premium Value (in PPP $)   86
4.1   Aggregate Patenting Trends by Priority Year at
       the EPO and USPTO   112
4.2   EP and US Financial Methods Patenting   112
4.3   Grant Rate at the EPO, Conditional on a Decision   123
4.4   Opposition Rates at the EPO, Conditional on Grant   124
5.1   Technological Diffusion by Application Sector   170
7.1   Inventor Workforce in the EPO/PCT System as
       Share of Business Intramural R&D Personnel   220
7.2   Foreign Employed Inventors in the EPO/PCT System
       as Share of Business Intramural R&D Personnel   222
8.1   Chinese Patents as Percentage of all Patents   263
8.2   Chinese Patents According to Institutional Sector   264
8.3   Technological Specialization of Chinese Patenting
       over Time   266

Preface

Technologies acquire economic value when they are taken to market with an effective business model. When research discoveries are driven by scientific inquiry and are not connected to any business purpose, the commercial value will be serendipitous and unforeseeable. Unsurprisingly, most of these discoveries will be worth very little, although a few may be worth a great deal— once they are connected to the market through some viable business model.

(Chesbrough 2003, 161)

Much of the literature on the patent valuation has attempted to appraise the intrinsic value of an underlying technological invention (Nagaoka et al. 2010). However, the value the innovator can extract from a patent depends to a significant extent also on the appropriability conditions and complementary assets required for the commercial translation of that invention (Teece 1986; McGahan and Silverman 2006). More in general, the innovator can put in place strategies to ameliorate the conditions that directly affect the value of an invention (Chesbrough 2003; Gans and Stern 2003). With the exception of few works, the role that the innovator's strategic behaviour and business model play in determining the value of patents has been overlooked by previous literature (Gambardella and McGahan 2010). This book aims to build on this gap by analysing how strategic factors— intrinsic and extrinsic to the business model of the firm—affect the value of patents.

There are several approaches for patent value assessment according to the rationales of the valuation. For instance, the asset value of patents has been first analysed in the context of the market valuation of publicly listed firms (Lanjouw and Schankerman 2004; Hall et al. 2005) or in the case of initial public offerings, mergers, and acquisitions (Cockburn and Macgarvie 2009). Second, there is a growing literature on the return of the premium value of patent protection (Arora et al. 2008; Bessen 2008). Third, several scholars have advanced indicators for ranking patents according to their value and quality (Lanjouw and Schankerman 2004; Nagaoka et al. 2010).

Fourth, the signaling value of patents has been scrutinized with respect to firm's financing decisions (Hsu and Ziedonis 2013; Haussler et al. 2014). Fifth, in specific industries patents have been shown to hold significant collateral value (Graham et al. 2009). More recently, patents have been valued in accordance to other intellectual property strategies pursued by the innovator (Alvarez Garrido and Dushnitsky 2013; Block et al. 2014). Nevertheless, previous literature has seldom debated how the strategic behaviour of the innovator affects the valuation of the patented inventions.

The analysis presented in this book scrutinizes the strategic behaviour of the innovator at various levels. Beforehand the analysis of the intrinsic strategic factors has regarded the valuation of the patent real options. In fact, a significant option value emerges from patent strategies when the innovator can postpone the complementary investment required for the successful exploitation of the patented invention. Furthermore, the combined usage of several intellectual property strategies regarding the same innovative project constitutes an intrinsic strategic factor for the decision maker that does affect patent valuation. Multiple complementary intellectual property strategies can be put in place in order to enhance the value of patenting, including formal strategies (trademarks, design patents, and copyright) or informal ones (lead time, standardization actions, and trade secrets). Further, the valuation approach of this book analyses the so-called strategic patenting hypothesis, according to which innovators obtain patents not only with the goal to achieve protection for their inventions but also for other reasons, such as attracting venture capital, reducing the risk of being held up by other patent owners, achieving stronger contractual power towards competitors in licensing agreements, etc.

The second dimension of the analysis conducted in this book is constituted by other strategic factors affecting the value of the patented inventions which are extrinsic to a firm's business model. These factors reside at the outset of R&D process, yielding the patented invention, and in particular they are constituted by knowledge spillovers from R&D activities conducted externally by other innovators. Whereas there is a growing number of studies that have assessed the role of spillovers for firm performance and productivity (for a survey see Feldman and Kogler 2010), they hardly have been analysed in connection to the value of the patented R&D. To the extent that knowledge spillovers are a geographically localized phenomenon, the co-location of R&D activities is a typical mechanism for knowledge spillovers to unfold benign effects on the economic value of the patented inventions.

Multiple factors regarding the localization of knowledge spillovers and their impact on patent valuation are taken into the consideration. First new evidences are brought with respect to the localization of knowledge spillovers and its determinants at the national and regional context. Then I show that the geography of the R&D outsourcing decisions contributes significantly to the patentee's market value (represented by the Tobin's *q*) and productivity (measured as revenue productivity). Last, the analysis shows that the quality and value of single patents are significantly affected by the geography of innovative activities, including institutional factors, such as the strength of national legislation on patent protection.

Outline of the Book

The book is organized into three parts. The first part presents an overview of the patent valuation approaches, including both monetary and nonmonetary approaches. Chapter 1 starts with the traditional approaches relying on the quantification of costs, revenues, or market value of the patent assets. Particular attention is devoted to the market value model relying on the Tobin's *q* equation, and its applications in the literature are discussed. In addition, the chapter explains the patent real option approach that assesses the additional value spurring from the flexibility in time when the decision maker can delay the complementary investment required for the successful exploitation of a patent. This latter approach can be reconciled with the Tobin's *q* model, which is not affected by problems of timing of costs and revenues, and several econometric evidences are presented in support of this view. The nonmonetary approaches proposed by the literature on patent indicators are thoroughly discussed and tested in the Chapter 2. A composite value index is built up by combining twenty different patent indicators according to several dimensions: patent breadth and technology potential, prior art and background of the invention, and filing and procedural aspects of a patent. A novel selection approach of patent indicators and their validation with market value of patents is advanced, whereas the computation of the composite value index is estimated by the mean of the factor analysis.

The second part of the book is constituted by three additional chapters regarding the strategic dimension of patent valuation. Chapter 3 investigates further the role of patent indicators in appraising the premium value of patents as measured by the renewal fee decisions. The main goal of this chapter is the determination of patent valuation given by other complemental IP strategies, when the patentee combines the patenting strategy with trademarks and design patents regarding the same innovative project. The identification of pairing strategies of patents, trademarks, and design patents is advanced by the means of textual analysis of the legal documents using matching algorithms.

Chapter 4 analyses the valuation with patent indicators for the assessment of the General Purpose Technologies (GPTs), such as financial patenting and business methods. The number of financial patents has increased significantly in parallel with innovations in payment and financial systems, with many potential applications in several other industries. Scholars have argued that financial patents, like other business methods patents, have low value and are owned for strategic reasons rather than for protecting real inventions. To test this hypothesis, the probability of patent indicators (grant, refusal, and opposition) of financial patents is analysed as a function of age and industry of origin of the patentee (financial vis-à-vis nonfinancial sector), the relative size of the patent portfolio, and other patentee characteristics.

Chapter 5 advances an in-depth study from a management perspective of the firm's strategic behaviour that could make a GPT succeed or fail. In particular, the analysis considers the technological strategies, business model, and performance of the GPT provider and what factors can favour or hamper the diffusion of the GPT in the using industries. The chapter presents an historical perspective on a breakthrough technology, introduced in the last decades by a Silicon Valley start-up company.

The third and last part of the book includes three chapters on the geographic dimension affecting patent valuation. Chapter 6 presents new evidences on the localization of knowledge spillovers as proxied by patent citations for the North American and European regions. The econometric analysis investigates the simultaneous effect on the probability of being cited of both the geographical spatial distance and territorial borders at the country level, secondary and tertiary national level of aggregation, and cross-border neighbouring territorial units. Furthermore, the strength of the national legislation on patent protection is analysed as determinant of the localization of knowledge spillovers.

Chapter 7 develops a new method of quantifying the R&D investments by country of the inventive activity by relying on patent information with respect to location of a firm's inventors. Whilst R&D is becoming increasingly globalized, firm-level data capture R&D investments irrespective of the location. For the top European and US patenting firms, which conduct about 80 percent of national intramural R&D, all inventors and their locations at the time of the invention have been identified. This measurement approach of the firm's inventor workforce allows one to advance market value regressions based on the Tobin's q equation against the geographical distribution of a firm's inventive activities across countries. Then the consistency of the valuation of R&D investment by location is assessed using the production function framework.

Chapter 8 investigates the rapid growth of patenting in an emerging geographical area such as China, which has experienced several institutional changes with respect to the increasing strength of the national legislation on patent protection. Relying on several patent value indicators, an econometric model is built up in order to analyse patent granting, prior-art searches, opposition to patents granted, and renewal decisions of patent maintenance according to the demographic characteristics of the patentees and their geographic origin: domestic firms performing indigenous R&D activities in China, foreign multinational firms off-shoring R&D activities in China, and Chinese firms employing foreign inventors.

References

Alvarez-Garrido E., G. Dushnitsky 2013. "Publications and Patents in Corporate Venture Backed Biotech." *Nature Biotechnol* 31(6):495–497.

Arora A., M. Ceccagnoli, W. Cohen 2008. "R&D and the Patent Premium." *Int J Ind Organ* 26(5):1153–1179.

Block J. H., G. De Vries, J. H. Schumann, P. Sandner 2014. "Trademarks and Venture Capital Valuation." *J Business Venturing* 29:525–542.

Chesbrough H. 2003. *Open Innovation: The New Imperative for Creating and Profiting from Technology*. Cambridge (MA): Harvard Business School Press.

Cockburn I., M. McGarvie 2009. "Patents, Thickets and the Financing of Early-Stage Firms: Evidence from the Software Industry." *J Econ Manag Strat* 18(3):729–773.

Feldman M., D. Kogler 2010. "Stylized Facts in the Geography of Innovation." In *The Handbook of the Economics of Innovation*, edited by B. H. Hall, N. Rosenberg, 13443–14547, Amsterdam: Elsevier, Kindle edition.

Gambardella A., A. McGahan 2010. "Business-Model Innovation: General Purpose Technologies and Their Implications for Industry Structure." *Long Range Plan* 43:262–271.

Gans J. S., S. Stern 2003. "The Product Market and the Market for Ideas: Commercialization Strategies for Technology Entrepreneurs." *Res Pol* 32:333–350.

Graham S. J. H., R. P. Merges, P. Samuelson, T. M. Sichelman 2009. "High Technology Entrepreneurs and the Patent System: Results of the 2008 Berkeley Patent Survey." *Berkeley Technol Law J* 24(4):255–327.

Hall B. H., A. Jaffe, M. Trajtenberg 2005. "Market Value and Patent Citations." *Rand J Econ* 36:16–38.

Häussler C., D. Harhoff, E. Mueller 2014. "How Patenting Informs VC Investors—The Case of Biotechnology." *Res Pol* 43(8):1286–1298.

Hsu D., R. Ziedonis 2013. "Resources as Dual Sources of Advantage: Implications for Valuing Entrepreneurial-Firm Patents." *Strat Manag J* 34:761–781.

Lanjouw J. O., M. Schankerman 2004. "Patent Quality and Research Productivity: Measuring Innovation with Multiple Indicators." *Econ J* 114:441–465.

McGahan A. M., B. S. Silverman 2006. "Profiting from Technological Innovation by Others: The Effect of Competitor Patenting on Firm Value." *Res Pol* 35(8):1222–1242.

Nagaoka S., K. Motohashi, A. Goto 2010. "Patent Statistics as Innovation Indicators." In *The Handbook of the Economics of Innovation*, edited by B. H. Hall, N. Rosenberg, 10973–12068, Amsterdam: Elsevier, Kindle edition.

Teece D. 1986. "Profiting from Technological Innovation." *Res Pol* 15(6):285–305.

Acknowledgments

This book emerged from my research activities in the last decade following my doctoral dissertation at the Sant'Anna School of Advanced Studies. During this period I faced the challenge of deepening the research topics that I started with my doctoral studies and opening some new avenues for further research. Although this task was accompanied undoubtedly by a kind of tension, it has been particularly fruitful in fuelling my interest around the general theme of the valuation of patent strategies.

I would like to thank for their extremely valuable discussions and various support Alessandra Colecchia, Dominique Guellec, Kazuyuki Motohashi, Mark Schankerman, and Andrew Wyckoff.

I am grateful to my colleagues Bronwyn Hall, Dietmar Harhoff, and Salvatore Torrisi, who have coauthored with me two chapters of this book. Chapter 4 has been jointly written with Bronwyn and Salvatore and chapter 6 with Dietmar.

I am responsible for all errors and limitations of the book.

Contributors

Bronwyn H. Hall is professor of economics emerita at the University of California at Berkeley and professor of economics of technology and innovation at the University of Maastricht, Netherlands. She is a research associate of the National Bureau of Economic Research and the Institute for Fiscal Studies, London, and a visiting fellow at the National Institute of Economics and Social Research, London.

Dietmar Harhoff is professor and managing director at the Max Planck Institute for Innovation and Competition in Munich and honorary professor at the University of Munich. He is a research associate at the Center for Economic Policy Research in London and the Zentrum für Europäische Wirtschaftsforschung in Manheim.

Grid Thoma is assistant professor with tenure of economics and management and rector delegate on intellectual property management at the University of Camerino. He is a research associate at CEFIN of University of Modena and Reggio Emilia in Modena.

Salvatore Torrisi is professor of economics and management and coordinator of the doctoral program in management at the University of Bologna. He is research associate at the 'L. Bocconi' University of Milan and program director of the Italian National Agency for the Evaluation of University Research.

Part I

The Valuation of Patent Assets

1 The Market Value of Patents and R&D

Grid Thoma

1.1 Introduction

One implication of the growth of the 'knowledge economy' is that the composition of the assets of a modern corporation has shifted away from tangibles and towards intangibles. Intangible assets account for one-third to one-half of the market value of US corporate securities, and R&D expenditures alone account for over 3 percent of nonfinancial corporate operative revenues (Blair and Wallman 2001; Nakamura 2003). Furthermore, it has been noted that receipts from intellectual property have grown much faster than the growth of R&D investments (Robbins 2006).

The increasing role played by intangibles can be seen beyond the US context as well. The figure below reports the share of intangible assets as part of total assets in a balanced panel of European publicly listed firms in low-tech industries and high-tech ones, such as chemicals and pharmaceuticals, computers and communication equipment, electrical machinery, instruments, telecommunication services, and software and other business services.

However, this figure understates the true share of intangible assets because accounting standards do not allow R&D capitalization, and because only intangible assets actually on the balance sheet are measured. In the United States, the generally accepted accounting principles (GAAP) set by the Financial Accounting Standard Board (FASB) prescribe that R&D costs be treated as current expenditures rather than investments. R&D costs cannot be capitalized according to the International Accounting Standard Committee (IASC) Foundation either. Only development costs (under given conditions) and in-process R&D acquired through merger or acquisition (IPR&D) can be capitalized because their value is determined objectively by the exchange price in the market.[1]

Another factor that makes it difficult to quantify the value of intangibles is the lack of accounting data on R&D expenditures in many countries whose legislation does not require disclosure of these outlays, even for the publicly listed companies (Toivanen et al. 2002). Furthermore, it is worth recalling that R&D investment is only an input to innovative activity and the output is highly uncertain, and thus it would be useful to have reliable indicators of R&D outcomes as well.

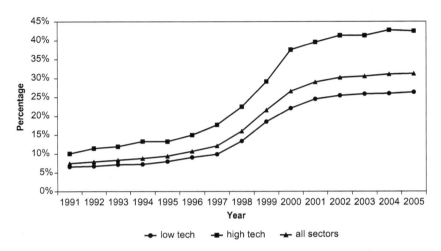

Figure 1.1 Intangible assets as percentage of total fixed assets over time for the European firms

Source: Thomson Financials' Global Vantage database, 562 firms and 8,430 observations.

Given these difficulties, patents have become the most popular and widely used indicator of R&D 'success' (Nagaoka et al. 2010), as information on patents is objective, the result of standards applied by patent offices that are intended to be uniform across technologies, and also accessible, because most patent information is published not long after the date of filing. However, the book value of patent assets is also unavailable, with the exception of those acquired through mergers and acquisitions, and this lack of information makes it difficult to assess the value of a firm (Chan et al. 2001; Lev et al. 2005).

In the absence of any kind of book value of R&D-related intangible assets (including internally generated patents), scholars in a number of countries have used the relationship between various innovation measures and the market value of the firm that performs the R&D and obtains the patents to estimate the contribution of those patent assets to current and future corporate earnings (Griliches 1981; Cockburn and Griliches 1988; Griliches et al. 1991; Hall 1993). Under the assumption that financial markets possess (and use) all relevant information needed to correctly estimate the future net cash flows generated by a firm's assets, patent-related information should affect a firm's market value (Hall 2000). Nevertheless, the distribution of the economic value of patents is very skewed, with only a few patents yielding significant value to their owners and many being nearly worthless *ex post*. This is why some empirical studies have made use of indicators of patent value, most notably citations received (forward citations) and patent family size (the number of different patent systems in which protection for a single invention is sought) (Lanjouw and Schankerman 2004; Hall et al. 2005). Such measures can be used to 'weight' the patent counts for each firm in order to partially correct for the heterogeneity in patent value.

Extending this exercise beyond US firms is problematic because of the limited availability of data on R&D spending. In Europe, with the exception of the UK (Bloom and Van Reenen 2002; Toivanen et al. 2002; Greenhalgh and Rogers 2006), accounting and fiscal regulations do not require publicly listed corporations to report R&D expenditures. For this reason, the evidence on the market valuation of R&D and patents for European continental firms has been quite limited, with some rare exceptions (Hall and Oriani 2006). For other countries, the unavailability of R&D data and their reduced comparability over time have limited the market value analysis to some industrial contexts for Japanese firms (Haneda and Odagiri 1998) or solely in a cross-section dimension for Australian firms (Bosworth and Roger 2001). More recently, the market value approach has been used to investigate R&D in developing countries (Chada and Oriani 2010; Kanwar and Hall 2015). Notwithstanding these partial and incomplete attempts in other countries, it is still important to question whether financial markets properly value innovation investments, including R&D and patents.

The goals of this chapter are threefold. First, the rationales of the market value model based on Tobin's q equation are presented together with a succinct review of the empirical literature on R&D activities and patents. Second, the various approaches to patent valuation are discussed, including cost-based approaches (based on the estimates of the investments required to obtain a patent asset), market-based approaches (based on the existence of an efficient public market for the patent asset), and revenue-based approaches (based on estimation of future cash-flows generated by the patent asset). Recently there has been a revival of the real option approach in the patent valuation literature, which can be seen as an advancement of the cost and revenue approaches. Further, the real option approach can also be reconciled with a forward-looking market approach such as the Tobin's q model, which overcomes problems of the timing of costs and revenues (Bloom and Van Reenen 2002).

The third goal of the chapter is to present some novel comparative evidence on the market value of R&D, patents, and patent indicators for European, US, and Japanese firms. To do so, a new dataset has been developed, integrating various primary and secondary sources, including company books, stock price information, corporate ownership structure, patent information, and other country-specific variables. A new patent value index is proposed: It looks at the breadth of the patent family (that is, the number of countries where the patent protection has been sought) weighted by the relative GDP of those countries. For the first time in the literature, this study reports cross-country analysis based on Tobin's q model to disentangle the market valuation of the stocks of granted patents vis-à-vis patent applications. An additional contribution to the literature is constituted by fact that these stocks of patents originate from multiple issuing authorities: Whilst the granted patents have been identified at the national issuing authority, the patent applications are defined at the international level, identified through filings deposited under the procedure of the Patent Cooperation Treaty (PCT).

The chapter presents four new findings. First, substantial evidence of the strong impact of R&D stocks on a firm's market value is reported across the three geographical segments of Europe, the United States, and Japan. In line with previous studies in the literature, the impact of R&D stocks is larger than patent variables. Second, patents granted at the domestic level contribute significantly to a firm's market value above and beyond R&D, except for the Japanese firms. Third, financial markets are particularly sensitive to the heterogeneity of patent value, rather than merely the number of patents, considered separately, and this effect is twice as strong for the US firms. Fourth, the patent application stocks at the international level significantly affect market value independently of the geographical context. This finding does not contradict the view that filings under the PCT procedure hold a large option value for the applicant, one that is incorporated in the firm's market value.

The chapter proceeds as follows. Section 2 presents a baseline version of Tobin's q model and discusses linear and nonlinear estimation methods. Then the various patent-asset valuation approaches are introduced, including monetary and nonmonetary methods. Section 3 explains the various data sources used in the analysis, compares the patent strategies pursued by the sample firms, and concludes with the econometric specification and the definition of the variables. Finally, the descriptive and multivariate results are shown.

1.2 Estimating the Economic Value of Innovation Assets

There are two main streams of studies that attempt to evaluate the economic returns on innovative activities. The first adopts the production function approach in order to relate innovation as proxied by R&D and patents to total factor productivity or profitability, in most cases capturing a measure of private returns, although in principle this approach can also yield social returns if prices are properly accounted for. The second, which will be discussed thoroughly in this chapter, measures the private returns on innovation using a forward-looking measure of firm performance, namely, the valuation in the stock market. Each approach has its merits and weaknesses.

1.2.1 Productivity

Total factor productivity (TFP) is simply the ratio of outputs to inputs, both expressed in real terms. Assuming only two inputs (capital C and labour L)

and taking the natural logs of all variables, the TFP of a firm can be expressed as follows:

$$log(TFP) = log(S) - \alpha \cdot log(L) - \beta \cdot log(C) \qquad (1)$$

This is an appropriate measure of productivity under conditions of constant returns to scale and competition in the markets for inputs and outputs.[2] Many studies during the past fifty years have estimated the returns on R&D using this approach and documented the importance of technology, measured by R&D expenditures, for the growth of total factor productivity of firms. Hall et al. (2010) recently provided a comprehensive survey of the empirical studies on productivity and reported their conclusions about the positive impact of R&D investment for a firm.

A major problem with this approach is that there is usually a long lag between R&D and its impact on productivity or profits, and thus the outcome is difficult to predict. This can give rise to serious measurement problems when the data are not available over a long period of time and when the process relating input and output is not stationary. In addition, the productivity approach that relies on accounting data often fails to allow for the effects of differences in systematic risk, temporary disequilibrium effects, tax laws, and accounting conventions. Much empirical work, therefore, has turned to alternative methods for measuring production functions, which will be investigated in Chapter 7 (this volume).

1.2.2 Market Value Approach

Some of these limitations are less important with the market value approach, which combines accounting data with measures of the value of the firm on the financial markets (Lindenberg and Ross 1981; Montgomery and Wernerfelt 1988). By relying on financial market valuation, this approach is inherently forward looking and overcomes a major drawback of the productivity approach, the problem of timing when the costs and revenues occur.

The market value approach draws on the idea, derived from hedonic price models for heterogeneous goods, that firms are bundles of assets (and capabilities) that are difficult to disentangle and to price separately on the market. These assets include plants and equipment, inventories, knowledge assets, process and product innovation, managerial skill, human capital in the workforce, customer networks, brand names, reputation, and other aspects of the firm. The assumption is that financial markets assign a correct valuation to the bundle of a firms' assets that is equal to the present discounted value of their future cash flows, because investors are forward looking and efficient in taking into the account all available information and do not make systematic errors. This approach has been used in several studies to calculate the marginal shadow value of knowledge assets relying on various datasets (Griliches 1981; Griliches et al. 1991; Hall 1993; Lanjouw and Schankerman 2004; Hall et al. 2005).

1.2.2.1 Baseline Model

The general functional form of the value function for an intertemporal maximization program with several capital goods is difficult to derive and in most cases does not have a closed form (Wildasin 1984). Starting with the work of Griliches (1981), most econometric studies have assumed that the market value equation takes a linear separable specification. The typical market value model relies on the assumption that a firm's assets enter additively:

$$V_{it}(A_{it}\ K_{it}) = q_t(A_{it} + \gamma_t K_{it})^{\sigma t} \tag{2}$$

Where A represents the book value of total tangible assets of firm i at time t and K is stock of the knowledge assets not included in the balance sheet, q is the average market valuation coefficient of a firm's total assets, and σ a time varying scaling factor. Under constant returns to scale ($\sigma_t = 1$), equation (2) in log form can be written as:

$$logV_{it} = logq_t + logA_{it} + log(1 + \gamma_t K_{it} / A_{it}) \tag{3}$$

or

$$logQ_{it} = logV_{it} / A_{it} = logq_t + log(1 + \gamma_t K_{it} / A_{it}) \tag{4}$$

The left-hand side of equation (4) is the log of Tobin's q, defined as the ratio of market value to the replacement cost of the firm, which is typically measured with the replacement value of the firm's tangible assets. On the right-hand side, γ_t is the marginal or shadow value of the ratio of knowledge capital to tangible assets at a given point in time (i.e., $(\partial V/\partial K)/(\partial V/\partial A)$). They measure the expectations of investors about the impact of the knowledge capital intensity (i.e., relative to tangible assets) on the discounted future profits of the firm. The intercept ($log\ q_t$) represents the average logarithm of Tobin's q for the sample firms, and it captures the adjustment of the overall macro-economic effects in the stock market. The absolute hedonic price of the knowledge capital is given by the product $q_t\gamma_t$, which is made up by the market expectations on the total effect of K_{it} on the discounted value and present and future returns of the firm.

Note that in general, the shadow prices implied by the estimated relationship are equilibrium prices resulting from the interaction between the firm's demand and the market supply of capital for a specific asset at a given point in time. This implies that no structural interpretation should be attached to estimates of the market value equation. However, the values obtained by estimation of the market value equation are still informative, in the sense that they do measure the average elasticity of value with respect to R&D or patents filed at a particular point in time. For a more detailed discussion of various problems concerning the estimation and interpretation of the market value equation, see Hall (2000).

1.2.2.2 Empirical Studies of Market Valuation

Both linear and nonlinear empirical strategies have been advanced to estimate the relationship implied by equation (4).

NONLINEAR MODELS

The Hall et al. (2005) study considered the Compustat dataset of about five thousand US-listed firms from manufacturing industries during the period from 1976 to 1995, including firms that performed R&D investments and held patents and noninnovating firms that did neither of these activities. Similarly to Hall (1993), they built capitalized measures of R&D expenditures and patent counts (see below). In addition, more sophisticated indicators of technological assets such as citation-weighted patents were elaborated to account for the great dispersion of the patent value distribution. This study used three ratios: R&D intensity, patent productivity, and citation yield. The first measure is the discounted R&D investment normalized by the tangible assets, which can grasp the cumulative nature of the knowledge-generation process. The second ratio, patent productivity, is a factored measure that captures investor expectation regarding the number of patents per dollar of R&D. Third, because citations correlate well with patent value distribution, investors form similar expectations based on citation yield given by the number of citations per patent.

Hall et al. (2005) reported several new findings. First, they demonstrated that R&D investment stock is more closely correlated with Tobin's q than patent and citation stocks. Nevertheless, they found that citation-weighted patents were more informative than mere patent counts about the market value of innovation, even after controlling for R&D stock variable. Further, they argued that the relative statistical explanatory power of citation stocks had been increasing over time, in particular since the beginning of the '80s, parallel to legislative changes strengthening the protection provided by patent rights. When they focused the analysis exclusively on patenting firms, they found that one additional citation generates a 3 percent growth of the firm's market value. Although this impact of the citation yield was very large, it is worth remembering that from a statistical point of view, it is a very extreme move, because the typical patent receives about three citations along its lifecycle and about one-quarter of patents receive none. A further major finding was that firms with a citation yield greater than the median show a more-than-proportional increase in market value. Quite interestingly, citations made to patents already owned by the same company had an additional positive value impact above the average cita-tion yield, although this relationship weakened with the size of the firm's patent portfolio.

In the absence of direct measures of the economic value of patents, Lan-jouw and Schankerman (2004) provided a useful method for exploring the relationship between the technological importance of a patent and the firm's market value. More specifically, they advanced a composite value index of several patent indicators. These indicators include, on the one hand, citation-weighted patents as in Hall et al. (2005), and on the other, family size in terms of the number of jurisdictions where the protection is sought, the quality of the patent prior art, and the number of claims depicted on the front page of a patent.[3] With reference to the US-listed firms drawn from the Compustat database over the years from 1980 to 1993, they showed that a similarly built index was highly correlated with Tobin's q even after controlling for the ratio of patent stocks to tangible assets. In this study, the measure of patent quality was an average measure at the firm level, that is similar to the citation yield of Hall et al. (2005). Estimation by technologi-cal field revealed that the composite value index was more predictive of the market value of pharmaceutical firms than that of firms in electronics and mechanical technologies.

LINEAR MODELS

The second stream of studies, which instead focuses on linear models of the valuation in the stock market, includes many more works than the former. Among the first in this stream was the study by Griliches (1981), which approximated the term $log(1 + \gamma_t K_{it} / A_{it}) \approx \gamma_t K_{it} / A_{it}$. In doing so, they could estimate the market value equation (4) with the mean of ordinary least squares, although with the disadvantage that this approximation becomes more inaccurate the larger the value of K_{it} / A_{it}. In another study, Cockburn and Griliches (1988) analysed a cross-section of firms from a balanced panel of the US Compustat dataset. They confirmed that the impact of the patent stock on assets was very large and significant, although the size of the coef-ficient was halved when a measure of recent R&D investment was consid-ered. The R&D flow measure had a greater impact than the stock measure, but this did not contradict the assumption that the former was a stronger signal to financial investors of the future profitability of the firm. By look-ing at the different knowledge appropriability conditions across industries, they found that the impact of knowledge variables on market value differed largely according to the industry in which the firm was active. Whereas the interaction effect with appropriability was positive and highly significant for the R&D measures, it was insignificant for patents. This finding does not contradict the view that the patent stock depreciation rates vary according to the industry in question, because of the way knowledge appropriability varies in different industries.

Hall (1993) conducted an exhaustive analysis of the return of R&D investment on market value. Her sample was the universe of US-listed firms over a two-decade period, from 1973 to 1991. In particular, she analysed two measures of R&D investment. The first, the annual flow measure, was taken from the expenditure category of the company annual reports, whereas the second, a capitalized R&D measure, was computed with the perpetual inventory method at the rate of 15 percent. Assuming a constant R&D growth rate, she demonstrated that the stock measure was fivefold greater that the flow measure, a statement that was fully supported by the empirical evidence. The year-by-year estimations revealed that during the '80s there was a drastic drop of the R&D return and an increase of depreciation, which she associated to the expansion of new industries characterised by a more rapid pace of technical change, such as computers and electronics.[4]

The market value of intangible assets in knowledge-intensive industries was analysed by Haneda and Odagiri (1998) with a balanced panel of ninety Japanese firms during the eleven-year period from 1981 to 1991. Both R&D and patents were considered as proxies of intangible assets, excluding other sources, such as goodwill or advertisement. Allowing for industry specific knowledge depreciation rates, they found that both past and recent R&D investment affected the market value of the firm and that recent R&D had a larger impact in industries characterised by a more rapid pace of technical change and a greater rate of knowledge depreciation. Only in pharmaceuticals did patents significantly enhance a firm's market value, unlike firms specializing in chemical or electrical technologies. Haneda and Odagiri attributed these findings to the role played by different appropriability conditions across industries, and the intrinsic heterogeneity of the knowledge-generating mechanisms in various industries.

Griliches et al. (1991) conducted a factor analysis of the time series of firm market valuation, patent counts, R&D investment, sales, and tangible assets over the decade ending in 1980. They argued that whereas demand side conditions could determine the existence of a common factor among these variables, there was limited evidence for the existence of a second factor in the time series dimension. Potentially, the second factor could be associated with a shift in technological opportunities, which takes place as an acceleration of the patent counts and is mirrored in the growth of firm market value. Nevertheless, they found that much of the growth of patenting was determined by R&D expenditure, which in turn was directly affected by the evolution of demand. Therefore, firm market value was only enhanced to a limited extent by the surprises of the variability of patent counts, considered separately from R&D investment.

The market value approach rests on the restrictive hypothesis of capital market efficiency, and therefore it can be used only for firms quoted in well-functioning stock markets with intense trading. In fact, financial markets are not always perfect, and there are persistent institutional differences across countries which may result in different evaluations of intangible assets. Not surprisingly, most empirical studies that follow the market value approach rely on data from the United States, where the stock markets are larger and characterised by more intense trading than those of the European and other OECD countries.[5] For related reasons, studies based on data from the United States also benefit from the availability of large datasets.

Regarding Europe, the few studies that used firm market value to analyse the economic value of R&D or patents focused for the most part on UK firms (Bloom and Van Reenen 2002; Toivanen et al. 2002; Greenhalgh and Rogers 2006); notable exceptions are the works by Czarnitzki and Hall (2006) and Hall and Oriani (2006), who looked at the market value of R&D for the continental countries as well. Most of these market valuation studies relied on measures of R&D expenditure, which is usually considered a measure of innovation input rather than innovation output or success of innovative activities. However, in the case of European firms, data on R&D expenditures are often lacking because accounting and fiscal regulations in most European countries do not require them to report these expenditures. The UK is probably the only European country where an explicit accounting practice recommendation encourages firms to disclose their R&D expenditures.[6]

Tovainen et al. (2002) analysed a sample of 877 UK firms over the period 1989–1995, which is of particular interest because there was no compulsory revelation of R&D investment prior to 1988. In addition to knowledge variables, they accounted for many others defined at the firm and industry level.[7] They broadly confirmed the findings of Hall (1993), although they did not report any time trend of the reduction of the R&D return on market value. Compared to Hall's measurements of the impact of R&D intensity on market value, the flow measures of Tovainen et al. indicated that R&D had one-third greater impact. They found that firms that disclose their R&D investment information for the first time experience a premium on the R&D return, compared to those firms that have previously reported R&D in their accounts. This evidence is consistent with the observation that the benefits accruing from R&D investments are markedly long-lasting over time, and the market has already capitalized on the information that firms have already disclosed, whereas ". . . for new announcers much less of the information content of the R&D announcement has been so capitalized" (Tovainen et al. 2002, 55). Last, the patent variable did not affect market value above and beyond R&D investment, which could be explained by the fact that this study only took into account UK patent applications, not grants. In fact, in order to have an objective measure of the patent rents a firm receives, it may be better to consider patent grants rather than patent applications.

The impact of patenting on market value was analysed more thoroughly by Greenhalgh and Rogers (2006), who focused on the population of UK-listed firms that disclosed R&D information in their accounts from 1989 to 2002. Similarly to Tovainen et al. (2002), they relied on flow measures of R&D investment and showed a comparable impact of R&D on market value, above other investment in intangibles. They examined patents granted in the UK by the UK Intellectual Property Office, and those granted under the aegis of the European Patent Convention (EPC) issued by the European Patent Office (EPO), and found that European patents had a large and positive impact on market value, whereas patents granted solely in the UK did not. There were significant differences on the market valuation of patenting, according to the industry category of the 'Pavitt's taxonomy' in which the firm was engaged. They found that a firm's market share was an important mediator of the impact of patenting on market value; it helped to disentangle the reported differences in the valuation of patents across industries.

Czarnitzki and Hall (2006) explored for the first time the market valuation of patent applications and grants for a sample of 186 patenting firms from fourteen manufacturing industries in Germany during the decade 1986–1995, although without conditioning for R&D investment.[8] They found that both types of patent stocks significantly affected the Tobin's q, although patent grants had three times the impact of applications. Whereas the R&D investment of a firm could be more appropriately approximated by the application stock, patent grants were indicative of the private value of inventive activities.[9] Quite interestingly, the results were solely valid when the regressions were implemented by the mean of fixed effect at the industry level, which confirmed that there were different knowledge depreciation rates and appropriability mechanisms across industries (Cockburn and Griliches 1988; Hall 1993).

Hall and Oriani (2006) looked at the market value of R&D for France, Germany, Italy and the United Kingdom. Given the long period considered (from 1989 to 1998), they were able to construct capitalized measures of R&D using the perpetual inventory method with a depreciation rate of 15 percent and an implied growth rate of 8 percent. Significant differences of the valuation of R&D intensity across countries were shown: R&D intensity in the UK had three times the impact of that in continental Europe, whereas in Italy no statistically significant impact could be traced. Nevertheless, these differences were mitigated when they took into consideration the ownership structure of the continental firms, that is, whether the corporation was governed by a single shareholder with majority control or without such a governance mechanism. Whereas the presence of majority shareholders showed a positive premium value on Tobin's q, R&D intensity in those firms was not valued at all. This finding can be explained considering the greater risk and uncertainty for the other shareholders in appropriating rents generated by a firm's investments in innovation.

In concluding this review of studies on the linear estimations of Tobin's q equation, it is worth recalling that some of them considered patent indicators as a proxy for the value of patents. Bloom and Van Reenen (2002) analysed the market valuation of patent citations together with patent counts of the major R&D-doers in the UK from 1969 to 1990. They did not find an additional positive impact of citations above and beyond patent counts, but it was difficult to reach a definitive conclusion about the market valuation of citation-weighted patents because both of these measures were normalized by tangible capital, given the absence of information on R&D expenditures in the UK in that period. In fact, Hall and MacGarvie (2010) and Belenzon (2012) showed for US firms that patent and citation stocks normalized by R&D affected market valuation even when a linear approximation of the Tobin's q equation was used. Hirschey et al. (2001) extended the analysis based on patent indicators by considering not only citations received but also the citations made to patent prior art and non-patent references.

1.3 Patent Valuation Methods

Three main approaches for assessing the value of IP assets, such as patents, are cost-based, market-based, and revenue-based (see, for example, Smith and Parr 2000). Further, some contributions have argued that patents can be considered as real options in the process of making future investments, and hence the financial option theory could be suitable for valuing patents as well (Pakes 1986; Bloom and Van Reenen 2002).

In this section I will present the rationales of these approaches, with particular focus on patents as real options. Whereas the goal of these approaches is to formulate a monetary valuation of a patent asset, there is a large stream of literature on patent indicators that concerns nonmonetary valuations. The next two chapters will provide deeper scrutiny of the literature on patent indicators; this section discusses the rationales of two main indicators of patent value, namely patent citations and the patent family size.

1.3.1 Cost-Based Approaches

Valuation under the cost approach is based on the so-called principle of substitution, the goal of which is to assess the investment required to replace an existing focal asset with a new asset that enables the innovator to have the same future service capability as that provided by the focal one (Smith and Parr 2000). The valuation process of the focal asset can proceed in two ways. One way is to look at the 'reproduction cost' required to produce the exact duplicate of the focal asset. Another examines the 'replacement cost' when the other asset ensures benefits equivalent to those afforded by the focal asset. If the surrogate asset does not provide a perfectly equivalent benefit, then the replacement cost should be reduced by an amount proportional to the value of the reduced productivity that comes from adopting an asset with inferior characteristics. In this second case, the value of the new asset is typically affected by the availability of technical alternatives, market conditions, and legal aspects.

These two techniques can yield different service characteristics of the focal asset under valuation and the new asset on which the valuation is based. For example, the reproduction cost disregards the technological advances that could have taken place since the issuance of the focal asset, whereas the replacement cost leaves aside the characteristics of the focal asset that do not ensure any benefit when the valuation is made. In other words, the cost-based approaches have to consider obsolescence from a technical, functional, and economic point of view, because rarely does valuation take place for an existing brand-new asset. In the case of patents, functional obsolescence could happen much faster than technical obsolescence, because technologies covered by patents often face rapid changes.

It is noteworthy that much of the reproduction costs of innovation regard wages for the inventor workforce. From survey data collected in the OECD countries, it is well known that R&D labour costs account for roughly 60 percent of the overall R&D budget (see Chapter 7, this volume). Materials make up roughly 30 percent, and capital goods approximately one-tenth of R&D expenditures. Obtaining patent protection for the innovation output is accompanied not only by R&D investment but also by procedural and maintenance costs, which should be factored into the reproduction cost. Also, the exact composition of the reproduction costs could differ by industry, technology, and possibly other factors, but it is expected to be relatively stable over time.

The use of the cost-based approaches for the valuation of patents is significantly hampered by the difficulty of correctly quantifying the economic obsolescence triggered by market conditions (Murphy et al. 2012). Intangible assets and patents could be of little value outside a particular line of business or industry (low asset versatility). Typically, patents are used together with other patents within a firm's portfolio and other nonpatented inventions along a technological trajectory pursued by the firm. Second, although the firm has made a significant investment in the patented technology, market conditions may not be ready to adopt the advancement covered by the patent. Last, whereas the implementation of the cost approach is typically more convenient than other approaches, it tends to provide more conservative—albeit less subjective—valuations than the other approaches. For a proper asset valuation, therefore, cost-based approaches should be combined with market and revenue approaches when the economic benefits ensured by the patent or by its wide use in the market far exceed the R&D costs.

1.3.2 Market-Based Approaches

The market approach aims to appraise the present value of future benefits. It evaluates the market price paid by the participants in the marketplace and formulates an average benchmark value. Much has been said regarding the stock market valuation relying on the Tobin's q equation, which focuses on a particular combination of the revenue- and market-based approaches. Under the assumption of efficient capital markets, the estimated impact of R&D and patents on the market value of the firm incorporates the discounted future cash flows generated by the firm's assets, including those created by R&D. Put differently, the Tobin's q approach assumes the market prices for the shares of the firm can be used to price its component assets. Other market value studies have investigated changes in stock prices in reaction to major news about a company's patents (Hall and MacGarvie 2010; Korkeamäki and Takalo 2013) or pre-money equity valuation given by entrepreneurial financiers (Hsu and Ziedonis 2013; Häussler et al. 2014).

Whereas the stock market value constitutes an indirect or implicit valuation of patents, market-based approaches could advance with a direct valuation of innovation when there is an active and public market and an exchange of a comparable asset. Some examples are patent auctions, competitive exchanges, and ratio analysis of comparable transactions, among others (Murphy et al. 2012). However, given the unique and intrinsic characteristics of intellectual property, the direct market approach has serious drawbacks when applied to the valuation of patents. The problem of identifying a comparable replica asset is twofold. Typically, technologies covered by patents yield positive effects when they are used together with other technologies; this makes it more difficult to find a comparable replica. The issue of comparability becomes even more severe when the patent assets under valuation are from different cohorts and have a different number of years remaining before expiration. Because of the highly skewed distribution of patent value, royalty rates defined at the industry level might not be a useful benchmark for the valuation of highly valuable inventions.

Second, even assuming that a replica asset exists, information about the specification of the exchange pricing should be known or discoverable. In the case of a patent transaction, the pricing value is not made public or is difficult to disentangle from other factors, such as confidentiality, the impact of goodwill, collateralization and insurance against litigation risk, and other exchange arrangements, including cross-licensing, and market transactions with other IP assets, nonpatented technologies, and tangible property (Zur and Squires 2015). Hence, uncertainty about future economic performance of patents is profoundly important in the context of patent exchanges.

1.3.3 Revenue-Based Approaches

The revenue approach concerns essentially the revenue-producing capability of the asset to be valued. In particular, this approach considers that the value of an asset is worth what it can yield in terms of revenues. These revenues can take the form of sales when the firms commercialize a product covered by the patent, or they can be royalties from licensing when the patent is licensed out. When the revenues are generated with the interaction of other assets, the contribution to the total revenues of each single asset should be identified.

The valuation of the asset is conducted with the discounted cash flow method, the computation of which requires the definition of the amount of incomes, the timing of the future cash flow, and the assumption of a proper discount rate that can also quantify the risk profile of the investment.[10] Typically, the discount rate is determined through a comparison to alternative and similarly risky investments. A simplified version of the discount rate that takes into account an average risk premium at the level of the firm is the so-called weighted average cost of capital.[11]

There are several techniques that resemble the revenue approach (Goddar and Moser 2011). Incremental revenue analysis aims to compute and evaluate the direct incremental cash flow due to the technologies covered by the patent. The revenues obtainable without the contribution of the patented technologies serve as a baseline situation. Next, the value of patents is computed as a difference of the discounted value of the revenues using those technologies and the baseline situation. The application of this technique is hampered by the fact that patents are characterised by intrinsic complementarities with other assets, including other types of IP, and this makes it extremely difficult to identify a proper baseline situation.

These drawbacks could be overcome by residual value analysis, which computes the value of the focal asset as difference from the total revenues of the contribution of all the other assets excluding the focal asset. The main assumption of this residual value analysis is that all other assets are identifiable and can be valued with at least one another approach based on cost, market, or revenue. Because of the risk of overvaluating the focal asset, this technique is typically implemented in combination with others, such as relief-from-royalty and profit-split analysis (see Layne-Farrar and Lerner 2006; Goddar and Moser 2011).

1.3.4 Patent Real Options

New products and processes that are covered by patents may take time to reveal their productive use. The patentee may be required not only to invest further in additional R&D to perfect the invention but also to expend effort on marketing and brand building to promote these new products and services in the marketplace. These activities typically involve sunk costs and irreversible investments once they have been incepted. Given that patents assign an exclusive right to their owners, the patentee has the option of waiting and partially or fully postponing some of these investments until the market or other conditions are more economically viable for the targeted business model.

One typical market condition that affects the emergence of the so-called real options is uncertainty or volatility about the future level of demand (Rosenberg 1996; Bloom and Van Reenen 2002). Similarly, the extension of the marketing and commercialization of the patented technology in a foreign market involves a patent real option as well. Further, the real option effect exists when the firm can delay the replacement of old technology in case of qualitative changes of demand. Other significant conditions that affect the emergence of patent real options regard the regulatory, approval, certification, and maintenance requirements that must be met before the patented technologies can be employed in production processes or brought into the marketplace (Oriani and Sereno 2011). Last but not least, whereas these examples regard the option to use the patents, the enforceability of a patent right could be seen as a real option—that is, the option to exclude others from using the patented technology (Marco 2005).

Traditional valuation techniques appraise the value of a technology covered by the patent, which includes both the value of the unprotected technology and the value of the patent right (Smith and Parr 2000). In the case of patent real options, the goal is to assess the additional value being created from the flexibility in time when the complementary investment for the successful exploitation of the patent can be postponed. Usually the delay in time to invest depends on the statutory limit of the exclusive protection given by patents, which is generally twenty years from the filing date. The more time that passes before expiration, the greater the value of the patent real option. The value of the patent real option increases with the increasing uncertainty about net future benefits of the technology covered by the patent.

Because patent real options to a large extent concern the decision to defer the use of the patented technology, they can be modeled as a call option (Murphy et al. 2012). Financial theory has seen two main approaches to the valuation of call options. On the one hand, there is the Black and Scholes (1973) method (BS method) with application to the so-called European-type options (Hull 2012), which are one-period options that can be exercised not before the maturity date. In the case of patents, the implementation of the BS method demands more information inputs than the other methods. In fact, both the cost and revenue approaches must be performed before the valuation of a patent real option. The potential benefits of the new technology are quantified with the revenue approach, whereas the investment required for the marketing of the new technology is computed with the cost approach. Furthermore, the implementation of the BS method also requires the volatility of the cash flow of the underlying investment project, and two other parameters, namely the maturity time to the expiration of the patent right and the risk-free interest rate, which are jointly considered as exogenous (Hull 2012).[12] The determination of the volatility parameters depends on future uncertainty related to the patent returns, which is spurred by the difficulty of anticipating the future commercial success of a patent, the technical viability of the underlying invention, and legal aspects regarding the enforceability of the patent (Marco 2005; Schwarz 2004)

Second, American-type call options and compound options can be valued with methods based on decision trees (Whaley 2003; Copeland and Tufano

2004). These types of options offer a more realistic model of the decision-making process in the case of patents. In fact, similarly to an American option, the decision to exercise the patent real option could be triggered any time before expiration, and usually the maintenance of the patent involves several subsequent decisions, as in the case of a compound option. Similarly to the BM method, the main assumption of decision tree methods is the so-called replicating portfolio, according to which the value of an option equals a particular dynamic hedging combination of activities by the patentee, which is made up by a partial investment in the underlying asset and the remaining part of the investment based on a debt financing at the risk-free rate having the same maturity time of the option. Generally, the decision tree methods result in higher valuation of patent real options than the BM method, because the former assign a positive value to the additional flexibility emerging from the exercise of the option before the expiration of the patent right.

The application of financial theory for the valuation of patent real options is still hampered by several drawbacks (Oriani and Sereno 2011). First, the interpretation of the replicating portfolio technique is blurred in the case of patents, because the underlying asset on which the option is based is the value in new business opportunities, and the dynamic hedging combination of activities might not be available. Second, the determination of the volatility parameter should be defined at the patent level, which encounters the same drawbacks of finding a comparable replica patent asset with a similar cash flow (see above the discussion on market approaches). Third, because patent real option valuation demands the completion of other valuation approaches, more information inputs, and a bigger computation effort, it is associated with a greater cost of implementation than other approaches.

1.3.5 Patent Valuation with Indicators

In this section, I discuss the rationales of two patent indicators—patent citations and family size—as nonmonetary indices of the value of patents (Lanjouw and Schankerman 2004; Hall et al. 2005). Citations have been found to correlate well with firm performance indicators such as stock market capitalization (see discussion in section 1.2). This does not necessarily imply that investors directly observe the value of inventions protected by patents, but they probably have access to qualitative information that is correlated with patent citations. Recently, financial investors have obtained greater access to patent information through specialized services offered by consulting firms and information providers (Dushnitsky and Klueter 2011; Ouellette 2012). Hence, patent indicators provide useful information about the value of the underlying inventions, information which is likely to be incorporated into the firm's market prices.

Forward citations received by a patent indicate that the knowledge in an invention has served as a foundation for a subsequent invention along a technological trajectory. If patent B cites patent A as previous prior art, the knowledge pool traced in the cited patent A can be assumed to have 'spilled over' to the inventor of the citing patent B. A patent with a large number of such forward citations is assumed to have spilled over a great deal of knowledge and therefore to be more valuable. However, the practice of citing earlier patents differs across patent offices, and this significantly hampers efforts to devise internationally comparable indicators based on citations.

Citations can be supplied by the inventor and the examiner (Alcacer and Gittelman 2006; Thompson 2006). Inventors should disclose all potentially known previous prior art when they file a patent application with the US Patent and Trademark Office (USPTO),[13] and typically patent citations in the United States can be numerous. In the case of the European Patent Office (EPO), inventors are not required to cite prior art, and references to earlier patents are usually added by patent examiners. Although the EPO citations tend to be more consistent and objective than those of the USPTO, the fact that examiners tend to minimize the total number per patent reduces the statistical power of EPO citations as a value indicator, due to the lower dispersion. The citation practices of the Japanese Patent Office (JPO) are more nuanced, with the patent reviewer assigning the citations included in the patent search report on which the granting decision is based, whereas the inventor may add citations to the patent description with the purpose of making the invention better understood (Motohashi and Goto 2007).

A second variable that has been shown to be highly related to the value of the underlying patented invention is the family size of the patent, which is the number of jurisdictions for which the patent protection has been sought (Lanjouw et al. 1998; Harhoff et al. 1999). Applying in multiple jurisdictions can be expensive, and so firms will tend to do so only when they have a sufficiently valuable invention. For instance, the patentee has to pay patent fees in each system (e.g., EPO, JPO, USPTO), and in the case of EPO patents, the amount of patent fees varies with the number of European countries covered by the patent protection. Because the patentee is likely to be more informed than the market about the real value of the underlying invention, family size can be viewed as a credible signal of the worth the applicant attributes to the invention. More precisely, family size is a proxy for the patentee's expectations regarding the size of the invention's potential market.

However, the patent's family size does not account for possible signaling differences across patent systems. Protecting an invention in national patent offices such as those of France or Germany does not provide the same prospective benefits as protecting the patent in the US system, because filing an application with the USPTO reveals the intention to exploit the invention in a market larger than a European national one. Moreover, the decision to protect an invention in a large market like that of the United States could constitute a preemptive strategy for value appropriation, which influences the financial market's expectations about the future benefits of the firm's R&D and patent assets. Thus, a very good prediction of a firm's market value should be obtainable by using family size as a value weight (in order to measure a market size-weighted version of family size to account for the fact that coverage in a large market is more valuable).

1.4 Setting and Variables

1.4.1. Sample

The sample is constituted by three separate datasets for European-, Japanese-, and US-listed firms over the period 1991–2005. To construct these datasets, I integrated several sources (Box 1.1). The European dataset

---

Box 1.1   Information sources for the listed firms over the period 1991–2005

Information type	Europe	United States	Japan
Company books	– Thomson Financials' Global Vantage database	– Thomson Financials' Compustat database	– Thomson Financials' Global Vantage database
Identification and ownership structure	– December annual issues of Amadeus 1998–2006 – Who Owns Whom 1985	– Who Owns Whom 1985–2005, available from NBER patent data project (update)	Securities Identification Code Committee in Japan (see Thoma et al. 2010 A)
R&D expenditures	– Bureau van Dijk's Amadeus database – Thomson Financials' Global Vantage database – UK Department of Industry's R&D Scoreboard	– Thomson Financials' Compustat database	– Thomson Financials' Global Vantage database
Market capitalization	Thomson Financial's Datastream database	Thomson Financial's Datastream database	Thomson Financial's Datastream database

Information type	Europe	United States	Japan
Patent information	– PatStat, April 2012 – EPO weekly XML files, from www.epoline.org	– PatStat, April 2012 – USPTO weekly XML files from Google Patents	– PatStat, April 2012 – IIP database, Dec. 2009 (Goto and Motohashi 2007)
	– Name matching from Thoma et al. (2010 B)	– Name matching from the NBER patent data project (update)	– Name matching from Thoma et al. (2010 A)
Coverage	R&D disclosing firms	Patenting firms	R&D disclosing firms
Domestic patent protection	Patents granted by the EPO & validated at national level°	Patents granted by the USPTO	Patents granted by the JPO
International patent protection	PCT patent applications	PCT patent applications	PCT patent applications
Firms with useful information	1,270	3,798	1,701
Useful observations	7,739	27,933	6,083

Notes: ° It includes PCT application filings designating the EPO as an ISA.

includes a large variety of countries with different accounting regulations and levels of financial development, ranging from the United Kingdom, a common-law country with an active equity market, to emerging Eastern European countries with a very small market capitalisation-to-GDP ratio. I consolidated some of the countries with small numbers of firms into larger groupings in order to reduce the number of dummies needed, thus for example, all Eastern European countries form one group, and Spain and Greece another.

As discussed above, the generally accepted accounting principles (GAAP) in the United States require the disclosure of R&D costs, and the relative proportion of R&D-disclosing firms in the United States is far greater than in other countries. Only one-fifth of the European-listed firms reported data on R&D expenditures for one or more of the sample years, whilst for Japan about one-half of the listed firms disclosed R&D data.[14] In addition, small and technology-based firms in the United States have much more exposure to financial markets than do such firms in other countries (IMF 2007). Therefore, I have restricted the dataset to the R&D-disclosing firms in Europe and Japan, whereas in the United States solely the patenting firms have been considered.

Company patent counts in all technological classes were obtained by matching the name of the assignee from patent databases with the company names (Thoma et al. 2010 A and B). For companies with subsidiaries, the patents of the ultimate parent company have been consolidated on the basis of the ownership structure. Further information on corporate structure was collected from Hoovers and company websites. Holding companies have been reclassified according to the main line of business or their most important subsidiaries, using additional information from business directories and company websites.

1.4.2 Patent Strategies

Firms in the proposed sample (Box 1.1) pursue several types of patent strategies. Patents granted by the USPTO and JPO ensure 'automatic' protection under the respective national legislation for twenty years from the date of filing. Unlike the USPTO, the JPO examination and granting processes take place only if the patentee deposits a request for substantive examination. Since 2001, that request should be filed within three years from application, instead of seven years. JPO applications are characterised by a relatively small number of claims: In fact, the multiple claim system was introduced only in 1988, and since then the number of claims has grown noticeably but has not yet reached that of the USPTO or EPO (Goto and Motohashi 2007). As a consequence, a patentee might need to combine several applications at the JPO as compared to a single filing from elsewhere in order to achieve a comparable level of protection.

Similarly to the JPO, all application filings under the European Patent Convention (EPC) are published by the EPO within eighteen months from the filing date, whereas at the USPTO the application cannot be published if the protection is not extended to foreign legislations. There are three ways to file an application at the EPO. The applicant can choose an extension of an earlier application filing in one of the EPC member countries or she can deposit a direct and central filing at the EPO.[15] An additional possibility is an application under the aegis of the Patent Cooperation Treaty (PCT) through a EURO-PCT procedure (see below). Once the patent application and the related search report have been published by the EPO, the patentee can request the substantive examination within six months. A patent granted by the EPO provides protection in the member countries of the EPC solely if the patent is validated at the national level by paying the corresponding fees and providing an official translation.

The three systems differ substantially in terms of costs for obtaining a standard patent (OECD 2009). The least expensive is the JPO, with about € 5,460 per patent in 2003, whereas a grant by the USPTO will cost about € 10,250. The EPO system is much more expensive, costing about € 30,530 for a granted patent of a direct filing or an extended national application. The EURO-PCT is the most expensive patent protection strategy, costing about € 46,700.[16] Further costs regard the maintenance of the patent at the national level, which depends on the number of validation countries. Typically the renewal fees are paid annually, but in the case of the USPTO, the renewal decisions are made 3.5, 7, and 11.5 years after the grant.

The procedure for filing a PCT application deserves particular attention, because only one centralized procedure is required to obtain international patent protection. When the patentee deposits a first filing in a national office, she has the benefit of a period of up to twelve months before she has to file for the international extension. The PCT procedure is managed by the World International Patent Office (WIPO), which receives the priority application and publishes it as an international application within eighteen months of the priority date. The publication is accompanied by an International Search Report (ISR) prepared by an International Search Authority, which is one of the appointed national offices, including the EPO, JPO, and USPTO that in turn will proceed with a EURO-PCT, JP-PCT, and US-PCT filing, respectively. The substantive examination and granting process starts at least thirty months after the priority date, when the applicant enters into the national phase by paying the appropriate fees in the designated countries. The effective transfer process in the national phase may still take several months depending on specific rules set by the national or regional offices (Guellec and Van Pottelsberghe de la Potterie 2007).

The PCT procedure allows the applicant to recoup time in order to choose the countries for protection, enforcement, and commercial exploitation of an invention. By delaying the decision for examination and in which countries to have it, the applicant can investigate the technical viability of the technology, its commercial potential, and other aspects related to enforceability. Obtaining international protection of an invention involves significant costs, including procedural costs (fees before grant, translation, and attorney fees) and maintenance costs (renewal fees after grant). The possibility of having thirty or more months for deciding the countries in which to sustain these costs, which are typically sunk and irreversible, generates a large option value for the applicant when a PCT procedure has started. In this direction, it could be concluded that the PCT procedure constitutes a quintessential example of how important patents are for identifying real option value.

1.4.3 Econometric Specification and Variables

The econometric specification in this study is built by means of a log-linear model, which can be reconciled with a Cobb-Douglas form of the market value equation of a firm (Hall 2000; Hall and McGarvie 2010). In particular, the basic definition of the market value equation with two terms, tangible assets A_{it} and knowledge assets K_{it}, is given by

$$log\ V_{it} = f\ (A_{it}, K_{it}) \tag{5}$$

Knowledge assets are assumed to be a function of R&D, patents, and the value weighted patents:

$$K_{it} = g(R_{it} \frac{P_{it}}{R_{it}}, \frac{I_{it}}{P_{it}}) \tag{6}$$

Where R_{it} is the firm i's R&D capitalized stock in year t, P_{it} is a measure of patent stock in year t, and I_{it} is a measure of a value index for the weighted patent stocks in year t.

Substituting expression (6) into (5) and performing a first-order logarithmic expansion, the following estimating equation can be obtained:

$$log\ Q_{it} = log\frac{V_{it}}{A_{it}} = log q_t + \sigma log A_{it} + \gamma_K\ log\frac{R_{it}}{A_{it}} + \gamma_P\ log\frac{P_{it}}{R_{it}} + \gamma_I\ log\frac{I_{it}}{P_{it}} + \varepsilon_{it} \tag{7}$$

In this log-linear model of the firm's market value, the relevant coefficients are measured as elasticities, and therefore they can be easily compared across different variables and samples, and the interpretation of the results is more straightforward. Furthermore, by using a robust functional form, the effects of outliers are reduced. Last, tangible assets control for scale effects, and the other effects are taken into account with the mean of industry dummies, country dummies, and year dummies.

The dependent variable is given by Tobin's q for the firm—that is, the ratio of the firm's market value to tangible assets. A firm's market value is defined as the sum of market capitalization (price multiplied by the number of outstanding shares at the end of the year) and noncurrent liabilities less a correction for net current liabilities plus inventories.[17] Tangible assets are the net costs of tangible fixed property and inventories used in the production of revenue and are obtained as the sum of gross fixed assets plus inventory stocks less depreciation, depletion, and amortization (accumulated), investment grants, and other deductions.[18]

Corporate finance scholars have developed alternative, more complex estimations of the Tobin's q which rely on estimated market value of the firm compared with that used in this study (e.g., Perfect and Wiles 1994). These alternative approaches to Tobin's q measurement produce more precise estimations but are computationally costly. Moreover, their greater precision is traded off by a larger selection bias. DaDalt et al. (2003) used the

Compustat dataset and found that the Perfect and Wiles' approach produces a 20 percent loss in sample size. It is important to note that DaDalt et al. (2003) estimated that simple methods such as the one used here, and complex ones, like that of Perfect and Wiles, agree in approximately 90 percent of cases for values of Q below 0.8 and above 1.2. As Table 1.1 clearly shows, for most firms and observations in the sample, the Tobin's q value falls above 1.2.

In this study, the R&D expenditure history of each firm was used to compute R&D stock. Missing R&D numbers for these firms were filled using data from the multiple sources. As mentioned earlier, non US firms are not required or recommended to disclose information on their R&D expenditures, and thus one could think that the availability of data on R&D expenditures is potential source of sample selection bias. Reporting R&D, therefore, is an endogenous variable, because the decision of whether or not to disclose this information is at the firm's discretion. Hall and Oriani (2006) found that selection was not a factor for most of the European countries they considered.

Because the stock of the key regressors cannot be measured directly from the firm books, proxies obtained from current and past flows of R&D and patent-related variables have been advanced. R&D stocks (K) were obtained using a declining balance formula and the past history of R&D spending:

$$K_t = R_t + (1 - \delta)K_{t-1} \tag{8}$$

Where δ is the depreciation rate, which is usually assumed to be 15 percent. The starting R&D stock of the sample was calculated for each firm at the first available R&D observation year as $K_o = R_o/(\delta + g)$. This assumes that real R&D had been growing at a constant annual growth rate g prior to the sample, where $g = 8$ percent. Patent stocks were obtained using the same method, except that the initial available patent counts were not discounted to obtain an initial capital stock because of the longer pre-sample history of patenting (back to the '70s) than for R&D, so the impact of the initial stock is minimal.[19]

This study uses several categories of patent stocks: i) Patents granted by the EPO; ii) patents granted by the USPTO; iii) patents granted by the JPO; iv) application filings under the PCT procedure at the WIPO. A caveat is in order with respect to the JPO patent counts. Because the 1988 reform shifted the unitary breadth of an invention as represented by the number of claims, the raw patent counts would not provide a coherent measure over time. In order to correct for this bias, the JPO patent counts in this study have considered only those patents that received at least one citation within five years from priority, thus allowing for more comparable patent counts for the years before the reform.[20]

The PCT applications encompass partial inventions which are likely to be included in the other types of patent stocks as well. In fact, PCT applications are extensions of domestic filings, when the patentee intends to obtain protection with the same domestic priority, but at the international level. To the extent that a PCT application has been granted by the national office, it is also taken into account in the computation of the domestic patent stock. This measurement approach can disentangle the additional impact of the PCT applications on a firm's market value above and beyond the other categories of patent stocks. The stock of PCT applications represents a proxy of the real option capability of the firm, because these types of filings hold a large option value as compared to other patent strategies. As discussed above, the PCT procedure gives the applicant more time to decide whether to request a substantive examination and to choose the countries in which to seek a granting decision. Because the Tobin's q approach is forward looking and is not hampered by problems of the timing of costs and revenues, the patent real option effect deriving from the PCT application filing stock will be incorporated into the market value of the firm.

Nevertheless, the stock of PCT applications is likely to be correlated with the breadth of patent protection and more in general with patent value and quality. Thus, the regression analysis has considered a patent value index based on the breadth of the patent family—that is, the extent of countries where the patent protection has been granted. This index measures the potential market size of an invention and it is constructed by summing up the real GDP of the countries covered by the patent family as defined by the INPADOC type of patent family.[21] The GDP of each covered country for the period 1950–2007 was drawn from the PENN World Table (http://pwt. econ.upenn.edu/), normalized to that of the United States, with the US GDP set to unity. For each focal patent taken out in the EPO, JPO, and USPTO, the normalized values for the countries covered (as of the patent's priority year) are summed to create the index. To form the portfolio stock of family values, the values for all the firm's patents in each year have been added, and the usual declining balanced formula has been used to construct the stock.

An additional note about the PCT applications is appropriate here. This variable also encompasses patents that have reached a definitive status of nonpatentability (refusal or abandonment) and a residual category of the patents not yet granted.[22] There is a protection premium on the underlying inventions, notwithstanding the fact that an application is still pending. These applications are likely to be more controversial because there is uncertainty about their technical viability or subject matter regarding their patentability. The uncertainty could also regard the economic potential when further investment is demanded to exploit the underlying inventions through brand building, publicity, customer networks, and so on. Typically, this type of investment is idiosyncratic country by country and takes time to be developed. Although the invention could be patentable, the extra investment required for its commercial exploitation could prove to be economically prohibitive for the patentee. The uncertainty related to this type of PCT application prior to attainment of a definitive status should increase the value of the real option effect and its impact on the market value of the firm.

Finally, the regression analysis has also considered a value index of the patent family breadth of the PCT application stock in order to account for the value heterogeneity of the PCT filings. This variable is indicative of the size of patent real option effect. Once the PCT application has entered the national phase and the application has been published as a domestic filing, the greater the number of countries where the protection is sought, the larger the expected value of the application.

On the basis of these considerations, the final econometric specification form looks like the following equation:

$$\log Q_{it} = \log \frac{V_{it}}{A_{it}} = \log q_t + \sigma \log A_{it} + \gamma_K \log \frac{R_{it}}{A_{it}} + \gamma_P \log \frac{P_{it}}{R_{it}} + \gamma_I^P \log \frac{I_{it}^P}{P_{it}} + \gamma_F \log \frac{F_{it}}{R_{it}} + \gamma_I^F \log \frac{I_{it}^F}{F_{it}} + \varepsilon_{it}$$

(9)

The meaning of the variables is as follows:

— Tobin's q (V/A)—the ratio of the firm's market value to tangible assets;
— Tangible assets (A)—annual book value of the tangible assets;
— R&D stock (R)—the stock of past R&D spending;
— Patent stock (P)—the stock of granted patent at the domestic level by priority date;
— Application filing stock (F)—the stock of PCT application filings by priority date;
— Patent value index (I^P)—the stock of granted patent at the domestic level weighted by the family value index;
— Application filing value index (I^F)—the stock of PCT application filings weighted by the family value index.

1.5 Results

This section presents the descriptive statistics and the multivariate econometric results. The final sample for the period 1991 through 2005, after eliminating a few observations with extreme outliers with respect to the patent data, firms with unconsolidated accounts, and firms with no sales information available, consists of 1,270 firms for Europe, 1,701 for Japan, and 3,798 for the United States.

Table 1.1 reports some descriptive statistics for the final sample of the three unbalanced panels (from one to fifteen years per firm). The firms in the sample are large, with median sales of about three hundred million euros for Europe and Japan, and the US panel is characterised by a broader presence of start-ups, as demonstrated by median sales four times smaller than

Table 1.1 Descriptive statistics

	Mean	S.D.	Median	1Q	3Q	Min	Max
Europe: 7,739 observations, 1,270 firms, 15 country/regions, 1991–2005							
Sales^	3,818	13,088	280	62	1,787	0.004	246,859
Assets^	2,903	10,346	148	30	1,161	0.087	204,112
Tobin's q	3.021	3.558	1.739	1.162	3.177	0.101	24.901
R&D expenditures^	127	496	8	2	34	0.002	7,463
R&D stock^	650	2,522	39	10	178	0.007	35,313
R&D stock/assets	0.694	1.155	0.275	0.093	0.694	0.000	5.607
EPO Patent-R&D stock ratio	0.502	1.135	0.174	0.031	0.459	0.000	8.484
Family value per EPO patent	0.264	0.169	0.287	0.173	0.361	0.000	0.804
PCT filing-R&D stock ratio	0.577	1.308	0.186	0.041	0.509	0.000	9.525
Family value per PCT filing	0.584	0.328	0.681	0.430	0.802	0.000	1.216
United States: 27,933 observations, 3,798 firms, 1991–2005							
Sales^	1,372	7,702	71	14	393	0.001	264,147
Assets^	1,901	14,429	92	24	478	0.015	623,379
Tobin's q	2.312	2.810	1.427	0.874	2.542	0.100	24.990
R&D expenditures^	62	342	6	1	21	0.000	10,785
R&D stock^	294	1,696	25	6	90	0.002	44,077
R&D stock/assets	0.537	0.878	0.244	0.089	0.568	0.000	5.688
US Patent-R&D stock ratio	0.645	1.469	0.198	0.014	0.608	0.000	11.048
Family value per US patent	0.329	0.305	0.284	0.169	0.419	0.000	1.674
PCT filing-R&D stock ratio	0.331	0.970	0.058	0.000	0.243	0.000	7.622
Family value per PCT filing	0.515	0.413	0.585	0.000	0.810	0.000	1.722
Japan: 6,083 observations, 1,701 firms, 1991–2005							
Sales^	2,625	9,831	310	115	985	1.542	144,854
Assets^	2,690	12,798	159	58	484	0.574	207,950
Tobin's q	1.562	2.065	1.103	0.799	1.534	0.101	24.944
R&D expenditures^	94	453	4	1	15	0.000	5,901
R&D stock^	451	2,140	21	6	81	0.032	25,413
R&D stock/assets	0.255	0.479	0.143	0.057	0.298	0.000	11.625
JPO Patent-R&D stock ratio	0.135	0.241	0.000	0.000	0.187	0.000	1.450
Family value per JPO patent	0.174	0.189	0.000	0.000	0.320	0.000	0.626
PCT filing-R&D stock ratio	0.099	0.281	0.000	0.000	0.064	0.000	2.049
Family value per PCT filing	0.282	0.363	0.000	0.000	0.669	0.000	1.077

Notes: The sample includes only firms that conduct R&D in the three geographical contexts. All the US firms are active in patenting, whereas 24.2 percent of the European firms and 56.0 percent of the Japanese ones have no national patent stock.

^In millions of current €.

those of the other panels. Another way of looking at the differential size distribution of a typical firm across the three panels is in terms of tangible assets, although it is noteworthy that the typical US firm is twice more capital intensive than the other firms, as revealed by comparing the assets to sales ratios. Firms in the US and European dataset are fairly R&D intensive, having a similar median R&D to tangible assets ratio of about one-fourth, whereas the Japanese firms follow more distantly in terms of R&D intensity (0.14). These differences are also reflected in their median Tobin's q, which is well above unity in the European and US panel, and not far from unity for the Japanese dataset.

Descriptive statistics for the ratio of patent stocks to R&D stocks and the ratio of family value index stocks to patent stocks are shown for the domestic granted patents and for the PCT application filings. In this table, the statistics for all of the patent variables are based on the entire subsample for each panel, but it is worth mentioning that the three panels report a different number of nonpatenting firms. All the US firms are active in patenting, whereas 24.2 percent of the European firms and 56.0 percent of the Japanese ones have no national patent stock. The regression analysis included several dummies of non R&D–reporting firms and zero patenting stocks in order to tackle any selection bias deriving from missing or incomplete information, possible firm differences, or errors in matching, although these binary variables cannot be interpreted directly (Hall and MacGarvic 2010).

A typical US firm has greater patenting productivity than a European one, respectively 0.20 and 0.17, perhaps because EPO patent filings are more costly than US patents. Given that there are many more nonpatenting firms in the Japanese panel, the relative patent productivity is the lowest in the sample. In turn, the patent productivity of the PCT filings is very heterogeneous for the three panels, revealing that the EURO-PCT route is a typical patent strategy for the European firms to achieve global and regional protection. Last, the family value indices for granted patents and PCT filings are very similar across the European and US dataset, but on the contrary they are zero for Japan, which can be explained again by the fact that over half of the observations of this panel are not linked to any patent stock.

Table 1.2 depicts the multivariate econometric results for the three samples. Each sample is represented separately, and five similarly built models are regressed for each sample, for a total of fifteen models. First, it can be noted that the scaling factor represented by the log asset is insignificant or small in the various regressions. Regardless of the patent variables included, the R&D elasticity of the European firms is the largest in the sample, with a coefficient of about 0.20, followed by the elasticities of the US and Japanese firms with 0.14 and 0.12, respectively. Under the assumption of efficient markets and optimal investment policies, we can compare the elasticity with the R&D stock to value ratio (the share of value due to capitalized R&D expenditure). For Europe and the United States, the median value of this ratio is distant from the estimated elasticities, implying underinvestment in

Table 1.2 Market value regressions: Dependent variable = log Tobin's *q*

	(1)	(2)	(3)	(4)	(5)
Europe: 7,739 observations, 1,270 firms, 15 country/regions, 1991–2005					
Log assets (millions of euros)	−0.012	−0.014	−0.022***	−0.017*	−0.018**
	[0.008]	[0.009]	[0.009]	[0.009]	[0.009]
Log R&D stock-assets ratio	0.197***	0.215***	0.199***	0.205***	0.204***
	[0.017]	[0.017]	[0.017]	[0.017]	[0.017]
Dummy for zero R&D stock	−0.845***	−0.940***	−0.843***	−0.871***	−0.865***
	[0.081]	[0.080]	[0.080]	[0.082]	[0.083]
Log EPO Patent-R&D stock ratio		0.086***	0.077***	0.043**	0.040**
		[0.015]	[0.015]	[0.018]	[0.018]
Dummy for zero EPO patent stock		−0.279***	−0.537***	−0.342***	−0.285**
		[0.061]	[0.080]	[0.112]	[0.120]
Log family value per EPO patent			0.207***	0.173***	0.156***
			[0.041]	[0.042]	[0.044]
Log PCT filing-R&D stock ratio				0.046**	0.047**
				[0.019]	[0.019]
Dummy for zero PCT filing stock				−0.169**	−0.218**
				[0.084]	[0.093]
Log family value per PCT filing					0.044
					[0.035]
Std. error (adj. R-squared)	0.254	0.271	0.280	0.282	0.282

(*Continued*)

Table 1.2 (Continued)

	(1)	(2)	(3)	(4)	(5)
United States: 27,933 observations, 3,798 firms, 1991–2005					
Log assets (millions of euros)	-0.020*** [0.006]	-0.006 [0.006]	-0.015** [0.006]	-0.009 [0.007]	-0.011* [0.007]
Log R&D stock-assets ratio	0.135*** [0.010]	0.155*** [0.010]	0.138*** [0.010]	0.141*** [0.011]	0.140*** [0.011]
Dummy for zero R&D stock	-0.489*** [0.06]	-0.604*** [0.061]	-0.522*** [0.059]	-0.543*** [0.061]	-0.538*** [0.061]
Log US Patent-R&D stock ratio		0.058*** [0.008]	0.040*** [0.008]	0.028*** [0.009]	0.027*** [0.009]
Dummy for zero US patent stock		0.003 [0.028]	-0.197*** [0.036]	-0.148*** [0.037]	-0.130** [0.038]
Log family value per US patent			0.203*** [0.024]	0.183*** [0.024]	0.171*** [0.025]
Log PCT filing-R&D stock ratio				0.030*** [0.008]	0.029*** [0.008]
Dummy for zero PCT filing stock				-0.120*** [0.031]	-0.143*** [0.032]
Log family value per PCT filing					0.043*** [0.015]
Std. error (adj. R-squared)	0.137	0.144	0.153	0.155	0.156

Japan: 6,083 observations, 1,701 firms, 1991–2005

Log assets (millions of euros)	-0.006	-0.005	-0.013**	-0.016***	-0.016**
	[0.005]	[0.006]	[0.006]	[0.006]	[0.006]
Log R&D stock-assets ratio	0.124***	0.126***	0.119***	0.116***	0.117***
	[0.011]	[0.011]	[0.012]	[0.012]	[0.012]
Dummy for zero R&D stock	-0.326***	-0.331***	-0.309***	-0.299***	-0.300***
	[0.045]	[0.050]	[0.051]	[0.051]	[0.051]
Log JPO Patent-R&D stock ratio		0.004	0.009	0.005	0.005
		[0.010]	[0.010]	[0.010]	[0.010]
Dummy for zero JPO patent stock		-0.002	-0.276***	-0.044	-0.048
			[0.061]	[0.075]	[0.075]
Log family value per JPO patent			0.219***	0.128***	0.131***
				[0.048]	[0.048]
Log PCT filing-R&D stock ratio				0.022***	0.022***
				[0.007]	[0.007]
Dummy for zero PCT filing stock				-0.214***	-0.207***
					[0.036]
Log family value per PCT filing					-0.014
					[0.018]
Std. error (adj. R-squared)	0.204	0.204	0.208	0.212	0.212

Notes: Ordinary least squares estimation with standard errors robust to heteroskedasticity and grouped by firms. All regressions include twenty-three industry dummies and fourteen-year dummies. The regressions for the European firms include also fourteen country dummies. *** indicates statistically significant at 1 percent level, ** 5 percent level, and * 10 percent level.

R&D by the average firm. For Japan, a smaller level of underinvestment in R&D is found because the median value is just above the estimated elasticity.

Second, EPO patents held by the European firms are more important than domestic patenting by the US firms, as seen in the greater elasticity of three percentage points for the unweighted patent counts. The patent coefficients are reduced slightly by the inclusion of the patent family value index, but otherwise these patent coefficient results are unchanged. The family value index is normalized by the patent stock, so it is roughly orthogonal to the unweighted patent stock. Quite interestingly, the indices' elasticity is exactly the same, about 20 percent for both the European and US firms. For Japan, the family value index of domestic patenting matters more, with an additional two percentage points, although the patent productivity is positive but not significant. These observations are consistent with the assumption that financial investors are capable of discriminating the heterogeneity of the value distribution of the granted patent stocks. The finding that domestic patenting by the Japanese firms is uninformative for market value above and beyond the R&D cumulative stock could be explained by the fact that the unit of invention at the JPO has been more limited than in the other countries and therefore the raw patent counts are a poorer proxy of the output of innovation activities (Haneda and Odagiri 1998; Goto and Motohashi 2007).

The family value index effects are fairly large. Doubling the average value index increases the value of European firms by 16 to 21 percent, the value of US firms by about 17 to 20 percent, and the value of Japanese ones by about 13 to 22 percent. However, the interquartile range for these variables is about 0.2 for Europe and 0.3 for the US and Japan, so doubling the value index is a fairly extreme move. In terms of one standard deviation increase of the family value index, the increases of market valuation are on the order of 2.5 percent for European and Japanese firms and 5 percent for the US firms (compare model 5). A one standard deviation impact of family value index yields a greater impact than patent productivity for the US firms, whereas the relative size of the impact of these two variables is reversed for the European firms. This finding is consistent with previous studies in the literature that have argued that the US financial markets are more efficient than other countries in the valuation of innovation activities (Hall and Oriani 2006).

The results regarding the domestic patent stock and family value index hold when the stock of PCT application filings is included in the regressions. The biggest elasticity of PCT filings above the domestic patent stock is found for the European panel, followed by the US firms and then the Japanese ones. The last model of Table 1.2 also includes the family value index for the PCT filings, which is significant solely for the US firms. Combining the joint effect of the two PCT filing–related measures, the largest elasticity on market value is seen for the US firms. Overall, these observations do not contradict the patent real option view, according to which the Tobin's q approach incorporates the option value because it is forward looking and unhampered by problems of timing of costs and revenues (Bloom and Van Reenen 2002). The real option capability of the firm is satisfactorily proxied by the PCT filing stocks, because a PCT filing application allows for a longer time span before entering the granting procedure and deciding the countries in which to seek patent protection.

1.6 Summary

The chapter has presented the rationales for the Tobin's q market value model of the firm. This model describes the value of the firm according to various assets that a firm holds, and therefore, it allows computation of the marginal or shadow value of the ratio of a knowledge asset to tangible assets. Computation of the Tobin's q requires a firm to be listed in financial markets characterised by intense trading and significant level of efficiency. For this reason and because the accounting standards for the disclosure of R&D information are more stringent in the US and the UK than elsewhere, previous research has regarded in large extent these two Anglo-Saxon economies. I discussed several linear and nonlinear estimation strategies for implementing the market value model of the firm. Most of the previous empirical studies have shown that R&D investment, patent counts, and average value of the firm's patent portfolio matter significantly for the firm's market valuation.

The accounting literature has seen the development of other approaches beyond market value to appraise the value of R&D and patents. First, it is worth recalling that the market value approach can proceed with a direct computation of the value of a patented technology when there is an active market of the focal asset or comparable replica asset(s). Second, there is the cost approach, which proceeds with an assessment of the level of investment required to obtain the same patent asset or an asset with the same future service capability. Third, the revenue approach typically estimates the future cash flow generated by the patent asset formulating an average benchmark value.

The real option approach for the valuation of a patent asset has been proposed repeatedly in the literature, although its empirical implementation is far from perfected. This approach seeks to establish the additional value gained by being able to delay the complementary investment for the successful exploitation of the patent. One of the main drawbacks of the patent real option is the fact that it demands far more information and hence its implementation costs more than other approaches. In fact, it requires computation of the costs and revenues deriving from the economic exploitation of a patented technology, consideration of the volatility of the future cash flow generated by the patent asset, and determination of some other exogenous conditions.

Innovation scholars have started to rank patents through the use of indices built with the mean of patent indicators; in doing so they also advance nonmonetary valuations of patents. In fact, patents are very informative about the breadth and technology potential of an invention, as well as other aspects. The two most widely used indicators for breadth and technology potential are based on the number of citations received (forward citations) and number of jurisdictions where the patent protection has been sought (family size). A full-fledged discussion of the patent indicators' literature and relative applications will be presented in the next chapters.

The last goal of the chapter has been to introduce some new and comparative empirical evidences regarding the market valuation of R&D and patents in three geographical contexts (the United States, Europe, and Japan), reconciling the Tobin's q model of the firm with the real option approach of patent valuation. Furthermore, I have used a nonmonetary index for the valuation of patent assets in order to take into the account the large heterogeneity of the value of patents. This index measures the geographical breadth of protection, given by the GDP-weighted number of countries where the patent protection has been sought, whereas the real option capability of the firm is proxied by the portfolio size of the PCT application filings, as the PCT allows the decision maker to wait many more months before requesting a substantive examination and choosing the countries in which to have a granting decision.

Several new findings are presented in this chapter. First of all, R&D stocks show a larger impact than patent variables independently from the geographical context. Second, with the exception of Japan, national patent stocks significantly affect a firm's market value above and beyond R&D. Third, financial investors can gauge the strong skewness of the value of patents and adjust their investment decisions accordingly. This effect is particularly pronounced in the US context. Last but not least, in the three geographical contexts, a firm's market value correlates significantly with the PCT application filing stocks. This finding does not contradict the assumption that these kinds of filings at the international level hold a large option value for the decision maker, one which is incorporated in the firm's market value.

Notes

1 The costs incurred during the research phase are considered as an expense and not capitalized, whereas patent filing fees and the related procedural costs (e.g., legal expenses) are recorded as an asset. For a full-fledged discussion see Murphy *et al.* (2012).
2 Note that it is possible to relax the assumptions of constant returns and perfect competition in the output market and derive a version of this equation that will still yield a measure of productivity (or profitability) that can be related to innovation inputs (Bloom and Van Reenen 2002).
3 See chapter 2 (this volume) for a fuller discussion on the Lanjouw and Schankerman (2004)'s methodology.
4 These results are shown to be robust even after controlling for advertisement investment, which in turn is characterised by a growing return on market value. During the time period of the second part of the Hall (1993)'s sample advertisement has an almost comparable return to R&D.

5 Among the European countries the financial market in the UK is more similar to the US than to the continental European countries (Toivanen *et al.* 2002); see Haneda and Odagiri (1998) for Japanese firms and Bosworth and Rogers (2001) for Australian firms.

6 See Toivanen *et al.* (2002).

7 In particular, these controls are debt structure, sales growth, firm's market share, investment in financial activities from external sources, cash flow ratio, growth of tangible assets, and others. For further details see Toivanen *et al.* (2002).

8 The construction of the firm patent portfolios has considered not only the direct ownership of patents by a firm but also indirect links given by the patent activities pursued by their subsidiaries.

9 Nevertheless, this study does not allow us to posit a definite conclusion regarding which of these two effects is stronger because the relative variables are not entered simultaneously in the regressions but one at a time.

10 The Discounted Cash Flow (DCF) method is based on the computation of the Net Present Value (*NPV*) of the focal asset under valuation with the mean of the following formula:

$$NPV = \sum_{t=0}^{T} \frac{CF_t}{(1+r)^t}$$

where T is the expected lifecycle of the asset, CF_t is the net cash flow in year t and r the discount rate adjusted for the risk profile attributable to the asset (Ross *et al.* 2009).

11 The weighted average cost of capital (WACC) of a firm is linear combination of the cost of equity R_E and the cost of debt R_D, that are weighted by the relative proportion of equity *(E)* and debt *(D)* in the capital structure of the firm:

$$R_{WACC} = \frac{E}{E+D} R_E + \frac{D}{E+D} R_D (1 - t_c)$$

where the $(1 - t_c)$ represents a tax shield yielding when a firm faces a corporate tax rate t_c. For a fuller presentation of the WACC theory see Ross *et al.* (2009).

12 Given an European-type call option with expiration date T, current value of the underlying asset V, and the exercise price I, the Black and Scholes (1973) formula is computed as $C = VN(d_1) - Ie^{-rT}N(d_2)$, where σ is volatility of the underlying asset value, r is the risk-free interest rate continuously compounded, and $N(\cdot)$ is cumulative standard normal distribution with:

$$d_1 = \frac{ln \, V/I + (r + \sigma^2 / 2)T}{\sigma\sqrt{T}}$$

$$d_2 = d_1 - \sigma\sqrt{T}$$

The term $\sigma\sqrt{T}$, known as cumulative volatility, measures how much the stream of cash flow of the underlying asset can vary before a decision must finally be taken (Luehrman 1998). For a wider presentation of this result and relative applications on binomial decision trees see Hull (2012) and Whaley (2003).

13 This is also known as duty-of-candor rule.

14 Author's elaboration from the respective sources depicted in Box 1.1.

15 Since the January 2013 the EPO under the aegis of a recent legislative initiative of the European Parliament has provided a new application procedure for the so-called unitary patent that is a European patent with unitary effects. This procedure has effects in the vast majority of the member states and will be effective with the entry in force of the Unified Patent Court. For more information see www.epo.org.
16 For a comparison in terms of purchasing power parities see chapter 8 (this volume).
17 Outstanding shares include both common shares and preferred shares.
18 All values expressed in domestic currencies have been converted into current € by using annual average exchange rates reported by Thomson Financial's Datastream database.
19 Because sample patent data begin in 1978 and the first year used in the regressions is 1991, the effects of omitted initial conditions will be small ($0.85^{14} \approx 0.10$).
20 Citation information has been drawn from the JPO Patent Gazette that goes back up till year 1981 (Goto and Motohashi 2007).
21 See also the measurement methodology described in Box 2.1 (chapter 2, this volume).
22 Given that patent counts are cumulative stocks, the fraction of the not-yet-granted patents should be increasing towards the end of the sample. In the regressions a full set of annual dummies is included in order to control for cohort effects.

References

Alcacer J., M. Gittelman 2006. "Patent Citations as Measure of Knowledge Flows: The Influence of Examiner Citations." *Rev Eco Stat* 88(4):774–779.
Belenzon S. 2012. "Cumulative Innovation and Market Value: Evidence from Patent Citations." *Econ J* 559(122): 265–285.
Black F., M. Scholes 1973. "The Pricing of Options and Corporate Liabilities." *J Pol Econ* 81(3):637–654.
Blair M., S. M. H. Wallman 2001. *Unseen Wealth: Report of the Brookings Task Force on Intangibles*. Washington (DC): Brookings Institution Press (Brookings Task Force on Intangibles).
Bloom, N., J. Van Reenen 2002. "Patents, Real Options and Firm Performance." *Eco J* 112:C97–C116.
Bosworth, D., M. Rogers 2001. "Market Value, R&D and IP: An Empirical Analysis of Large Australian Firms." *Econ Record* 77:323–337.
Chada A., R. Oriani 2010. "R&D Market Value Under Weak Intellectual Property Rights Protection: The Case of India." *Scientometrics* 82:59–74.
Chan L. K. C., J. Lakonishok, T. Sougiannis 2001. "The Stock Market Valuation of Research and Development Expenditures." *J Finan* LVI(6):2431–2456.
Cockburn I., Z. Griliches 1988. "Industry Effects and Appropriability Measures in the Stock Market's Valuation of R&D and Patents." *Am Econ Rev* 78:419–423.
Copeland T., P. Tufano 2004. "A Real-World Way to Manage Real Options." *Harv Bus Rev* March 82(3):90–99.
Czarnitzki D., B. H. Hall 2006. "Comparing the Market Valuation of Innovative Assets in U.S. and German Firms." Working Paper, University of California, Berkeley.
DaDalt P. J., J. R. Donaldson, J. L. Garner 2003. "Will Any *q* Do?" *J Finan Res* 4:535–551.

Dushnitsky G., T. Klueter 2011. "Is There an eBay for Ideas? Insights from Online Knowledge Marketplaces." *Eur Manag Rev* 8:17–32.

Goddar K., U. Moser 2011. "Traditional Valuation Methods: Cost, Market and Income Approach." In *The Economic Valuation of Patents Methods and Applications*, edited by F. Munari, R. Oriani, 109–140, Cheltenham: Edward Elgar Publishing.

Goto A., K. Motohashi 2007. "Construction of a Japanese Patent Database and a First Look at Japanese Patenting Activities." *Res Pol* 36(9):1431–1442.

Greenhalgh C., M. Rogers 2006. "The Value of Innovation: The Interaction of Competition, R&D and IP." *Res Pol* 35:562–580.

Griliches Z. 1981. "Market Value, R&D and Patents." *Econ Letters* 7:183–187.

Griliches Z., B. H. Hall, A. Pakes 1991. "R&D, Patents and Market Value Revisited: Is There a Second (Technological Opportunity) Factor?" *Econ Inno New Tech* 1:183–202.

Guellec D. Van Pottelsberghe de la Potterie 2007. *The Economics of the European Patent System.* Oxford: Oxford University Press.

Hall B. H. 1993. "The Stock Market's Valuation of R&D Investment During the 1980's." *Am Econ Rev* 83:259–264.

Hall B. H. 2000. "Innovation and Market Value." In *Productivity, Innovation, and Economic Performance*, edited by R. Barrell, G. Mason, M. O'Mahoney, 177–198, Cambridge: Cambridge University Press.

Hall B. H., A. B. Jaffe, M. Trajtenberg 2005. "Market Value and Patent Citations." *Rand J Econ* 36:16–38.

Hall B. H., M. MacGarvie 2010. "The Private Value of Software Patents." *Res Pol* 39:994–1009.

Hall B. H., J. Mairesse, P. Mohnen 2010. "Measuring the Returns to R&D". In the *Handbook of the Economics of Innovation*, edited by B. H. Hall and N. Rosenberg, Amsterdam: Elsevier, Kindle edition.

Hall B. H., R. Oriani 2006. "Does the Market Value R&D Investment by European Firms? Evidence from a Panel of Manufacturing Firms in France, Germany." *Int J Ind Organ* 24:971–993.

Haneda S., H. Odagiri 1998. "Appropriation of Returns from Technological Assets and the Values of Patents and R&D in Japanese High-Tech Firms." *Econ Inno New Tech* 7:303–322.

Harhoff D., F. Narin, K. Vopel 1999. "Citation Frequency and the Value of Patented Inventions." *Rev Econ Stat* 81(3):511–515.

Häussler C., D. Harhoff, E. Mueller 2014. "How Patenting Informs VC Investors— The Case of Biotechnology." *Res Pol* 43(8):1286–1298.

Hirschey M., V. J. Richardson, S. Scholtz 2001. "Value Relevance of Nonfinancial Information: The Case of Patent Data." *Rev Quant Finan Acc* 17(3):223–235.

Hsu D., R. Ziedonis 2013. "Resources as Dual Sources of Advantage: Implications for Valuing Entrepreneurial-Firm Patents." *Strat Manag J* 34:761–781.

Hull J. C. 2012. *Options, Futures and Other Derivatives, 8e.* Harlow: Pearson Publishing.

IMF 2007. *Global Financial Stability Report. Market Development and Issues.* Washington, DC: International Monetary Fund, September. Accessed July 30, 2014, www.imf.org/External/Pubs/FT/GFSR/2007/01/index.htm

Kanwar S., B. Hall 2015. "The Market Value of R&D in Weak Innovation Regimes: Evidence from India." NBER Working Paper No. 21196, National Bureau of Economic Research Inc., Cambridge (MA).

Korkeamäki T., T. Takalo 2013. "Valuation of Innovation and Intellectual Property: The Case of iPhone." *Eur Manag Rev* 10:197–210.

Lanjouw J. O., A. Pakes, J. Putnam 1998. "How to Count Patents and Value Intellectual Property: The Uses of Patent Renewal and Application Data." *J Ind Econ* 46(4):405–432.

Lanjouw J. O., M. Schankerman 2004. "Patent Quality and Research Productivity: Measuring Innovation with Multiple Indicators." *Econ J* 114:441–465.

Layne-Farrar A., J. Lerner 2006. "Valuing Patents for Licensing: A Practical Survey of the Literature." Accessed September 30, 2014, http://papers.ssrn.com/sol3/papers.cfm?abstract_id=1440292

Lev B., D. Nissim, J. Thomas 2005. "On the Informational Usefulness of R&D Capitalization and Amortization." Columbia Business School Working Paper. Accessed on June 30, 2014, https://www0.gsb.columbia.edu/mygsb/faculty/research/pubfiles/3277/On%20the%20informational%20usefulness%20of%20R&D%20capitalization%20and%20amortization%202005.04.17.pdf

Lindenberg E. B., S. A. Ross 1981. "Tobin's *q* Ratio and Industrial Organization." *J Bus* 54:1–32.

Luehrman T. A. 1998. "Strategy as a Portfolio of Real Options." *Harv Bus Rev* September–October 76(5):87–99.

Marco A. C. 2005. "The Option Value of Patent Litigation: Theory and Evidence." *Rev Finan Econ* 14(3–4):323–351.

Montgomery C. A., B. Wernerfelt 1988. "Diversification, Ricardian Rents, and Tobin's *q*." *Rand J Econ* 19(4):623–632.

Murphy W. J., J. L. Orcutt, P. C. Remus 2012. *Patent Valuation: Improving Decision Making*. Hoboken (NJ): John Wiley & Sons.

Nagaoka S., K. Motohashi, A. Goto 2010. "Patent Statistics as Innovation Indicators." In *The Handbook of the Economics of Innovation*, edited by B. H. Hall, N. Rosenberg, 10973–12068, Amsterdam: Elsevier, Kindle edition.

Nakamura L. 2003. "A Trillion Dollars a Year in Intangible Investment and the New Economy." In *Intangible Assets*, edited by J. R. M. Hand, B. Lev, 19–47, Oxford: Oxford University Press.

OECD 2009. *OECD Patent Statistics Manual*. Paris: OECD.

Oriani R., L. Sereno 2011. "Advanced Valuation Methods: The Real Options Approach." In *The Economic Valuation of Patents Methods and Applications*, edited by F. Munari, R. Oriani, 141–168, Cheltenham: Edward Elgar Publishing.

Ouellette L. L. 2012. "Do Patents Disclose Useful Information?" *Harv J Law Tech* 25(2):531–545.

Pakes A. S. 1986. "Patents as Options: Some Estimates of the Value of Holding European Patent Stocks." *Econometrica* 54(4):755–784.

Perfect S., K. Wiles 1994. "Alternative Construction of Tobin's q: An Empirical Comparison." *J Emp Finan* 1:313–341.

Robbins C. A. 2006. *Measuring Payments for the Supply and Use of Intellectual Property*. Washington DC: Bureau of Economic Analysis of the US Department of Commerce.

Rosenberg N. 1996. "Uncertainty and Technological Change." In *Technology and Economic Growth*, edited by J. Fuhrer, J. Little, 91–125, Boston (MA): Federal Reserve Bank of Boston.

Ross S. A., R. W. Westerfield, J. Jaffe 2009. *Corporate Finance, 9e*. New York: McGraw Hill.

Schwartz E. 2004. "Patents and R&D as Real Options." *Econ Notes* 33(1):23–54.

Smith G., R. Parr 2000. *Valuation of Intellectual Property and Intangible Assets, 3e*. New York: John Wiley & Sons.

Thoma G., K. Motohashi, J. Suzuki 2010 A. "Consolidating Firm Portfolios of Patents Across Different Offices. A Comparison of Sectoral Distribution of Patenting

Activities." In Europe and Japan, University of Tokyo IAM Discussion Paper Series No. 2010/19.

Thoma G., S. Torrisi, A. Gambardella, D. Guellec, B. H. Hall, D. Harhoff 2010 B. "Harmonizing and Combining Large Datasets—An Application to Firm-Level Patent and Accounting Data." NBER Working Paper No. 15851, National Bureau of Economic Research Inc., Cambridge (MA).

Thompson P. 2006. "Patent Citations and the Geography of Knowledge Spillovers: Evidence from Inventor- and Examiner-Added Citations." *Rev Econ Stat* 88:383–388.

Toivanen, O., P. Stoneman, D. Bosworth 2002. "Innovation and Market Value of UK Firms, 1989–1995." *Oxford Bul Econ Stat* 64:39–61.

Whaley R. 2003. "Derivatives." In *Handbook of the Economics of Finance*, edited by G. Costantinides, M. Harris, R. Stulz, 1131–1206, Amsterdam: Elsevier.

Wildasin D. E. 1984. "The q Theory of Investment with Many Capital Goods." *Am Econ Rev* 74(1):203–210.

Zur E., J. A. Squires 2015. "Why Investment-friendly Patents Spell Trouble for Trolls." Accessed September 24, http://knowledge.wharton.upenn.edu/article/why-investment-friendly-patents-spell-trouble-for-trolls/

2 The Composite Value Index of Patent Indicators

Grid Thoma

2.1 Introduction

The literature on patent indicators has proposed several approaches to devising nonmonetary indices for patent valuation, advancing our understanding about the intrinsic value of a technology (Nagaoka *et al.* 2010). As discussed in the previous chapter, a first group of studies has analysed the market value return of R&D investments and weighted patent counts through indicators for publicly listed firms (Bloom and Van Reenen 2002; Lanjouw and Schankerman 2004; Hall *et al.* 2005). Other contributions, later discussed in chapter 3 (this volume), have estimated the value of patent rights relying on renewal decisions of patent maintenance (Schankerman 1998; Bessen 2008). Furthermore, patent indicators have been analysed in connection to the external financing of start-ups (Hsu and Ziedonis 2013; Häussler *et al.* 2014). Nevertheless, the current debate is far from reaching definite answers on how to gauge the heterogeneity of patent value and what are the determinants of the market value of the R&D output (Abrams *et al.* 2013).

This chapter aims to fill this gap by proposing a new composite index of patent value which aggregates several patent indicators that are typically used in the literature with respect to patent breadth and technology potential, prior art and background of the invention, and filing and procedural aspects of the patent (Nagaoka *et al.* 2010). These indicators are validated with market value information of patents obtained from a survey (Gambardella *et al.* 2008). Subsequently, I aggregate the selected indicators into a single composite value index following the methodology proposed by Lanjouw and Schankerman (2004). I show that the resulting composite value index summarizes effectively the variability of the indicators taken separately, because the reduction in the explanatory power of the estimated market value model is only about 10 percent, which is quite limited considering that I have combined eight distinct indicators.

In addition, by relying on opposition and renewal decisions, I conduct a robustness analysis of the composite value index and the survey's market value dataset. I have opted to keep opposition and renewal decisions apart from other patent indicators, because they are known only after the grant of a patent. I do find that both of them are positively correlated with the market value of patents, confirming the validity of the proposed analysis. The inclusion of the composite value index doubles the explanatory power of the estimated model. Conversely, when the composite value index is solely considered, adding the opposition and renewal decisions increases the goodness of fit of the model of only 14 to 16 percent.

2.2 Patent Indicators and Patent Asset Value

Previous studies have relied on direct survey estimates to gauge market value information of a patent asset. In spite of the high cost of data collection, this methodology can offer more precise estimates of the patent asset value as compared to the indirect market value approaches (Bessen and Meurer 2008). Scherer and Harhoff (2000) showed that the value of patent assets is extremely skewed, with the top decile of the patents holding 84 percent of the economic value, and they stylized this finding with the log normal distribution. Harhoff *et al.* (1999) argued that counts of patent citations can mimic significantly the tail of the patent value distribution. However, the relationship is mediated also by the premium value of patent protection—that is the additional value that the patent-protection strategy generates as compared to the nonpatenting strategy of the invention output. In particular, citation counts of patents maintained till the end of their statutory life have a three times larger return on value than other patents on average. More recently, other studies have argued that citations are characterised by a curvilinear relationship with respect to value, with fewer citations at the tail of value distribution than at the middle (Abrams *et al.* 2013).

Beyond patent citations, other patent indicators have been shown to correlate significantly with the value of patent assets. Analysing a panel of patents invented in Germany of the 1977s cohort and maintained up to the full-term, Harhoff *et al.* (2003) find that successful defence against opposition action is a particularly strong predictor of patent value. They argue that the survival to a two-tiered selection process such as grant and opposition is a highly reliable indicator of value. Other variables matter as well, including international priorities of patents, backward citations provided during the examination, and—for science-based inventions—nonpatent references. One limitation of this study consists in restrictive assumptions required for extrapolating market value information also for those patents which have not been targeted by the survey.

This methodology has been extended and fully developed by Gambardella et al. (2008), who administrated a questionnaire to inventors at the pan-European level, and they overcame potential restrictive assumptions by scrutinizing a representative sample of the population of patents before the end of their statutory life (see section 2.3.4 for further details on this survey).

Gambardella et al. argue that patent indicators can predict ex-ante the asset value of a patent, including patent references backward and forward, patent families as measured by the number of jurisdictions in which the protection is sought, and number of claims, although the unexplained variability of the patent value distribution is considerable. Further, they confirm that patent citations could mimic significantly the skewness of the value distribution. These results have been confirmed by Fischer and Leidinger (2014), who analysed the impact of patent indicators on the market value of patent assets exchanged through public auctions (see also Odasso et al. 2015).

It is noteworthy that these studies are largely silent about the impact of innovator's strategic behaviour on patent valuation. More in general, it can be argued that the patentee can put in place strategies in order to ameliorate the conditions affecting the value of an invention. For example, Gambardella et al. (2012) question to what extent patent value depends on the effort dedicated to the underlying R&D project—as measured by the workload of inventors—in relation to the innovative breadth of the project, which is given by the number of patent filings related to the same invention (being part of the same patent family). They find that the second effect is larger than the former, and it is mitigated by the technological field of the invention (science based vis-à-vis traditional sectors), and the mode of the invention process (e.g., decentralized technological problem solving as compared to noncollaborative R&D projects).

2.3 Data and Variables

This section describes data sources and variables that are then included in the multivariate econometric analysis. The data sources have originated from different repositories: i) patent indicators from the EPO Worldwide Patent Database; ii) opposition decisions from the EPOLINE XML files; iii) procedural information on renewals of patents from the EPO Patent Register (EPR) Database; iv) market value estimates of patents from survey information.

2.3.1 Patent Indicators

The main source of patent indicators has been the EPO Worldwide Patent Database (PatStat 2012) and the related Patent Register Data regarding procedural information (see also section 2.3.3). From PatStat, bibliometric information has been extracted regarding claims, references, patent classifications, inventors, and renewal decisions. Due to data availability, in the econometric analysis the sample is limited to patents originating from the European Patent Office (EPO). In fact, for this dataset I have complete procedural information on applications, grants, oppositions, and renewals. Limiting the sample to one single patent office allows more homogeneity and precision in the definitions and computations of the variables. Box 2.1 depicts the patent indicators of the econometric multivariate analysis.

2.3.2 Opposition

Opposed patents are more likely to create potential economic losses for opponents and thus have bigger value (Harhoff *et al.* 2003). Indeed, the average cost of an opposition action has been estimated around € 25 thousand

---

Box 2.1 Uni-dimensional patent indicators

Group I: Breadth and technology potential

Patent family size	Number of patents that share the same INPADOC priority. Economic value is related to the willingness of the owner to seek protection for the same invention across multiple jurisdictions (Lanjouw et al. 1998). When the EPC patent documents are not typically published as internal documents of a European national office, family size has been combined with information on the designation decisions for that country.
Patent family value	It is measured as the patent family size variable where each jurisdiction has been weighted by the GDP of the country where the protection is sought. The GDP of each covered country was normalized to that of the US, with the US GDP set to unity. For more details see chapter 1 (this volume).
Claims	A count variable of the number of claims of the patent at the moment of grant or application.
Patent classes	Number of technology classes (European Patent Classification) in which the patent was classified by the patent reviewer (Lerner 1994).
Forward citations	The number of forward cites received by the patent or its equivalents during the first five years (Hall *et al.* 2005).
Generality	One minus the Herfindhal index measuring the distribution of forward citing patents over their technology classes—four digits of the International Patent Classification—during the first five years of the patent life cycle (Hall 2005).

Group II: Prior art and background of the invention

Inventors	Number of inventors in a patent (Guellec and Van Pottelsberghe de la Potterie 2000).
Backward citations	Number of citations to other patent documents. A bigger number of cites indicates that an invention relies on a broader knowledge base, and hence it is more important (Lanjouw and Schankerman 2004).
XY type backward citations	A count variable of cites made to other patents whose claims overlap completely (X type) or partially (Y type) with at least one claim of the focal patent. It measures the degree of importance of prior art to the focal patent.

Group II (continued)	
Non patent literature	Number of citations to the nonpatent literature prior art, which proxies the closeness to 'science' knowledge (Meyer 1999).
Originality	One minus the Herfindhal index measuring the distribution of backward-citing patents over their technology classes—four digits of the International Patent Classification (Hall 2005).
Citation lag	A measure of the average age of the backward citations in days (Henderson *et al.* 1998).
Group III: Filing and procedural aspects of the patent	
Grant	A binary variable that takes the positive outcome if a patent has been granted by the office (Harhoff and Wagner 2009).
Grant lag	Number of days between the priority date and the grant date.
PCT route	A binary variable that signals whether the patent owner has filed an international application via the Patent Cooperation Treaty agreement, which allows one to achieve global protection by filing a unique application.
Supplementary search report	A binary variable if the patent application process has been accompanied with a supplementary search report by the examiner. The examiner can optionally choose to elaborate an additional prior art search, when she thinks that an EPC patent filing still lacks relevant prior art in the matter.
Divisional application	A binary variable if the patent has at least one divisional application with a common priority patent.

and the opposition action can account for the potential litigation risk connected to that invention (Graham and Harhoff 2006). To this end I have built a binary variable whether a patent has been opposed using information extracted from the weekly XML files available from EPOLINE (2012). These files have been parsed and structured in a SQL relational database and then linked with the patent indicators dataset through the publication numbers.

2.3.3 Renewal Decisions

Patent renewals consist in the payment of renewal fees every fixed number of periods, which in the case of European patents are annual periods. As not all patents are maintained until the end of their statutory life, then the fee costs structure could be considered as lower bound revenue that the patent can ensure to its owner. Drawing on this assumption, an advancement of the patent family value indicator is proposed, which takes into the account the years of validity of a patent in each covered country:

$$R = \frac{\sum_{t=1}^{T}\sum_{c=1}^{C}G_p\left(c,t\right)}{C * T} \tag{1}$$

Where C is the number of the covered countries in which the patent p is valid in time t, and T coincides with the years of maximum maintenance of a patent (i.e., the statutory limit of twenty years from filing date). In addition $G(.)$ is assumed to be dependent on the GDP of the country where the protection is sought and renewed, which can approximate the time evolution of the potential market size of an invention. Due to the bigger statistical dispersion, the patent family maintenance value index is then expected to correlate with the market value of patents at a bigger extent than the patent family value index. In the current analysis, information on renewal decisions is drawn from the EPO Patent Register Database (PatStat 2012), whereas the national GDP information originates from the PENN World Table (http://pwt.econ.upenn.edu/).

2.3.4 Survey Data

For the validation of the patent indicators, I consider the market value information of patents originating from the survey discussed by Gambardella et al. (2008). This dataset includes value estimates for about 8,277 European-granted patents through a questionnaire directly administrated to the population inventors resident in the eight largest countries Europe. Patent value estimates are obtained by administrating the following question to the first listed inventor in a patent: *"Suppose that on the day on which this patent was granted, the applicant had all the information about the value of the patent that is available today. In case a potential competitor of the applicant was interested in buying the patent, what would be the minimum price (in euro) the applicant should demand?"* (Gambardella et al. 2008, 70). Ten intervals of patent values in current Euros are provided: Less than € 30K; 30–100K; 100–300K; 300K–1M; 1–3M; 3–10M; 10–30M; 30–100M; 100–300M; more than 300M. It is noteworthy that the survey is statistically representative at the country and technology level for the cohorts of patents 1993–1997. Patents have been oversampled among those that have been at least cited once or opposed. In the regressions I used weights to account for oversampling of most valuable patents and for potential respondent bias at the country level.

2.4 Detrending Indicators for Time and Technology Effects

Previous econometric evidence has shown that technological and time effects account for a large and significant share of the variability of patent asset value (Gambardella et al. 2008; Fischer and Leidinger 2014). To reduce these effects, I have log transformed the value estimates and patent indicators, once they have been normalized by the geometric mean computed over technological classes and years. In particular the resulting detrended log indicator reads as follows:

$$
I^D_{pct} = Log\left(1 + \frac{I_{pct}}{e^{\frac{\sum_{i=1}^{n}\log(1+I_{ict})}{n}}}\right) \tag{2}
$$

Where I_{pct} is the patent indicator of the focal patent p in technology class c and year t, I_{ict} is the indicator of a given patent i in c and t, and n is the number of all patents in same class and year.

The direct computation of (2), however, is limited by the fact that the identification of a unique technological class of a patent is not always viable. Whereas for the US patent documents examiners typically define a single main international patent class, in other patent offices—such as the EPO—the international patent classes can be multiple, and their order of listing in a patent document does not necessarily follow a technological relevance criteria (PatStat 2012). The computation of patent indicators at the family level further complicates the problem, because within a patent family the inventions can be classified in multiple patent classes within and between the offices. To this end I computed (2) for all the m classes listed in a patent family, and then I took the averages across those classes, having the resulting transformation:

$$
I^D_{pct} = \frac{\sum_{j=1}^{m} Log\left(1 + \frac{I_{pct}}{e^{\sum_{i=1}^{n}\frac{\log(1+I_{ict})}{n}}}\right)}{m} \tag{3}
$$

The transformation (3) has been implemented at several levels of technological disaggregation. In particular, I have followed a computation cascade procedure from level one to level four of the international patent classification, which allows one to smooth more effectively technological and time trends.

2.5 Composite Value Index of Patent Indicators

I develop a novel patent composite value index relying on several patent indicators, typically used in the literature (Nagaoka *et al.* 2010). In particular I consider three macro groups of uni-dimensional patent indicators:

patent breadth and technology potential; prior art and patent background; filing and procedural aspects of a patent (see Box 2.1 for more details). Then, I aggregate these variables into a single composite indicator following the factor analysis methodology proposed by Lanjouw and Schankerman (2004), who showed that a similarly built index is positively and significantly associated with the market value of publicly quoted companies. I build upon these stream of studies, and I advance improvements regarding the selection and validation (STAGE I) of patent indicators to be used in the computation of the composite value index (STAGE II).

2.5.1 Selection and Validation of Patent Indicators

The selection and validation task of the patent indicators (Ernst and Omland 2011) has consisted in comparing them with survey-based value estimates by the mean of a stepwise regression. As dependent variable I used the log of the midpoint of each interval of the patent value from the survey that is in current Euros: 15K, 65K, 200K, 650K, 2M, 6.5M, 20M, 65M, 200M, and 650M for the last interval. The log transformation allows one to regress the impact of patent indicators on the value estimates by least squares: As robustness check I consider also the log-log transformation. It is noteworthy that the log transformation of the midpoint of each interval provides also a more conservative estimate of the value of patents against various factors: misclassification of a patent in a given value interval, extreme tail of the value distributions, and presence of outliers and influential observations.

The stepwise regression's results are reported in Table 2.1 (Model 1–2). Only the patent indicators which are statistically significant at 5 percent level are shown. All regressions include also two dummies for no backward and forward citations.

We can notice that the selected indicators are eight, and the results are confirmed even when I consider the log-log specification (Model 2). In particular, they are:

i) Patent family size given by the number of patents that share the same priority;
ii) Patent family value, a weighted measure of family size by the mean of the GDP of the country where the protection is sought;
iii) Number of claims in the front page of a patent;
iv) Number of forward citations received within five years from priority year;
v) Number of backward citations, excluding nonpatent references;
vi) Number of XY type backward citations;
vii) PCT route dummy, indicating whether the patent originates from an international filing;
viii) Supplementary search report dummy.

Table 2.1 Patent asset value: log linear regression with patent indicators

(8,277 EPO patents from the survey dataset)

Dependent variable	(1) log(value)	(2) log-log(value)	(3) log(value)	(4) log-log(value)	(5) log(value)	(6) log-log(value)
Constant	0.169*** [0.010]	0.179** [0.005]	0.229*** [0.003]	0.218*** [0.002]	0.245*** [0.006]	0.219*** [0.003]
No forward citations	0.000 [0.003]	-0.002 [0.002]	-0.004** [0.001]	-0.005*** [0.001]	-0.001 [0.003]	-0.002 [0.001]
No backward citations	0.010 [0.007]	0.006** [0.003]	-0.005** [0.003]	0.004* [0.002]	0.012** [0.003]	0.007** [0.001]
Patent family size	0.042*** [0.007]	0.021*** [0.004]			0.006** [0.003]	0.007** [0.003]
Patent family value	0.024*** [0.011]	0.013*** [0.006]				
Forward citations	0.011*** [0.003]	0.005*** [0.001]				
Claims	0.012*** [0.004]	0.007*** [0.002]				
Backward citations	0.005** [0.003]	0.003** [0.001]				
XY type backward cites	0.005** [0.002]	0.002* [0.001]				
D (SSR)	-0.070*** [0.032]	-0.036*** [0.014]				

	(1)	(2)	(3)	(4)	(5)	(6)
D (PCT route)	0.013*** [0.005]	0.008*** [0.003]				
Composite index (computed in all EPO dataset)					0.028*** [0.002]	0.014*** [0.001]
Composite index (computed in the survey dataset)			0.007*** [0.001]	0.009*** [0.001]		
Std. error (adj. R-squared)	0.052	0.050	0.032	0.031	0.046	0.044
R-squared relative reduction			39.4%	37.5%	11.3%	11.8%

Notes:
1) *** indicates statistically significant at 1 percent level, **5 percent level, and *10 percent level.
2) Standard errors are clustered at the level of the patentee.
3) Regressions include statistical weights for respondent bias at the country level and oversampling of the most valuable patents.

As in Gambardella et al. (2008) I find that patent family size is the main positive predictor of patent value, followed more distantly by patent citation variables. The patent family value indicator adds further explanatory power to the model with an elasticity about half of that of the unweighted family size indicator. This is not a small amount and confirms that the market size of the legislation where protection is sought can be considered a direct demand-size measure of the future profitability of a given invention (Harhoff et al. 2003).

The PCT route is positively correlated with patent value, which suggests that patent owners typically achieve global protection by the mean of a unique international application when they think ex-ante that the focal invention is more valuable. The fact that the PCT route is the most expensive type of filing is indicative of the larger economic potential of these kinds of inventions, and on average it associated with bigger success regarding the granting decision.[1] Furthermore, the PCT route applications are expected to hold a large option value (see the analysis conducted in chapter 1, this volume), because the decision to start the substantive examination and granting process of the international application into national phase can be postponed for thirty months or more from filing. In turn, this real option effect of PCT applications is likely to be positively correlated with the asset value of patents.

Patent citations affect positive patent value, although the relative coefficient is smaller than the patent family indicators. The forward and backward citations have an overall elasticity of about one-third of the two indicators of patent family taken together.[2] The supplementary search report variable, which represents also a measure of prior art, is negatively related to patent value; in absolute terms its effect is even larger than forward cites, and it is comparable to the combined elasticities of the two measures of patent family.

The overall goodness of fit of the model is limited as reflected by the R squared ratio, which is only of about 5.2 percent, not very high but in line with the model proposed by Gambardella et al. (2008), who have found that four indicators—forward cites, backward cites, claims, and family size—account for about 2.7 percent of total variability of patent value. The present analysis improves along several dimensions: i) include additional indicators such as the weighted family size indicator, XY backward cites, PCT route, and supplementary search report; ii) detrend the patent indicators along time and technology effects by the geometric mean; iii) take into the account the overall technology classes in a patent and not only the primary listed class. As in Gambardella et al., I find that the goodness of fit of the log specification is higher than the log-log transformation, and the difference is of a similar order of magnitude (about 0.2 percentage points).

2.5.2 Aggregation of the Composite Value Index
with Factor Analysis

The construction of the composite value index of patent indicators relies on the factor analysis (STAGE II). In factor models each series of data is decomposed into a common component driven by some common features and an idiosyncratic component, which represents the remaining unexplained variability in the population. To estimate the factors I use principal component analysis, a methodology that seeks a linear combination of variables that maximizes the variance of the sample for the first factor, then the remaining of the variance for the second factor, and so on. Furthermore, I use a multiple indicator model with the unobserved factors and error terms normally distributed (Lanjouw and Schankerman 2004). The assumption of normality allows one to estimate by maximum likelihood, which ensures the uniqueness of the solution of the factor analysis. Estimation of the factors is based on information extrapolated from the covariance matrix of patent indicators (for a fuller discussion see Jolliffe 2002).

The descriptive statistics and correlation matrix of patent indicators are reported in Table 2.2. All indicators are correlated at 5 percent level of statistical significance. The family indicators are highly correlated with forward and backward cites, and in part also with the PCT route dummy pointing to the fact that owners rely on the World Intellectual Property Office in order to achieve broader protection. XY type backward citations are correlated with claims and with the SSR dummy, which in turn is positively correlated with all the other indicators.

The positive correlation of the SSR dummy with other indicators does not necessarily contradict the results of Table 2.1, where it is shown that the SSR dummy has a negative impact on the patent value estimates. Indeed, all indicators are affected by the presence of many null values and small number biases. As expected, the SSR dummy is mainly correlated with the PCT route, revealing that in large majority of cases the SSR comes in presence of International Search Authorities other than EPO. By including the PCT dummy in the regressions of Table 2.1, I can identify the net effect of the SSR on the patent value compared to the other indicators.

The results of the factor loadings are reported in Table 2.3. We can notice the existence of three factors which can be associated to the macro groups of uni-dimensional indicators proposed in Box 2.1 respectively:

- F1: Breadth and technology potential mainly constituted by patent family and citations indicators;
- F2: Filing and procedural aspects of the patent such as the PCT route and SSR dummies;
- F3: Prior art and background of the invention such as the two measures of backward citations.

2.5.3 Robustness Analysis

Robustness analyses of the composite index with estimates of patent value from the Gambardella's et al. (2008) dataset are also reported in Table 2.1 (see Models 3–6). I find that the composite value index summarizes effectively the variability of the indicators taken separately (Model 5–6). The

Table 2.2 Descriptive statistics and correlation table of the patent indicators

Overall EPO patents with priority years 1978–2007, n = 2,008,134 patent applications

	Mean	S.D.		(1)	(2)	(3)	(4)	(5)	(6)	(7)	(8)
(1) Patent family size	0.527	0.154	(1)	1.000							
(2) Patent family value	0.703	0.337	(2)	0.629	1.000						
(3) Forward citations	0.565	0.566	(3)	0.438	0.383	1.000					
(4) Claims	0.694	0.420	(4)	0.130	0.165	0.180	1.000				
(5) Backward citations	0.702	0.490	(5)	0.514	0.489	0.552	0.198	1.000			
(6) XY type backward cites	0.500	0.456	(6)	0.018	0.047	0.080	0.124	0.166	1.000		
(7) D (PCT route)	0.414	0.493	(7)	0.163	0.233	0.037	0.071	0.062	0.091	1.000	
(8) D (SSR)	0.109	0.312	(8)	0.077	0.073	0.079	0.064	0.123	0.195	0.400	1.000

Notes: All coefficients are statistical significant at 5 percent level. The continuous variables are log transformed.

Table 2.3 Factor loadings of the principal component analysis with maximum likelihood

Overall EPO patents with priority years 1978–2007, n = 2,008,134 patent applications

		Factor 1	Factor 2	Factor 3
(1)	Patent family size	0.273	−0.048	−0.255
(2)	Patent family value	0.329	0.020	−0.464
(3)	Forward citations	0.158	−0.094	0.198
(4)	Claims	0.036	0.014	0.057
(5)	Backward citations	0.354	−0.159	0.497
(6)	XY type backward cites	0.022	0.078	0.148
(7)	D (PCT route)	0.061	0.435	−0.122
(8)	D (SSR)	0.050	0.465	0.209
	Eigenvalues of variance covariance matrix	2.257	0.836	0.410

reduction in R squared ratio is of order of about 10 percent, which is quite limited considering that I have combined eight distinct indicators. Further, estimating the composite value index using the overall EPO dataset provides informational improvements compared to the case of reducing the estimation of the index by the mean of a smaller scale dataset (compare Models 5–6 with Models 3–4).

An additional robustness check has been that of including the opposition and renewal decisions, which are considered by the literature relevant measures of patent value (Harhoff *et al.* 2003; Graham and Harhoff 2006). However, they are known only after the grant of a patent, and for this reason I have opted to keep them separate from other patent indicators, which are the base for the composite value index. Including these two variables in the value regressions constitutes a robustness check of the survey dataset as well.

Table 2.4 reports the results of these regressions. The opposition and patent family maintenance value index are positively correlated with the patent market value, confirming the validity of the survey information (Model 7 and 8). The inclusion of the composite value index doubles the explanatory power of the estimated model (Model 9 and 10). However, compared to the case of the index solely considered (Model 5 and 6), the goodness of fit of the model increases of only 14 to 16 percent. Put differently, not considering as value determinants opposition and renewal decisions which can be traced only after the grant of a patent implies a loss in the explanatory power of model which is comparable to the case of all patent indicators taken separately.

2.6 Conclusions

The analysis conducted in this chapter contributes to the research agenda on proposing novel timely indicators of innovation activities (OECD 2013). I devised a composite value index that aggregates information from several patent indicators regarding patent breadth and technology potential,

Table 2.4 Patent asset value: log linear regression with patent indices

(8,277 EPO patents from the survey dataset)

Dependent variable	(7) log(value)	(8) log-log(value)	(9) log(value)	(10) log-log(value)
Constant	0.252*** [0.007]	0.222** [0.003]	0.233*** [0.007]	0.213*** [0.003]
No forward citations	−0.013*** [0.003]	−0.008*** [0.001]	−0.002 [0.003]	−0.002 [0.001]
No backward citations	−0.020*** [0.005]	−0.009*** [0.002]	0.010* [0.006]	0.006** [0.003]
D (No Renewals index)	−0.002 [0.005]	−0.001 [0.003]	−0.004 [0.005]	−0.003 [0.003]
Renewals index (log)	0.209*** [0.035]		0.118*** [0.037]	
Renewals index (log-log)		0.119*** [0.020]		0.066*** [0.021]
D (Opposition)	0.010*** [0.004]	0.005*** [0.002]	0.008** [0.004]	0.005*** [0.002]
Composite index (computed in all EPO dataset)			0.025*** [0.002]	0.013*** [0.001]
Std. error (adj. R-squared)	0.024	0.025	0.053	0.052
R-squared relative change[4]			116.4%	106.4%
R-squared relative change w.r.t. (Table 2.1)[5]			13.8%	16.5%

Notes:
1) *** indicates statistically significant at 1 percent level, **5 percent level, and *10 percent level.
2) Standard errors clustered at the level of the patentee.
3) Regressions include statistical weights for respondent bias at the country level and over-sampling of the most valuable patents.
4) The comparisons regard Model 7 with 9, and Model 8 with 10.
5) The comparisons regard Model 5 with 9, and Model 6 with 10.
6) The renewals index is the patent family maintenance value index as defined in section 2.3.3.

prior art and background of the patent, and filing and procedural aspects of the patent (Nagaoka *et al.* 2010). Beforehand these indicators are validated with respect to market value of patents obtained from survey information. Then the factor analysis advances their aggregation into a single composite. The composite value index summarizes effectively the variability of the indicators taken separately: when I regress the composite index against the market value of patents, the relative reduction in goodness of fit of the predictive model is only about 10 percent.

These results are robust when post-grant information of a patent such as opposition and renewal decisions are taken into the account. First, I found that both oppositions and patent family maintenance value index are positively correlated with the market value of patents originating from the survey dataset adopted in this study. Second, the inclusion of the composite value index doubles the explanatory power of the estimated model. Conversely, when the composite value index is solely considered, adding information on opposition and renewal decisions increases the goodness of fit of the model by only 14 to 16 percent.

Future research could advance in several directions. Beforehand additional robustness analyses are required with respect to patent datasets originating from other legislations beyond the European Patent Convention. Further research could regard the aggregation methodology of the composite value index, which can take into the account also second-order conditions and interaction terms of single-patent indicators (Ozer-Balli and Sorensen 2010).

Finally, it is of high interest to elaborate more fine-grained measures of the impact of citations and prior art to patent value and the combination of these variables to other indicators. This task could include measures of self-citations at the level of the same patent owner, origin of the cited prior art in terms of sectoral activity of patentee, experience with the patent system, availability of complementary assets, and others. Chapter 3 (this volume) analyses how other complemental IP strategies pursued by the innovator, such as trademarks and design patents, affect the valuation of patents.

Notes

1 For a comparison of patenting costs in current currency see chapter 1 (this volume), whereas for a comparison in terms of purchasing power parities see chapter 8 (this volume).
2 In a nonreported regression I analyse the backward citations by different categories, that is the inventor-added citations at the moment of filing, XY type citations added by the examiner, and other examiner-added citations. Whereas the impact of two count variables of examiner citations are positive and highly significant, the number of inventor citations is not significantly correlated with patent value, but there is evidence at 10 percent level of significance that patents that include at least one inventor-added citation are more valuable. These findings do not contradict the assumption that inventions with a bigger number of inventor citations are more connected to the local dimension of the innovation relative to the geographic and technological distance and therefore those inventions could be more derivative in nature and less valuable on average (Criscuolo and Verspagen 2008). On the other hand, inventions with larger technological breadth are characterised by a bigger number of examiner-added citations, and typically they are better drafted by the applicant and their law firm representative (i.e., they already provide prior art at the moment of the filing).

References

Abrams D., U. Akcigit, J. Popadak 2013. "Patent Value and Citations: Creative Destruction or Strategic Disruption?" NBER Working Paper No. 21196, National Bureau of Economic Research Inc., Cambridge (MA).
Bessen J., M. Meurer 2008. *Patent Failure: How Judges, Bureaucrats and Lawyers Put Innovators at Risk*. Princeton (NJ): Princeton University Press.

Bloom N., J. Van Reenen 2002. "Patents, Real Options and Firm Performance." *Eco J* 112:C97–C116.

Criscuolo P., B. Verspagen 2008. "Does It Matter Where Patent Citations Come from? Inventor vs. Examiner Citations in European Patents." *Res Pol* 37(10):1892–1908.

EPOLINE 2012. "EPO Raw Product: XML Weekly Files." European Patent Office, December edition, Accessed January 7, 2014, www.epoline.org.

Ernst H., N. Omland 2011. "The Patent Asset Index—A New Approach to Benchmark Patent Portfolios." *World Pat Inform* 33:34–41.

Fischer T, J. Leidinger 2014. "Testing Patent Value Indicators on Directly Observed Patent Value: An Empirical Analysis of Ocean Tomo Patent Auctions." *Res Pol* 43:519–529.

Gambardella A., D. Harhoff, B. Verspagen 2008. "The Value of European Patents." *Eur Manag Rev* 5(2):69–84.

Gambardella A., D. Harhoff, B. Verspagen 2012. "What Are the Determinants of the Private Value of Patented Inventions?" CEPR Discussion Paper No. 9462, Center for Economic Policy Research, London.

Graham S., D. Harhoff 2006. "Can Post-Grant Reviews Improve Patent System Design? A Twin Study of US and European Patents." CEPR Discussion Paper No. 5680, Center for Economic Policy Research, London.

Guellec D., B. Van Pottelsberghe de la Potterie 2000. "Applications, Grants, and the Value of Patent." *Econ Let* 69(1):109–114.

Hall B. H. 2005. "A Note on the Bias in the Herfindahl Based on Count Data." *Rev Econ Ind* 110:149–156.

Hall B. H., A. Jaffe, M. Trajtenberg 2005. "Market Value and Patent Citations." *Rand J Econ* 36:16–38.1364.Harhoff D., F. Narin, F. M. Scherer, K. Vopel 1999. "Citation Frequency and the Value of Patented Innovation." *Rev Econ Stat* 81: 511–515.

Harhoff D., F. M. Scherer, K. Vopel 2003. "Citations, Family Size, Opposition, and the Value of Patent Rights." *Res Pol* 32:1343–64.

Harhoff D., S. Wagner 2009. "Modelling the Duration of Patent Examination at the European Patent Office." *Manag Science* 55(12):1969–1984.

Häussler C., D. Harhoff, E. Mueller 2014. "How Patenting Informs VC Investors—The Case of Biotechnology." *Res Pol* 43(8):1286–1298.

Henderson R., A. Jaffe, M. Trajtenberg 1998. "Universities as a Source of Commercial Technology: A Detailed Analysis of University Patenting, 1965–1988." *Rev Econ Stat* LXXX(1):119–127.

Hsu D., R. Ziedonis 2013. "Resources as Dual Sources of Advantage: Implications for Valuing Entrepreneurial-Firm Patents." *Strat Manag J* 34:761–781.

Jolliffe T. 2002. *Principal Component Analysis, 2e*. New York: Springer Verlag.

Lanjouw J. O., A. Pakes, J. Putnam 1998. "How to Count Patents and Value Intellectual Property: The Uses of Patent Renewal and Application Data." *J Ind Econ* 46(4):405–432.

Lanjouw J. O., M. Schankerman 2004. "Patent Quality and Research Productivity: Measuring Innovation with Multiple Indicators." *Econ J* 114:441–465.

Lerner J. 1994. "The Importance of Patent Scope: An Empirical Analysis." *Rand J Econ* 25:319–333.

Meyer M. 1999. "Does Science Push Technology? Patents Citing Scientific Literature." *Res Pol* 29:409–434.

Nagaoka S., K. Motohashi, A. Goto 2010. "Patent Statistics as Innovation Indicators." In *The Handbook of the Economics of Innovation*, edited by B. H. Hall, N. Rosenberg, 10973–12068, Amsterdam: Elsevier, Kindle edition.

Odasso C., G. Scellato, E. Ughetto 2015. "Selling Patents at Auction: An Empirical Analysis of Patent Value." *Ind Corp Change* 24(2):417–438.

OECD (2013). *Entrepreneurship at a Glance*. Paris: OECD Publishing.

Ozer-Balli H., B. Sorensen 2010. "Interaction Effects in Econometrics." CEPR Discussion Paper No. 7929, Center for Economic Policy Research, London.

PatStat 2012. *EPO Worldwide Patent Statistical Database and the EPO Patent Register*, April edition. Vienna: EPO.

Schankerman M. 1998. "How Valuable Is Patent Protection: Estimates by Technology Fields." *Rand J Econ* 29(1):77–107.

Scherer F. M., D. Harhoff 2000. "Technology Policy for a World of Skew-Distributed Outcomes." *Res Pol* 29:559–566.

Part II

The Strategic Dimension of Patent Valuation

3 Combined IP Strategies and the Valuation of Patent Premium

Grid Thoma

3.1 Introduction

According to the findings of recent research on entrepreneurial finance, the value of patents goes beyond the sole protection of the intellectual property because patents can serve as quality signals for external financing (Hall and Harhoff 2012; Gambardella 2013). Hsu and Ziedonis (2013) argue that firms with more patents receive relatively more venture funding, whereas Häussler et al. (2014) claim that external investors gauge the value of patents even before granting. Cockburn and Macgarvie (2009) document that patents are used for external financing also in the case of an initial public offering, merger, or acquisition. When combined with other IP strategies external investors have a better understanding about the value of patents (Alvarez Garrido and Dushnitsky 2013; Block et al. 2014), and several procedural aspects of patents are indicative for their proper valuation (Deb 2013). Nevertheless, with the exception of the study of Block et al. (2014), previous literature has seldom debated how marketing and commercialization activity directly linked with a patented invention affect its valuation. In particular, there is scarce evidence on the determinants of patent value when several IP strategies are combined regarding the same innovative project.

Building over entrepreneurial finance literature this chapter analyses how trademark strategies impact the value of patented inventions. Similarly to Block et al. (2014) I argue that by enhancing the signaling function of patents and expanding the breadth and length of protection trademarks increase the value of patented R&D. In this context I introduce a novel concept, namely patent and trademark pair, when the output of the invention process is protected by a combined IP strategy represented by patenting and also filing a trademark. I argue that patent and trademark pairs have a significant signaling value, and hence they are corresponded with higher valuations. Furthermore, signals from patents and trademarks are featured by a different strength and effectiveness, which account for the heterogeneity of the patent value distribution.

To advancing this task I develop a new method and database integrating several sources: bibliographic information from patent and trademark records, patent renewal decisions and corresponding fee payments, patentee demographic information from business directories, and others. The context is constituted by the population of the European patenting firms, who have filed at least one European Patent Convention (EPC) application. The new method for the computation of the patent and trademark pairs is given by a textual matching algorithm which integrates the trademark and patent data on two levels. First, it considers the patentee who files patents and trademarks (i.e., the business company that owns the intellectual property). For this purpose I draw from a database previously developed by Thoma et al. (2010 B), that provides a direct identification of the business companies and their patent and trademark portfolios. A subsequent layer of integration of patents and trademarks is based on the textual analysis of the description of the legal documents. Because patents and trademarks are very rich information sources regarding the technological and commercial activities of a firm, their combination allows one to uniquely assess to what extent the patent portfolio of a company has been actively translated in commercial activities and to measure its economic potential.

The dependent variable is constituted by patent valuation, which is estimated by the mean of a model on renewal decisions of the payment of patent fees. By adopting the approach of Schankerman (1998), I compute dollar estimates of the value of patent protection, relying on annual renewal decisions and historical information on fee costs. This dataset allows one to disentangle the valuation of patent and trademark strategies and sheds light on the determinants of patent value when multiple IP strategies are jointly combined. In fact, I analyse the impact on patent valuation of an additional combined IP strategy. That is when the innovator pursues a pairing strategy with design patents extending the protection of the invention patents. As controls I take into the account several patentee demographic characteristics which correlate with the value of patents, such as: sector of activity, firm's size and experience, country of origin, growth of R&D investment, and others.

This study reports several new findings. First, I document that patent and trademark pairs are statistically associated with higher patent valuation above and beyond the effect of the indicators typically used in the literature, such as those discussed in chapter 2 (this volume) regarding patent breadth and technology potential, prior art and patent background, and filing and procedural aspects of a patent. Second, I find that the signaling from patent and trademark pairs is stronger when highly visible textual information from legal documents is considered; patents linked to trademarks with exactly the same title and wordmark have the largest impact on the patent premium value with a return of PPP $115 thousand above the average value. With other types of pairing strategies—such as linking patent textual information with goods and services description in trademarks—the increase of patent valuation is more distant in absolute number than the strongest patent and trademark pair strategy. This latter finding confirms that the strength of the signaling strategy accounts for the heterogeneity of the patent value distribution. Last, I assessed the robustness of the results by analysing the impact of the IP pairing strategies on the renewal value of trademarks, and the former analysis of patent valuation is fully supported.

3.2 Theoretical Background: IP Strategies and Signaling

Recent literature has analysed firm performance with respect to the combination of IP strategies of patents and trademarks, positing the hypothesis that trademarks are a proxy of the marketing and commercialization ability of a firm. Helmers and Rogers (2010) show that the trademark stock yields two percentage point higher impact on firm survival as compared to patents. Buddelmeyer et al. (2010) claim that trademarks are positively associated with survival both over the short term and the long run, whilst patent stocks positively affect survival only in the latter case. Helmers and Rogers (2011) find that trademarks impact also the asset growth after having controlled for several demographic and market characteristics of the firm, whereas a positive impact of patenting on growth is traced solely in the manufacturing and R&D intensive sectors, and when the most valuable filing strategies are taken into account—such as patents having international breadth.

A full-fledged sectoral investigation of the impact of patenting and trademark strategies is constituted by Greenhalgh and Rogers (2006), who claim that technological trajectories given by the so-called Pavitt's taxonomy can disentangle the differential impact of the two IP strategies on firm market value as measured by the Tobin's q ratio. With the exception of the software industry and other high value-added services, the trademark stock contributes positively and significantly to the Tobin's q beyond the investment in R&D and intangibles, whereas patents affect market value solely for specialized suppliers and science-based firms.

Sander and Block (2011) extend the Tobin's q analysis by considering indirect indicators for the valuation of trademarks in the same fashion of those used for patents, such as the breadth of protection and opposition decisions. Sander and Block find that the size of trademark portfolio contributes significantly to the firm's market value, after having controlled for the effect of patenting and size of operative activities. Furthermore, the trademark value indicators have a significant impact as well, although some caveats are in order with respect to patenting: the Tobin's q is correlated with the number of jurisdictions where the trademark protection is sought as the only proxy of breadth of protection and the number of opposition actions undertaken by the focal firm but not those received.

Korkeamäki and Takalo (2013) analyse how patents and trademarks of the Apple's iPhone product platform affect the market capitalization of the firm and that of its network of suppliers, service providers, and competitors. Their approach consists in an event study using daily data on stock market value and some key events, such as the publication of patent applications, granting decisions, and filing of trademarks. They find that the iPhone-related capabilities and resources account for about 15 percent of Apple's total market capitalization, and patents and trademarks constitute about one-fourth of the iPhone's overall market value. There is also a positive effect on the market capitalization of the Apple's suppliers but not on that of its competitors and service providers.

The combination of patent and trademark strategies has been analysed also in the context of the pre-money valuation by venture capitalists. Block et al. (2014) argue that trademarks can constitute a quality signal—in the same vein as patents—between the inventor and the potential financier in order to reduce information asymmetries *à la* Spence (1973). To corroborate this hypothesis they analyse the population of venture-backed US start-ups from 1998 to 2007, which have obtained at least one financial round at the seed or early investment stage. They confirm that the combination of patents and trademarks affect the pre-money valuation of startups, although they argue that the signaling intensity decreases with the size of the trademark portfolio and in the latter rounds of financing, when the financier could assess the growth potential of a start-up also through other mechanisms.

These results are line with the entrepreneurial finance literature, which has claimed that the value of patents goes beyond the mere protection of the intellectual property (Hall and Harhoff 2012; Gambardella 2013). It has been argued that venture capitalists assess the quality of start-ups by the mean of their patent portfolios (Hsu and Ziedonis 2013; Häussler et al. 2014). Patenting attracts financing from prominent VCs who can contribute with a larger share of nonfinancial capital (Hsu and Ziedonis 2013). Although patents are valuable signals for new investors but not old ones (Conti et al 2013 B), only patents held by the inventor prior to first round of financing have the largest signaling value (Hoenen et al. 2014), and the intensity of the signal decreases with the size of the patent portfolio (Mann and Sager 2007). Furthermore, Cockburn and Macgarvie (2009) have claimed that patents increase the external financing during an IPO or M&A, although they are not valuable signals for private investors (Conti et al. 2013 B) and other entrepreneurial financiers except VCs (Conti et al. 2013 A).

Nevertheless the entrepreneurial finance literature has seldom debated how the firm valuation is affected when patent and trademark strategies are jointly combined by the focal firm (Block et al. 2014). An additional gap in the literature is constituted by the fact that the unit of analysis is the firm level, and the potential reinforcing effect of other IP strategies on the valuation of a single patent can be inferred only indirectly. In other words, previous literature has not analysed how marketing and commercialization activity directly linked with a patented invention affect its valuation. There is scarce evidence on the determinants of patent value when trademark strategies are combined regarding the same innovative project, although complemental investments in marketing and commercialization are essential for the economic success of an invention (Teece 1986; Chesbrough 2003; McGahan and Silverman 2006).

Because trademark strategies have the typical goal to build brand awareness and publicity among consumers (Krasnikov et al. 2009), the commercial potential of a patented invention is enhanced in several ways when it is paired with a trademark filing. Trademark strategies anticipate the commercial translation of a technology when it requires novel complementary assets with respect to the incumbent business model (Gans and Stern 2003). More in general, an IP strategy articulated through a patent and trademark pair (hereafter PTP) signals to customers and competitors in an industry about the market success of an invention project, and therefore it is associated with higher economic return and valuation of the underlying invention. An analyst claimed that *"it is no coincidence that many of the world's best known and most valuable brands have other IP traits in common: Their reputation for quality, innovation, and consistency not only facilitates product sales and shareholder interest, but to enhance the value of their patents."* (Berman 2008).[1]

Second, patent strategies which are combined with trademarks facilitate communication across technological producers and consumers by establishing a trust relationship (Rujas 1999) and reducing uncertainty about product performance (Bao et al. 2008), which in turn directly affects the financial return the innovator obtains by the patent. A patent and trademark pair strategy can be used to signal product quality not only in the sale and distribution phase but also in advertisement and publicity activities. In fact, brand names play a critical role for the commercial success of a new product lunch, because consumers use preconceived beliefs with respect to what categories of brand names could be associated to specific product types, and it is known that the relevance of an appropriate name extends well beyond the consumer goods industries (Kohli and LaBahn 1997). In this direction, by increasing the information available to consumers about product categories trademarks sustain the consumer preference regarding a technological product (Bao et al. 2008) and stimulate learning in the marketplace during the product launch (Ching 2010), and therefore the integration of the invention phase with commercialization is facilitated.

Last, from a legal point of view trademarks perpetuate the commercial success of a patented product beyond the statutory limit of the patent right if the consumers still perceive a differential value of the branded product after patent expiration. Indeed, the validity of trademarks can be prolonged without an end, although the owner has to demonstrate that the mark is continuously used in commercial activities. Managing intellectual property rights during filing, renewals, and legal disputes has relevant costs, but the patentee can scale up the investment by combining several strategies together. Trademarks increase the bargaining power of the innovator for technology licensing and trading (Graham et al. 2014). In conclusion, trademarks easy the knowledge transfer even in the nonbusiness sector by improving the innovator's reputation (Squicciarini et al. 2012).

Thus, on the basis of the debated considerations the following ceteris paribus testable hypothesis can be advanced:

HP 1: A patent and trademark pairs provides useful signaling infor-mation about the success of an invention project and therefore they impact positively the value of the underlying patent.

3.2.1 Signaling Strength

The theory of signaling suggests that signals function properly when they are costly for the issuers (Spence 1973). Typically, the benefits obtained by the receiver from the signal varies according to its strength (Deb 2013). In order for the signaling to create a separating equilibrium for high- and low-quality issuers, the signal should be more costly at issuing for the low-quality and less-productive issuers. The cost could regard various aspects: investment or expenditure in the issuing process, opportunity cost of the investment, and nonmonetary and quantifiable costs related to status or social networks. In addition, Spence (1973) argues that strong signals should generate com-mitment in order to be credible as sorting mechanism. The definition of the separating equilibrium implies some kind of strategic complementarity across issuers when signals take time to be developed and involve irrevers-ible investments. In this case the issuers will continue to use the signals in subsequent periods.

Then there is certifiability when an independent and neutral organization certifies the issuing of the signal according to specific and predetermined guidelines. In the case of patent and trademark offices, expert reviewers ver-ify that IP applications comply to standard criteria of patentability before approval. For example according to the European Patent Convention (EPC), which serves as the leading International Search Authority under the Patent Cooperation Treaty (PCT), agreement patents should be novel, not obvious to experts, and susceptible of industrial applicability. In the same vein, regis-tration requirements are in order for the trademark-approval process, where very often the most critical one is the distinctiveness from previously reg-istered marks. An additional functioning principle of the patent and trade-mark offices is the publication of the filing and examination results, which ensures the visibility of the signals to external investors and other parties. The publication of the EPC and PCT patent filings is made within eighteen months from the earliest date of application or priority, which are then fol-lowed by the publication of the search reports and patentability opinions by the examiners. For trademarks the publication schedules are even shorter than patents. The granting process is finalized when the application has entered the official register of granted rights, which is visible and accessible to external parties in all aspects of the approved intellectual property.

Furthermore, strong signals are featured by clarity or measurability. Gans et al. (2008) argued that a significant share of the licensing agreements takes place around the grant date, because the granting decision facilitates the commercialization of knowledge by establishing the breadth of the intellectual property rights. Greenberg (2013) found that granted patents have positive impact on the premoney evaluation by VCs above and beyond patent applications. These studies are in line with the interpretation that uncertainty and ambiguity exist as long as the intellectual property application has not been granted or officially approved. During the patent prosecution the examiner can ask amendments to various aspects of the invention, including the number and breadth of patent claims. If the application does not comply with the patentability (or registration) criteria, the examiner will not ultimately approve the request of protection in full or partial terms.

Last, Deb (2013) argues that signals from patents should be consistent in order to be credible for external investors. This means that the signals need to be stable and not to deteriorate over time when investors have subsequent interactions with the issuing firms. Whereas patents could be maintained to the statutory limit, trademarks can be renewed for an endless number of times. Moreover, the protection deriving from trademarks can be extended in novel markets beyond those current in use, although firms typically do extensions in later periods of the product life cycles (DeGraba and Sullivan 1995), in the case of multi-product umbrella branding,[2] and in presence of well-known and strong parent brands (Völckner and Sattler 2006).

Assuming these signal characteristics I posit an additional ceteris paribus testable hypothesis regarding the strength of signals issued by the focal firm:

HP 2: The strength of the signaling of a patent and trademark pair provides additional useful information about the success of an invention project that will be incorporated in the value of the underlying patent.

3.3 A Case Study

Patents and trademarks are very informative on the timing of the technological and commercial activities of the firm. In patents priority date documents when the invention processes and R&D investments have taken place, whereas in trademarks the filing date can approximate the timing when a product or a service started to be commercialized. Hence, whereas patents can be considered an output variable of the R&D process, trademarks typically are filed at the inception of the investments in marketing and brand building (Mendonça et al. 2004). The intercurrent period from patent filing to trademark filing indicates the average time lag needed to a company to translate an idea from laboratory to market (i.e., the generation of a valuable commercial product or service). Previous survey evidence has shown that four out of five companies complete the name-branding process during the product development phase, which typically gives birth to the filing of a trademark (Kohli and LaBahn 1997).

A quintessential example of combined strategies of patents and trademarks is the AMINEXIL product by the L'OREAL Corporation, which is a cosmetic treatment against the hair loss. The product is based on a new class of organic chemical compounds, called *diaminopyrimidines*. It was launched in the market in May 2006, when a mark was filed at the USPTO (serial number 78883916, AMINEXIL), which has been officially registered by the patent office in about three months. The wordmark of the trademark is exactly labeled 'AMINEXIL', and the 'goods and services' description explicitly mentions the term 'diaminopyrimidine'. Quite interestingly, L'OREAL had filed a patent application (serial number 2006/097359, Hair and/or eyelash care composition containing AMINEXIL) through the PCT system some months before the registration of the mark. As in the case of the trademark, the functionality and composition of AMINEXIL are clearly described in the title and abstract of the patent with the same names and words: The title of the patent includes the term 'AMINEXIL', whereas 'diaminopyrimidine' reads in the abstract. Thus the US mark 78883916 and the PCT patent 2006/097359 are clearly directed to obtain protection for the same innovative project, being that an invention or product targeted to final consumers.

The case of AMINEXIL shows how we can define a patent and trademark pair. The time-to-market of this product is very limited, around one year. The managers of L'OREAL confirm that the patent and trademark pair strategy is deliberate and not an isolated example (Legendre 2010). Patenting inventions related to a given product and contemporaneously filing a trademark regarding the same product is a typical IP strategy in cosmetics industry. They also monitor the competitors' IP strategies with particular focus on patents, in order to predict the average time-to-market of new products, because in their view patents constitute a unique source of information to understand the dynamics of new products in this industry.

The textual structure of the legal documents related to AMINEXIL deserves some additional comparative analysis because it reveals some interesting insights about strength of the PTP signaling strategy. As discussed, strong signals are characterized by cost, commitment, certifiability, clarity, visibility, and consistency. Patent and trademark pairs that use similar wording in titles and wordmarks are stronger signals than those pairs that have similar wording solely in the patent abstracts or in the description of trademarks (e.g. the token AMINEXIL appears in the title and wordmark, whereas diaminopyrimidine is reported solely in the abstract and goods and services description). In fact, the former type of pairs is intrinsically featured by a bigger visibility, clarity, and measurability. In this case, firms can cross label and reference their commercial products using both trademarks and patents. With respect to certifiability of the signal, it is worth recalling that examiners approve the registration of a mark if the wordmark has sufficient distinctiveness from other marks in the same goods and services categories which the mark has been requested for. Moreover, the category descriptions are created by the patent office and listed in a publicly available register (USPTO 2013). During the filing process the applicant can propose new categories, but the trademark reviewer can advance objections when she thinks they are not sufficiently definite.

Stronger signals of patent and trademark pairs are more costly to be issued, because it means that the underlying invention is somehow in an advanced stage and closer to the market. Approval of the registration of a trademark needs to be featured by some degree of intrinsic distinctiveness for the consumers. In this case the patent owner could have done investments for its commercialization or supported cumulative R&D along a technological trajectory (Kohli and LaBahn 1997), which is often associated to irreversible investments, and there is commitment that the inventor will continue to invest along that trajectory in the future (Von Graevenitz 2013). Furthermore, when multiple trademarks are paired with one or multiple patents, these strategies can be assimilated to an umbrella branding and brand extension (Völckner and Sattler 2006), which often take place in the case of highly distinctive and identifiable words (i.e., there is consistency in the usage of the same wording across patent titles and wordmarks).

3.4 Patent Premium Value

To assess the valuation of the patent and trademark pairs, I relied on renewal fee data. For patents kept in force renewal fees are considered as lower bound revenues that the patent ensures to the owner, and more specifically they concern the incremental premium value that the patent protection strategy generates as compared to a world without patents (Arora et al. 2008; Bessen and Meurer 2008). The analysis on actual data at the patent level allows one to compute of the premium value of patent rights once some assumptions on the functional form of the patent value distribution have been made (Schankerman 1998; Bessen 2008).

Similarly built models as that of Schankerman (1998) assume that the patenting agent maximixes the benefits derived from the protection strategy by choosing how many years to keep a patent in force. In particular, the net benefits of a patent from cohort j in age t are represented as current returns Y_{tj} minus the costs of renewal fees X_{tj}. Thus the agent optimizes the discounted value on T:

$$max_{T \in [1,2,...,\bar{T}]} V(T) = \sum_{t=1}^{T} \left(Y_{tj} - X_{tj} \right) \left(1 + i \right)^{-t} \tag{1}$$

Where $\bar{T}$ is the statutory limit to patent protection and i is the discount rate, which is typically assumed at the level of 10 percent. The optimal patent maintenance T^* is the first age when $Y_{tj} - X_{tj} < 0$. Otherwise it coincides with the statutory limit. Renewal fees, X, are non/decreasing in age, whereas returns, Y, are non-increasing in age meaning that in each time t the returns can be expressed as function of initial returns Y_{0j}. Assuming that the benefits from patents decay with a time invariant rate d, then the patentee will renew the protection in time t solely when $Y_{0j} \geq X_{tj} \prod_{\tau=1}^{t} (1 - d_{\tau})^{-1}$.

If $F(Y_{0j}, \theta_j)$ denotes the cumulative distribution of initial returns, where θ_j indicates a vector of parameters, then the proportion of patents from cohort j renewed in age t is $P_{tj} = 1 - F(Y_{0j}, \theta_j)$, and the log of the initial returns is distributed as $y_{0j} \sim N(\mu_j, \sigma_j)$ with mean μ_j and standard deviation σ_j. The owner will renew the patent protection if and only if:

$$\frac{y_{0j} - \mu_j}{\sigma_j} \geq \frac{lnX_{tj} - t * \ln(1 - d) - \mu_j}{\sigma_j} \tag{2}$$

Which implies that the proportion of patents in cohort j that drops out by age t is given by $1 - P_{tj} = \Phi(z_{tj}, \theta)$ where $\Phi(.)$ is the standardized normal distribution function with $z_{tj} = lnX_{tj} - t*ln(1 - d)$.

For the computation of dollar estimates of the premium value imposed by equation (1), I analyse the historical fee schedules for the cohorts 1985–1994 in the UK and Germany, whose renewal decisions have been observed from 1986 to 2013. Limiting the analysis to these economies does not constitute a serious drawback because they represent a sufficiently large market to attract the lion's share of designation and renewal decisions at the European level. With respect to the above cohorts around 87.3 percent and 94.4 percent of the European patents have designated the UK and Germany respectively (PatStat 2015). Further, patents are maintained for a longer period in the largest European economies than in the other EPC member countries.[3] More broadly, these patterns are consistent with anecdotal evidence which has suggested that patentees could save fee costs by renewing patents solely in a limited number of legislations, if this strategy is effective in preempting market presence in overall Europe (Burt 2010).

Because a deflator for business investment is not available for the overall period, the renewal fees have been deflated using a production index for services with the 2010 as base year. This year has been also the time reference for the exchange rate in PPP US dollars. The decay rate is assumed to be 15 percent, and the central moments of the distribution have been estimated parametrically. Then I drew fifty thousand pseudo-random variables from a lognormal distribution and calculate V for each of them using equation (1). In the value computations the granting fees have not been included and the starting time has been year three in Germany and year four in the United Kingdom. The mean and median of patent value have been estimated respectively in about PPP $84 thousand and $16 thousand for the combination of patent designations.

3.5 Data and Variables

The data sources have originated from three different repositories: i) patent indicators from the EPO Worldwide Patent Database (PatStat, April 2015); ii) bibliographic and procedural information on trademarks from the USPTO data files; iii) patentee demographic information from the Amadeus business directory of the Bureau Van Dijk.

3.5.1 Patent Indicators

The main source of patent data is constituted by the EPO Worldwide Patent Database (PatStat, April 2015) and the related EPO Patent Register. First, textual information on patent titles and abstracts has been drawn. When patent abstracts are not written in English, the abstracts of their patent equivalents have been considered.[4] Second, procedural information on renewal decisions from the EPO Patent Register has been linked with the historical fee cost structure of the designations in Germany and the United Kingdom. Third, additional information has been extracted regarding claims, references, patent classifications, inventors, priorities, and opposition decisions. Patent classifications have been aggregated in thirty groups of the categorization proposed by OST (2008). The multivariate econometric analysis controls for the same patent indicators proposed in chapter 2 (this volume), whose description is depicted in Box 2.1.[5] With the exception of the binary variables, all the indicators have been detrended for time and technology effects.[6]

3.5.2 Trademarks

Bibliographic information on US trade and service marks has been extracted from the SGML files of the USPTO trademark database (CASSIS 2007). This data source collects complete bibliographic information on the universe of US mark registrations since 1977, including date of filing and priority, goods and services description of a mark, sectoral classification, and mark ownership. On the other hand, updated procedural information about the trademark life cycle has been drawn from the CASE file.[7] This file comprehends detailed information on the examination process by trademark reviewers, office actions, publication dates regarding opposition and maintenance, decisions with respect to renewal, cancellation and expiration of a mark, and other information (Graham et al. 2013).[8] Moreover, I harmonized and integrated trademarks with the patent dataset described in Thoma et al. (2010 B), which identifies the business companies who file patents in EPC, PCT, and USPTO systems. I opted to include US trademark documents, and not those of the European Office for Harmonization in the Internal Market (OHIM) because of the substantially longer and wider coverage of the USPTO with respect to the OHIM during the '90s.

To identify a patent and trademark pair and measure the strength of the signaling strategy I analysed the textual content of patent and trademark documents. In this task I deviced a matching algorithm relying on string similarity analysis which accounts for differences due to the position of the same word between otherwise identical strings (e.g., AMINEXIL diamino-pyrimidine as compared to diaminopyrimidine AMINEXIL). I implemented the string similarity J^w index proposed by Thoma et al. (2010 B), which computes the fraction of common words after breaking up the strings into words at the blank spaces.[9]

In order to gauge the PTP strategies, the J^w index algorithm has been applied to the three textual information sets of the legal documents in a decreasing order of the signaling strength. The first textual information set is consituted by all the words appearing in patent titles as compared to wordmarks, which typically represent very unique and distinctive words. In fact, titles are succinct categorisations of a patent reporting its most salient feature. On the other hand, wordmarks are carefully scrutinized by expert reviewers who approve their registration under strict criteria regarding their distinctiveness and being not similar or identical to any earlier mark.[10]

The second information set is given by all the words of patent titles as compared to the goods and services description of a mark. These category descriptions are officially maintained by the USPTO in the Manual of Acceptable Identifications of Goods and Services, which is harmonized with the other member offices of the World Intellectual Property Organization (USPTO 2013). During the filing process the applicant can include novel categories with respect to that manual, but the examiner can request amendments when she thinks the descriptions are not sufficiently definite. The third and last information set is residual to the other two, and it is made of the words occurring in the abstract of a patent as compared to the wordmark and goods and services of a mark.

Whereas it can be argued that these variables measure only incidental text similarity across patent and trademark documents, and thus the matching algorithm could generate false positives, two kinds of caveats are worth mentioning. On the one hand, the matching of patent and trademark documents employs the weighted J^w index (Thoma et al. 2010 B), which takes into the account the statistical frequency of the tokens in the overall dataset, and thus it can overcome spurious matching of frequent and nondiscriminating words. On the other hand, the wording in trademarks is featured by an intrinsically distinctive nature, and hence the potential false positives spurring from the matching of trademarks should be more limited than when other types of documents are analysed (such as the matching patents with scientific publications).[11] In conclusion, to avoid collinearity across string measures the weighted J^w index has been computed as mutually exclusive with the other information set in a decreasing order of the signaling strength.

3.5.3 Design Patents

In order to account for potential heterogeneity deriving from other IP strategies that could affect patent valuation, I considered design patent rights which protect purely decorative and ornamental products. It is been argued that patentees actively achieve a proliferation of overlapping intellectual property rights regarding the same innovative project in order to enlarge the amount of remedies that can be requested in patent disputes (Heller and Eisenberg 1998; Lanjouw and Lerner 1998). In this case it is not the patent and trademark pair strategy per se that affects the value of patents but the ability of the patentee to obtain protection with a combination of several IP strategies.

Using data from PatStat (April 2015) I built patent pairs when an owner of an European patent obtains an US design patent having the same or similar title.[12] In the same fashion, I applied the string similarity weighted J^w index discussed in Thoma et al. (2010 B) in order to compute pairs of invention patents with design rights. Again focusing only on the USPTO dataset does not constitute a limitation because the OHIM, who is in charge of receiving filing requests for European design patents, started its relative activity only in 2003.

3.5.4 Firm Level Controls

In the multivariate econometric analysis I control for the patentee's demographic characteristics which could have an impact on the premium value of patents. The task is eased by the fact that the database described in Thoma et al. (2010 B) allows one to link the patentee names with external information on firm's characteristics. In particular, I have drawn information from the Amadeus business directory (amadeus.bvdep.com) of the Bureau Van Dijk, and I have built several control variables at the level of the patenting firm, which are depicted in Box 3.1 jointly with a short description about the measurement methodology.

Box 3.1   Patent pairing strategies and controls for the patenting firm

Patent pairing strategies

Patent title ∩ Wordmark	The weighted J^w index computed over the tokens appearing in the title of a patent as compared to the wordmark of a mark.
Patent title ∩ Mark goods and services description	The weighted J^w index computed over the tokens appearing in the title of a patent as compared to the goods and services description of a mark.

Patent pairing strategies	
Patent abstract ∩ Wordmark and mark goods and services description	The weighted J^w index computed over the tokens appearing in the abstract of a patent as compared to the wordmark and goods and services description of a mark.
Design patent pair	The weighted J^w index computed over the tokens appearing in the title of a patent as compared to the title of a design patent right.

Controls for the patenting firm	
Country of origin	Dummies for the country where the firm has been incorporated.
Listed firm	Binary variable whether the firm is publicly listed in financial markets, zero otherwise.
Large firm	Binary variable with the positive outcome when the firm has more than 250 employees, zero otherwise.
Cohort dummies	Dummies for firm's experience according to the year when a firm was founded: between 1971 and 1980, 1981 and 1985, 1986 and 1990, 1991 and 1995, after year 1996, with those founded prior to 1971 the left-out category.
Sector of activity	Dummies for the main activity code of the firm. The activity codes have been aggregated as the industry grouping of the 'OECD, STAN database' relying on the main activity code of the firm (Thoma *et al.* 2010 A).
Growth of R&D investment	Lagged growth of R&D personnel over five-year window. The R&D personnel counts are measured according to the methodology discussed in chapter 7 (this volume).

3.6 The Determinants of the Patent Premium Value

In order to test the hypotheses, I regressed a series of linear equations against the log premium value of patents of the three proposed measures of the patent and trademark pair strategies. The analysis has considered all granted patents filed from 1985 to 1994, and those patents that have been validated at least once in the UK or Germany.[13] I have limited the analysis only to the European business patenting firms, excluding also sole inventors and non-business organizations. Thus the dataset is reduced to about 154,852 patents, that is 45.2 percent. Second, I discarded also those patents for which I could not identify the business company who filed the patent application: for 83,948 patents (24.5 percent) I could not retrieve any matched record in the Amadeus business directory, or when there is matched record demographic information on the patent owner is not available. The final sample is constituted of 103,805 patents: 13.9 percent of these patents designate only Germany, whereas 3.9 percent of them only the United Kingdom.[14]

Table 3.1 and Table 3.2 depict respectively the descriptive statistics and the correlation results of the patent and trademark pairs with patent valuation and the controls for the patenting firm. As we can notice, the PTP measures are positively and significantly correlated with the value of patents. To ease the interpretation of IP pairing measures from a managerial perspective, I have transformed them in binary variables. In particular, I have considered as the positive outcome only when an IP pairing measure equals the top quartile of the relative distribution in terms of the textual similarity. Although this threshold is conservative, the correlation analysis of the binary variables with the patent valuation reports very similar results to the case when the PTP measures have been computed as the J^w similarity index in absolute terms.

The multivariate results of the linear regressions are depicted in Table 3.3. I have included several control variables defined at the level of the patent owner, such as cohort, size, sector of the activity, country of origin, listing in financial markets, and growth of R&D investment. Furthermore I have considered a complete set of patent indicators regarding patent breadth and technology potential, prior art and patent background, and filing and procedural aspects of a patent.[15] All regressions include dummies to condition for fixed effects with respect to patent cohorts, two-digit technological classification, and year-technology interaction effects. The standard errors are clustered using the robust estimator at the patentee level in order to take into the account potential omitted factors. In all regressions there is also a dummy whether the patentee has not filed any utility patent, trademark, or design patent at the USPTO during the considered period. These variables condition for the potential selection biases deriving from the fact that I am considering only trademarks and design patents filed under the US legislation and not other systems. As it is shown in Table 3.3, these variables do not enter significantly in the regressions.

For the controls at the patent level I find that the indicators of patent breadth and technology potential have the largest positive impact on patent value for a standard deviation change. In particular forward citations have the biggest impact on the log premium value of patents with about one-fifth increase, which is then followed by the two measures of patent family breadth, that is patent family size and patent family value (the GDP weighted family size indicator). It is quite interesting that the importance of the breadth of protection is shown also in the case of filing a divisional application that is accompanied with about 54.2 percentage points increase on the average premium value.[16] Other variables which measure patent breadth—such as the number of technology classes and number of claims— have a positive impact on patent valuation for a standard deviation increase,

Table 3.1 Descriptive statistics

Variables	Mean	Median	S.D.	Min	Max
Dependent variable: Patent value (log)	9.804	9.716	2.072	4.404	14.021
Patent and trademark pair as J^w index					
Patent title ∩ Wordmark	0.010	0.000	0.046	0.000	0.990
Patent title ∩ Goods & services	0.050	0.021	0.077	0.000	1.498
Patent abstract ∩ Wordmark and goods & services	0.036	0.003	0.080	0.000	4.057
Patent and trademark pair as binary variable					
Patent title ∩ Wordmark	0.028	–	–	0.000	1.000
Patent title ∩ Goods & services	0.128	–	–	0.000	1.000
Patent abstract ∩ Wordmark and goods & services	0.133	–	–	0.000	1.000
Patentee level variables and other controls					
Design patent pair as $J^w index$	0.016	0.000	0.067	0.000	1.582
Design patent pair as binary variable	0.025	–	–	0.000	1.000
D (Patentee w/o US utility patents)	0.110	–	–	0.000	1.000
D (Patentee w/o US trademarks)	0.189	–	–	0.000	1.000
D (Patentee w/o US design patents)	0.884	–	–	0.000	1.000
D (Large firm)	0.962	–	–	0.000	1.000
D (Listed firm)	0.330	–	–	0.000	1.000
R&D investment 5 years growth	0.778	0.530	0.799	-0.813	6.399

Patent breadth and technology potential indicators

Log (Patent family size)	0.695	0.659	0.232	3.812
Log (Patent family value)	0.545	0.577	0.139	1.495
Log (Claims)	0.623	0.601	0.266	2.669
Log (Patent classes)	0.557	0.516	0.287	2.785
Log (Forward citations)	0.557	0.469	0.469	4.552
Generality index	0.277	0.000	0.369	1.000

Patent prior art and background of the invention indicators

Log (Inventors)	0.523	0.508	0.233	2.153
Log (XY type backward citations)	0.355	0.000	0.431	3.369
Log (Inventor-added backward cites)	0.243	0.000	0.375	2.539
Log (Other examiner-added backward cites)	0.658	0.629	0.458	5.480
Log (Nonpatent literature references)	0.331	0.000	0.450	4.306
Originality index	0.557	0.643	0.308	1.000

Filing and procedural aspects of the patent

Log (Grant lag)	0.676	0.659	0.204	1.923
D (Patent opposed)	0.083	–	0.000	1.000
D (PCT route)	0.173	–	0.000	1.000
D (Supplementary search report)	0.003	–	0.000	1.000
D (Divisional application)	0.014	–	0.000	1.000
D (No forward citations)	0.180	–	0.000	1.000
D (No backward citations at all)	0.003	–	0.000	1.000
D (No inventor-added backward cites)	0.668	–	0.000	1.000

Notes: n=103,805 EPC patents designating Germany and the UK from the cohorts 1985–1994.

Table 3.2 Pairwise correlations

Variables	1	2	3	4	5	6	7	8	9	10	11	12
1. Patent value (log)	1.000											
Patent and trademark pair as J^w index												
2. Patent title ∩ Wordmark	0.022	1.000										
3. Patent title ∩ Goods & services	0.030	-0.090	1.000									
4. Patent abstract ∩ Wordmark and goods & services	0.038	-0.045	0.171	1.000								
Patent and trademark pair as binary variable												
5. Patent title ∩ Wordmark	0.021	0.863	-0.086	-0.043	1.000							
6. Patent title ∩ Goods & services	0.029	-0.056	0.782	0.119	-0.052	1.000						
7. Patent abstract ∩ Wordmark and goods & services	0.034	-0.048	0.119	0.697	-0.041	0.090	1.000					
8. Design patent pair as J^w index	0.001	0.066	0.083	0.053	0.065	0.056	0.050	1.000				
9. Design patent pair as binary variable	-0.005	0.049	0.070	0.044	0.053	0.044	0.038	0.813	1.000			
10. D (Large firm)	0.015	0.041	0.027	0.045	0.033	-0.009	0.035	0.025	0.024	1.000		
11. D (Listed firm)	-0.022	0.109	0.023	-0.013	0.087	-0.035	-0.031	0.038	0.008	0.139	1.000	
12. R&D investment five years growth	0.031	-0.026	-0.014	0.015	-0.019	0.003	0.021	0.022	0.021	-0.016	-0.123	1.000

Notes: a) n=103,805 EPC patents designating Germany and the UK from the cohorts 1985–1994. b) Coefficients in bold are statistically significant at 5 percent level.

Table 3.3 Patent premium value: log linear regression results

Dependent variable: log value of patent rights based on historical renewal fee costs (US 2010 PPP $)

	(1)	(2)	(3)	(4)	(5)	(6)	(7)	(8)
Patent and trademark pair as J^w index								
Patent title ∩ Wordmark	0.621** [0.309]	0.733** [0.311]	0.691** [0.305]	0.790** [0.307]				
Patent title ∩ Goods & services		0.568*** [0.156]		0.525*** [0.152]				
Patent abstract ∩ Wordmark and goods & services			0.497*** [0.118]	0.455*** [0.116]				
Patent and trademark pair as binary variable								
Patent title ∩ Wordmark					0.183** [0.082]	0.193** [0.083]	0.194** [0.082]	0.204** [0.083]
Patent title ∩ Goods & services						0.100*** [0.032]		0.097*** [0.032]
Patent abstract ∩ Wordmark and goods & services							0.081*** [0.027]	0.078*** [0.026]
Design patent pair as J^w index	-0.224 [0.262]	-0.273 [0.258]	-0.235 [0.261]	-0.280 [0.258]				
Design patent pair as binary variable					-0.141 [0.102]	-0.143 [0.100]	-0.137 [0.101]	-0.145 [0.100]
D (Patentee w/o US utility patents)	-0.065 [0.071]	-0.065 [0.071]	-0.064 [0.071]	-0.064 [0.071]	-0.065 [0.071]	-0.065 [0.071]	-0.064 [0.071]	-0.063 [0.071]
D (Patentee w/o US trademarks)	0.003 [0.043]	0.036 [0.045]	0.026 [0.044]	0.055 [0.045]	0.002 [0.044]	0.020 [0.044]	0.017 [0.043]	0.033 [0.044]

(Continued)

Table 3.3 (Continued)

Dependent variable: log value of patent rights based on historical renewal fee costs (US 2010 PPP $)

	(1)	(2)	(3)	(4)	(5)	(6)	(7)	(8)
D (Patentee w/o US design patents)	-0.014 [0.078]	-0.019 [0.078]	-0.014 [0.078]	-0.018 [0.077]	-0.016 [0.077]	-0.015 [0.077]	-0.013 [0.077]	-0.014 [0.077]
D (Large firm)	0.226*** [0.082]	0.228*** [0.083]	0.221*** [0.082]	0.224*** [0.083]	0.227*** [0.082]	0.232*** [0.082]	0.225*** [0.082]	0.229*** [0.083]
D (Listed firm)	-0.104** [0.052]	-0.098* [0.053]	-0.101* [0.052]	-0.095* [0.052]	-0.104** [0.052]	-0.098* [0.053]	-0.102* [0.052]	-0.096* [0.053]
R&D investment 5 years growth	0.009 [0.018]	0.009 [0.018]	0.008 [0.018]	0.009 [0.018]	0.009 [0.018]	0.008 [0.018]	0.008 [0.018]	0.008 [0.018]
Log (Patent family size)	0.651*** [0.084]	0.653*** [0.084]	0.652*** [0.084]	0.653*** [0.084]	0.650*** [0.084]	0.650*** [0.084]	0.650*** [0.084]	0.650*** [0.084]
Log (Patent family value)	1.114*** [0.144]	1.103*** [0.144]	1.110*** [0.144]	1.100*** [0.144]	1.116*** [0.144]	1.110*** [0.144]	1.114*** [0.144]	1.109*** [0.144]
Log (Claims)	0.087** [0.043]	0.087** [0.043]	0.082* [0.043]	0.082* [0.043]	0.088** [0.043]	0.087** [0.043]	0.084* [0.043]	0.083* [0.043]
Log (Patent classes)	0.157*** [0.038]	0.156*** [0.038]	0.155*** [0.038]	0.155*** [0.038]	0.157*** [0.038]	0.157*** [0.038]	0.156*** [0.038]	0.156*** [0.038]
Log (Forward citations)	0.423*** [0.027]	0.422*** [0.027]	0.419*** [0.027]	0.418*** [0.027]	0.423*** [0.027]	0.423*** [0.027]	0.421*** [0.027]	0.421*** [0.027]
Generality index	0.089*** [0.022]	0.089*** [0.022]	0.089*** [0.022]	0.090*** [0.022]	0.089*** [0.022]	0.089*** [0.022]	0.089*** [0.022]	0.089*** [0.022]
Log (Inventors)	0.225*** [0.053]	0.223*** [0.053]	0.225*** [0.053]	0.224*** [0.053]	0.225*** [0.053]	0.225*** [0.053]	0.226*** [0.053]	0.225*** [0.053]
Log (XY type backward citations)	0.134*** [0.016]	0.134*** [0.016]	0.135*** [0.016]	0.135*** [0.016]	0.134*** [0.016]	0.134*** [0.016]	0.134*** [0.016]	0.134*** [0.016]
Log (Inventor-added backward cites)	0.148*** [0.044]	0.145*** [0.044]	0.147*** [0.044]	0.145*** [0.044]	0.148*** [0.044]	0.147*** [0.044]	0.147*** [0.044]	0.146*** [0.044]

	(1)	(2)	(3)	(4)	(5)	(6)	(7)	(8)
Log (Other examiner-added backward cites)	0.029 [0.023]	0.029 [0.023]	0.029 [0.023]	0.030 [0.023]	0.029 [0.023]	0.029 [0.023]	0.029 [0.023]	0.029 [0.023]
Log (Nonpatent literature references)	0.028 [0.022]	0.027 [0.022]	0.028 [0.022]	0.026 [0.022]	0.028 [0.022]	0.027 [0.022]	0.028 [0.022]	0.026 [0.022]
Originality index	−0.054** [0.026]	−0.056** [0.026]	−0.054** [0.026]	−0.056** [0.026]	−0.051* [0.026]	−0.054** [0.026]	−0.052* [0.026]	−0.055** [0.026]
Log (Grant lag)	0.578*** [0.062]	0.579*** [0.061]	0.580*** [0.061]	0.580*** [0.061]	0.580*** [0.061]	0.580*** [0.061]	0.581*** [0.061]	0.581*** [0.061]
D (Patent opposed)	0.083*** [0.031]	0.085*** [0.031]	0.084*** [0.031]	0.087*** [0.031]	0.080** [0.031]	0.084*** [0.031]	0.083*** [0.031]	0.086*** [0.031]
D (PCT route)	0.046 [0.038]	0.047 [0.038]	0.047 [0.038]	0.047 [0.037]	0.046 [0.038]	0.046 [0.038]	0.046 [0.038]	0.047 [0.037]
D (Supplementary search report)	−0.076 [0.136]	−0.077 [0.135]	−0.074 [0.136]	−0.074 [0.135]	−0.082 [0.136]	−0.079 [0.135]	−0.078 [0.136]	−0.075 [0.135]
D (Divisional application)	0.542*** [0.060]	0.541*** [0.059]	0.543*** [0.060]	0.542*** [0.060]	0.539*** [0.059]	0.539*** [0.059]	0.541*** [0.060]	0.541*** [0.060]
D (No forward citations)	−0.006 [0.021]	−0.006 [0.021]	−0.006 [0.021]	−0.006 [0.022]	−0.006 [0.021]	−0.006 [0.021]	−0.006 [0.021]	−0.006 [0.022]
D (No backward citations at all)	−0.135 [0.094]	−0.139 [0.094]	−0.132 [0.094]	−0.136 [0.094]	−0.133 [0.094]	−0.138 [0.094]	−0.131 [0.094]	−0.135 [0.094]
D (No inventor-added backward cites)	0.029 [0.038]	0.029 [0.038]	0.029 [0.038]	0.029 [0.038]	0.029 [0.038]	0.029 [0.038]	0.029 [0.038]	0.029 [0.038]
Constant	7.096*** [0.261]	7.110*** [0.261]	7.102*** [0.261]	7.120*** [0.261]	7.088*** [0.262]	7.106*** [0.261]	7.099*** [0.262]	7.119*** [0.262]
F-test geographic origin dummies (15)	6.24***	6.28***	6.29***	6.32***	6.20***	6.25***	6.20***	6.27***
F-test sector dummies (33)	2.28***	2.29***	2.31***	2.32***	2.31***	2.29***	2.32***	2.31***
F-test founding year dummies (6)	2.09*	2.08*	2.17*	2.17*	2.12*	2.09*	2.19*	2.17*
F-test all firm characteristics' dummies (60)	3.93***	3.98***	4.00***	4.06***	3.95***	3.96***	3.99***	4.03***
Std. error (adj. R-squared)	0.099	0.098	0.098	0.098	0.099	0.098	0.098	0.098

Notes: 1) n=103,805 EPC patents designating Germany or the UK from the cohorts 1985–1994. 2) *** indicates statistically significant at 1 percent level; **5 percent level and *10 percent level. 3) Standard errors are clustered at the patentee level. 4) Weights have been computed because of the oversampling observations as compared to the universe of patents. 5) All regressions include ten-year dummies, thirty technology-fixed effects, and a complete set of year-technology interaction dummies.

with about 4.5 and 2.2 percentage points respectively. Also more general patents, as represented by those being cited by more diverse inventions from a technological point of view, hold a bigger value on average.

With respect to prior art and background of the invention, several indicators enter significantly into the regressions, although they have smaller benign effects. Beforehand, citations that are provided by the inventor at the moment of the filing have a significant and larger impact than those added by the examiner, which is consistent with the assumption that better-drafted and higher-quality patents are more valuable. Also XY type citations, which are typically introduced by the examiners during the elaboration of the search report, have a positive and significant impact at least as big as inventor-added citations. This finding could be interpreted with the fact that these patents hold a high strategic value, and hence they are maintained for a longer period than other patents on average. A further finding that does not contradict this view is constituted by the positive impact of the granting lag and opposition decisions, which concern the uncertainty related to the patent protection strategy and the risk of a patent dispute. In other words, patents which are approved after a relatively longer period from filing and those that are considered more controversial have a significant strategic value for their owners. Last, patents invented by more numerous teams of inventors are more valuable with a similar impact to one standard deviation change of the inventor-added citations, whereas patents that stand on the shoulders of a more diverse pool of prior knowledge as proxied by the originality index have a negative first-order effect on patent valuation.[17]

Patentee demographic characteristics positively account for a significant variability of the patent premium value. On the one hand, as shown by the F-tests on model restrictions differences across industries, cohorts, and locations are relevant to disentangle the value distribution of patents. In addition, patents held by large firms are associated with higher valuations than those inventions patented by small and medium-sized ones. In particular I find a difference of PPP $153 thousand in the patent valuation across the two groups of firms. This evidence is line with the assumption that patent premium is positively mediated by firm's size, because large firms have better access to other appropriability mechanisms—such as lead time, complementary assets, and secrecy—reinforcing the protection obtained from patents (McGahan and Silverman 2006; Bessen and Meurer 2008). The moderate impact of financial market listing can be explained with the fact that listed firms have a higher patent propensity, as represented by number of patents for unit of R&D investment, and hence the relative average patent value is smaller than patents owned by non-listed patentees (Hall and Ziedonis 2001).

Regarding Hypothesis 1 that argues on the signaling function of the patent and trademark pairs, I find that the PTP strategies are positively and significantly associated with the premium value of patents according to all the proposed measures. Models 1–4 include the variables measuring the IP pairing strategies in terms of J^w similarity index, whereas Models 5–8 consider them as binary variables. The results of Table 3.3 suggest that the joint use of patents and trademarks constitutes a signal for competitors, investors, or commercial partners that the underlying focal invention is highly valuable from a commercial point of view. More in general these findings confirm the validity of the patent and trademarks pairs in predicting patent valuation as compared to the typical indicators adopted in the literature (Nagaoka et al. 2010).

The combination of trademarks with patenting increase the value of patent rights by expanding the breadth of the intellectual property protection. In fact, trademarks can prolong the commercial success of a patented product beyond the statutory limit, enlarge the bargaining power of the patentee for the technology licensing and trading, and improve the plaintiffs' conditions during litigation. Heller and Eisenberg (1998) have argued that combined strategies of overlapping intellectual property rights could increase the amount of remedies that can be requested in legal disputes. The present analysis shows that whereas trademarks are positively associated with patent valuation, design patents have an insignificant impact. These findings do not falsify the view that design patents offer a second-tier protection (Greenhalgh and Rogers 2010), and hence they do not further ameliorate the appropriability conditions of the patentee above the granting of an invention patent. On the other hand, trademarks play a quintessential role in the branding and commercialization activities of the innovator, and thus they complement the protection obtained from patents. Because design patents do not slack the impact of the PTP strategies, it can be concluded that the increase in patent premium value, which is generated from pairing patents with trademarks, goes beyond the effect of the mere combination of multiple IP strategies.

Also Hypothesis 2 on the strength of signaling strategy cannot be rejected. In particular, the PTP strategy which relies on the most narrow information set (title of a patent vis-à-vis wordmark) has the largest marginal effect on patent value. These results are valid both when a patent and trademark pair is measured as a J^w similarity index or as a binary variable. In particular, one additional patent and trademark pair of the first type generates an increase of 20.4 percentage points on the log premium value of patents (i.e., PPP $115 thousand in absolute number or increasing the average patent value more than twice) (Model 8). When I consider the patent abstracts the marginal effect reduces to 7.8 percentage points, whereas the estimate of the other pairing strategy—which combines patent titles vis-à-vis goods and services description—is about half of the pairing strategy based on combining patent titles with wordmarks. These results can be explained with the heterogeneity of the strength of the signals issued by patent and trademark pairs (i.e., the impact of the signaling is stronger when patent titles and wordmarks include the same wording and labelling). In absolute number the additional increase for the pairing strategies of patent titles with goods and services description is about PPP $28 thousand. When patent abstracts are analysed, the

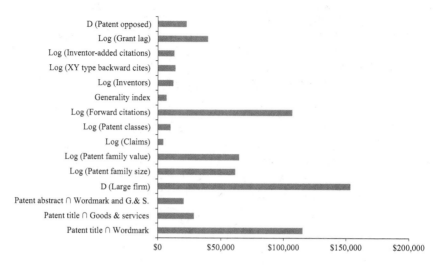

Figure 3.1 Absolute impact of patent indicators on patent premium value (in PPP $)

Notes: The impact of the continuous variables has been measured for one standard deviation change.

additional increase of patent premium value is about PPP $20 thousand. In conclusion, Figure 3.1 compares the absolute impact of the most relevant variables of the proposed multivariate analysis.

3.7 Robustness Analysis

To assess the robustness of the results, I extended the analysis to trademark renewals. Similarly to patenting, trademark owners face fee costs to maintain a mark registration in force, and additionally they are required to demonstrate that the focal mark is actively used in commercial activities.[18] Because trademarks can be renewed for an endless number of times, an analysis based on renewal decisions could shed light not solely about the central moments of the value distribution of the invention but also on its upper tail, if a sufficiently long time period is taken into the consideration.

To advance this task, I regressed a series of probit regressions on the probability of trademark renewal for the registration cohorts from 1978 to 1983, whose renewal decisions have been observed up to year 2013. That is a life cycle of about thirty years. The dataset is constituted by the universe of trademarks registered at the USPTO by the European patenting firms, that is 7,031 registrations out of which 2,109 (30.0 percent) have been kept alive up to year 2013. The regression analysis has employed similarly built variables at the patentee level to those depicted in Box 3, such as firm size, listing in financial markets, and dummies whether the patentee has not filed any utility or design patent at the USPTO—and several other controls computed at the mark level. A complete list of the control variables and a brief measurement methodology is presented in Appendix 3.2, whilst the relative descriptive statistics in Appendix 3.3.

In the regressions I conditioned for fixed effect regarding Nice classes, design search codes, registration cohorts, and year-Nice classes interaction variables. As we can notice from Table 3.4, marks having longer word-marks are less likely to be maintained during the life cycle, although this relationship has a curvilinear effect as shown by the positive impact of the second-order term. As in the case of the analysis of the patent premium value, breadth measures—such as the number of categories in which a trademark is classified—have a positive impact on maintenance. Further, trademarks held by multiple owners and reassigned after registration are more valuable, and hence they are renewed for a longer a period. In par-ticular, a reassigned trademark is one-third more likely to be maintained over its life cycle. Quite interestingly, I find that trademarks characterised by acquired distinctiveness—that is the usage of common and generic words as wordmarks—have longer renewal patterns, which does not contradict the view that consumers rely on preconceived beliefs regarding what categories of brand names could be indicative of specific products (Kohli and LaBahn 1997). An additional finding is given by the fact that a higher value of IP protection is associated with incontestable trademark registrations, which typically take place when no litigation action is pending during registration process and for five years the mark has been employed in commercial activi-ties by its owner in an exclusive way.

The results with the patent and trademark pairs are presented in Models 3–4, whereas Models 5–6 include also the pairing strategies with design patents. Because the number of observations of the dataset is reduced drasti-cally, I have computed the pairing strategies comparing patent titles not only with wordmarks but also with goods and services description of a trade-mark, in order to have a bigger number of nonzero values in absolute terms. In addition I have transformed the J^w similarity index of the paring strate-gies in binary variables.

As we can notice, both measures of patent and trademark pairs are posi-tively and significantly associated with the renewal value of trademarks. Furthermore, the results hold even when the regressions condition for the pairing strategies of design patents with trademarking, which in turn have an insignificant impact. In particular, one patent and trademark pair is 6.5 percent more likely to be renewed over its life cycle than other trade-marks on average (Model 6). These evidences do not contradict the posited hypotheses and previous findings with respect to the renewal value of pat-ents. Last, it is worth mentioning that the magnitude of the absolute impact of a patent and trademark pair on renewal is about two-thirds the impact of the firm size effect—that is when the trademark owner is represented by a large firm—and a similar differential impact is also found by the prior analysis on the determinants of the renewal value of patents.

Table 3.4 Probability of trademark renewal: probit marginal effects

Dependent variable: Binary variable with the positive outcome if the trademark has been renewed up to 2013

	(1)	(2)	(3)	(4)	(5)	(6)
Patent and trademark pair as J^w index			0.095** [0.045]		0.096** [0.046]	
Patent and trademark pair as binary variable				0.062** [0.033]		0.065** [0.033]
Design patent and trademark pair as J^w index					-0.007 [0.054]	
Design patent and trademark pair as binary variable						-0.024 [0.038]
D (Patentee w/o US utility patents)			0.046 [0.079]	0.041 [0.078]	0.047 [0.079]	0.043 [0.077]
D (Patentee w/o US design patents)			-0.033 [0.022]	-0.037* [0.021]	-0.033 [0.022]	-0.038* [0.021]
D (Patentee w/o US patents)			-0.021 [0.072]	-0.019 [0.072]	-0.022 [0.072]	-0.020 [0.071]
D (Large firm)		0.113*** [0.015]	0.107*** [0.016]	0.109*** [0.015]	0.107*** [0.016]	0.109*** [0.015]
D (Listed firm)		-0.013 [0.020]	-0.028 [0.020]	-0.025 [0.020]	-0.028 [0.020]	-0.025 [0.020]
D (Trademark)	0.022 [0.063]	0.033 [0.060]	0.035 [0.060]	0.035 [0.060]	0.034 [0.060]	0.035 [0.060]
D (Service mark)	-0.027 [0.073]	-0.020 [0.074]	-0.011 [0.077]	-0.012 [0.076]	-0.011 [0.076]	-0.013 [0.076]
Wordmark length	-0.007*** [0.002]	-0.007*** [0.002]	-0.007*** [0.002]	-0.007*** [0.002]	-0.007*** [0.002]	-0.007*** [0.002]
Wordmark length squared/100	0.004*** [0.002]	0.004*** [0.001]	0.004*** [0.001]	0.004*** [0.001]	0.004*** [0.001]	0.004*** [0.001]

	(1)	(2)	(3)	(4)	(5)	(6)
D (Use basis at filing)	0.007	0.009	0.012	0.012	0.012	0.011
	[0.022]	[0.022]	[0.022]	[0.022]	[0.022]	[0.022]
D (Acquired distinctiveness)	0.072**	0.071**	0.069**	0.068**	0.069**	0.068**
	[0.035]	[0.035]	[0.035]	[0.035]	[0.035]	[0.035]
D (Incontestability acknowledged)	0.330***	0.328***	0.327***	0.328***	0.327***	0.328***
	[0.013]	[0.013]	[0.014]	[0.013]	[0.014]	[0.013]
D (Supplemental register)	0.175***	0.177***	0.172***	0.175***	0.172***	0.176***
	[0.054]	[0.055]	[0.055]	[0.056]	[0.055]	[0.056]
D (Opposition decision)	0.016	0.020	0.017	0.018	0.017	0.018
	[0.050]	[0.050]	[0.050]	[0.050]	[0.050]	[0.050]
D (Foreign filing)	-0.039*	-0.038*	-0.036*	-0.035*	-0.036*	-0.036*
	[0.022]	[0.021]	[0.021]	[0.021]	[0.021]	[0.021]
D (Priority filing)	0.008	0.001	-0.001	-0.001	-0.001	-0.001
	[0.016]	[0.015]	[0.015]	[0.015]	[0.015]	[0.015]
Number of categories – US classification	0.064***	0.063***	0.062***	0.063***	0.062***	0.063***
	[0.007]	[0.007]	[0.007]	[0.007]	[0.007]	[0.007]
Number of goods & services categories	0.023	0.015	0.010	0.013	0.009	0.012
	[0.026]	[0.025]	[0.026]	[0.026]	[0.026]	[0.026]
Number of owners (log)	0.153***	0.131***	0.133***	0.133***	0.133***	0.133***
	[0.026]	[0.026]	[0.026]	[0.026]	[0.026]	[0.026]
D (Reassignment of the trademark)	0.299***	0.292***	0.296***	0.295***	0.296***	0.295***
	[0.018]	[0.018]	[0.018]	[0.018]	[0.018]	[0.018]
Chi-squared Nice classes (42)	250.21***	290.65***	241.65***	246.10***	298.84***	288.36***
Chi-squared design search codes (29)	41.36**	42.84**	40.72**	40.92**	40.67**	40.92**
Chi-squared firms country (15)	47.66***	43.17***	38.76***	39.64***	38.72***	39.50***
Pseudo R-squared	0.369	0.378	0.379	0.379	0.379	0.379

Notes: 1) n=7,031 trademark registrations issued during 1977–1983, positive outcome 2,109. 2) *** indicates statistically significant at 1% level; **5% level and *10% level. 3) Standard errors clustered at the patentee level. 4) All regressions include 7 year dummies, 42 Nice classes fixed effects, and year-Nice classes interaction dummies.

3.8 Conclusions

This study is among the first attempts to analyse what are the determinants of patent premium value with respect to a complemental IP strategy, such as trademarks. I elaborate a novel method and database to identify combinations of patent and trademark strategies regarding the same innovative project. In particular, I define a new concept, namely patent and trademark pair, when the innovation process yields both a patent and a trademark. By relying on previous research on quality signals in entrepreneurial finance, I propose a theoretical framework which argues that trademarks improve the signaling function of patents and, therefore, increase the value of the patented R&D. In this framework the signaling from patent and trademark pairs is characterized by different levels of strength, which is positively associated with patent valuation. Furthermore, I elaborated a taxonomy of pairs which categorises the strength of signals according to their cost, commitment, certifiability, clarity, visibility, and consistency, and I operationalize it by comparing the textual similarity of the legal documents.

I do find ample evidences that the IP strategies based on patent and trademark pairs are associated with higher valuations after controlling for a full-fledged set of other variables. First, I account for the traditional patent value indicators proposed in the literature on patent valuation regarding patent breadth and technology potential, prior art and patent background, and filing and procedural aspects of a patent. Second, I analysed design patents as an additional IP strategy which is pursued in combination with patenting. The econometric results are in line with the view that design patents constitute a second-tier protection mechanism for smaller and incremental inventions, and hence they do not conflate into a greater patent valuation. Last, I condition for multiple characteristics defined at the level of the patent owner which are expected to correlate with patent value, such as sector of activity, firm's size and experience, listing in financial markets, country of origin, growth of R&D investment, and others.

The largest impact on the patent premium value is obtained when I analyse the trademark strategy issuing the strongest type of signaling: In particular when patent and trademark pairs are linked through patent titles and wordmarks, then the protection value of the underlying invention is augmented twice, that is PPP $115 thousand above the average value. On the other hand, when patent and trademark pairs are jointly combined relying on other textual information—such as patent abstracts and goods and services description in trademarks—the increase is positive and statistically significant, but more distant in absolute number than the former combined IP strategy.

Notwithstanding the robustness analysis confirmed that IP pairing strategies impact also the premium value of trademarks beyond that of patents, there are several limitations of this study. Although it analyses the IP strategies of European business patentees, only US trademarks are taken into the account. Whereas this limitation could not constitute a serious drawback for the cohorts of patents from 1985 to 1994, the usage of the trademark filings at the OI IIM has increased rapidly after year 1996, and not necessarily these trademark filings could have been extended at the USPTO. Second, this study has disregarded EPC patents from non-European patentees. In fact, the valuation analysis of these other inventions could gauge a differential impact of patent indicators, in particular those related to filing and procedural aspect of the patent. A third limitation is given by the limited number and static nature of the controls at the patentee level. Other characteristics could influence patent valuation, such as financial and ownership structure of the patenting firm. This kind of information has become available in digitalized format only recently, but the analysis which focuses on the latter cohort of patents is likely to benefit at great extent by looking to these firm characteristics. A fourth area for further research is the inclusion of the competitive landscape in the patent valuation—that is, how the IP strategies by competitors affect the patent premium value by the focal firms. At the current stage I have proxied for the sector of the activity of the patentee by the mean of time invariant variables. A significant contribution in this area would require a redefinition of the measurement approach, taking into the account the dynamic nature of competition. In conclusion, it is interesting to disentangle from a policy persepective whether the combined IP strategies are accompanied with any impact on the growth of R&D investment or its intensity relative to sales at the firm level (Bessen and Maskin 2009): whereas in a static context combined IP strategies could encourage R&D spending, there could be less-benign effects when the innovation process is sequential and demands complementaries across the research lines pursued by different innovators.

Appendix 3.1
Textual Similarity Index

To identify a patent and trademark pair, I semantically compared and matched textual information of the legal documents. In this task I deviced a matching algorithm relying on string similarity analysis, which accounts for differences due to the position of the same word between otherwise identical strings (e.g., AMINEXIL diaminopyrimidine as compared to diaminopyrimidine AMINEXIL). In particular I implemented the string similarity J index proposed by Thoma et al. (2010 A), which computes the fraction of common words after breaking up the strings into words at the blank spaces and it reads as the following:

$$J(X,Y) = \frac{|X \cap Y|}{|X \cup Y|} \cong \frac{2|X \cap Y|}{|X| + |Y|} \tag{A.1}$$

Where $X \cap Y$ computes the number of common words between strings X and Y whereas $X \cup Y$ computes the total number of distinct words. To reduce the computational complexity the second term of the Eq. (A.1) has been approximated, and the denominator is stylized as the sum of all words, including those words that are contained in both strings. This may result in some double counting and thus the numerator is multiplied by two in order to preserve a comparable scale.

To account for frequent words, I normalize each word i by its statistical weight w_i in the dataset

$$w_i = \frac{1}{\log(n_i) + 1} \tag{A.2}$$

Where n_i is the frequency of the token in the dataset. Thus, the weighted J^w index is equal to the following expression:

$$J^w(X,Y) = \frac{2\sum_{k|x_k \in X \cap Y} w_k}{\sum_{i|x_i \in X} w_i + \sum_{j|y_j \in Y} w_j} \tag{A.3}$$

Where $x_i \in X$ and $y_i \in Y$ and w_i and w_j are the weights inversely correlated with the frequency of tokens x_i and y_i in the dataset; the terms x_k and w_k are respectively the kth token and relative weight belonging to the intersection set $X \cap Y$.

Appendix 3.2
Trademark Indicators

Trademark characteristics and classification

Trademark	A binary variable if the mark is associated to a good product.
Service mark	A binary variable if the mark is associated to a service.
Wordmark length	Number of characters of the wordmark of a mark.
Wordmark length squared	The squared number of characters of the wordmark of a mark.
Nice classes	Dummies for each of the forty-five categories of the Nice classification.
Design search codes	Dummies for each of the twenty-nine categories of the US design search codes.
Time dummies	Annual dummies for the period from 1977 to 1983.
Nice-time dummies	Interaction dummies for each Nice classification and annual period.

Filing and procedural aspects of the trademark

Use basis at filing	A binary variable with the positive outcome if a declaration of 'use in commerce' has been submitted at the date of filing.
Acquired distinctiveness	A binary variable with the positive outcome if an affidavit of acquired distinctiveness has been filed.
Incontestability acknowledged	A binary variable with the positive outcome if an affidavit of incontestability has been acknowledged.
Supplemental register	A binary variable with the positive outcome if the mark has been filed for or registered on the supplemental register.
Opposition decision	A binary variable with the positive outcome if an opposition action has been pending after registration.

Geographical and activity breadth of the trademark

Foreign filing	A binary variable with the positive outcome if the trademark registration involves at least one foreign or international application/registration.
Priority filing	A binary variable with the positive outcome if the trademark registration involves at least one prior application/registration.
Number of categories	A count variable of the number of the categories of the US classification which have been assigned to a mark. These categories are more detailed than the Nice classification, and thus can account for a larger variability of the commercial breadth of a mark.
Number of goods and services categories	A count variable of the number of categories of the goods and services categories which are reported by the mark at the time of registration.
Number of owners	A count variable of the number of owner of the trademark. For more clarity I have considered only those owner names that have been matched to the Amadeus business directory.
Reassignment of the trademark	A binary variable with the positive outcome if the mark has changed ownership during its lifecycle.

Appendix 3.3

Descriptive Statistics of the Trademark Dataset

Variables	Mean	Median	S.D.
Dependent variable: Trademark renewal°	0.300	–	–
IP paring variables			
Patent and trademark pair as J^w index	0.093	0.000	0.152
Patent and trademark pair as binary variable	0.049	–	–
Design patent and trademark pair as J^w index	0.023	0.000	0.127
Design patent and trademark pair as binary variable	0.017	–	–
Patentee level variables and other controls			
D (Patentee w/o US utility patents)	0.203	–	–
D (Patentee w/o US design patents)	0.727	–	–
D (Patentee w/o US patents)	0.191	–	–
D (Large firm)	0.754	–	–
D (Listed firm)	0.234	–	–
Trademark characteristics and classification			
D (Trademark)	0.975	–	–
D (Service mark)	0.033	–	–
Wordmark length	8.429	8.000	6.505
Wordmark length squared/100	1.134	0.640	5.649
Filing and procedural aspects of the trademark			
D (Use basis at filing)	0.574	–	–
D (Acquired distinctiveness)	0.033	–	–
D (Incontestability acknowledged)	0.524	–	–
D (Supplemental register)	0.019	–	–
D (Opposition decision)	0.011	–	–
Geographical and activity breadth of the trademark			
D (Foreign filing)	0.518	–	–
D (Priority filing)	0.187	–	–
Number of categories—US classification	1.415	1.000	1.150
Number of goods & services categories	1.259	1.000	0.818
Number of owners (log)	0.813	0.693	0.258
D (Reassignment of the trademark)	0.328	–	–

Notes: n = 7,031 trademark registrations issued during 1977–1983, positive outcomes 2,109.
° Binary variable with the positive outcome if the trademark has been renewed up to 2013.

Notes

1 B. Berman (2008), interviewed in IP Close UP, November 15, 2012.
2 Umbrella branding consists in including a single name in many different wordmarks.
3 For the cohorts 1985–1994 I tested this assumption with the renewal decisions drawn from PatStat (April 2015). I do find significant differences that patents are maintained for a longer period in Germany, France, and the United Kingdom than in the other EPC member countries.

4 Whereas about 3.3 percent of EPC patent applications are not filed with an English abstract, this ratio is reduced to 0.5 percent once the abstracts of their patent equivalents have been considered as a surrogate. For the cohorts 1985–1994 which have been validated at least once in the UK or Germany, with the exemption of twenty-two observations the complete population of patents has been linked to an English abstract.

5 In addition, the backward citations have been disaggregated in three mutually categories in order to disentangle their differential impact: XY type backward citations, inventor added backward citations, and other examiner added backward citations.

6 For further details on the detrending methodology see the discussion reported in section 2.5 (chapter 2, this volume).

7 The analysed USPTO CASE file comprehends updated trademark records up to January 7, 2015. For more information see www.uspto.gov/economics.

8 For a fuller presentation and discussion about the CASE file see Graham *et al.* (2013).

9 See Appendix 3.1 for a deeper discussion.

10 Another criteria for approval of the registration of a mark is that it should not be deceptive and contrary to law or morality.

11 I attempt to manually assess the false positives for about twenty patent and trademark pairs that have flagged the highest J^w similarity index when I compare patent titles and wordmarks. These pairs are included in the top quartile of the relative PTP distribution. I found that two cases could be considered as false positives, which are linked through a single nondiscriminating and nonfrequent word ('electronics'). In all other cases I obtained a high level of similarity across the portfolio of patents and trademarks originating from: a) discriminating token(s) in the patent title and wordmark, such as the case study of AMINEXIL and diaminopyrimidine by the L'OREAL Corporation; b) combination of nondiscriminating tokens from a patent title, that could appear in one single wordmark or in combination of wordmarks in distinct trademarks (within the same portfolio); c) one single and nondiscriminating token from a patent title repeated in many trademarks from the same portfolio, which can be assimilated to an umbrella branding.

12 Furthermore the patentee must provide drawings and/or photographs depicting the characteristics of the design in order to obtain patent protection. The statutory limit of protection for US design patents is fourteen years, and no payment of renewal fees is required.

13 In terms of the renewal fee payment I computed the present value rule starting in year three in Germany and in year four in the United Kingdom, and I did not consider the grant fee in the value computations.

14 In the regressions I use weights in order to tackle selection biases arising from the fact of analysing the dataset with a reduced number of observations compared to the universe of patents.

15 See the Box 2.1 for more details. The backward citation variables—XY type backward citations, inventor-added backward cites, and other examiner added backward cites—are computed as mutually exclusive.

16 Two kinds of caveats are in order to interpret the divisionals' large impact. On the one hand, divisional applications constitute a rare filing strategy during the period from 1985 to 1994: About 1.4 percent of the patent dataset is made of divisional applications (see Table 3.1). The largest share of divisionals are held by chemical, pharmaceutical, and medical instrument firms whose patents are maintained typically for a longer period than other patents on average. In the latter years these filing strategies would have been used more intensively in computer and semiconductor technologies, which are characterized by a higher patent propensity than other fields, and the output of invention activities would

have shifted towards less important patents (Hegde *et al.* 2009). Second, Graham (2004) argued that the use of fractional application could proxy the ability of the patentee to protect the output of the invention process not only through formal IP mechanics but also informal ones, most notably secrecy. More in general, it has been claimed a complementary view across patenting and secrecy, when the patent publication could be delayed by filing a fractional application or when part of the knowledge to make the patented invention fully operational has not been disclosed yet (Arora 1996; Graham 2004). In fact, the large impact of the divisional application is consistent with the empirical evidences brought by Searle (2010), who claimed that the value an invention which is protected also with secrecy is one order of magnitude bigger than the value of the inventions protected only through patenting.

17 An additional robustness analysis has been that of including interaction and second-order terms of the patent indicators with respect to patent breadth and technology potential, prior art and patent background, and filing and procedural aspects of a patent. The patent valuation results of the patent and trademark pairs are in line in terms of sign, impact, and significance to those presented in this section. For simplicity I have omitted this robustness analysis, which is available upon request.

18 Renewal decisions for trademarks are maintained through a ten-year period from the date of registration, and contemporaneously a filing of an affidavit of continued used or excusable nonuse is required to the owner.

References

Alvarez-Garrido E., G. Dushnitsky 2013. "Publications and Patents in Corporate Venture Backed Biotech." *Nature Biotechnol* 31(6):495–497.

Arora, A. 1996. "Contracting for Tacit Knowledge: The Provision of Technical Services in Technology Licensing Contracts." *J Dev Econ* 50(2):233–256.

Arora A., M. Ceccagnoli, W. Cohen 2008. "R&D and the Patent Premium." *Int J Ind Organ* 26(5):1153–1179.

Bao Y., A. T. Shao, D. Rivers 2008. "Creating New Brand Names: Effects of Relevance, Connotation, and Pronunciation." *J Advertising Res* 48(1):148–162.

Berman B. 2008. *From Assets to Profits: Competing for IP Value and Return.* Hoboken (NJ): John Wiley & Sons.

Bessen J., E. Maskin 2009. "Sequential Innovation, Patents, and Imitation." *Rand J Econ* 20(4):611–635.

Bessen J., M. Meurer 2008. *Patent Failure: How Judges, Bureaucrats and Lawyers Put Innovators at Risk.* Princeton (NJ): Princeton University Press.

Block J. H., G. De Vries, J. H. Schumann, P. Sandner 2014. "Trademarks and Venture Capital Valuation." *J Business Venturing* 29:525–542.

Buddelmeyer H., P. Jensen, E. Webster 2010. "Innovation and the Determinants of Company Survival." *Oxford Econ Pap* 62(2):261–285.

Burt R. 2010. "Personal Communication to the Author by Roger Burt, Chief of the IBM legal office in the U.K.", Vienna, Austria, November 17–18.

CASSIS 2007. *US Bibliometric Trademark Database: SGML Files in the CD Version*, October edition. Washington (DC):US Patent and Trademark and Office.

Chesbrough H. 2003. *Open Innovation: The New Imperative for Creating and Profiting from Technology.* Cambridge (MA): Harvard Business School Press.

Ching A. T. 2010. "Consumer Learning and Heterogeneity: Dynamics of Demand for Prescription Drugs after Patent Expiration." *Int J Ind Organ* 28:619–638.

Cockburn I., M. McGarvie 2007. "Patents, Thickets and the Financing of Early-Stage Firms: Evidence from the Software Industry." *J Econ Manag Strat* 18(3):729–773.

Conti A., M. Thursby, F. Rothaermel 2013 A. "Show Me the Right Stuff: Signals for High-Tech Startups." *J Econ Manag Strat* 22(2):341–364.

Conti A., M. Thursby, J. Thursby 2013 B. "Patents as Signals for Startup Financing." NBER Working Paper No. 19191, National Bureau of Economic Research, Inc., Cambridge (MA).

Deb P. 2013. "Signaling Type and Post-IPO Performance." *Eur Manag Rev* 10:99–116.

DeGraba P., M. W. Sullivan 1995. "Spillover Effects, Cost Savings, R&D and the Use of Brand Extensions." *Int J Ind Organ* 13:229–248.

Gambardella A. 2013. "The Economic Value of Patented Inventions: Thoughts and Some Open Questions." *Int J Ind Organ* 31:626–633.

Gans J. S., D. H. Hsu, S. Stern 2008. "The Impact of Uncertain Intellectual Property Rights on The Market for Ideas: Evidence from Patent Grant Delays." *Manag Science* 54(5):982–997.

Gans J. S., S. Stern 2003. "The Product Market and the Market for Ideas: Commercialization Strategies for Technology Entrepreneurs." *Res Pol* 32:333–350.

Graham S. 2004. "Hiding in the Patent's Shadow: Firms' Uses of Secrecy to Capture Value from New Discoveries." Georgia Institute of Technology TI:Ger Working Paper. Accessed at tiger.gatech.edu. Accessed date June 30, 2014.

Graham S., H. Galen, A. Marco, A. F. Myers 2013. "The USPTO Trademark Case Files Dataset: Descriptions, Lessons, and Insights." *J Econ Manag Strat* 22(4):669–705.

Graham S., A. Marco, A. F. Myers 2014. "Monetizing Marks, Insights from the USPTO Trademark Assignment Dataset." USPTO Economic Working Paper No. 2014–2. Office of the Chief Economist, Patent and Trademark Office, Alexandria, VA.

Greenberg G. 2013. "Small Firms, Big Patents? Estimating Patent Value Using Data on Israeli Start-ups' Financing Rounds." *Eur Manag Rev* 10:183–196.

Greenhalgh C., M. Rogers 2006. "The Value of Innovation: The Interaction of Competition, R&D and IP." *Res Pol* 35:562–580.

Greenhalgh C., M. Rogers 2010. *Innovation, Intellectual Property and Economic Growth*. Princeton (NJ): Princeton University Press.

Hall B. H., D. Harhoff 2012. "Recent Research on the Economics of Patents." *Annu Rev Econ* 4:541–565.

Hall B. H., R. Ziedonis 2001. "The Determinants of Patenting in the US Semiconductor Industry, 1980–1994." *Rand J Econ* 32:101–128.

Häussler C., D. Harhoff, E. Mueller 2014. "How Patenting Informs VC Investors—The Case of Biotechnology." *Res Pol* 43(8):1286–1298.

Hegde D., D. Mowery, S. Graham 2009. "Pioneering Inventors or Thicket Builders: Which US Firms Use Continuations in Patenting?" *Manag Science* 55(7):1214–1226.

Heller M. A., R. S. Eisenberg 1998. "Can Patents Deter Innovation? The Anticommons in Biomedical Research." *Science* 280:698–700.

Helmers C., M. Rogers 2010. "Innovation and the Survival of New Firms in the United Kingsom." *Rev Ind Organ* 36:227–248.

Helmers C., M. Rogers 2011. "Does Patenting Help High-Tech Start-Ups?" *Res Pol* 40:1016–1027.

Hoenen S., C. Kolympiris, W. Schoenmakers, N. Kalaitzandonakes 2014. "The Diminishing Signaling Value of Patents Between Early Rounds of Venture Capital Financing." *Res Pol* 43:956–989.

Hsu D., R. Ziedonis 2013. "Resources as Dual Sources of Advantage: Implications for Valuing Entrepreneurial-Firm Patents." *Strat Manag J* 34:761–781.

IP CloseUp 2012. "Leading Brands Increasingly Have the Most Valuable Patents." by Bruce Berman. Accessed November 15, 2012, http://ipcloseup.wordpress.com/2012/11/15/leading-brands-increasingly-have-the-most-valuable-patents/

Kohli C., D. W. LaBahn 1997. "Creating Effective Brand Names: A Study of the Naming Process." *J Advertising Res* 37:67–75.

Korkeamäki T., T. Takalo 2013. "Valuation of Innovation and Intellectual Property: The Case of iPhone." *Eur Manag Rev* 10:197–210.

Krasnikov A., S. Mishra, D. Orozco 2009. "Evaluating the Financial Impact of Branding Using Trademarks: A Framework and Empirical Evidence." *J Marketing* 73(6):154–166.

Lanjouw J. O., J. Lerner 1998. "The Enforcement of Intellectual Property Eights: A Survey of the Empirical Literature." *Annals Econ Stat* 49/50:223–246.

Legendre J. Y. 2010. "Combination of Patent Indices and Product Data Can Help Understanding Product Innovation Strategies." Paper presented at the Conference on Patent Statistics on Decision Makers, Vienna, Austria, November 17–18.

Mann R. J., T. W. Sager 2007. "Patents, Venture Capital, and Software Start-Ups." *Res Pol* 36:193–208.

McGahan A. M., B. S. Silverman 2006. "Profiting from Technological Innovation by Others: The Effect of Competitor Patenting on Firm Value." *Res Pol* 35(8):1222–1242.Mendonça S., T. S. Pereira, M. M. Godinho 2004. "Trademarks as an Indicator of Innovation and Industrial Change." *Res Pol* 33(9):1385–1404.

Nagaoka S., K. Motohashi, A. Goto 2010. "Patent Statistics as Innovation Indicators." In *The Handbook of the Economics of Innovation*, edited by B. H. Hall, N. Rosenberg, 10973–12068, Amsterdam: Elsevier, Kindle edition.

OST 2008. *Science and Technology Indicators*. Paris, France: Observatoire des Sciences et des Techniques.

PatStat 2015. *EPO Worldwide Patent Statistical Database and the EPO Patent Register*, April edition. Vienna: EPO.

Rujas J. 1999. "Trademarks: Complementary to Patents." *World Pat Inform* 21:35–39.

Sander P., J. Block 2011. "The Market Value of R&D, Patents, and Trademarks." *Res Pol* 40:969–985.

Schankerman M. 1998. "How Valuable Is Patent Protection: Estimates by Technology Fields." *Rand J Econ* 29(1):77–107.

Searle N. 2010. "The Economics of Trade Secrets: Evidence from the Economic Espionage Act." PhD diss., University of St. Andrews. St Andrews, Scotland. DOI: https://research-repository.st-andrews.ac.uk/handle/10023/1632?mode=full&submit_simple=Show+full+item+record

Spence M. 1973. "Job Market Signaling." *Quart J Econ* 87:355–374.

Squicciarini M., V. Millot, H. Dernis 2012. "Universities Trademark Patterns and Possible Determinants." *Econ Innov New Technol* 21(5–6):473–504.

Teece D. 1986. "Profiting from Technological Innovation." *Res Pol* 15(6):285–305.

Thoma G., K. Motohashi, J. Suzuki 2010 A. "Consolidating Firm Portfolios of Patents Across Different Offices. A Comparison of Sectoral Distribution of Patenting Activities in Europe and Japan." IAM Discussion Paper Series No. 2010/19, University of Tokyo. Tokyo.

Thoma G., S. Torrisi, A. Gambardella, D. Guellec, B. H. Hall, D. Harhoff 2010 B. "Harmonizing and Combining Large Datasets—An Application to Firm-Level Patent and Accounting Data." NBER Working Paper No. 15851, National Bureau of Economic Research Inc., Cambridge (MA).

USPTO 2013. "Trademark Manual of Examining Procedure." Accessed on October 1, 2014, www.uspto.gov.

Völckner F., H. Sattler 2006. "Drivers of Brand Extension Success." *J Marketing* 70:18–34.

Von Graevenitz G. 2013. "Trade Mark Clustering–Evidence from EU Enlargement." *Oxford Econ Pap* 65(3):721–745.

4 Patent Valuation of a General Purpose Technology

An Analysis of Financial Patents and Business Methods[1]

Grid Thoma, Bronwyn H. Hall, and Salvatore Torrisi

4.1 Introduction

The advent and fast growth of the Internet economy has been accompanied by innovation in traditional forms of financial payments. These changes have been propelled on the one hand by the emergence of new commercial relations conveyed through the Internet which require new and secure modes of payments (e.g., digital marketplaces and e-commerce). On the other hand, traditional markets and industries have experienced the diffusion of new business practices within their procurement and marketing activities (Tufano 2003; Lerner 2004).

The potential benign impact of innovation in the payment and financial systems is very high and extends well beyond the banking sector. It is worth remembering that changes in short-term payment and financial systems were at the base—among others—of the commercial revolution in Europe during the fifteenth and sixteenth centuries (Rosenberg and Birdzell 1986). The relationship between the development of an economy's financial structure—financial instruments, markets, and institutions—and economic growth in the modern economy is well documented in the literature (Levine 1997). More recently, scholars have suggested that innovation in payment and financial systems has some of the features of a General Purpose Technology (GPT) (Hall 2007). GPTs are technologies characterized by use in a wide range of sectors, the need for complementary investment when adopted, and scope for productivity enhancement in diverse sectors of the economy, leading to increasing returns on both the supply and demand side (Bresnahan and Trajtenberg 1995).

Here, as in most areas, the strengthening of patent coverage can have both positive and negative effects. On the one hand, it can increase the incentive to devote resources to inventive activity. On the other hand, it may discourage or raise the cost of combining and recombining of inventions to make new products and processes, in particular in cumulative innovations such as GPTs and technologies that are part of a standard setting process (see, among others, Scotchmer 1996; Cohen and Lemley 2001; Lemley

2007). These considerations are of particular relevance for financial patents and software and business methods in general (Hall 2003), due to the importance of standards for technologies enabling web-based interactions and financial transactions, whether conducted via the web or over other telecommunications networks.

Patenting in this area has increased significantly in the last two decades. According to evidence documented by Hall (2007), 5,393 patents were issued by the United States Patent and Trademark Office (USPTO) in Class 705 (Data Processing: Financial, Business Practice, Management, or Cost/ Price Determination) during the decade 1995–2004, corresponding to approximately 2,918 patentees. Patenting in this class accelerated after the key decisions taken by the Courts of Appeals for the Federal Circuit (CAFC) in 1998, which removed most of the exceptions to the patentability of software and other business methods 'as such'—that is, methods that are independent of a particular physical embodiment (State Street v. Signature Financial Group 1998, ATT v. Excel Communications 1998). Such patents have proved particularly contentious and subject to litigation, especially those related to financial innovations. For example, Lerner (2006) reported a litigation rate on financial patents twenty-seven times larger than the rate found by Lanjouw and Schankerman (2001) for a sample of all patents.

Even in the United States, the question of exactly what types of software or business methods may be patented remains controversial. The CAFC—prompted by a series of Supreme Court decisions—decided to reconsider the question of patentable subject matter by scheduling an *en banc* hearing (before all judges of the court) to consider an appeal *in re* Bilski.[2] A decision was issued in October 2008. This decision is viewed as restricting business method and financial patenting at the USPTO to some extent (Managing Intellectual Property, 31 October 2008b). In particular, the court found that if an invention relates to a 'pure' business method that is not limited to performance on a computer and produces only abstract results, such as manipulation of documents, information, or data, it is not patentable subject matter.[3]

At the EPO the treatment of software and intangible business methods is different, with these inventions excluded 'as such' from patentable subject matter according to the European Patent Convention (Article 52). Nevertheless, when we analysed a large dataset of EPO patents, we found an increasing number of what appeared to be software-related patents during the '90s (Hall et al. 2007). This suggests that, despite the different legal environment, barriers to patenting on software and intangible business methods may have fallen somewhat in Europe as well.[4]

Another notable difference between the two patent systems, US and European, concerns the process for post-grant validity challenges. The US system has two main ways to challenge validity: *Ex-parte* re-examination available to anyone, and litigation over validity, which can only be initiated by a party that has been accused of infringement.[5] The EPO system relies on an *inter partes* opposition system which allows third parties to actively provide evidence of prior art that may have been missed during the examination process. Oppositions can be filed by any party at the EPO within nine months after the patent is granted; in practice they are generally filed on the last eligible day. The input provided by third-party oppositions complement the pre-grant search process conducted by the EPO, especially in new subject matter areas such as software and business methods, where information on prior art is not easily accessible to patent examiners (Janis 1997; Hall 2003). As in the United States, opposition may or may not be followed by litigation, but in this case, the jurisdiction shifts to national courts rather than being European-wide, which makes it a somewhat less attractive option for invalidating a patent.[6]

In the USPTO context the heterogeneity of the actors involved in financial patents can be seen along a number of dimensions (Hall 2007). About 20 percent of the patentees are alliances or R&D consortia of financial firms, suggesting the importance of the standards-setting process in payment and financial systems. Other patentees are older and larger firms active in non-financial and nonsoftware sectors, such as oil and gas or machinery. Newer patentees are typically small firms, and only three of them—E-Trade, eBay, and Verisign—have more than one billion dollars of revenue annually by 2005. Another dimension of heterogeneity is the importance of financial patents relatively to the overall portfolio of the patentee: only 0.7 percent of patents in this class are granted to firms that specialize in financial patenting, whereas the remaining patents are held by large patentees that operate in a number of other sectors, such as Exxon Mobil, Chevron, NCR, Lockheed Martin, Diebold, etc. This picture is quite similar to that of software-related patents, a large proportion of which are held by non-software firms. The small share of patents held by financial institutions in the United States is at odds with the importance of these institutions in the creation of financial innovations (Tufano 2003). Moreover, patent-holding firms specialized in licensing and litigating patent awards are the most frequent plaintiffs in patent litigations, whereas financial innovators (investment banks, trading exchanges, and other financial institutions) are mostly involved as defendants (Lerner 2006).

Based on this body of evidence, scholars have raised concern about the growing number of financial and business method patents whose average quality is considered low because of the limited examination capacity of the US patent office, the lack of prior art databases (both patent and nonpatent literature), and a declining severity of the nonobviousness test in court decisions. Several authors have then suggested that the standard of patentability should be raised especially in subject matters like software and business methods (Barton 2000; Dreyfuss 2001; Lunney 2001; Hall 2007; Bessen and Meurer 2008).[7]

Following on the results for the United States, in this chapter we look at the ways in which firms in Europe are dealing with the increase of financial patenting, given the differences they face in patentability in their home markets. The differences between US and European patenting systems—such as (possibly) more thorough search of prior art, the exclusion of software and business methods 'as such' from the patentable subject matter, and the opposition system—offer a fertile ground for examining the ways in which firm patenting strategy reacts to different institutional incentives.

In this context, the following exploratory questions drive our empirical research.

1 How can we define financial patents at the EPO, and how many are issued, given the definition?
2 Which firms obtain financial patents? What are their characteristics—sector, size, age, listed versus nonlisted, and the size of their patent portfolio?
3 Do nonfinancial firms own a large share of these patents, as in the United States?
4 How do financial patents differ from other patents in their scope, citation of patent and nonpatent literature, forward and backward citations, family size, and other characteristics?
5 Are European firms patenting financial innovations at the USPTO? How many also succeed at the EPO? That is, what is the pattern of equivalents?

This chapter contributes to the literature on the economics and management of patents in ways discussed below. First, whereas a growing body of evidence has focused on business method patents in the US system, the analysis of business methods patents in Europe is still in its infancy (e.g., Wagner 2008). Looking at financial patenting in particular is important because business methods encompass a highly heterogeneous set of technological and 'intellectual' innovations. When aggregating such different types of innovations one runs the risk of overlooking important peculiarities of innovation and patenting strategy in the financial sector.

Second, the patent literature distinguishes between patent quality and economic value or importance of patents. Patent quality refers to the statutory definition of a patentable invention—novelty, nonobviousness, and usefulness (or the production of a technical effect). Moreover, to be patentable an application must disclose sufficient information about the invention. The economic value of a patent depends on the expected profits accruing to its owner. Earlier studies have found that litigation and opposition are correlated with various indicators of patent value or importance (Harhoff et al. 2003; Harhoff and Reitzig 2004; Lerner 2006). Therefore, we estimate probit models for the probability of a decision by the EPO conditional on an application, a grant conditional on a decision, and oppositions conditional on a grant that are similar to those in the literature, but focusing on our sample of financial patents.

The chapter is organized as follows. Section 4.2 describes the background literature and sets out some research hypotheses. Section 4.3 describes the data, whereas Section 4.4 reports the results of the empirical analysis that compares financial patents to other patents, and Section 4.5 presents an analysis of the outcomes at the EPO for financial patent applications. Section 4.6 concludes.

4.2 Background and Hypotheses

To understand the quality and value of financial patents, we need to clarify the peculiarities of financial innovations and to link these peculiarities to the economics of patenting. The main social function of the patent system is to increase private incentives for innovation by granting temporary monopoly power to inventors. In return for exclusivity, the patent owner is required to make the invention public rather than keeping it secret. In principle then the potential negative consequences for efficiency in the market for products due to the temporary monopoly are counterbalanced by the disclosure of information about the innovation.

Thus in theory the patent system yields several social benefits: providing greater incentives for R&D and diffusion of innovation, reducing the entry barriers faced by innovative startups with limited complementary assets, and increasing the efficiency in the market for intellectual property (Arora et al. 2001). There are corresponding social costs in the form of the transactional and other costs patents may impose on those who wish to build on earlier inventions or combine several together in a new innovation. This problem is particularly important in technological areas characterized by cumulative, sequential innovations (Hall 2003, among others). Moreover, patents favour an excessive fragmentation of intellectual property and increasing transaction costs due to enforcement and litigation (Heller and Eisenberg 1998; Ziedonis 2004). Finally, in industries characterized by strong network externalities and the requirements for standards, patents reinforce the monopoly power of the winners and may reduce future innovation.

The extension of patent coverage to business methods and software in the US system has raised concerns that the imbalance between the benefits and costs of the patent system may be unfavourable in this technological area. *"If it has been a policy experiment, could we determine today that it was successful? Probably not"* (Hunt 2008, 1). One may ask, however, whether the alleged imbalance between costs and benefits of patents is specific to this particular technology. To help to answer this question with reference to financial patents, we have to note some important differences between innovation in financial services and manufacturing.

First, historically legal protection of financial innovations has been particularly weak relative to manufacturing. Trade secret has been the primary legal instrument to protect financial innovations, but unlike software, the use of trade secrets has become more difficult over time because the regulation of the financial sector has required a rising level of product and process transparency (Duffy and Squires 2008). Moreover, financial institutions are subject to detailed scrutiny by public regulatory agencies, and this may distract resources from innovation, especially for younger, small financial firms (Lerner 2004). The weak appropriability regime and the use of the Internet favour a rapid diffusion and imitation of financial innovations by competitors. This weakens the incentives for innovation, especially in sectors like insurance where innovators bear the costs of developing a new product and obtaining the regulatory approvals but cannot prevent competitors from imitating its innovations very quickly (Hunt 2008). In general, however, the lack of legal protection has not prevented the introduction of important product innovations (such as a multitude of financial instruments) and process innovations (such as trading platforms and pricing algorithms) in the financial industry, similar to the situation in the software industry prior to 1994/1995 (Torrisi 1998). The history of this industry clearly shows that "the creation of new financial products and processes has been an ongoing part of economies for at least the past four centuries, if not longer" (Tufano 1989, 312).

Second, financial services are characterized by network externalities and strong demands for standardization. For instance, for financial exchanges and payment cards, both attractiveness and efficiency (cost) depend on the number of users of the service. In other financial services, such as paper checks and automated clearinghouses, network externalities arise from interoperability, which is achieved by standard setting (e.g., standardized message formats). Standardization and compatibility between products typically give rise to strong market power for the owner of the standard. Patents can reinforce network effects and induce the accumulation of large patent portfolios for cross-licensing purposes. In turn, this raises entry barriers and may hamper innovative entrants. Many financial innovations also require collaboration among financial institutions, for example, in syndications of innovative securities or standard setting for secure communication and transaction exchanges, implying a need to share access to patented inventions. In financial markets an innovator's success often relies on the existence of different versions of the innovation developed by competitors. These derivative, complementary innovations are important to *"share the risk, increase market depth, liquidity, and price transparency"* (Kumar and Turnbull 2008). By patenting an innovation with a high potential for sequential innovations, a first-mover then can hamper market growth. Patents may hinder competitors from investing in cospecialized assets because of the hold-up risk (Kumar and Turnbull 2008). By the same token, financial innovators who bear significant up-front costs to develop coinventions compatible with an industry standard may be discouraged by the cost of licensing in the necessary patents. In the case of litigation for patent infringement with a patent-holding company, the innovator finds it necessary to settle at relatively high cost because of their sunk R&D costs and the costs of abandoning a standard that is already established. Litigation risk can therefore reduce investment in new standards (Hunt 2008).

Finally, financial patents, like other business method patents, are often characterized by high uncertainty about enforceability. This is due to a number of factors. First is the absence of good nonpatent prior art databases. Prior to the State Street v. Signature Financial decision in 1998, business method patent applications were very rare at the USPTO, so that there was little prior art on financial methods in the patent databases. In addition, most business method inventions have a practical nature and can be realized without much written documentation or are simply a known and used process transferred to the Internet (Hunt 2001; Wagner 2008). Another reason for uncertainty arises from the use of ambiguous claims in patent applications which make it difficult to determine the boundaries of property rights for business methods and financial innovations. The importance of this problem for business method patents in general is emphasized by the fact that appeals over claims definition in this area are over six times more likely to occur compared with patents in general (Bessen and Meurer 2008). Uncertainty over patent validity reduces the incentives to invest in innovation for both the patent holder and for the developers of competing inventions. These effects are strengthened in the presence of cumulative innovation like that in software and financial services. The inventors of subsequent, cumulative inventions may be discouraged by previous inventions that are covered by patents of uncertain validity—because they are obvious or have an indeterminate breadth.

This theoretical and empirical literature overall does not provide clear-cut evidence about the quality and economic importance of financial patents. However, various scholars have raised concerns about the lowering of barriers to business method and financial patents in the US institutional context. We wonder whether the evolution of the US patent system has produced any substantial effect on the application and granting of financial patents at the EPO, although the differences between the two systems remain significant. More precisely, our critical review of the literature on financial patents leads to a set of testable hypotheses that we present below.

The literature suggests that compared with other patents, financial patents are characterized by a higher level of uncertainty arising from the difficulty of establishing the novelty of financial inventions relative to prior art and the ambiguity of their claims. This uncertainty should affect both the application process and the post-grant litigation. An additional source of uncertainty for financial patent applications filed at the EPO arises from article 52 of the EPC, which excludes business methods and software 'as such' from patentable subject matters. Examination of financial patents at the EPO then is likely to be particularly complex because examiners have to distinguish pure business methods, which are not patentable, from patentable financial inventions. We expect then that the likelihood that we observe a larger grant lag or a rejection is larger for a financial patent than for another patent with identical quality or value characteristics, such as the number of citations received by other patents. These considerations lead to the following two hypotheses:

> *Hypothesis 1a. Ceteris paribus*, financial patent applications should have longer decision lags than patent applications in other technological areas.
>
> *Hypothesis 1b. Ceteris paribus*, financial patent applications should have a lower probability of grant than patent applications in other technological areas.

The literature also suggests that the extension of patent coverage to subject matter where patents are difficult to define and to enforce gives rise to large litigation costs. Previous empirical evidence based on US patents suggests that financial patents, like other business method patents, are a case in point (Lerner 2006). As mentioned before, the opposition system at the EPO is an important instrument for first-instance challenges to the validity of granted patents. As Harhoff and Reitzig (2004, 445) have noted, this instrument offers a 'fast and inexpensive resolution of legal disputes'.[8] Working on patents data in biotech and pharmaceuticals, Harhoff and Reitzig have found that opposition rates are particularly high in new technical areas, such as special areas of biotechnology. Their results are in line with the predictions of the theory of legal disputes and settlement. (For a survey see Cooter and Rubinfeld 1989). Looking at the oppositions filed to the EPO, we ask whether the probability that a financial patent is opposed is larger than the probability for nonfinancial patents of similar quality or value. The uncertainty and claim ambiguity that characterize business method patents in general and the limitations to patentability of business methods 'as such' in Europe suggest that financial patents that have been granted should be litigated more often than other patents. More precisely, we test the following hypothesis:

> *Hypothesis 2. Ceteris paribus*, the probability that a financial patent is opposed is greater than that for patents in other technological areas.

Thus far we have focused on the differences between financial patents and other patents, controlling for the quality or importance of patents. One may also ask, however, whether and how quality affects the examination outcome and the post-grant opposition probability in the case of financial patents.

Various studies have demonstrated that the outcome of the examination process (grant, refusal to issue, or withdrawal by the applicant) is only an imperfect measure of the quality or economic importance of a patent (e.g., Lanjouw and Schankerman 2004 B; Hall et al. 2005). And as discussed before, several scholars have cast doubts on the quality of financial patents granted by the USPTO.[9] To better understand financial patenting at the EPO we need to look at more precise indicators of quality and importance of patents. Earlier studies have proposed several measures, such as the number of inventors, the number of backward and forward citations, the number of claims, and family size or the number of patent systems worldwide where patent protection is sought for the same invention. The empirical evidence shows that all these indicators, to various degrees, are associated with the importance or economic value of patents (e.g., Lerner 1994; Harhoff et al. 1999; Hall et al. 2005). Other studies have also found that a linear combination of these indicators can serve as a proxy for the economic value of patents (see discussion in chapter 2, this volume, on Lanjouw and Schankerman 2004 B; Gambardella et al. 2008).

Finding measures of patent 'quality' is somewhat more difficult. For example, references to prior patent art (backward citations) can be a somewhat ambiguous measure. Some scholars have suggested that large numbers of citations to others reveal that a particular invention is likely to be more derivative in nature and therefore, of limited importance (Lanjouw and Schankerman 2004 A). However, a large number of backward citations may also indicate a novel combination of existing ideas. This is probably the reason why Harhoff et al. (1999) have found that backward citations are positively correlated with patent value. A more precise indicator is provided by the number of X-type and Y-type citations that are references to prior art potentially challenging the novelty claims of the patent.[10]

The lack of documented prior art and the uncertainty surrounding financial patents may make it difficult for EPO examiners to identify patents which provide a significant, nonobvious contribution to prior art. This suggests the possibility that financial patents may be granted that are of low quality (lack novelty or are obvious). Such patents are also likely to be of low value, social or economic. We expect that, despite the difficulties mentioned before, the traditional severity of the EPO examination system (see, e.g., Quillen et al. 2002) and the EPC restrictions on business method patentability help patent examiners to distinguish important patents (e.g., patents that will receive many citations) from patents that provide a modest contribution to prior art (e.g., the patent cites prior art potentially challenging its novelty claims).[11] Moreover, we expect that the number of claims, a proxy for patent complexity (Harhoff and Reitzig 2004), will slow the patent office decision and reduce the likelihood of grant. These considerations lead to the following hypothesis:

> *Hypothesis 3. Ceteris paribus*, financial patents are less likely to be granted if they have fewer citations received, contain a large number of claims, or have several overlapping claims with earlier patents (many XY type backward citations).

Our final hypothesis concerns the probability that a financial patent will be challenged by an opposer after it is issued. The theory of legal disputes suggests that patent oppositions are likely to occur under conditions of high uncertainty and imperfect information. This is one reason why we expect that the complexity and problematic enforceability of financial patents relative to other patents make them more likely to be opposed.[12] However, the theory of legal disputes and their resolutions also argues that valuable patents will be litigated more frequently because there is more at stake (for a survey see Cooter and Rubinfeld 1989).

Empirical studies on US patents (Lanjouw and Schankerman 2001, 2004 A, B), US financial patents (Lerner 2006), and EPO patents in biotech and pharmaceuticals (Harhoff and Reitzig 2004) have found evidence on the association between the value of patents and litigation. All of these studies found that citations received (a proxy for value) are positively associated with litigation. However, the findings using backward citations (a proxy for the quality of disclosure or for the crowdedness of the technological space) vary considerably. Lanjouw and Schankerman (2004 A) finds that backward citations per claim are negatively associated with litigation probability, whereas Lanjouw and Schankerman (2004 B) finds that other value measures are positively correlated with litigation. However, Lerner (2006) found that backward citations in financial patents are positively associated with litigation. Harhoff and Reitzig (2004) provide a potential resolution of this conundrum using EPO patents, where it is possible to distinguish among the types of citations made. They found that it is the citations to patent literature that potentially challenge the novelty claims of the patent (X-type citations) and not the other backward citations which predict opposition. This finding suggests that more incremental (less valuable) patents or patents with a technologically close competitor are more likely to be opposed

The probability of litigation in the United States has also been found to increase with the number of claims both for all patents (Lanjouw and Schankerman 2004 A) and for financial patents (Lerner 2006). The economic interpretation of claims is quite controversial. It is unclear whether they are a measure of patent complexity (Harhoff and Reitzig 2004) or a proxy for potential profitability (Lanjouw and Schankerman 2004 B), or most likely, a combination of both. In any case, we expect the number of claims to be related to opposition.

Finally, the potential economic value of an invention will determine the applicant's willingness to file for a patent in multiple jurisdictions, because doing so involves substantial expenditure (not just the patent office fees, but also the costs of attorneys, translation fees, etc.). For this reason, and beginning with the work of Putnam (1996), the number of patent applications that share the same priority date as the patent in question (the family size) is a frequently used proxy for patent value (Harhoff et al. 2003; Harhoff and Reitzig 2004).

These considerations lead to the following two hypotheses:

Hypothesis 4a. Ceteris paribus, more valuable financial patents (that is, those with more forward citations or a larger family size) are more likely to be opposed.

Hypothesis 4b. Ceteris paribus, more controversial financial patents (those with more claims or more XY type backward citations) are more likely to be opposed.

The above concludes the presentation of our hypotheses. In order to test them, we need to identify financial patent applications at the EPO and a corresponding sample of nonfinancial patents for comparison. This task is described in the next section of the chapter.

4.3 Data and Variables

As in the case of software or business method patents (Hall 2003; Hall and MacGarvie 2006; Hall et al. 2007; Bakels et al. 2008), identifying financial patents precisely (with no Type I or II error) is difficult. To some extent, the difficulty lies in the fact that we do not have a precise definition of what we mean by a financial patent, although we are fairly sure we can tell one when we see it. The most important IPCs in which the patents we identify as financial may be found are described as 'complete banking systems', 'mechanisms activated by other than coins . . . to actuate vending, etc. . . . by credit card', 'office automation or reservations', 'finance, e.g., banking, etc.', 'payment schemes', but also by more generic terms such as 'digital computing or data processing equipment'. Many, but not all, of these patents are associated with payment systems, cash machines, or vending machines, but some are more related to innovation in financial instruments. As can be seen in Appendix 4.1, we found it essential to use keywords to restrict any set of patents identified using simply technology classes.

Duffy and Squires (2008) have examined a sample of one hundred patents granted by the USPTO, with a USPC class 705/35 and issue date from June to September 2008.[13] They found that only a few of these patents are about sophisticated trading mechanisms, valuation metrics, or innovative financial products. The innovations described are all relevant to the financial industry, but they are not pure financial innovations. Moreover, among the patents closely connected with finance, only a few disclosed *"cutting edge financial engineering . . . cognizable as a significant development in financial theory"* (Duffy and Squires 2008, 26). Their evidence suggests that it may be important to develop robust definitions to identify financial patents in the US and European patent offices. We begin such an exploration here but are aware that there is room for further work in this area.

Our investigation explores three different methods of choosing such patents: A) EPO equivalents of USPTO patents in certain finance-related class/subclass combinations;[14] B) EPO patents in a set of IPC/ECLA finance-related classifications; C) EPO patents in technology classes where 'pure play' financial firms patent. Financial patents at the EPO seem to be scattered among a large number of classes, and there was relatively little overlap across the three sets. Therefore we used the union of the three sets as our definition, but at the same time we restricted the sample to those with one of eight specific keywords in the title or abstract: *transaction, financial, credit, payment, money, debit card, portfolio*, and *wallet*. After dropping a few observations due to missing applicant information, this yielded a sample of 3,298 patents with priority year between 1978 and 2005, about 4 percent of the initial 87,719 patents in the union of sets A, B, and C. The details of the patent selection algorithm are given in the Appendix 4.1.

The analysis in the next section of the chapter is based on a comparison of financial patents with all other patents. To form the comparison group of all patents, we took a random 1 percent sample of the EPO database (excluding financial patents), obtaining 18,523 patents. The relatively large size of the sample ensured that the sampling variability of the comparison group was rather small. The description of the main variables employed in the analysis is depicted in Box 4.1, whereas Box 2.1 has already presented the measurement approach of the patent indicators.

Box 4.1 Description of variables employed in the analysis

Variable	Description
Dependent variables	
Decision reached	A dummy variable which takes the value one if the patent application has been granted, rejected, or withdrawn. Knowing whether a decision has been reached for a patent application provides useful information about the complexity and uncertainty of the examination process.
Grant	A dummy variable which takes the value one if a patent has been granted at the EPO.
Grant lag in years	Number of years between the priority date and the grant date.
Refusal	A dummy variable which takes the value one if a patent has been rejected for grant at the EPO.
Withdrawn	A dummy variable which takes the value one if a patent has been withdrawn by the applicant before grant at the EPO.
Opposition	A dummy variable which takes the value one if a patent has been opposed at the EPO. Oppositions can be filed at the EPO within nine months from the granting date.

Independent variables describing the patent owner	
Stock of EPO patents	Log stock of EPO patents of the patentee (depreciated at 15 percent annual rate).
Stock of XY type backward cites	Log stock XY type backward citations of the patentee (depreciated at 15 percent annual rate).
Stock of forward cites per patent	Log stock of forward cites per patent of the patentee. This variable is obtained by dividing EPO patent citations received (first three years only, depreciated at 15 percent annual rate) by the stock of patents depreciated at same annual rate.
Size of the patentee	A categorical variable for firm size. Small: 1–50 employees; medium: 51–250 employees; large: more than 250 employees.
Age of the patentee	Dummies for firms that were founded between 1981 and 1995, and after 1995, with those founded prior to 1981 the left-out category.
Sector of the patentee	Dummies for the six leading sectors plus the remainder in the left-out category.
Country of the patentee	Dummies for the United States, Japan, Germany, France, and the UK, with the remaining countries as the left-out category.

4.4 Trends and Descriptive Statistics

The trends of aggregate and financial methods patenting at the USPTO and EPO are displayed in Figures 4.1 and 4.2 respectively. Figure 4.1 shows aggregate EPO grants and applications and USPTO patent grants (all by priority year), whereas Figure 4.2 shows the trends in financial methods patenting at the two agencies.[15] Note that prior to about 1991 or 1992 the trends in all patents and financial patents are very similar. The growth of EPO financial patenting follows the growth of US financial patents closely, although the latter set accelerates more rapidly in 1999 and 2000 and decelerates more quickly after that.

Relative to overall patenting activity, financial patents show a very rapid growth in the years 1994 and 1995, which are the years of the main software patentability decisions in the United States, and also the years during which use of the Internet took off in that country. Both in the EPO and USPTO, by 2006 there were approximately three times as many patents as in 1991 overall, and six times as many financial patents. Although the EPO subject matter restrictions in the software and business method area are narrower than in the United States, the growth of financial patents at the EPO doubtless reflects the impact of the State Street decision in the United States in 1998 and the changing attitudes toward patenting among business services and financial firms which that decision engendered.

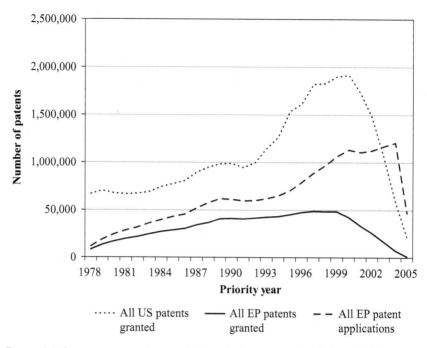

Figure 4.1 Aggregate patenting trends by priority year at the EPO and USPTO

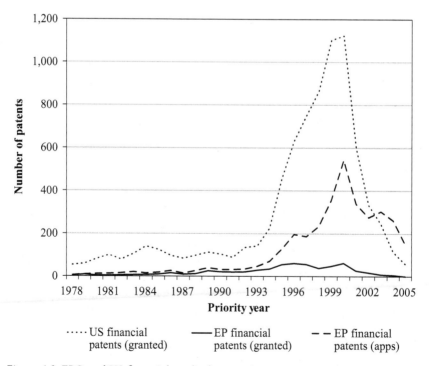

Figure 4.2 EPO and US financial methods patenting

Note also that at the end of the period (after about 2001), there is a substantial falling off in all types of patents, due to the lag between priority year and publication (at the EPO) or grant (at the USPTO). Nevertheless, there also appears to be real decline in the growth rate of patent applications at both offices which is not accounted for by the grant lag. This trend may be only partially due to a change in the application strategy after the Business Patent Initiative was announced by the USPTO in year 2000. Because the aim of this initiative was to raise the examination standards for patent applications in class 705, applicants may have tried to avoid filing applications in this class by a careful choice of wording. However, this does not explain the decline in the growth rate of total patent applications.

To illustrate the characteristics of the patentees who take out financial patents at the EPO, we focus on the 90 percent that are taken out by businesses.[16] We look at the country of origin, the business sector, and the size of firm.[17] In our regression analysis we ask how these variables are related to outcomes at the EPO. To save space, we relegate several tables to Appendix 4.2 and summarize their results here.

Appendix Table 4.2.1 shows that a large share of EPO financial patents are filed by US applicants (49 percent versus 34 percent for European patentees and 13 percent for Japanese patentees), with the surge from the United States beginning some four to five years earlier than that from the EU. Prior to 2000, applicants from the United States accounted for over half (57 percent) of the financial patents at the EPO, and after 2000, only 45 percent. The overall decline in patenting and the shifting shares probably reflects two things: the dotcom bust in 2001, which had a bigger impact in the United States, and the diffusion of patenting activity in this area to European firms.

This distribution, however, remains clearly more asymmetric in favour of US applicants than overall patenting activity or even patenting in Information and Communication Technologies (ICT) at the EPO (see *Patent Compendium*, OECD 2008). The persistent large share of US assignees probably reflects the differences in the treatment of financial and business method patents between the US patent system and other systems. Another plausible explanation is the high intensity of financial innovations in the US economy vis-à-vis other economies. For comparison, we also show in Appendix Table 4.2.2 the distribution of assignee country for financial patents filed at the USPTO, which is even more skewed towards to the United States. It also shows that most of the patenting at this office is accounted for by applicants in the United States, Japan, and the EU. The share of financial patents held by US patentees rose during the '90s and then fell somewhat after that as European applicants increased their share. About two-thirds of European-owned financial patents come from the largest three countries, the UK, Germany, and France.

Table 4.1. in the text depicts the distribution of financial patents by the main activity of the patentee. We used different sources to identify the main

Table 4.1 Financial patents by the country and sector of the patentee

Sector+	Overall		EU 27		US	
	N	Share*	N	Share*	N	Share*
Office, accounting & computing machinery	624	20.8%	45	4.5%	378	25.3%
Computer services & related activities	570	19.0%	212	21.3%	323	21.6%
Finance & insurance	532	17.7%	106	10.7%	388	26.0%
Post & telecommunications	290	9.7%	182	18.3%	67	4.5%
Other business services	227	7.6%	69	6.9%	132	8.8%
Radio, television & communication equip.	226	7.5%	123	12.4%	47	3.1%
Electrical machinery & apparatus, nec	162	5.4%	108	10.9%	6	0.4%
Medical, precision & optical instruments	91	3.0%	44	4.4%	23	1.5%
Wholesale & retail trade repairs	65	2.2%	33	3.3%	23	1.5%
Machinery & equipment, nec	60	2.0%	23	2.3%	28	1.9%
Chemicals excluding pharmaceuticals	24	0.8%	1	0.1%	22	1.5%
Pulp, paper products, printing and publishing	21	0.7%	18	1.8%	1	0.1%
Health & social work	11	0.4%	0	0.0%	10	0.7%
Motor vehicles, trailers & semi-trailers	10	0.3%	3	0.3%	2	0.1%
Coke, petroleum products & nuclear fuel	9	0.3%	0	0.0%	6	0.4%
Air transport	9	0.3%	2	0.2%	6	0.4%
Manufacturing nec recycling (in. Furniture)	8	0.3%	1	0.1%	5	0.3%
Aircraft & spacecraft	7	0.2%	1	0.1%	6	0.4%
Other community, social & personal services	7	0.2%	4	0.4%	2	0.1%
Food products, beverages and tobacco	6	0.2%	1	0.1%	5	0.3%
Land transport, transport via pipelines	6	0.2%	1	0.1%	3	0.2%
Research & development	6	0.2%	3	0.3%	1	0.1%
Rubber & plastics products	5	0.2%	1	0.1%	4	0.3%
Construction	4	0.1%	2	0.2%	1	0.1%
Production and distribution of electricity	3	0.1%	2	0.2%	1	0.1%

Sector+	Overall		EU 27		US	
	N	Share*	N	Share*	N	Share*
Supporting and auxiliary transport activities	3	0.1%	1	0.1%	2	0.1%
Real estate activities	3	0.1%	3	0.3%	0	0.0%
Pharmaceuticals	2	0.1%	1	0.1%	0	0.0%
Fabricated metal products (no machinery)	2	0.1%	2	0.2%	0	0.0%
Mining and quarrying (energy)	1	0.0%	0	0.0%	0	0.0%
Mining and quarrying (non-energy)	1	0.0%	1	0.1%	0	0.0%
Iron & steel	1	0.0%	0	0.0%	0	0.0%
Non-ferrous metals	1	0.0%	0	0.0%	0	0.0%
Hotels & restaurants	1	0.0%	0	0.0%	1	0.1%
Top 6 business sectors	2469	82.4%	737	74.2%	1335	89.4%
Total for all business sectors	2998	85.2%	993	80.3%	1493	88.4%
Individuals & nonbusiness organizations	511	14.5%	240	19.4%	191	11.3%
Patents held by nonclassified business firms	11	0.3%	4	0.3%	5	0.3%
Total, including double counting for copatenting	3520		1237		1689	

Notes: *The share of business sector financial patents is shown in these columns, with the exception of the last three rows, where the share of all financial patents is shown. + The sector categorisation is based on the 'OECD, STAN database'.

activity of the applicant, successfully obtaining this information for almost all (99.7 percent) of the financial patents owned by businesses.[18] There is a very high concentration of patents in a few sectors: in particular, only six sectors account for about 70 percent of the financial patents overall and 82 percent from the business sector, with four of them being services—computer services including software, financial services, telecommunications, and other business services—and the remaining computer-related hardware. This is in line with the concentration of software patents reported by Hall et al. (2007).

The concentration of patents in these six sectors is higher for US applicants than for EU applicants. Moreover, the two leading sectors in Europe differ significantly from the ones in the United States: in the former case telecommunication firms, computer-related services, and communications equipment are responsible for 52 percent of the business sector financial patents, whereas in the United States, firms in the computer hardware, computer services, and financial sectors hold 73 percent of them. In Europe, firms in the financial sector account for only 11 percent of business sector financial patents. These differences in distribution doubtless reflect the strength of the telecommunications sector relative to the software and financial sectors in Europe vis-à-vis the United States.

Prior to 1994/1995 there was little patenting in this area. After the US Court of Appeals of the Federal Circuit (the CAFC) removed the restriction on patentability of software as such in 1995 and then again after the State Street decision in 1998, there were spikes in financial patent applications, the first due to computer hardware, telecommunications, and other business sectors, and the second mostly from computer hardware and finance and insurance. Between 1993 and 1998 average annual patenting in this technology jumped from twenty patents per year to one hundred patents per year. However, in the period after 2000 the growth appears to have moderated somewhat and a higher share come from software and finance/insurance firms. The breakdown by sector and firm age shown in Appendix Table 4.2.3 demonstrates that the service firms that hold financial patents tend to be much younger than the manufacturing firms. Thus even in Europe, there appears to be a shift in attitudes towards patenting among the newer entrants in business service sectors.

Table 4.2.4 in Appendix 4.2 looks at the size of the firms taking out financial patents.[19] The majority of financial patents are obtained by large patentees. However their role decreased somewhat after 1999 in favour of the small-sized firms. Moreover, the small patentees are concentrated in a few sectors. Indeed, about 78 percent of the financial patents held by small-sized firms are held by firms in three service sectors—software, financial, and other business services—whereas these sectors account for less than half (40 percent) of patents filed by large firms. It is interesting to note that SMEs account for about 24 percent of financial patenting at the EPO.

The small patentees operating in the service sectors are also new firms: firms born after year 1995 account for over 60 percent of the financial patents by small patentees, whereas their role in the overall patenting is minimal (Appendix Table 4.2.5). In contrast, the great majority of patents held by large firms are held by firms that were founded prior to 1970, as one might expect. Typically the emergence of smaller firms active in financial patenting is associated with the advent of the so-called Internet economy. Their business models often rely on licensing transactions and financial models embodied in a software application that uses nonexclusive technology contracts. This can be seen in Appendix Table 4.2.3, where firms founded after 1990 that take out financial patents are more likely to be found in the service sector. In contrast, a large share of the communication equipment and telecommunications firms that have financial patents were born during the 1981–1990 period with the advent of wireless and cell telephony.

A higher propensity to patent is consistent with the active participation in technology markets, where IP protection of the goods being traded is important. Ongoing research has not yet reached a definitive conclusion on the sustainability in the long run of such a business strategy. However, the development of specialized technology providers in the financial area could be considered a quintessential example of the vertical disintegration that takes place when ownership of innovation assets becomes available (Arora et al. 2001).

Table 4.2 shows the approximately fifty largest patentees in our sample; almost all of them are large and old firms. Nevertheless, there are a number of newer entrants among the next fifty, such as Bitwallet (electronic money service provider in Japan), Orbis Patents (patent holding company in Ireland), Trintech (transaction software provider in Ireland), and Contentguard (DRM technology in the US).

4.4.1 Comparing Financial Patents to Other Patents

In this section the characteristics of financial patents are compared with all patents at the EPO, in order to explore potential differences regarding the prior art base and to get some idea of the economic value or importance of this kind of patenting.

Because most of the variables we consider will vary systematically over time, and because financial patents are disproportionately represented in the later years, we normalized each of the variables by its overall year mean before performing tests for differences between the two samples. Table 4.3 shows the results of our analysis: it contains some simple statistics on the unadjusted data for the two sets of patents, and the results of t-tests comparing financial patents with all other patents. These tests were conducted using the priority year normalized variables. We used a conventional two-sample t-test for differences in the mean, allowing the two samples to have different variances.

The upper panel of Table 4.3 reports some measures of the prior art base for the two sets of patents. Financial patents cite slightly newer prior art than patents as a whole (average age about sixty months versus sixty-four months), and the difference is significant. They also have significantly fewer backward citations (whether XY type or otherwise) and citations to the nonpatent literature. They have the same number of inventors on average, suggesting that the resources invested in them are roughly comparable with resources invested in other patents.

The middle panel of Table 4.3 shows some indicators that are commonly associated with patent value: the number of claims, the number of technology classes (IPCs) in which the patent is classified, the number of patents in the rest of the world with the same priority date (the number of equivalents), whether there are one or more divisionals at the EPO associated with the patent, the number of countries in which coverage was requested at the EPO, the number of citations received by the patent, and the composite value index (based on the combination of family size, IPC classes, and forward citations).

Table 4.2 Top financial patentees and their patent portfolio composition

Rank	Company	Country	Industry	Entry	Fin Pats	All Pats	Fin pat share*
1	IBM	US	Comp serv	pre-1970	111	14950	very low
2	**CITICORP**	US	**Fin & ins**	**pre-1970**	96	101	**high**
3	NCR	US	Machinery	pre-1970	86	1588	low
4	FUJITSU	JP	Comp serv	pre-1970	85	8707	very low
5	SIEMENS	DE	Elec. eq	pre-1970	76	28497	very low
6	HITACHI	JP	Comp mach	pre-1970	69	8733	very low
7	SONY	JP	Comm. eq	pre-1970	47	14246	very low
8	HEWLETT PACKARD	US	Comp mach	1981–1990	47	7312	very low
9	SAP	DE	Comp serv	1971–1980	47	1011	low
10	SUN MICROSYSTEM	US	Comp mach	1971–1980	40	1415	very low
11	ATT	US	Post & tele	pre-1970	40	5053	very low
12	FRANCE TELECOM	FR	Post & tele	1981–1990	39	1915	very low
13	MICROSOFT	US	Comp serv	1981–1990	38	2847	very low
14	PITNEY BOWES	US	Comp mach	pre-1970	34	789	low
15	ALCATEL	FR	Comp mach	pre-1970	34	3847	very low
16	NOKIA	FI	Comm. eq	pre-1970	33	6587	very low
17	**FIRST DATA**	US	**Fin & ins**	**1991–1995**	33	69	**high**
18	DEUTSCHE POST TELEKOM	DE	Post & tele	pre-1970	33	746	low
19	**VISA**	US	**Fin & ins**	**pre-1970**	32	65	**high**
20	**MASTERCARD INTERNATIONAL**	US	**Oth bus**	**pre-1970**	30	47	**high**
21	LM ERICSSON	SE	Comm. eq	pre-1970	29	6502	very low
22	ACCENTURE	US	Comp serv	1981–1990	27	333	low
23	LUCENT TECHNOLOGY	US	Comp serv	1985–1990	26	3812	very low
24	KONINKLIJKE PTT NEDERLAND	NL	Post & tele	1981–1990	25	569	low
25	DIEBOLD	US	Comp mach	pre-1970	25	83	medium
26	MATSUSHITA ELEC INDUSTRIAL	JP	Elec. eq	pre-1970	22	16921	very low
27	NTT	JP	Post & tele	pre-1970	22	1390	very low
28	SWISSCOM	CH	Post & tele	1996–2000	21	266	low

#	Company	Country	Industry	Period		Value	Level
29	TOSHIBA	JP	Comp mach	pre-1970	18	10047	very low
30	AMERICAN EXPRESS	US	Fin & ins	pre-1970	18	47	medium
31	PHILIPS	NL	Elec. eq	pre-1970	17	4382	very low
32	SAGEM	DE	Instruments	pre-1970	17	281	low
33	NEC	JP	Comp mach	pre-1970	16	8272	very low
34	**WESTERN UNION**	US	**Fin & ins**	**pre-1970**	**16**	**20**	**high**
35	KODAK	US	Instruments	pre-1970	15	11187	very low
36	GOLDMAN SACHS	US	Fin & ins	pre-1970	14	44	medium
37	**US BANCORP**	US	**Fin & ins**	**pre-1970**	**14**	**16**	**high**
38	OMRON	JP	Instruments	pre-1970	13	1197	very low
39	GEMPLUS	FR	Comm. eq	1981–1990	12	478	very low
40	GIESECKE DEVRIENT	DE	Printing	pre-1970	12	665	very low
41	AXALTO	FR	Comm. eq	pre-1970	11	261	low
42	NOKIA SIEMENS NETWORKS	FI	Comm. eq	pre-1970	11	1318	very low
43	BRITISH TELECOM	UK	Post & tele	1981–1990	11	1908	very low
44	SCHLUMBERGER	FR	Instruments	pre-1970	11	1049	very low
45	MOTOROLA	US	Comm. eq	pre-1970	11	5300	very low
46	LA POSTE	FR	Post & tele	1981–1990	10	60	medium
47	SUMITOMO MITSUI BANKING	JP	Fin & ins	pre-1970	10	32	medium
48	**METAVANTE**	US	**Comp serv**	**pre-1970**	**10**	**14**	**high**
49	OKI	JP	Elec. eq	pre-1970	10	1026	very low
50	EBAY	US	Comp serv	1991–1995	10	39	medium
51	GE CAPITAL	US	Fin & ins	pre-1970	10	27	medium
52	ELECTRONIC DATA SYSTEM	US	Comp serv	pre-1970	10	148	low

Notes: * High: >50 percent; Medium: 10–50 percent; Low: 3–10 percent; Very low: 0–3 percent. Country codes are based on the ISO 2-digit classification.

Table 4.3 Comparing financial to all other patents

	All patents			T-test† fin pat vs all other	Financial patents		
	18,523 observations#				3,298 observations		
	mean	sd	median		mean	sd	median
Indicators of Prior Art Base							
Inventors	2.44	1.79	2.0	--	2.53	2.08	2.0
Nonpatent literature references	0.49	1.4	0.0	--	0.46	1.13	0.0
Backward citations to patents	3.75	2.98	3.0	--	3.34	3.27	3.0
Backward citations per inventor	2.28	2.32	1.7		2.05	2.45	1.3
XY type backward citations	0.88	1.6	0.0	--	0.87	1.44	0.0
XY type backward citations per inventor	0.51	1.06	0.0		0.53	1.03	0.0
Citation Lag in Months @	63.6	42.7	52.5	--	59.5	37.0	50.0
Indicators of Patent Value							
Number of claims	14.89	12.77	11	++	21.78	17.78	17
Technological classes	7.16	6.96	6.0	--	5.77	4.61	4.0
Patent family size (worldwide equivalents)	11.03	74.05	6.0		11.40	30.54	6.0
Divisionals rate	0.05	0.21	0.0		0.05	0.21	0.0
Designated countries	11.95	9.10	9.0	+++	14.50	9.88	18.0
Application via PCT route (dummy)	0.40	0.49	0.0	+++	0.44	0.50	0.0
Forward citations received in 3 years	0.41	0.97	0.0	+++	0.67	1.81	0.0
Composite value index	0.00	0.54	-0.1		0.12	0.65	-0.1

Status

Decision reached	0.760			0.580	
Granted, conditional on decision	0.640			0.341	
Refused, conditional on decision	0.033			0.071	
Withdrawn, conditional on decision	0.327			0.588	
Grant lag in years‡	3.91	1.78		5.10	2.23
Opposition if granted‡	0.065	3.59	++	0.090	4.77

Notes:
† T-test for the hypothesis that the mean for financial patents differs from that for all patents. Significant at 1 percent (+++), 5 percent (++), or 10 percent (+) level if the mean is larger; similarly for smaller but with a minus (−). Before testing, all variables have bee
@ Computed for nonzero lags only. Numbers of observations are 1077 and 833.
‡ Computed for granted patents only. Numbers of observations are 9,003 and 736; for grant prior to 2001, they are 8,883 and 642.
# This is a 1 percent sample of all patents.

On a number of these value measures, financial patents differ substantially from other patents. Financial patents have similar equivalents (family size), divisionals, and number of designated states. They have more claims, are more likely to be cited, and are more likely to reach the EPO via the PCT route. The composite value index is higher on average than that for other patents, once we adjust for differences across priority years. Note that the higher rate at which financial patents are cited may indicate higher social value as well as higher private value, because it implies greater 'spillovers' of knowledge to future inventors than yielded by the typical patent. We should notice that small population of financial patents at the EPO reduces the likelihood of citations between financial patents. The high number of citations received then suggests that these patents are mostly cited by patents from different technological classes. The larger number of citations received by financial patents is in line with the large number of forward citations of business method patents reported by Wagner (2008).

Financial patents are classified into significantly fewer IPC classes than all patents, which is a bit surprising, because business methods and software inventions are excluded from the patentability 'as such' in EPO according to article 52 of the statute, and hence there is a lack in EPO of a clear technological classification for this type of patenting; nevertheless, this fact seems to lead the examiner to place the patent in fewer rather than more classes.[20]

Finally, financial patents have a significantly larger number of claims compared with other patents, which suggests a greater complexity as compared to other patents.

4.4.2 Outcomes

Most of the analysis in this chapter is based on the published patent documents on the EPO website. These documents are patent applications that may ultimately be rejected, withdrawn, or granted by the EPO.[21] One indicator of the 'quality' or eligibility of these financial inventions for patenting is their experience in the EPO examining and granting process (Harhoff and Wagner 2009). In the bottom panel of Table 4.3, we show some simple statistics on this question for our two groups of patents. The first question is whether a decision has yet been rendered by the EPO. For three-quarters of all patents, the answer is yes, but for financial patents there are somewhat fewer decisions, partly because their applications are on average newer. When we adjust for this fact, these applications are just as likely to have received a decision.

Table 4.3 shows clearly that conditional on a decision having been reached, financial patents are far less likely to be granted than other patents, indicating that the EPO is finding these applications unpatentable more often than other patents, which is probably related to the subject matter restriction of article 52. Correspondingly, they are more likely to be either refused or withdrawn. If they are granted, the process takes longer than other patents (as suggested earlier). Once again, after adjusting for the differences in time profiles, these differences are not statistically significant. Note that granting rates for business methods patents overall are significantly larger than for overall patents (Wagner 2008).

The final step in the EPO process before the patent becomes a set of national patent rights that can be enforced in national courts is the nine-month post-grant window during which any third party may file an opposition against the patent showing that it should not have been granted. The overall rate at the EPO for opposition during the 1978–2005 period is about 6.5 percent, but financial patents have been opposed 9.0 percent of the time, which is significantly higher.

The aggregate numbers mask some interesting changes that have occurred over time. In Figures 4.3 and 4.4 we show the evolution of the grant rates and opposition rates for the two groups of patents at the EPO between 1978 and 2002.[22] Three periods can be discerned. In the first, roughly 1978–1985, financial patents were much less likely to be granted than the other patents, but also less likely to face opposition, once granted. Between 1986 and 1993, grant rates for all types of patents were roughly comparable, whereas financial patents were about three times as likely to be opposed once granted. Then beginning around 1994, the grant rate for financial patents fell precipitously along with the opposition rates. Financial patents now face the same rate of opposition as other patents. The conclusion is that

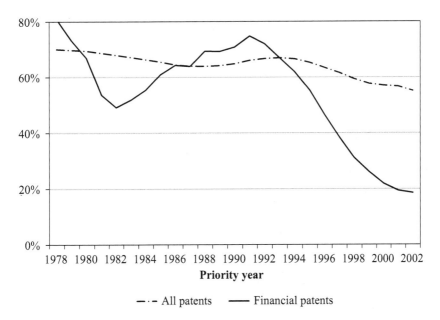

Figure 4.3 Grant rate at the EPO, conditional on a decision

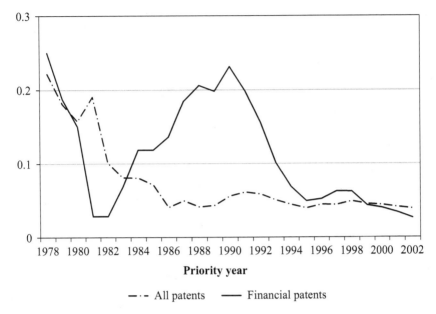

Figure 4.4 Opposition rates at the EPO, conditional on grant

greater scrutiny at the EPO has led to a decrease in the issuance of controversial patents; the question remains whether this has also eliminated more valuable patents.

4.5 The Determinants of Outcomes for Financial Patents

In order to test hypotheses 1 and 2 and to explore the determinants of a successful application at the EPO, we estimated a series of probit equations for the probability of a decision conditional on an application, a grant conditional on a decision, and opposition conditional on a grant. Controlling for average differences across time, whether a decision has yet been reached can be an indicator of the quality of the original application and of the speed with which the patentee pursues the application. Given a decision, whether or not the patent is granted is first and foremost an indicator of invention quality, and also of whether the invention is viewed as satisfying the subject matter restrictions. Finally, opposition has been shown repeatedly to be an indicator of the economic value and importance of the patented invention (Harhoff et al. 2003; Harhoff and Reitzig 2004).

The explanatory variables for these equations are a selection from the variables described previously, plus a dummy for financial patents. That is, in order to test hypotheses 1a, 1b, and 2, we ask whether financial patents are more or less likely to receive a decision, be granted, and be opposed given their prior art and value characteristics and priority year. All variables except the divisional and PCT dummies are in logarithms to facilitate inter-pretation. We also included a complete set of priority year dummies in the regressions.

The results are shown in Table 4.4. As expected, the sample sizes get successively smaller, from decision conditional on application, grant condi-tional on decision, and opposition conditional on grant. In the latter case we removed a few observations for 2004 and 2005, because there were too few grants corresponding to those priority years for opposition to be observed. The three groups of variables (priority year dummies, prior art indicators, and value indicators) were always highly jointly significant using a Wald-type test. In general, the results for these variables agree with those in prior work: backward references increase the probability of receiving a timely decision, but not if they are of the XY type, whereas backward references to patents increase the probability of a grant, with XY type backward cita-tions reducing the probability substantially and increasing the probability of opposition, once the patent is granted.

Almost all the value indicators reduce the probability of receiving a decision and of having that decision to grant the patent, whereas increas-ing the probability of opposition significantly, as expected. The one impor-tant exception is the size of the patent family: this has no impact on the speed with which a decision is reached but a substantial impact on the probability of a grant (an increase of 0.37 from a doubling of the family size). This may reflect the fact that the inventions associated with patents that have been applied for in many jurisdictions are more important (have greater novelty) and are more likely to have satisfied the subject matter restrictions.[23]

Financial patents are strikingly different from other patents with the same characteristics, being less likely to receive a decision, less likely to be granted, and slightly more likely to be opposed. Thus hypotheses 1a and 1b, which state that financial patents will have longer decision lags and are less likely to be granted, fail to be rejected. The evidence in favour of hypothesis 2, that financial patents are more likely to be opposed, c. p., is somewhat weaker, but that may be due to the relatively small sample of oppositions (fifty-three for the financial patents).

All of this suggests that these patents are of lower quality technologically than the others and simultaneously more valuable or at least more con-troversial, other things equal. Because of the higher opposition rate faced by financial patents, which concords with the value indicators shown in Table 4.3, we can conclude that these patents, once granted, are expected to be of higher economic value than other patents. As we argued earlier, the outcomes of financial patents relative to other patents reflect a more strin-gent scrutiny of this category of patent applications by the EPO. The longer decision lag, however, may also depend on the complexity and uncertainty

Table 4.4 Probability of decision, grant, and opposition conditional on grant 1978–2005. Financial patents vs. a 1 percent sample of other patents

Dependent variable	Decision		Grant conditional on decision		Opposition conditional on grant by 2003	
	Marginal effect	s.e.	Marginal effect	s.e.	Marginal effect	s.e.
D (Financial patent)	-0.054	[0.008]***	-0.240	[0.014]***	0.018	[0.011]*
Log (Inventors)	-0.050	[0.006]***	0.017	[0.011]*	0.001	[0.006]
Log (Nonpatent literature references)	0.013	[0.006]**	-0.042	[0.009]***	-0.016	[0.006]***
Log (Backward citations to patents)	0.064	[0.005]***	0.077	[0.009]***	0.005	[0.005]
Log (XY type backward citations)	-0.015	[0.005]***	-0.104	[0.008]***	0.016	[0.005]***
Log (Claims)	-0.055	[0.005]***	-0.091	[0.007]***	0.007	[0.004]
Log (Technological classes)	-0.010	[0.005]**	-0.083	[0.008]***	-0.010	[0.004]**
Log (Family size)	0.006	[0.005]	0.369	[0.016]***	0.020	[0.005]***
D (Divisional)	-0.181	[0.020]***	-0.085	[0.026]***	0.021	[0.012]**
Log (Designated countries)	-0.033	[0.003]***	-0.017	[0.006]***	0.026	[0.005]***
D (PCT route)	-0.086	[0.006]***	-0.143	[0.011]***	-0.018	[0.006]***
Log (Forward cites received in 3 years)	-0.014	[0.007]**	0.051	[0.009]***	0.026	[0.005]***
Number of observations (number=1)	23,011 (16,689)		16,689 (10,034)		9779 (705)	
Pseudo R-squared	0.454		0.173		0.051	

Notes: Marginal effects and their robust standard errors are shown. Significance at 1 percent ***, 5 percent **, 10 percent *.

surrounding these patents compared to others. Finally, the lack of documented prior art may contribute to the difficulty of obtaining a patent grant for financial innovations.

Hypotheses 3 and 4 concern the variation across financial patents, and we test these hypotheses in Table 4.5, where we repeat the analysis of Table 4.4 but restrict it to the 90 percent of the financial patents that are held by firms in order to include the influence of firm characteristics on outcomes at the EPO. The sample consists of 2,998 patent applications corresponding to 1,021 patentees that have priority year 2005 or earlier. Almost three-quarters of the patentees (998 observations) have applied for only one financial patent at the EPO, whereas one (IBM) has applied for more than one hundred.

There are two sets of explanatory variables included in these equations: the characteristics of the applicant firm and the characteristics of the patent application itself. We also include a reduced set of priority year dummies. Three probit regressions are shown: 1) predicting the 1,718 decisions for the 2,998 applications that have priority year 2005 and a decision prior to October 2008; 2) predicting the 618 grants that emerge from those decisions; 3) predicting the 53 oppositions filed against the 553 grants that have priority year 2000 or earlier.[24] All standard errors in Table 4.5 have been clustered by patent owner, although this makes relatively little difference to their estimates.[25]

Turning first to the probability of obtaining a decision on patentability at the EPO, controlling for patent characteristics and priority year the most important predictor among the owner characteristics are whether the firm is Japanese, which appears to delay the decision considerably; this may reflect delays associated with distance and translation. German firms seem to experience a correspondingly faster decision process. With the exception of medium-sized firms, who receive a somewhat quicker decision, the firm's size, sector, and past patenting history do not seem to matter much. The stock of patents and XY type backward citations have a quite limited impact on the likelihood of obtaining a decision. What does matter are the characteristics of the patent itself: Forward and backward cites raise the probability of a decision, whereas inventors and the number of designated states lower it.[26] This suggests that more valuable financial patents that have more resources behind them take longer to issue or be rejected, other things equal. This may reflect the applicant's willingness to extend the process at the EPO when more is at stake.

Once a decision has been reached, however, the probability of grant is more affected by the characteristics of the patent owner. Although size of firm does not matter in the presence of the size of the firm's patent portfolio, sector and country do matter. Patenting experience counts for a great deal: a doubling of the firm's patent portfolio is associated with a 16 percent increment in the probability that a financial patent is granted. Firms in

Table 4.5 Probability of decision, grant, and opposition conditional on grant 1978–2005. Financial patents only

2,998 observations for 1,021 patentees (1,718 decisions, 618 grants, 53 oppositions out of 553 pre-2001 grants)

Dependent variable	Decision		Grant conditional on decision		Opposition conditional on grant	
	Marginal	s.e.	Marginal	s.e.	Marginal	s.e.
Owner characteristics						
Log (stock of EP patents) +	-0.079	[0.045]*	0.157	[0.059]***	-0.036	[0.032]
Log (stock of XY backward cites) +	0.059	[0.031]*	-0.051	[0.034]	-0.001	[0.014]
Log (stock of forward cites per patent)+	-0.030	[0.046]	0.108	[0.077]	-0.029	[0.038]
D (small firm)	0.047	[0.045]	-0.048	[0.064]	0.040	[0.055]
D (medium firm)	0.108	[0.042]**	0.003	[0.073]	0.072	[0.071]
Founded 1981–1995	0.039	[0.039]	-0.031	[0.054]	-0.022	[0.020]
Founded after 1995	0.014	[0.049]	0.042	[0.074]	-0.051	[0.017]**
Software sector	-0.053	[0.044]	0.095	[0.058]*	-0.012	[0.026]
Other business services	-0.009	[0.051]	0.026	[0.072]	-0.032	[0.020]
Post & telecommunications	-0.002	[0.056]	0.086	[0.076]	0.011	[0.027]
Finance & insurance	0.070	[0.049]	-0.119	[0.060]*	0.016	[0.041]
Computing equipment	-0.034	[0.067]	0.254	[0.064]***	0.029	[0.036]
Communication equipment	-0.075	[0.075]	0.093	[0.066]	0.032	[0.050]
US owner	-0.040	[0.037]	-0.130	[0.066]**	-0.022	[0.027]
Japanese owner	-0.161	[0.060]***	-0.128	[0.066]*	-0.008	[0.031]
German owner	0.105	[0.049]*	0.076	[0.084]	0.110	[0.074]**
French owner	0.085	[0.053]	0.081	[0.094]	0.041	[0.048]
UK owner	-0.005	[0.061]	0.027	[0.097]	0.014	[0.052]

	(1)		(2)		(3)	
Chi-squared (2) size	5.5	[0.065]*	0.9	[0.637]	1.9	[0.389]
Chi-squared (2) founding year	1.1	[0.593]	1.1	[0.567]	5.2	[0.076]*
Chi-squared (6) sector dummies	8.5	[0.209]	25.1	[0.000]***	3.1	[0.830]
Chi-squared (5) region	21.0	[0.001]***	18.2	[0.003]***	9.2	[6.103]
Chi-squared (18) firm characteristics	49.9	[0.000]***	123.3	[0.000]***	31.0	[0.029]**
Patent characteristics						
Log (Inventors)	-0.053	[0.017]***	0.015	[0.024]	0.005	[0.015]
Log (Total backward cites)	0.093	[0.018]***	0.120	[0.023]***	0.005	[0.020]
Log (XY backward cites)	-0.025	[0.021]	-0.089	[0.025]***	0.021	[0.016]**
Log (Claims)	-0.041	[0.017]**	-0.095	[0.024]***	0.021	[0.013]*
Log (Family size)	-0.041	[0.026]	0.239	[0.031]***	0.045	[0.014]***
Log (N of designated states at EPO)	-0.093	[0.015]***	0.027	[0.021]	-0.009	[0.018]
D (PCT route)	-0.114	[0.033]***	-0.069	[0.038]*	-0.044	[0.016]**
Log (Forward cites received in 3 years)	0.042	[0.019]**	0.046	[0.021]**	0.041	[0.012]***
Priority year 1986–1990	*combined with pre–1986*		0.103	[0.103]	0.034	[0.049]
Priority year 1991–1995	-0.857	[0.013]***	0.011	[0.079]	-0.044	[0.028]
Priority year 1996–2000	-0.995	[0.002]***	-0.213	[0.078]***	-0.056	[0.037]
Priority year post-2000	-0.999	[0.000]***	-0.231	[0.061]***	*no oppositions*	
Pseudo R-squared	0.302		0.307		0.243	

Notes: The left-out category is a patent owned by a large firm in the rest of the world that was founded before 1981, and that operates in one of the remaining business sectors, with priority year prior to 1986 (prior to 1991 in the first set of columns). Marginal effects and their standard errors clustered on patentee are shown. Significance at 1 percent ***, 5 percent **, 10 percent *.
+ These variables are stocks for all the firm's patents as of the priority year of the current patent, constructed using a 15 percent depreciation rate.
# All patent characteristics excluding the priority year dummies, which control for selection over time.

computing hardware or software experience a higher probability of receiving a financial patent grant than firms in other business sectors, whereas firms in finance and insurance have a lower probability. This may reflect inexperience on the part of these firms, also when compared with software firms, but it is more likely to be due to the nature of their patent applications, which may fail the subject matter test more often. Patent application in the hardware sectors are more likely to be for the kinds of software-hardware combinations that are viewed as patentable subject matter by the EPO.[27] US and Japanese patent owners (who presumably are more likely to have patent applications outside the article 52 restrictions but acceptable to the USPTO) are somewhat less likely to receive a grant of their financial patent application, although the result is not very significant.

Looking at the patent characteristics themselves, our hypothesis 3 stated that financial patents with few forward citations, many overlapping claims with earlier patents, and a large number of claims are less likely to be granted. All of this finds confirmation in the regression, and we fail to reject the hypothesis. In addition, both designating more states at the EPO and being a member of a large patent family increases the likelihood of a grant once a decision has been reached, although both delay the decision. Again, this is consistent with greater effort by the patentee when more is at stake.

The final column reports on the predictors of opposition conditional on grant. Unfortunately, the sample size is fairly small and the results therefore somewhat weaker than some of those in the literature. It is noteworthy that patent owner characteristics do not predict the probability that a particular patent is opposed, with the exception of very young firms, who are less likely to be opposed, and German firms, who are more likely to be opposed. The main predictors of opposition are the number of forward cites received by the patent, and the family size, both of which are known to be significantly correlated with value, and the number of XY type backward cites, which suggests that the opposition occurs because there is some controversy over the extent of the inventive step above a competitor's patent. An additional X or Y type backward cite adds 2 percent to the probability that a patent will be opposed, which is a large effect given the average opposition probability of 9 percent for financial patents.[28] The positive sign on claims adds further evidence in favour of the view that more complex, controversial patents are more likely to be opposed.

Hypothesis 4a stated that more valuable patents were more likely to be opposed. These results provide strong evidence that fails to reject this hypothesis. Hypothesis 4b, that more controversial patents are more likely to be opposed, is more weakly supported, possibly because our indicators (claims and XY type backward cites) are somewhat weaker proxies for the underlying concept.

A better understanding of the relationship between value or importance, complexity or uncertain enforceability, and opposition would require a more qualitative, in-depth analysis which goes beyond the scope of this chapter. A casual inspection of our data, however, provides interesting insights about the opposition patterns. We found 106 oppositions to 53 financial patents that had a publication date 2000 or earlier.[29] The analysis of opponents and defendants shows that a large share of oppositions has occurred within the financial and insurance sector. Financial patents owned by financial firms receive the largest number of oppositions (33), followed by patents owned by computer hardware and software firms (29). Over half the oppositions (65) come from German firms, which is similar to what was found by Harhoff and Hall (2005) for the cosmetics industry.

Most of the opposers come from the same sectors as the active patentees (computing hardware and software, finance and insurance, and post and telecommunications). By far the most active opposer is Giesecke & Devrient (G&D), a German supplier of banknote paper, banknote printing, currency automation systems, as well as smart cards and complex system solutions in the fields of telecommunications, electronic payment, health care, identification, transportation, and IT security (PKI). This firm alone filed twenty-one oppositions to financial patents granted by the EPO, mostly during the first half of the '90s. In latter years both Swisscom AG and Siemens have been active opposers. These data suggest that opposition involves mostly firms that contribute to financial innovation in various ways—from the development of new financial products and platforms to the creation of the equipment and telecom infrastructure that is needed to implement financial innovations. It is possible that they feel threatened by patents on technologies related to standards in this area; more detailed analysis awaits future work.

4.6 Conclusions

This chapter analysed the financial patenting in the European Patent Office. It began by proposing a definition of such patents, drawing on earlier work using USPTO data. Although in the EPO system software 'as such' and business methods are excluded from the patentable subject matter, we found a substantial number of such patents in the European system. In principle, in order to be patentable at the EPO, these inventions should yield some technical effects, and some financial inventions like payment technologies indeed have links with electronic (hardware) devices, such as wireless systems. However, it has often proved to be difficult to establish a clear border between patentable inventions and 'pure' business methods.

Our investigation shows that financial patents are different from other patents in that they rely less on prior literature (patent or nonpatent), and the literature they do rely on is younger, which is reasonable given their newness in the patent system. They also are slower to receive a decision at the EPO, which can reflect both the uncertainty surrounding a new and possibly unpatentable subject matter as well as the applicant behaviour (i.e., her willingness to delay the disclosure of a valuable invention). Once a decision is reached, it is less likely to be a grant and more likely to be opposed if it is. All this may reflect greater economic value, and we do find that financial patents have several indicators of higher value than other patents. The higher opposition rate may also be due to higher uncertainty surrounding these subject matters, especially in Europe.

Then we have explored the characteristics of financial patentees. First, firms from a few sectors (computers, telecommunication equipment, finance and insurance, and software) account for the bulk of financial patents. Second, large, established firms maintain a large, albeit declining share of these patents whereas small, young firms have a smaller but rising share of these patents. Small firms include some specialized technology firms whose business model is largely based on technology licensing. Nonetheless, to a great extent these patents are held by the same large firms (IBM, Siemens, Hitachi, etc.) that hold the bulk of software patents at the EPO (Hall et al. 2007).

Finally, we have analysed how the main characteristics of the patentee and the invention impact on the outcome of the examiner's decision and probability of receiving an opposition. First we find that the probability of grant for financial patent applications—rather than reject (by the EPO) or withdrawal (by the applicant)—is influenced by the owner's stock of EPO patents, country of origin, and whether the applicant is in the computing sector (as opposed to the financial sector). This latter finding could reflect the relative lack of experience with patenting among financial firms. As expected, financial patent applications with more claims (a measure of complexity) or more XY type backward cites (an indicator of limited inventive step) are less likely to be granted, whereas patent applications with a large number of equivalents in other jurisdictions (a measure of value) are far more likely to be granted.

The analysis of patent oppositions shows that patent-level characteristics including family size, forward citations, and XY type backward citations have a significant predictive power but that the characteristics of the patent owner hardly matter. Our conclusion was the unsurprising one that more valuable financial patents were clearly more likely to be opposed. In addition, there was weaker evidence that more controversial financial patents were more likely to be opposed. Moreover, oppositions mostly involve, as opponents or as defendants, firms that are also important contributors to financial innovations and the underlying IT infrastructure. This result points to an important difference with the US system, where the most active plaintiffs in patent litigation are patent holder firms specializing in licensing and patent litigation (Lerner 2006).

Our findings overall offer intellectual property managers and senior managers useful insights into financial innovations and patenting. Our analysis tells the type of financial patent applications which are more likely to affect the decision lag and the probability of a rejection at the EPO. They also point out which financial patents are more likely to be opposed and by whom. This evidence can help managers in elaborating their patenting strategies, increasing the probability of granting at the EPO, and economizing on post-grant litigation costs.

In conclusion, the explosion of patents in this field produces contrasting effects on social welfare. On the one side, the increased number of financial patents has induced more oppositions (and possibly more litigation costs as in the United States) and may to some extent be a by-product of strategic patenting by large established computing firms. On the other side, financial patents open up new windows of opportunities for specialized technology firms. This trend is similar to what happens in other sectors such as security software and semiconductors (Hall and Ziedonis 2001; Giarratana 2007). In our future research we will explore more thoroughly the differences among the financial patents held by different types of firms. Moreover, we will examine the differences in patent exploitation strategies between specialized technology firms and vertically integrated firms. Our preliminary analysis shows that specialized technological firms are heavily involved in licensing out of their financial patents.

Appendix 4.1
Selecting Financial Patents at the EPO

As described in the text, our sample of financial patents is the union of patents selected using three different algorithms, intersected with patents selected using a set of financial process-related keywords.[30] Our methodology follows that used by Hall and MacGarvie (2006) to select software patents at the USPTO. The idea on which it is based is first to identify the universe in which such patents might lie using the relevant patent classification system and the patenting of 'pure play' firms, and then to select from this universe by means of keywords those patents that are clearly related to the technology area and sector under consideration.

The first set of financial patents (Set A) relies on Hall (2007) and Lerner (2006), who defined a financial patent based on the subclasses of the US class 705 and 902. We used a combination of those definitions obtaining a list of the following US class and subclasses: 705/14; 705/16–18; 705/21; 705/33; 705/35–45; 705/53–56; 705/61; 705/64–79; 902/1–41. Then we retrieved all the documents in the USPTO assigned to at least one of those class and subclass combinations. We obtained a sample of 9,549 utility patent documents granted in the USPTO, which correspond to about 1,350 equivalents of patent applications in EPO. A similar approach has been followed by Wagner (2008) to find EPO patents on business methods. Note that the use of this criterion by itself to identify a financial patent in EPO has the limitation of excluding EPO applications with no equivalent application filed in the USPTO or with an equivalent US application which has been rejected or not yet granted.

The second method of defining a financial patent at the EPO relied on other patent classification systems, the IPC and the ECLA systems (Set B). We started by retrieving all patent documents classified in the full digit IPCs corresponding to the above US classes and subclasses according to the USPC-to-IPC Concordance Table provided by the USPTO.[31] The validity of this task is hampered by the fact there is a many-to-many correspondence across the IPC and USPC. Hence, in order to check that these IPCs are appropriate for identifying financial patents, we consider how many other subclasses not identified by 705/902 end up in the same full digit IPCs. We found that no full digit IPC is related one-for-one to the US classes and subclasses of financial patents defined by Hall (2007) and Lerner (2006). The IPCs either include subclasses different from the US 705 subclasses considered by Hall and Lerner (e.g., IPC class G06F/11/34 corresponds to USPC class 705/11 which is about 'job performance analysis') or they are linked to other US classes such as 235, 186, 178, 380, which are not related with financial inventions. Hence, the use of the IPC classes only for defining a financial patent could generate some false positives.

Therefore we employed an extension of the IPC—the ECLA classification—which is administered by the EPO and is about twice as detailed as the IPC.[32] On the one hand, we used the Concordance Table provided by the USPTO (see previous paragraph) to choose the ECLA codes related to the IPCs corresponding the USPC classes of Hall (2007) and Lerner (2006). On the other hand we identified those ECLA codes in which the EPO equivalents of the US financial patents were classified. In particular we considered the top ten groups of ECLA codes which contain about 78 percent of the EPO equivalents of the US financial patents. This yielded the following ECLA codes for identifying financial system-related patents at the EPO (for the description see Appendix Table 4.1.5): G06Q20/00; G06F21/00N9A2P; G07F7/02; G07F7/08; G07F7/10D; G07F7/10E; H04L9/32. This subset of patents consists of circa 2,803 patent documents which are referred to as Set B in Table 4.1.

The third criterion used to define a financial patent was based on an analysis of the patenting activity of 'pure play' firms, that is, firms that specialize in financial services or software. To identify pure play firms we started with a list provided by Hall (2007) for the US patentees, and for the largest European patentees we considered those classified in investment banking and securities dealing (NAICS activity 523110).[33] We then retrieved all patent applications filed by these firms in the EPO. We found about 452 patents that could potentially be related to financial innovations, because they were filed by firms specializing in financial services. To these we added all patents having the same class/subclass areas where the chosen set of 'pure play' firms patent, as was done by Graham and Mowery (2004). This group consisted of 85,542 EPO patents labelled as Set C in Table 4.1.

The results of this complex search procedure are illustrated in Appendix Table 4.1.1. The union of the three search criteria yields 87,719 patent applications at the EPO, whereas the intersection yields only 141 patents. The largest similarity across methods is obtained when Set A and Set B are

Appendix Table 4.1.1 Number of patents in each set and their intersection sets

	Set A	*Set B*	*Set C*
Set A	1350	217	927
Set B	217	2803	1425
Set C	927	1425	85,994

Source: *Our elaborations using USPTO and EPO datasets*

taken together, yielding an intersection of about 217 patents, accounting for 16.1 percent of patents in Set A and 7.7 percent in Set B. Moreover, there is a very small intersection between Set C and the other two sets. This evidence points to the fact that the three search methods may include patents unrelated to financial innovations, and also that most of these patents are not held by pure play firms.

Hence, to minimize the number of false positives (Type I error), we analysed the text of the titles and abstracts of the selected patents and restricted our sample only to patent documents having as words or subwords (e.g., wallet in electronic-wallet) at least one these keywords: *transaction, financial, credit, payment, money, debit card, portfolio,* and *wallet.*

After this further refining of financial patent definition, our sample was reduced to about 3,446 patent applications at the EPO (see Appendix Table 4.1.2). This constitutes the final set of financial patents. Note that the table shows a greater similarity across the results obtained with the three different definitions.

The sample actually used in estimation was slightly reduced to 3,298 patents by restricting the priority year to be prior to 2006, and removing a few patents for whom we did not know the applicant name or type (Appendix Table 4.1.3).

Finally, in order to fully access the different kind of patents identified by the above searching strategy we read the titles, abstracts, and the description of the patent documents. In particular we classified them using a similar

Appendix Table 4.1.2 Including financial keywords in the title and abstract

	Set A	Set B	Set C
Set A	362	119	274
Set B	119	944	591
Set C	274	591	3,039

Source: *Our elaborations using USPTO and EPO datasets*

Appendix Table 4.1.3 Selecting the sample

Total number of financial patents on the PatStat (October 2007)	3,446
Less loss due to slight change in Set B (no bibliometric information)	–17
Less patents with priority year>2005	–40
Missing applicant code	–97
Other	–4
Sample of financial patents	3,298

taxonomy to that suggested by Duffy and Squires (2008) consisting of the following categories:

1) ATM (Automatic Teller Machine), mechanical, or electronic technologies that have some connection to the financial industry
2) Trading technologies including anti-fraud techniques, mechanisms for implementing trades, and trading structures and market microstructure. This also includes web transaction methods.
3) Valuation techniques or other financial strategies
4) Financial products, broadly construed to include sophisticated products such as a new credit default swap or a more consumer-oriented product.

We selected for reading the patent documents in Set A that had received a final decision—that is a grant, withdrawal, or rejection. The goal of this choice was twofold: on the one hand, the patents of Set A have by definition an equivalent in USPTO, which ensures potential comparability with current and future studies on the US patents. On the other hand, considering only those that have received a final decision allows us to document which technologies are considered patentable by the EPO.

As we can see from Appendix Table 4.1.4, a large share of the patents analysed are in category (2), which relates to the methods and technologies for implementing transactions and payments systems. In one sense, Appendix Table 4.1.4 helps to validate the keywords search algorithm proposed above, as we found almost no patents in Set A that were unrelated to finance and payments methods. In the same vein, there is little evidence of the presence of advanced financial engineering methods in the Set A patents. Thus we conclude that the methodology proposed provides a fairly robust definition for selecting patents related to technologies for trading and payment systems at the EPO.

Appendix Table 4.1.4 Financial patents by type of the technologies involved

Category	Granted		Rejected		Withdrawn	
	Number	Share	Number	Share	Number	Share
(1) ATM, etc.	14	14.7%	3	12.0%	13	10.2%
(2) Trading	72	75.8%	12	48.0%	94	74.0%
(3) Valuation	9	9.5%	6	24.0%	20	15.7%
(4) Fin prods	0	0.0%	4	16.0%	0	0.0%
Overall	95	100.0%	25	100.0%	127	100.0%

Sources: The taxonomy is based on Duffy and Squires (2008).

Notes: (1) ATMs or mechanical or electronic technologies that have some connection to the financial industry; (2) Trading technologies including antifraud techniques, mechanisms for implementing trades, and trading structures and market microstructure. This includes also the web transactions; (3) Valuation technique or other financial strategy; (4) Financial products, broadly construed to include sophisticated products such as a new credit default swap or a more consumer-oriented product.

Appendix Table 4.1.5 List of ECLA classes with financial patents

ECLA subclass	Description
G06Q20/00	Payment schemes, architectures, or protocols (apparatus for performing or posting payment transactions
G06Q20/00K	further characterised by the type of neutral party arbitrating, type of payment circuit used, architecture used, payment model or scheme applied, or details of specific step in the protocol
G06Q20/00K1	involving a neutral party (e.g., certification authority, notary or trusted third party [TTP])
G06Q20/00K2	characterised by the type of payment circuit
G06Q20/00K2B	in a public payment circuit (e.g., standard banking accounts)
G06Q20/00K2C	in a private payment circuit (e.g., electronic cash used only among participants of a common payment scheme or inside a defined community), money generated by private organizations
G06Q20/00K3	characterised by the architecture used
G06Q20/00K3A	Electronic funds transfer (EFT) systems; home banking systems
G06Q20/00K3B	Electronic shopping systems
G06Q20/00K3C	Billing systems
G06Q20/00K3D	Payments settled via telephone service provider
G06Q20/00K3E	Payments for services accessed through systems involving a self- service terminal (SST), a vending machine, or a multimedia terminal
G06Q20/00K3F	point-of-sale (POS) network systems (POS per se G07F or G07G)
G06Q20/00K4	characterised by the payment model or scheme
G06Q20/00K4C	Credit card scheme (e.g., pay after)
G06Q20/00K4D	Debit scheme (e.g., pay now)
G06Q20/00K4P	Prepayment scheme (e.g., pay before)
G06Q20/00K5	characterised by the use of a wireless device
G06Q20/00K6	characterised by details of the protocol
G06Q20/00K6A	Authorisation
G06Q20/00K6C	Confirmation
G06F21/00	Security arrangements for protecting computers or computer systems against unauthorised activity (multiprogrammingG06F9/46; protection against unauthorised use of memoryG06F12/14; dispensing apparatus actuated by coded identity card or credit cardG07F7/08)
G06F21/00N9A2P	. . . protecting personal data (e.g., for financial or medical purposes)
G07F7/00	Mechanisms actuated by objects other than coins to free or to actuate vending, hiring, coin or paper currency dispensing or refunding apparatus (handling coins or paper currencies apart from coin-freed or like apparatus G07D); complete banking systems G07F

ECLA subclass	Description
G07F7/02	by keys or other credit registering devices (for producing a coded signal for use together with coded identity cards G07F7/10)
G07F7/02B	. . . by active credit-registering devices (e.g., counters, memories)
G07F7/02C	. . . by means (e.g., cards), comprising cases representing monetary value (for cancelling tickets, see G07B11/11)
G07F7/02D	. . . by cards with numerical value (G07F7/08 takes precedence)
G07F7/02E	. . . by means (e.g., cards), providing billing information at the time of purchase (e.g., identification of seller or purchaser), quantity of goods delivered or to be delivered
G07F7/08	by coded identity card or credit card . . . or other personal identification means(without personal verification meansG07F7/02)
G07F7/08B	. . . by passive credit-cards adapted therefore: constructive particularities to avoid counterfeiting (e.g., by inclusion of a physical or chemical security-layer) (for security documents see G07D7/00; for the reading of record-carriers in general see G06K7/)
G07F7/08C	. . . by active credit-cards adapted therefor (G07F7/10D takes precedence)
G07F7/08C2	. . . Electronic wallets suitable to be connected to similar devices for mutual funds transfer, either with or without a terminal
G07F7/08C2B	. . . with central accounting to keep track of the electronic money in circulation
G07F7/08C2C	. . . the wallets having several accounts
G07F7/08C4	. . . the value being automatically decremented in function of a variable (e.g., time, distance)
G07F7/08C6	. . . Systems wherein such cards are used for payment
G07F7/08C8	. . . Separate devices accepting such cards for payment
G07F7/08D	. . . Details or accessories (e.g., reading, decoding, printing of data from the cards) (G06K takes precedence)
G07F7/08E	. . . Verification of the card (i.e., checking validity to avoid misuse, e.g., checking expiry date)
G07F7/08E2	. . . by comparing with other document or pass (e.g., with a bank-cheque)
G07F7/08E4	. . . by mutual comparing codes on the card
G07F7/08F	. . . Account status verification (e.g., checking solvency of the holder) (computers adapted for financial accounting G06Q40/00A)
G07F7/08F2	. . . Local credit-checking (e.g., with black-list on tape)

(Continued)

ECLA subclass	Description
G07F7/08F4	. . . Central credit-checking via terminal (G07F7/10 takes precedence)
G07F7/10D	. . . Active credit cards provided with means to personalise their use (e.g., with PIN-introduction/comparison system)
G07F7/10D2	. . . Personalisation or initialisation of card
G07F7/10D2K	. . . with securisation during issuing/transport phase
G07F7/10D2M	. . . for several users (e.g., hierarchical)
G07F7/10D2P	. . by application program downloading (G07F7/10D10M2 takes precedence)
G07F7/10D4	. . . Mutual authentication of card and transaction partner (e.g., terminal, host, other card)
G07F7/10D4E	. . . the card having encyphering/decyphering capabilities
G07F7/10D4E2	. . . used for an authentication protocol (means for verifying the identity or authority of the user of a communication system per se H04L9/32)
G07F7/10D4T	. . . with transaction monitoring means (e.g., deriving transaction authentication number); with registration of transaction
G07F7/10D6	. . . Identification of card user
G07F7/10D6F	. . . with means to protect against fraudulent identification attempts (e.g., counter for erroneous PIN attempts)
G07F7/10D6K	. . . by comparing other identifying data with reference data stored in the card chip (G07C9/00B6 takes precedence)
G07F7/10D6P	. . . by PIN check
G07F7/10D8	. . . Independent cards, capable to authorise a transaction without the intervention of a terminal (e.g., by self-checking of user identity or solvency)
G07F7/10D8C	. . . Cards only used as intermediate carriers for identification data of user and for transaction data
G07F7/10D8P	. . . Cards combined with portable reader/writer to constitute an independent assembly
G07F7/10D10	. . . Multiple service cards (e.g., for several accounts, applications of the same person, the card to be processed by different terminals/issuers)
G07F7/10D10M	. . . with protecting memory zones, assigned to one service, against access (read/write/delete) by terminals of other services (protection against unauthorised access of computer memory areas in general G06F12/14; circuits for protecting data [e.g., PIN])
G07F7/10D10M2	. . . Zone-allocation and setting access conditions of zones

ECLA subclass	Description
G07F7/10D12	. . . Means to guarantee integrity of card data, not provided for in G07F7/10D2 to G07F7/10D10, (e.g., digital signatures, check numbers
G07F7/10D14	. . . Details or accessories concerning data transfer and storing, (e.g., error detection, self-diagnosis) (G06K19/07 takes precedence)
G07F7/10D16	. . . Multiple-card systems, the cards having either different or identical functions
G07F7/10E	. . . Devices and methods for securing the PIN and other transaction-data (e.g., by encryption) (arrangements for secret communication, see H04L9/00)
H04L9/00	Arrangements for secret or secure communication
H04L9/32	including means for verifying the identity or authority of a user of the system (computer systems G06F; coin-freed or like apparatus with coded identity card or credit card G07F7/08)
H04L9/32A	involving a third party or a trusted authority
H04L9/32B	using a nonpublic key algorithm
H04L9/32C	using a zero-knowledge proof
H04L9/32H	using hash functions
H04L9/32M	for message authentication (H04L9/32S takes precedence)
H04L9/32P	involving the concurrent use of a plurality of channels of different nature
H04L9/32R	using challenge-response
H04L9/32R2	for mutual authentication
H04L9/32R4	involving splitting up or repeating the challenge and/or response
H04L9/32S	using electronic signatures
H04L9/32S1	using blind signatures
H04L9/32S3	involving a plurality or a group of signers
H04L9/32S5	with message recovery
H04L9/32S5P	with partial message recovery
H04L9/32T	using time stamps or public key certificates

Appendix B
Additional Tables

Appendix Table 4.2.1 Time evolution of EPO financial patents by region of the patentee

3,127 EPO patent documents*

Country	Number with priority year equal to				
	before 1990	1990–1994	1995–99	2000–2005	Total
US	85	109	594	771	1559
Germany	17	14	68	202	301
France	23	23	60	100	206
UK	17	3	30	86	136
Other EU countries	18	18	120	260	416
EU27 total	75	58	278	648	1059
Japan	24	25	129	219	397
Rest of world	8	4	28	72	112
Overall	192	196	1029	1710	3127

Country	Shares with priority year equal to				
	before 1990	1990–1994	1995–99	2000–2005	Total
US	44.3%	55.6%	57.7%	45.1%	49.9%
Germany	8.9%	7.1%	6.6%	11.8%	9.6%
France	12.0%	11.7%	5.8%	5.8%	6.6%
UK	8.9%	1.5%	2.9%	5.0%	4.3%
Other EU countries	9.4%	9.2%	11.7%	15.2%	13.3%
EU27 total	39.1%	29.6%	27.0%	37.9%	33.9%
Japan	12.5%	12.8%	12.5%	12.8%	12.7%
Rest of world	4.2%	2.0%	2.7%	4.2%	3.6%

Source: our computations, see text for details.

Notes: *245 documents have more than one applicant but in all cases the applicants are from the same country.

Appendix Table 4.2.2 Time evolution of US financial patents by region of the patentee

Financial Patents based on Hall (2007) and Lerner (2006) classes plus financial keywords 4,460 US utility patent documents*

Country	Number with priority year equal to				
	before 1990	1990–1994	1995–99	after 2000	Total*
US	392	1829	283	1040	3544
Germany	15	16	6	6	43
France	19	27	12	6	64
UK	21	26	12	12	71
Other EU countries	11	52	8	42	113
EU27 total	66	121	38	66	291
Japan	179	144	51	75	449
Rest of world	23	90	16	73	202
Overall*	660	2184	388	1254	4486

Country	Shares with priority year equal to				
	before 1990	1990–1994	1995–99	after 2000	Total
US	59.4%	83.7%	72.9%	82.9%	79.0%
Germany	2.3%	0.7%	1.5%	0.5%	1.0%
France	2.9%	1.2%	3.1%	0.5%	1.4%
UK	3.2%	1.2%	3.1%	1.0%	1.6%
Other EU countries	1.7%	2.4%	2.1%	3.3%	2.5%
EU27 total	10.0%	5.5%	9.8%	5.3%	6.5%
Japan	27.1%	6.6%	13.1%	6.0%	10.0%
Rest of world	3.5%	4.1%	4.1%	5.8%	4.5%

Source: PATSTAT October 2007

Notes: *292 documents have more than one applicant but in almost all cases the applicants are from the same country.

Appendix Table 4.2.3 EPO financial patents by the sector and age of the patentee

2,945 EPO patent documents*

Sector+	Founding year of firm						
	pre-1970	1971–1980	1981–1990	1991–1995	1996–2000	2001–2005	Unknown
Office, accounting, computing machinery	492	44	67	5	4	8	4
Radio, television & comm. equipment	173	5	30	6	8	4	0
Equipment	665	49	97	11	12	12	4
Finance & insurance	325	6	25	60	61	40	15
Software & computer related activities	40	57	130	72	134	135	2
Post & telecommunications	125	0	91	23	39	12	0
Other business services	38	1	53	16	42	75	2
Services	528	64	299	171	276	262	19
Other business sectors	377	12	43	29	36	25	7
Sector unknown	0	0	0	1	1	0	9
Total	1570	125	439	212	325	299	39
	Within-sector shares of financial-patenting firms founded in each period						
Office, accounting, computing machinery	78.8%	7.1%	10.7%	0.8%	0.6%	1.3%	0.6%
Radio, television & comm. equipment	76.5%	2.2%	13.3%	2.7%	3.5%	1.8%	0.0%
Equipment	78.2%	5.8%	11.4%	1.3%	1.4%	1.4%	0.5%
Finance & insurance	61.1%	1.1%	4.7%	11.3%	11.5%	7.5%	2.8%
Software & computer-related activities	7.0%	10.0%	22.8%	12.6%	23.5%	23.7%	0.4%
Post & telecommunications	43.1%	0.0%	31.4%	7.9%	13.4%	4.1%	0.0%
Other business services	16.7%	0.4%	23.3%	7.0%	18.5%	33.0%	0.9%
Services	32.6%	4.0%	18.5%	10.6%	17.0%	16.2%	1.2%
Other business sectors	71.3%	2.3%	8.1%	5.5%	6.8%	4.7%	1.3%
Sector unknown	0.0%	0.0%	0.0%	9.1%	9.1%	0.0%	81.8%

Notes: *The sample includes double counting in case of copatenting and excludes patents held by individuals and governments. There are fifty-two patents with more than one applicant. + The sector categorisation is based on the 'OECD, STAN database'.

Appendix Table 4.2.4 Time evolution of financial patents by size of the patentee

*2,945 EPO patent documents**

Size of firm	With priority year equal to				
	before 1990	1990–1994	1995–99	2000–2005	Overall
	Number of patents				
Large (>249 employees)	130	151	800	1,191	2272
Medium (50–249 employees)	13	16	63	114	206
Small (<50 employees)	33	25	138	329	525
Size class not available	0	1	1	4	6
Total	176	193	1002	1638	3009
	Share of patents by size of firm				
Large (>249 employees)	73.9%	78.2%	79.8%	72.7%	75.5%
Medium (50–249 employees)	7.4%	8.3%	6.3%	7.0%	6.8%
Small (<50 employees)	18.8%	13.0%	13.8%	20.1%	17.4%
Size class not available	0.0%	0.5%	0.1%	0.2%	0.2%

Notes: *The sample includes double counting in case of copatenting and excludes patents held by individuals and governments. There are fifty-two patents with more than one applicant.

Appendix Table 4.2.5 EPO financial patents by the size and age of the patenting firm

*2,945 EPO patent documents**

Founding Year	Size of firm				Total
	Large	Medium	Small	Size unknown	
	Number of patents				
pre-1970	1559	5	6	0	1570
1971–1980	115	7	3	0	125
1981–1990	370	25	44	0	439
1991–1995	127	38	47	0	212
1996–2000	78	99	148	0	325
2001–2005	15	25	259	0	299
Not known	8	7	18	6	39
Total	2272	206	525	6	3009
	Shares by size in each founding period				
pre-1970	99.3%	0.3%	0.4%	0.0%	
1971–1980	92.0%	5.6%	2.4%	0.0%	
1981–1990	84.3%	5.7%	10.0%	0.0%	
1991–1995	59.9%	17.9%	22.2%	0.0%	
1996–2000	24.0%	30.5%	45.5%	0.0%	
2001–2005	5.0%	8.4%	86.6%	0.0%	
Not known	20.5%	17.9%	46.2%	15.4%	

Notes: *The sample includes double counting in case of copatenting and excludes patents held by individuals and governments. There are fifty-two patents with more than one applicant.

Notes

1 This chapter has been written in collaboration with Bronwyn H. Hall (University of California at Berkeley and University of Maastricht) and Salvatore Torrisi (University of Bologna and University 'L. Bocconi').

2 Bernard Bilski's patent application for an invention relating to a method for hedging commodity price risk was rejected by the USPTO as relating to an abstract idea without practical application. The applicants have then appealed to the CAFC.

3 Moreover the USPTO has issued clarifying guidelines with respect to business methods (May 15, 2008).

4 This process has been reinforced by some conflicting decisions at the various national European courts and the European Court of Justice. Nevertheless the EPO has announced some initiatives in order to clarify some patentability guidelines (Managing Intellectual Property, 24 October 008a).

5 There is also an *inter-partes* re-examination system that was introduced in 1999, but until very recently, it has been rarely used.

6 The new legislative initiative of the European Parliament (January 2013) has introduced a joint invalidation procedure with the entry in force of the Unified Patent Court. For more information see www.epo.org.

7 The CAFC decision in light of the Bilski case and the USPTO clarifying guidelines with respect to business methods may prelude to future potential changes in the patenting rules which add further uncertainty to the uncertainty arising from the ambiguous claims and unclear definition of the boundaries of financial patents and other business method patents. This ambiguity may slow down the investments on innovation because of hold-up problems that are especially important in the case of sequential innovations, a high risk of involuntary infringement, and high litigation costs (Hunt 2008; Bessen and Meurer 2008).

8 Harhoff and Reitzig (2004) estimate that an opposition case typically costs each party between fifteen thousand and twenty-five thousand euros—only a very small part of which is accounted for by opposition fees.

9 The term *patent quality* does not have a universally accepted definition, but we use it to mean an application that is more likely to satisfy the novelty, non-obviousness, and subject matter restrictions, and whose validity and ability to withstand subsequent challenges is therefore more certain (see Hall 2003 for a discussion).

10 It is important to note that at the EPO, references to the patent and nonpatent literature (scientific publications) are assigned by the examiner, not by the applicant. X type backward citations refer to patents containing claims that overlap with claims in the patent under examination. Y type backward citations refer to patent applications containing claims that combined with other claims overlap with claims in the patent examined.

11 That is, the patent has backward citations classified as X type or Y type by the EPO.

12 Later in this study we do find that the opposition probability for financial patents is significantly higher than that for other patents (9 percent versus 6.5 percent, without correcting for the overall decline in opposition probability during the period; the correction would increase the difference slightly).

13 Class 705 is 'Data processing: financial, business practice, management, or cost/price determination' and subclass 35 is 'Finance (e.g., banking, investment or credit)'.

14 Although this clearly biases the selection towards firms operating in the United States, because we use the union of this criterion with the other two (Sets B and C), we expect the bias to be small.

15 The precise definitions of the series shown are the following: all EP patents—patent grants and patent applications to the EPO; all US patents—patent grants by the USPTO; EP financial patents—the union of sets A, B, and C; US financial patents—the union of the sets defined by Hall (2007) and Lerner (2006). All series are shown by priority year or application year if the priority year is not available.

16 There are a total of 3,298 patents in our sample. Of these, 169 have more than one applicant (in a few cases more than two). In the next section we include all the patents, but only once each, so the total number of observations is 3,298. In this section we focus on those applicants that were in the business sector, excluding individuals and government applicants, for a total number of observations equal to 2,998, corresponding to 2,934 patent documents, of which fifty-two have more than one applicant. Note that the eleven observations where the sector of the applicant could not be identified were also removed from this sample.

17 For information on the patent owners we used a number of online company directories: Amadeus for European companies; Compustat for North American firms; Jade for Japanese and Who Owns Whom for other companies. We complemented these data with information from companies' websites.

18 In particular, we used Amadeus for European firms, Hoover's and Who Own Whom for US companies, Jade for Japanese firms, and the company's websites for any firms not found on one of these sites.

19 For firm size, we used three categories that are compatible with the definition given by the European Network for SME research (ENSR) of the EC SME observatory: i) small, having 1–49 employees; ii) medium, having 50–249 employees; iii) large, having more than 249 employees.

20 The suggestion is that these patents have less breadth of applicability. Nevertheless some caveats are in order with respect to the interpretation of this finding, because the IPC classes indicator is insignificantly correlated with the patent asset value above other indicators such as forward citations (see chapter 2, this volume). In fact, financial patents are found to be significantly more cited than other patents, and these citations are likely to originate from different technological classes (see above).

21 The possible outcomes for an application are that it is granted, that the EPO refuses it, or that the applicant withdraws it after negotiation with the EPO. The decision to withdraw a patent application can be considered equivalent to having received a rejection. In this way, the patentee can preempt a potential rejection decision of the examiner after the dispatch of the results of the examination process (Lazaridis and van Pottelsberghe 2007).

22 These periods are based on priority years, so there are too few granted patents in 2003–2005 to see much in the way of opposition. We therefore ended the detailed analysis at 2002.

23 The PCT dummy and family size are correlated because using the PCT route implies a desire to take out the patent in more than one country. Although the PCT coefficient is significantly negative, which will weaken the impact of family size, when it is removed, the coefficient falls only slightly (to 0.34).

24 There are no oppositions for the grants of financial patents with priority year after 2000, so we excluded those years from the analysis in the last column (fifty-three observations).

25 However, doing things this way has the advantage of making both our estimates and standard errors consistent even if there are random firm effects. Given the large number of firms (over one thousand) with only a single patent, using a fixed effect estimator is not very attractive as it would drop too many observations.

26 Because family size and the number of designated countries are correlated, in unreported regressions we tried with only one of these variables and the results do not change substantially.

27 In results not shown, when we combine the three ICT hardware sectors, we find that their probability of a grant is 0.15 higher than all other firms; the services sector probability is no different from that for other manufacturing firms.

28 In unreported regressions we entered a variable that measure the grant lag (the lag between the time of application and grant time) in the opposition equation. This variable has a negative and significant impact on the likelihood of opposition. This effect can be due to the fact that a long lag allows the patent office and the applicant to negotiate important modifications of the original application that prevent oppositions.

29 For patents held by business firms, there were one hundred oppositions to fifty-three patents, as in Table 4.5.

30 Our analysis is based on multiple sources. The identification of financial patents based on ECLA codes and keywords has been done using the ESPACE on-line database. Bibliographic data on EPO patents have been extracted from the Pat-Stat database (October 2007 version), whereas information on oppositions was drawn from EPOLINE files.

31 See http://www.uspto.gov/go/classification/international/ipc/ipc8/ipc_concordance/ipcsel.htm

32 For more information on the ECLA classification see: http://ep.espacenet.com/help?topic=classesqh&locale=en_EP&method=handleHelpTopic

33 For European firms we considered only NAICS 523110 because the other NAICS related to market of financial services are characterized by the presence of many holding companies of large industrial groups.

References

Arora A., A. Fosfuri, A. Gambardella 2001. *Markets for Technology: The Economics of Innovation and Corporate Strategy.* Cambridge (MA): MIT Press.

Bakels R., R. A. Ghosh, B. H. Hall, G. Thoma, S. Torrisi 2008. *Study of the Effects of Allowing Patent Claims for Computer Implemented Inventions.* UNU-MERIT, the Netherlands: Final Report to the European Commission.

Barton J. H. 2000. "Reforming the Patent System." *Science* 287:1933–1934.

Bessen J., M. J. Meurer 2008. *Patent Failure: How Judges, Bureaucrats, and Lawyers Put Innovators at Risk.* Princeton (NJ): Princeton University Press.

Bresnahan T. F., M. Trajtenberg 1995. "General Purpose Technologies: Engines of Growth." *J Econom* 65:83–108.

Cohen J. E., M. A. Lemley 2001. "Patent Scope and Innovation in the Software Industry." *Calif Law Rev* 89:1–57.

Cooter R. D., D. L. Rubinfeld 1989. "Economic Analysis of Legal Disputes and Their Resolutions." *J Econ Lit* XXVII:1067–1097.

Dreyfuss R. C. 2001. "Examining State Street Bank: Developments in Business Method Patenting." *Comput Recht Int* 1:1–9.

Duffy J. F., J. A. Squires 2008. "Disclosure and Financial Patents: Revealing the Invisible Hand." Paper presented at the Bank of Finland-CEPR Conference, Helsinki, October 16–17.

Gambardella A., D. Harhoff, B. Verspagen 2008. "The Value of European Patents." *Eur Manag Rev* 5:69–84.

Giarratana M. 2007. "Missing the Starting Gun: De Alio Entry Order in New Markets, Inertia and Real Option Capabilities." *Eur Manag Rev* 5:115–124.

Graham S. D., D. C. Mowery 2004. "Submarines in Software? Continuations in U.S. Software Patenting in the 1980s and 1990s." Econ Innov New Tech 13(5):417–442. http://www.tandfonline.com/doi/abs/10.1080/1043859042000188700

Hall B. H. 2003. "Business Method Patents, Innovation, and Policy." NBER Working Paper No. 9717, National Bureau of Economic Research Inc., Cambridge (MA).

Hall B. H. 2007. "Innovation in Non-Bank Payment Systems." Paper presented at the Kansas City Federal Reserve Conference, Santa Fe (NM): May 2–4.

Hall B. H., A. Jaffe, M. Trajtenberg 2005. "Market Value and Patent Citations." *Rand J Econ* 36: 16–38. Hall B. H., M. MacGarvie 2006. "The Private Value of Software Patents." NBER Working Paper No. 12195, National Bureau of Economic Research Inc., Cambridge (MA).

Hall B. H., G. Thoma, S. Torrisi 2007. "The Market Value of Patents and R&D: Evidence from European Firms." *Acad of Manag Best Paper Proc*, Philadelphia (PA): August 1, DOI:10.5465/AMBPP.2007.26530853.

Hall B. H., R. H. Ziedonis 2001. "The Determinants of Patenting in the US Semiconductor Industry, 1980–1994." *Rand J Econ* 32: 101–128.

Harhoff D., B. H. Hall 2005. "Intellectual Property Strategy in the Global Cosmetics Industry." *Ludwig-Maxmilians-Universität Muenchen and CEPR.* UC Berkeley and NBER: unpublished manuscript.

Harhoff D., F. Narin, F. M. Scherer, K. Vopel 1999. "Citation Frequency and the Value of Patented Inventions." *Rev Econ Stat* 81:511–515.

Harhoff D., M. Reitzig 2004. "Determinants of Opposition Against EPO Patent Grants—The Case of Biotechnology and Pharmaceuticals." *Int J Ind Org* 22:443–480.

Harhoff, D., F. M. Scherer, K. Vopel 2003. "Citations, Family Size, Opposition, and the Value of Patent Rights." *Res Pol* 32:1343–1364.

Harhoff D., S. Wagner 2009. "Modelling the Duration of Patent Examination at the European Patent Office." *Manag Science* 55(12):1969–1984.

Heller M., R. Eisenberg 1998. "Can Patents Deter Innovation? The Anticommons in Biomedical Research." *Science* 280 May:698–701.

Hunt R. 2001. "You Can Patent That? Are Patents on Computer Programs and Business Methods Good for the New Economy?" *Fed Reserve Bank Bus Rev* 1st Quarter:5–15.

Hunt R. 2008. "Business Method Patents and US Financial Services." Federal Reserve Bank of Philadelphia Working Paper No. 08–10. www.philadelphiafed.org

Janis M. D. 1997. "Rethinking Reexamination: Toward a Viable Administrative Revocation System for U.S. Patent Law." *Harvard J Law Technol* 11:1–122.

Kumar P., S. M. Turnbull 2008. "Optimal Patenting and Licensing of Financial Innovations." *Manage Science* 54:2012–2023.

Lanjouw J. O., M. Schankerman 2001. "Characteristics of Patent Litigation: A Window on Competition." *Rand J Econ* 32:129–151.

Lanjouw J. O., M. Schankerman 2004 A. "Protecting Intellectual Property Rights: Are Small Firms Handicapped?" *J Law Econ* 47:45–74.

Lanjouw J. O., M. Schankerman 2004 B. "Patent Quality and Research Productivity: Measuring Innovation with Multiple Indicators." *Econ J* 114:441–465.

Lazaridis G., B. van Pottelsberghe 2007. "The Rigour of EPO's Patentability Criteria: An Insight into the 'Induced Withdrawals'." Solvay Business School, Centre Emile Bernheim Working Paper No. 07–007.RS, Université Libre de Bruxelles. Brussels, Belgium.

Lemley M. A. 2007. "Ten Things to Do About Patent Holdup of Standards (And One Not To)." *Boston Col Law Rev* 48:1–49.

Lerner J. 1994. "The Importance of Patent Scope: An Empirical Analysis." *Rand J Econ* 25:319–333.

Lerner J. 2004. "The New New Financial Thing: The Sources of Innovation Before and After State Street." *J Fin Econ* 79:223–255.

Lerner J. 2006. "Trolls on State Street?: The Litigation of Financial Patents, 1976–2005." Harvard Business School Working Paper, Boston, MA.

Levine R. 1997. "Financial Development and Economic Growth." *J Econ Perspect* 35:688–726.

Lunney G. S., Jr. 2001. "e-Obviousness." *Michigan Telecommun Technol Law Rev* 7:363–422.

Managing Intellectual Property 2008a. "EPO to Address Software Patentability." Weekly News, October 24.

Managing Intellectual Property 2008b. "Federal Circuit Clarifies Test for Business Method Patents." Weekly News, October 31.

OECD 2008. *Patent Compendium*. Paris: OECD Publishing.

Putnam J. 1996. "The Value of International Patent Rights." PhD diss., Yale University, New Haven, CT.

Quillen C. D., O. H. Webster, R. Eichmann 2002. "Continuing Patent Applications and Performance of the U.S. Patent and Trademark Office—Extended." *Federal Circuit Bar J* 12:35–55.

Rosenberg N., L. E. Birdzell 1986. *How The West Grew Rich: The Economic Transformation of the Industrial World*. New York: Basic Books Inc.

Scotchmer S. 1996. "Protecting Early Innovators: Should Second Generation Products Be Patentable? *Rand J Econ* 27:322–331.

Torrisi S. 1998. *Industrial Organisation and Innovation. An International Study of the Software Industry*. Cheltenham: Edward Elgar.

Tufano P. 1989. "Financial Innovation and Dirst-Mover Aadvantages." *J Financ Econ* 25:213–240.

Tufano P. 2003. "Financial Innovation." In *Handbook of the Economics of Finance*, edited by G. Costantinides, M. Harris, R. Stulz, 307–335, Amsterdam: Elsevier.

Wagner S. 2008. "Business Method Patents in Europe and Their Strategic Use—Evidence from Franking Device Manufacturers." *Econ Innov New Technol* 17:173–194.

Ziedonis R. H. 2004. "Don't Fence Me In: Fragmented Markets for Technology and the Patent Acquisition Strategies of Firms." *Manag Science* 50:804–820.

5 Commercialization Strategies of a General Purpose Technology

Grid Thoma

5.1 Introduction

This study attempts to understand an important aspect of General Purpose Technologies (GPTs) that has been somewhat overlooked by the previous literature (Bresnahan 2010). In particular, the chapter analyses the business model, the profitability, and the economic performance of the GPT provider by presenting an in-depth and detailed case history of the processes involved in the commercialization of a GPT (Arora et al. 2001). Using multiple sources, I document the financial viability and sustainability of the business model of the GPT provider in the long run (Bresnahan and Trajtenberg 1995). Hence, this study contributes to a wider research agenda that aims to consolidate the understanding of GPTs, the conditions for their emergence, their organizational implications inside firms, and the effects on firm behaviour and performance (Lipsey et al. 1998; Gambardella and McGahan 2010).

The second goal of the chapter is to identify the factors that favour or hamper the diffusion of a GPT both on the supply side (Rosenberg and Trajtenberg 2004; Goldfarb 2005) and the demand side (David 1990; Bresnahan and Greenstein 1996). To this end I will discuss different factors that slack the GPT diffusion process when there is an existing substitute technology. I show how a producer firm can take advantage of an open standard business model in this process and how the coordination with technological adopters can be pursued without a complete integration into product markets.

The setting will be a particular GPT in action—*LonWorks*, a control technology introduced in December 1990 by Echelon, a Silicon Valley start-up company. Although until the inception of Echelon the various control network markets relied on different technologies, architectures, and market leaders, the founders of the new start-up launched the idea of an universal technological solution to the problem of control, based on a radical redefinition of the existing control technologies (Echelon Corporation 1990). Since then LonWorks has found many applications, mainly in utility services and building and residential automations, but also industrial and transportation controls.[1]

The articulation of this study follows the Schumpeterian distinction between invention, innovation, and diffusion. According to this distinction, invention concerns the first development of a new artefact or process. Innovation entails its advancement from economic point of view, and diffusion describes its introduction by buyers or competitors. Despite being rather a rough distinction, this can still be considered a useful point of departure. For example, invention is suggestive of some sort of exploited potential for technological progress, whereas innovation and diffusion hint at economic, social, and organizational incentives and impediments to the translation of technological advances into economic products and processes (Dosi 1991; Hall 2005 A).

5.2 Literature Background

5.2.1. Markets for Technology and Specialized Firms

Markets for technology are social welfare enhancers for several reasons. First, they simply avoid duplication of R&D among firms that use similar production processes (Stigler 1951). Second, they allow to internalize potentially public R&D outcomes, when specialized firms undertake that activity and license the technology to all members of the industry (Arrow 1975; Arora and Gambardella 2001). Third, in downstream markets for products markets for technology allow a more numerous entry of firms characterized by technological constraints, and they unbind resources for incumbent firms from internal R&D to a larger product diversification (Cesaroni 2004). Finally, market for technologies may create incentives for R&D specialized suppliers to increase the modularity and generality of their technologies for other possible applications (Bresnahan and Gambardella 1998).

However, there are also failures that affect technology markets (Arora 1996; Gambardella 2002). On the one hand, they are made up of some specific characteristics of technological transactions (Arrow 1962; Teece 1988). First, contracts for technology services are largely incomplete. Second, if a user develops tight interactions with one technology provider, the interplay may generate sunk investments, switching costs, and lock-in problems. Third, releasing precontract information may require the supplier to share valuable proprietary information, and this increases the risk of unintended appropriability.

On the other hand, an obstacle to the emergence and growth of markets for technology is intrinsically related to one of their benefits. In particular, the internalization of the R&D public good by specialized firms comes with a price related to the market power conferred on the provider in applying a markup for every technology input sold. Whereas the existence of this type of cost is justified by fixed idiosyncratic investments for the development of the public good, it leads to a market failure when the number of licensees in the market is small (Bresnahan and Gambardella 1998).

The specialized technology firm can increase the turnover by making its technology more general and searching for new potential markets. In this case, even low unitary royalties for every product sold in different markets can generate significant revenues to allow the licensor to reach the break-even point rapidly. Similarly, the greater the number of licensees across application sectors, the shorter the payback period of the individual fixed investments required for the development of a technology by the licensor.

The existent literature on the conditions of the emergence and profitability of the specialized technological firms with licensing in different markets is very limited, with few exceptions. In biotechnology Arora and Gambardella (1994) documented the effort of dedicated biotech firms to modularize their technology, which could enable them to change the business model from exclusively licensing chemical compounds to selling general purpose research tools to different manufacturers. In the software security industry, specialized technology firms have intensively patented generic encryption algorithms that they can license in very heterogeneous niches of that market (Giarratana 2004). Similarly, in the emergent industry of advanced materials Maine and Garsney (2006) analysed a couple of case studies of firms that actively have pursued active strategies to generalize its technology and to extract value by the mean of strategic alliances in different industries. However these studies are silent on the financial viability and sustainability of the business models of the licensor of a general technology in the long run.

5.2.2 Factors Affecting the Diffusion of a GPT

Following the taxonomy given by Hall (2005 A), factors affecting technological diffusion can be classified into four main groups according to: i) benefits received from the new technology; ii) costs of adopting the new technology; iii) network effects on the demand side; iv) information and uncertainty.[2]

5.2.2.1 Benefits Received from the New Technology

The benefits received from the adoption of a new technology are mostly related to the amount of improvement which the new technology offers over any previous technology. Put differently, they depend on the degree of substitutability of older technologies: if existing ones are close substitutes of the new technology, then adoption patterns will be slow. Rosenberg and Trajtenberg (2004) analysed the emergence and diffusion process of a new technological design of the steam engine—the Corliss model—during the second half of the nineteenth century. They argued that the diffusion of the Corliss engine was mainly triggered by the technical improvements embodied in the new design, and it contributed to the major reorganization process of industrial machinery and workflow in production and to speeding up urbanization and agglomeration dynamics in US cities.

Another factor affecting the potential benefits of a technology is *learning by doing or using*. If learning is significant then the innovation and diffusion can be characterized as strategic complements: whereas learning fosters adoption, the latter increases the former. The study by Goldfarb (2005) showed that the diffusion rate of electrical power in industry can be associated with advances of cumulative technical adaptations in specific applications, and developments of complementary technologies.

5.2.2.2 Costs of Adoption

Costs in the adoption of a new technology may arise from various sources, apart from acquisition costs. These can include complementary investment for use, management, maintenance, and ultimate discarding of the technology. Moreover, adoption costs are higher in the presence of (high) sunk costs for the initial use of the new technology. This is shown not only in the much longer payback periods of the investment but also in the cost-opportunities of switching technology after adoption.

In the case of the GPTs, different studies have argued that adoption costs are significantly related also to the technological and organizational learning processes that are required for an effective use of the new technology (David 1990; Bresnahan and Greenstein 1996, Bresnahan and Malerba 1997). This stream of literature considers the difficulties of reorganizing production around new technologies as one of the main factors in explaining the diffusion rate of a GPT. For example, in the computer industry, Bresnahan and Greenstein (1996) found that inventive activity of downstream users in adapting a general technology to localized need was the main predictor of the diffusion of client/server architecture in computing.

5.2.2.3 Network Effects

Positive networking effects could arise from the enhanced potential functionalities coming from a larger customer base and the network externalities in adoption due to scale economies. First, a larger customer base increases the direct attractiveness of adopting a new technology in the presence of goods that enable customers to communicate with others using the same technology, examples being the telephone or the word processor. Second, the role of indirect effects from network externalities in adoption are typical in markets characterised by a duality consumption system highlighted, for example, by the well-known competition of the VHS vs. Betamax standard in video recorders/players. Dominance of VHS was not explained by the intrinsic superiority of the winning standard but mainly by the availability of complementary conditions in consumption. A similar adoption dynamics has been documented in other industrial contexts related to the so-called Information and Communication Technologies, which often are considered a quintessential example of a GPT (for a survey see Katz and Shapiro 1994; Gandal 2006).

It is worth mentioning that others studies have argued how in industries characterized by competition among architectures, high levels of interdependence among technologies produced by independent firms, and very rapid change, firms consider the process of the emergence of interface standards or a so-called *dominant design* as a strategic variable and not as exogenous to their action (Khazam and Mowery 1994).

5.2.2.4 Information and Uncertainty

Diffused information about suitability and benefits, costs and limitations, and length of life will clearly influence the adoption rate of a new technology (Rosenberg 1996). In the diffusion process of a GPT, the role of information and uncertainty can be of particular relevance, because of the potential coordination failures between technological investment decisions by users and those concerning the general purpose characteristic of the GPT by the producer(s). Bresnahan and Trajtenberg (1995) argued that historically the coordination between user and producer(s) could be facilitated by the presence of exogenous factors, typically big contractors such as large firms, public procurement, or large public utilities. By committing themselves to specific technological trajectories and spurring the overall innovative collective action, big contractors can play a leading role not only in the design and development of GPTs but also in the encouragement of complementary innovations by users in specific directions. In this study I will argue on other strategic behaviours GPT producer(s) can follow to reduce uncertainty and increase coordination in downstream sectors.

5.3 The Emergence of a New Technological Paradigm in the Control industry

At the beginning of the '80s the existing control industries were characterized by different automation technologies and architectures, market structure, and leaders. Control systems were typically designed, manufactured, installed, and maintained by large original equipment manufacturer (OEM) firms that focused on one or more vertical markets, such as process or manufacturing control, or automations for heating, ventilating, and air conditioning (henceforth also as HVAC) equipment in buildings. Specialized technological and design firms were absent, whereas dedicated producers of control systems—also called small OEMs—concentrated on the production of specific components. These components could be integrated into the large control systems supplied to end users by large OEM firms, who established subcontracting agreements with small OEMs, once they had won a tender from the end user. Installation and maintenance were carried out by in-house installation and maintenance divisions of the large OEMs or by independent system integrators (SIs), who competed aggressively with the large OEMs.

Technical imbalances to the traditional technologies were occurring from the need of integration across existing applications.[3] For example, in building automation, potential synergies were being considered for HVAC with other automated building systems, including fire and safety, card access, lighting, security, and elevator control. Indeed, traditional technologies had been defined for creating ad-hoc large systems, and their ex-post expansibility was limited.[4] Second, there were difficulties in the application of traditional technologies for new uses of control systems—in transportation means, such as trains, buses, and trucks; in home automation, one of the largest markets for electronic goods and ICTs; in utility automations for meters and energy management. A third class of technical problems to the traditional technologies lay in the fact that they were based on an electronic/electric/pneumatic artefact, and their convergence in a communication network had not been considered at all.[5]

In the late '80s, a new paradigm emerged based on the so-called *FieldBus*, an all-digital, serial, and pair-to-pair two-way communications system that interconnected measurement and control equipment. At the base level in the hierarchy of a control network, it served as a Local Area Network (LAN) for sensors and actuators used in the control network and had a built-in capability to *distribute* the controlling functionality across the network. During the '90s, several *FieldBus* standards were defined.[6] Each bus definition had particular characteristics, and consequently, some bus standards were more suitable for some installations than others. Although the control industry is far from reaching a single standard, LonBus is considered one of the most diffused technologies in the market for different uses and for the number of nodes installed.

LonBus was launched in 1988 by Echelon, a Palo Alto start-up company, which was founded by Mike Markkula, a serial entrepreneur, early investor, and cofounder of several start-ups, among them respectively Apple Computers and ROLM (Box 5.1). Around 1985–86, Markkula had raised the question as to what business opportunities could arise when every device in whatever context was embodied with intelligence: industrial plants, buildings, homes, transportation means, and many others.

First, new control functions, applications, and uses could result from the integration of various devices on the net, which suggests some degree of interoperability. Once such interoperability was built, then by combining different kinds of devices, and allowing them to interact with one another, a more sophisticated and useful systems-level functionality can be created. A variety of potential tasks could be accomplished not only within systems but also between systems. For example, lights and shutters could be controlled automatically when a motion detector sensed that a space was no longer occupied.

Second, there are benefits of scale economies using a horizontal/multipurpose solution. On the production side, if different industries can use the

Box 5.1   Main facts of the Echelon Corporation and the LonWorks Platform

Place and date of company founding	San Jose, CA (USA), 1988 Mike AC Markkula					
Founder of the company	1993	1995	1997	1999	2001	2003
LonWorks Nodes Installed *(cumulated in millions*)*		0.5	2.3	4	16	40
Users *(cumulated*)*	300	700	2000	3500	4000	5000
R&D expenditures *(cumulated in millions US$*)*		14.1	28.7	45.5	73.7	130.3
Revenues *(cumulated in millions US$*)*		40.1	92.4	164.3	290.2	531.2
Profit/Loss *(cumulated in millions US$*)*		–18.2	–16.7	–11.4	–0.4	18.2
Capitalization *(in millions US$*)*			116.4	1977.6	554.1	452.6

Source: Elaboration from Echelon's 10-K reports and author's interviews

same technology, they can share the R&D efforts and manufacturing costs of producing it. Hence the producer can offer the technology at a lower price with respect to the case of an industry-specific solution. Moreover, a less-expensive technology can be used in contexts never employed before because of the lower price. This brings some positive feedbacks in the nature of scale economies. On the demand side, the integration of interoperable devices belonging to different industries could generate positive feedbacks in adoption (see discussion on sections 5.2.1. and 5.2.2.3).

Finally, the emergence of new application sectors increased the potential benefits by having a general solution. At the beginning of the '90s, new industries were demanding technologies for control, for example home automation, energy management, transportation, etc. Before the '90s, automation had a limited diffusion in residential homes, not only because of the cost but also because of radical sociological and psychological changes required in individual users' lifestyles. With the advent of the ICT era, many analysts claimed that the '90s were the moment of strong growth in this market (Business Week 1990).

5.3.1 Redefining the Unit of Operation

Echelon realized that every control process could be reconsidered and redefined as an event-driven control instead of traditional technologies, commonly known as command-based control,[7] and so they tried to redefine the unit of operation in control, moving from an electric/electronic problem to a telecommunication one.[8] In the event-driven system architecture invented by Echelon, every node communicates continuously to the net the status of the variables that have been assigned previously. A variable is the expression of a feature of the node, and every node can retrieve information and adapt to the status of other nodes if it has been programmed to it. The system adapts globally and continuously to the external environment, and the integration of different systems is favoured. On the basis of the flexibility and power of the new system architecture, Echelon was convinced that its LonWorks control technology could be used to solve problems in every industry mentioned earlier.

Markkula was not able to manage the company by himself because of other business commitments, so he hired Kenneth Oshman to be CEO of Echelon. Oshman was already considered a highly successful manager in Silicon Valley because of his past experience in ROLM, a company that he cofounded with Markkula. In 1969, ROLM entered the PBX market with the first digital PBX and became the second-largest supplier in the market after AT&T before being acquired by IBM in 1984. Markkula and Oshman hired a dozen engineers from ROLM, IBM, and Apple. This group designed the LonBus, defined by a communication protocol and a chip (called the Neuron Chip). The protocol, called LonTalk, was designed to be applicable in every device suitable for control (in buildings, home control, industrial applications, etc.) whereas the chip, called the Neuron Chip, contained the LonTalk protocol in firmware, was optimized for control applications and was sufficiently low cost that it could be sold widely for use in everyday devices regardless of context.

Echelon also designed hardware and software tools that could enable the whole development, implementation, and maintenance of a control network, thereby creating a complete technological platform called the LonWorks platform. An important component of the LonWorks platform were the so-called network connectivity devices—such as transceivers, adapters, switchers, and routers—across different communication channels, such as twisted pair cables, power lines, radio frequency communication, TCP/IP, etc. Thus, the potential demand for a control system could not be hampered by a lack of suitable communication infrastructure. Then, the LonWorks platform was extended to hardware and software development tools and network management software to enable the physical configuration, installation, and maintenance of the control network.

5.4 Patenting Strategies

Echelon started at a time when there was a modest degree of competition in distributed control, but it was not clear whether the FieldBus paradigm would have a future.[9] Moreover, LonWorks was the only horizontal solution in the control industry. The other control technologies were industry-specific and manufacturer-specific, based on traditional hierarchical architectures.[10]

The IP protection through patents has covered intensively all the main components of LonWorks: the communication standard protocol, computing and intelligence capacities, network connectivity devices, Internet gateways, and the development, configuration, and installation tools (see Table 5.1). A high share of continuations and divisional applications can also be noted, in particular with regard to communication standard protocol and computing modules. Continuations and divisional filings are patents that share a common priority date, and hence their use underlines the importance of considering LonWorks as a unique technological platform, not only 'de facto' but also 'de jure'. This evidence is consistent with the study of Hall and Ziedonis (2001), who documented the rising number of

Table 5.1 Main components of LonWorks technology and patenting strategy followed by Echelon

Function and Products	US patent counts[1]	US patent shares	First Priority Year	Continuations/ Divisional Patents[2]
Communication standard protocol (LonTalk[TM])	7	8.2%	1987	6
Computing and intelligence capacity (Neuron Chips[TM])	7	8.1%	1987	6
Network connectivity devices (e.g. Transceivers)	55	64.7%	1989	24
Hardware development tools for OEMs (LonBuilder[TM])	11	12.9%	1990	8
Software development tools for OEMs (LNS[TM])	2	2.3%	1991	1
Configuration and Installation tools for SIs (LonMaker[TM])	2	2.4%	1994	0
Communication enablers in Internet (i.Lon[TM] Internet Gateways)	1	1.2%	2000	0
Overall	85	100%		

Source: Author's elaboration on the LonWorks Product catalogue and www.uspto.gov

Notes: 1) Only utility patents invented by Echelon before 2005 are considered and not design patents. 2) Continuations include continuation applications, continuations in part, and divisional patents.

US patents for semiconductor technology in the decades, following changes in US patenting legislation in the mid-'80s that increased the value and range of patentability. They argued that new young firms, specialized in technology design and entering the semiconductor market during the '80s, demonstrated a higher propensity to patent compared with firms entering before. This is explained not only with a greater responsiveness towards licensing out but also the need to attract venture capital and to protect themselves from larger competitors.

The technological generality characteristics of LonWorks with respect to its competitors can be evaluated by the Echelon patent citation data, by relying on the so-called generality index (Hall and Trajtenberg 2004; Hall 2005 B; Bresnahan 2010). This index is a quadratic measure of dispersion of forward citations from other patents over their technology classes, and it reads as the following:

$$G_i = 1 - \sum_{j=1}^{n_i} s_{ij}^{\,2}$$

Where s_{ij} is the share of citations received by patent i that originate from patent class j, out of n_i citing patent classes.[11] Therefore, if the received citations originate from a wide number of patent classes, the generality index of the focal patent will be high, whilst the index will be low or approximating to zero if the focal patent is cited by patents from a few classes.

In order to appraise the technological generality, I isolated a pooled sample of patents from Echelon and its main competitors by application sector. In particular, I considered the patents of the top competitor of the most relevant application sectors as suggested in Echelon's 10k reports: Allen Bradley in industrial control, Robert Bosch in transportation, Intellon in the utilities, ABB in building automation, and Microsoft in home automation. Because some of these players are diversified and vertically integrated firms with large patent portfolios, I focused only on patents classified in the same main technological classes and subclasses as Echelon's patents.

Given the well-known skewness of patent value and the fact that the generality index is not defined from patents with no forward citations and zero for patents with only one citation, in the analysis I considered solely the patents of the top decile of the citation distribution.[12] More than half of these patents are assigned to Echelon. Thus, considering the top quartile in terms of generality index of the patents of this top decile of the citation distribution, I reported that more than two-thirds of them are assigned to Echelon. I repeated the same exercise for patents belonging to the 95th and 99th percentile of the citation distribution and the results hold. In other words, I found not only that Echelon's patents are highly cited—indicating a higher importance—but also that the received citations originated in quite different potential application sectors.

5.5 Commercialization Strategies

From the beginning, Echelon's management concentrated on creating a large market for LonWorks technology. The initial business model targeted the large majority of the control markets at that time[13] on the one hand, by targeting large existing industries—such as buildings, process industries, and manufacturing—and on the other hand, potentially big new application sectors—such as home automation, transportations, and utilities (Oshman 2005).

The management planned for the revenues to be derived from two main sources. First, they could come from licensing royalties. Echelon could license the production and distribution of Neuron Chips and network connectivity devices directly to silicon foundries, or just the use of the LonTalk protocol embedded in the Neuron Chips to the foundries, if they were willing to develop their own chips. Second, revenues could be generated from selling hardware and software tools for the development of control systems directly to OEMs.

In the next sections I will discuss the commercialization strategies in three potential large application sectors—buildings automation, home automation, and industrial controls. These application sectors are interesting case studies to analyse because they have attracted attention since the commercial launch of LonWorks and have continued to play an important role in the subsequent stage of Echelon's existence. First, I will argue on the initial difficulties that Echelon faced in the commercialization of its general technology, and then I will analyse what other strategies the management used to encourage a faster adoption of LonWorks and enable the creation of a large market for control applications, such as changes in the initial business model, technical adaptations, new product development, strategic alliances, vertical integration, and so on.

5.5.1 Early Adopters

Echelon began its marketing strategy with large OEM companies in different markets who could potentially ensure large orders and enable Echelon to break even more rapidly. Moreover orders by large OEMs could have activated some inertia and favour coordination in adoption also for other smaller-sized firms (see discussion in section 5.2.2.4). So they tried to convince these companies to move towards distributed and interoperable architectures, respectively FieldBus and LonWorks, stating that FieldBus could ensure a shorter time to market in product development, whereas the interoperability of LonWorks would favour a larger product differentiation and integration.

The technology was launched commercially by Echelon and a dozen partners on December 5, 1990, at a public conference in New York among hundreds of business leaders.[14] Partners included the silicon foundries of Motorola and Toshiba, to whom they licensed the production of Neuron Chips, and potential customers, such as: Allen-Bradley, the manufacturing control market leader; Johnson Controls and Landis & Gyr, two of the three largest producers of control systems for building automation;[15] Advanced Transformers and Lithonia Lighting, lighting systems manufacturers; Leviton, a home appliance manufacturer; Ziatech, a computer producer; Steal-case, an office furniture manufacturer; and finally, the military system integrator CACI.

5.5.1.1 Home Automation

Given the potential extent of the market, Echelon's management considered home automation to be one of the most attractive application sectors for LonWorks, together with building automation and industrial control. During 1989–93, Echelon's attention was focused on large OEMs that manufactured residential devices, such as Leviton and then Philips, who could ensure big orders. Later (1993–94), Echelon also tried to interact with other actors interested in entering this market, the OEMs manufacturing PCs. With the advent of the WinIntel paradigm, the PC was becoming widely diffused in the residential market. The idea was simple: a PC could be interconnected not only to its fellow artefacts, through the LANs, but also to other devices in the house, creating a single network, where PC technology would have a crucial role. With this in mind, Echelon signed an agreement with IBM and launched an exploratory working group with Novell.

However, the applications for LonWorks were scarce, and OEM orders dripped through slowly because of limited development in the home automation market. Moreover, at that time, LonWorks was a proprietary technology and OEMs were reluctant to accept a standard that they could not control. In the computer industry, after IBM's decision to use a standard operative system, such as Microsoft Windows, software vendors were able to obtain very high profit margins compared to hardware producers, who did not hold any leverage to appropriate some of those margins.[16]

5.5.1.2 Building Automation

As in the residential market, Echelon established relationships with large OEMs—Honeywell, Johnson Controls, Landis and Gyr, and Siebe—in order to convince them to move towards distributed and interoperable architectures, such as LonWorks.

Between 1991 and 1994—apart from a few advances with Honeywell— the large OEMs were reluctant to adopt LonWorks in their products and to substitute it for their own proprietary technologies, in spite of Echelon's claim of significant benefits for the new technology (see above). First, there seemed to be a sort of myopia of learning inside the organizational structure of OEMs which hampered its adoption. Echelon claimed that often the decisions were made by an individual designer, who could not see the global benefits of the technology for end-users but only the unit cost of the device, on which Echelon was not competitive. Had the marketing divisions taken the decisions as to what technology to include in their systems, they would have foreseen the larger benefits of LonWorks compared to other solutions, hence adopting it more widely.[17] This is one of the factors that led Echelon to try another approach and to stimulate demand for LonWorks products through system integrators (see section 5.5.3).

Second, LonWorks aimed to significantly reduce the installation and maintenance service costs of the systems that were twice the cost of the device. These services were the largest source of profits for large OEMs, who were able to impose monopoly prices on end-users for these services. Independent SIs could not offer these services once the system was developed because the technical specifications of the system were strictly proprietary, and the end-users were locked into a single supplier.

In order to compete with large OEMs, independent SIs had to work with very low margins, spending a great deal of effort integrating the systems of small OEMs that were not designed to work together. Had the large OEMs adopted an off-the-shelf policy and used an open technology such as LonWorks in their system, this would have favoured the entry of independent SIs into the market for installation and maintenance, increasing competition and lowering their profits.

Given the initial difficulties of getting adopted, Echelon was not able to capture the benefits of scale economies, and the cost of the technology remained high, especially that of the chips. The costs of the neuron chip can approximate the unit cost of LonWorks adoption at a lower level. However, other costs need to be carried over that we can roughly estimate to be twice the unitary cost of the Neuron Chips, mainly because of communication interfaces and customized software and hardware.[18] At the public launch in December 1990, Markkula had declared that they could bring down the cost of a chip to one dollar within five years, a price which was still not feasible in the market even two decades latter.

In building automation, the higher cost of technology with respect to traditional technologies based on induced them to reconsider their decision to initially target only large buildings of more than five thousand square metres.

5.5.1.3 Industrial Automation

In process industries and manufacturing, Echelon's management was convinced that LonWorks control networks could be used in specific industrial applications such as semiconductor fabrication plants, gas compressor stations, gasoline tank farms, oil pumping stations, water pumping stations, textile dyeing machinery, pulp and paper processing equipment, automated conveyor systems, and many other industrial environments.

As documented, since the commercial launch in 1990, Echelon had established an interesting partnership with Allen-Bradley, the OEM leader for industrial control systems. Initially, Allen-Bradley was very interested in the LonWorks technology, and a joint working group was created with the aim of exploring the deployment of an automation system embodying LonWorks. However, some divergences soon emerged within the working group because Echelon wanted to substitute traditional control solutions for new ones whereas Allen-Bradley was not willing to totally renounce traditional solutions and architectures. As a consequence, the partnership broke up, and Allen-Bradley went on to develop an industry-specific standard, called 'DeviceNet'. Thus, in the two application sectors for industrial automations, LonWorks had only a limited diffusion, in spite of some initial successful applications. One possible explanation for the diffusion of an industry-specific technological standard in manufacturing is related to the fact that the size of control applications in industrial plants is much larger than in other sectors: the larger the size of a single user, the greater the need for more localised technology (Bresnahan and Gambardella 1998).

5.5.2 Creating an Open Standard

At the beginning of 1995, Echelon decided to open up LonBus by committing legally to freely licensing the protocol to any potential user. Every silicon foundry was allowed to build a chip with the protocol inside without giving Echelon any royalty. By first patenting and then free-licensing, Echelon was able to prevent others from modifying the protocol and successfully ensure a fully standardized and interoperable technology for many possible uses. Moreover, Echelon sponsored the creation of an independent association, called *LonMark*, to "... *define guidelines that enable easy integration of LonWorks products made by multiple manufacturers without the need for development of custom application code, network management tools and hardware*" (LIA 1995).[19] In this case, LonWorks could be considered a technology that no actor could control unilaterally.

Echelon also launched a research and development programme called LonWorks Independent Developers (LIDs). In addition to being users of the technology for their own purposes, the LIDs became independent hardware and software design consultants approved by Echelon to provide LonWorks-based development services for product manufacturers in different application sectors and countries.

These changes in the business model significantly increased the attractiveness of the LonWorks technology. Particularly in the building automation market, they burst up the adoption rate of LonWorks compared to alternative solutions, making LonWorks a 'de-facto' standard. At the beginning of the '90s, the American Society of Heating, Refrigerating and Air-Conditioning Engineers decided to sponsor a different protocol from LonTalk, the Bacnet that claimed to ensure interoperability as good as LonWorks and to be a more stable and reliable technology for large systems. A standard battle took place, and by the beginning of 1999, more than four million LonWorks nodes had been installed, whereas Bacnet was still a long way behind.[20] An open standard strategy contributed strongly to this result, together with a new learning dynamics in this market. We will discuss this in the next section.

5.5.3 Stimulating Demand through Creative Destruction in the Value Network

In the building automation market, LonWorks technology could also be of interest to so-called low-level OEMs, like Carrier and York, which were producing sub-systems for large OEMs, on whose orders they were completely dependent. Indeed, the subsystems of low-level OEMs did not work autonomously and depended totally on integration with the systems produced by the large control companies. Had they adopted interoperable technologies, integration could have been done downstream by independent SIs, competing with the in-house installation and maintenance divisions of the large OEMs. In public tenders, independent SIs could bid up to 70 percent more competitively than the large OEMs, because they did not have to sustain a lot of effort in integrating, installing, and maintaining the systems. So Echelon tried to stimulate demand for LonWorks through system integrators, launching an intensive promotion activity: if they requested products embodying LonWorks, they would have to adopt Echelon's technology. The idea was simple: independent SIs such as Olivetti Solutions and M&E Sales could integrate multivendor, interoperable products containing LonWorks without the need to spend a lot of effort in building up special gateways for different products that were not designed to talk together.

The promotion activity started with the launch of national and regional user organizations to provide information to potential interested parties— the LonUser Groups—and an annual conference and trade fair, called Lon-World, where users could face directly with the top management of Echelon. However, Echelon realized that there were few products in the market embedding LonWorks; small OEMs were not independent of large ones in technological decisions because they produced systems without a stand-alone functionality and were integrated in the larger systems produced by the large OEMs or to a lesser extent by the independent SIs. Moreover, the small OEMs needed more time to acquire competencies to develop devices embedded with intelligence, because traditionally, this work had been done by large OEMs. Hence, independent SIs apparently did not have any leverage. How was it possible to solve this dilemma?

Thanks to experience accumulated with some LID partners, Echelon realized that the 'delay' in adoption choices by OEMs could be overcome if system integrators could simply attach LonWorks intelligence to devices downstream. At the end of 1996, Echelon launched the *LonPoint*, a box able to translate the input/output electrical signals of a HVAC component in the LonTalk protocol and vice versa and hence could enable the integration of the component developed by independent (small) OEMs into the

LonWorks net. The production of LonPoint boxes was quite expensive, but in big systems they turned out to be competitive.[21] They served as a starting point for diffusion in the automation of large buildings, associated with the emergence of a new industrial organization characterised by independent SIs, able to win autonomously in public tenders and commission-customized products based on LonWorks technology to small OEMs.[22]

The strategy achieved quite a significant success if we consider the number of nodes installed. During 1997, the orders doubled with respect to the previous year, and at the beginning of 1999, monthly adoptions of LonBus reached half a million units compared to seventy-five thousand in 1996. The total number of nodes installed increased from four million at the end of 1998 to sixteen million at the end of 2000. This led LonWorks to be considered a de facto standard in the automation market for large buildings.

In spite of this success in the automation of large buildings, the financial performance of Echelon was still poor, and the break-even point had not yet been reached. Hence, the management tried to increase the entry of independent SIs, especially for medium and small buildings. But there were very scarce technological competencies for handling a new technology which was very different from the traditional. Handling LonWorks required telecommunication and computing competences, whereas traditional solutions were based on electric and electronic technologies. Moreover, the implementation of a LonWorks system required the integration of various different competences: mechanical, electrical, plumbing, information technology, and controls.[23]

Mixing different competences created organizational challenges not only for the new entrants but also for existing system integration companies, such as Olivetti Solutions, where the capabilities of integrating and marketing data networks proved not to be easily transferable in the case of LonWorks control networks.[24] Individual technology training for product developers was required, whereas the marketing personnel had to reconfigure the distribution network with respect to final users. Traditionally, they used to commercialise their products for IT managers in companies or institutions, whereas in the case of LonWorks they were asked to interact with facility or security managers. The system integration companies required time to complete these organisational innovations, and this hampered the fast arrival of a significant level of orders for LonWorks-based products sufficient for Echelon to reach the break-even point.

Echelon launched a System Integrator training programme to transfer technological and organizational competencies downstream in the building automation market. Given the small size of the company, Echelon was not able to take on the costs of building its own distribution network of System Integrators. Hence, the process of entry of independent SIs was a slower and more gradual process, conditioned significantly by national and regional specificities and path-dependencies.

5.5.4 *Transferring Competences by (Quasi) Integrating Downstream*

As we have seen, transferring competences downstream to a system integrator in the building automation was very costly for Echelon and required time. In 2001, Echelon still had not reached the break-even point. The home automation market had the potential for larger orders, but this market was still emerging, and the amount of system integration capabilities to be fuelled was even higher given the size of the market. Echelon had to search for big orders elsewhere. But from where?

At the launch, Echelon's management considered that utility providers, in particular energy utilities, might show significant interest in the LonWorks platform. Echelon's technology would enable them to establish direct low-cost connection—through power lines—to residential devices to read the energy meters remotely and to introduce some demand side energy management services. During 1993–95, some utilities showed particular interest in LonWorks and disclosed ongoing test projects.

However, during 1995–96, the interest of utilities in LonWorks decreased, mostly due to the fact that these applications involved only the remote reading and management of energy meters, whereas integration with home automation systems was not considered—if this were the case, there were less-expensive solutions, such as those offered by Intellon and Cellnet.

Indeed, integration across utility services and home automation was the core of a production and commercial agreement between Echelon and Enel, the largest Italian utility and the second worldwide for installed generation power at that time. In June 2000, Enel and Echelon launched the 'Contatore Elettronico' project to provide digital electricity meters and a home automation infrastructure based on LonWorks to over thirty million customers in Italy.

Two kinds of factors enabled this project. First, important institutional innovations had taken place in the utilities sector in Europe starting in the '80s. Historically, the supply of electricity had been considered to have the features of a public good, and many state-owned monopolies had been built up. However, the rapid emergence of new technological paradigms and the evolution of the needs towards new frontiers pushed European policy makers towards a greater liberalization and privatization of the sector. In the past, these policies had been hampered by important technological difficulties in the metering process of energy consumption, whereas by the end of the '90s, some companies were announcing solutions to these technological bottlenecks, among them Echelon and Enel.[25]

The second set of favourable factors was constituted by the organizational competencies of the Italian partner. Enel was of one of the first actors to move in the direction of developing new metering technologies in the '80s. Although experiencing failure in the first years, Enel became more and more convinced that the implementation of new metering technologies in the residential market had to be integrated with indoor home automation systems, so that payback periods could be much shorter and service costs lower. LonWorks was the general solution that Enel was looking for. According to Enel, the power line transceivers designed by Echelon to enable digital transmission across power wires were the only commercialized technological solution suitable for implementation of remote metering and home automation.[26]

The 'Contatore Elettronico' project not only developed new metering services for public utilities but also home automation applications, such as energy management, safety, and Internet access. Echelon launched a new product called Network Energy Services (NES), that tried to exploit the synergies with home automation systems, and this had become the most important line of business for the company by the beginning of 2004. Other utilities have since announced their intention to adopt the NES products in Germany, in Scandinavia, in Australia, and in China, just to mention a few examples.

The importance of the production and commercial agreement with Enel is highlighted by the fact that the number of nodes to be installed was double those deployed in 2001, and Echelon finally broke even in 2003. Moreover, Echelon greatly improved its core technology with the development of Smart Transceivers, a new type of product that incorporates a Neuron Chip and a transceiver, able to integrate the unit into the control net without the need for supplementary interfaces. Integration efforts have been very significant, making them suitable for deployment also in very small devices such as residential appliances for home automation. Agreements to this end have been disclosed by appliance manufacturers that have decided to adopt LonWorks in their products: Merloni, Samsung Electronics, and Goregne in household white appliances, Riello and Carrier in the residential HVAC market, and Bticino, Vimar, and Gewiss in lighting and safety systems. In short, thanks to its partnership with Enel, Echelon has delivered a better, more general, and less expensive technology not only for the utility market but also for the home automation market, generating horizontal innovational spillovers, such as Smart Transceivers.

5.6 Discussion of the Commercialization Strategies

The initial model of Echelon involved a few large OEMs in different application sectors that Echelon considered were able to use the technology off the shelf. However, the early adopters initially paid little attention to the new technology for various reasons. First, it was a proprietary technology and OEMs were reluctant to accept a standard that they could not control because of the high risk of the 'hold-up problem'. Second, a sort of short-sightedness within the organizational structure of the OEMs slowed down orders for LonWorks, because the adoption decisions were not taken by their marketing divisions, who would see the overall benefits to be gained by the end-users from the new technology, but by the individual designers who were put off by the unitary cost of a control system. Third, had the OEMs adopted LonWorks, they could have generated competition for their own products and services, because LonWorks aimed to reduce significantly the installation and maintenance service costs of the control systems that were the main source of revenues for the large OEMs.

Hence, Echelon decided to open up the technology by creating an open standard. This change in the business model had multiple effects. First, as we said, it aimed to overcome the reluctance of some OEMs to adopt Lon-Works because the protocol was a proprietary technology at that time. With the decision to create an open standard, LonWorks could be considered a technology that no actor could control unilaterally.

Second, in terms of the model suggested by Bresnahan and Trajtenberg (1995), this can be interpreted as an attempt to enlarge the market by stimulating the entry of the existing marginal application sectors. On the GPT producers' side, when the potential market is very large, the decision to freely license part of the technology can increase profitability of the GPT producer if this allows an increase in demand for additional parts of the technology, such as Neuron Chips and communication enablers. Indeed, royalties from the silicon foundries made up a large part of the revenues for Echelon in the years following the launch.

Third, the open standard strategy aimed to create a 'bandwagon' effect in the creation of a 'de facto' technological standard. Hence, Echelon's strategy is consistent with the finding of Khazam and Mowery (1994), who argued that in fast-evolving industries firms consider the process of the emergence of interface standards or a dominant design as a strategic variable and not as exogenous to their action (see discussion in section 5.2.2.3).

The lack of vertical integration between technological providers and the producers of complementary technologies required for the implementation of a LonWorks net catalysed the launch of a 'bandwagon-creation' strategy. On the one hand, there were the network connectivity devices such as transceivers and routers; with respect to such components Echelon established supply contracts, producing LonWorks products with the Echelon brand, thus changing the initial business model. Revenues would not be derived from royalties but rather from the increased sales of Echelon products such as sales of communication interfaces and software management systems. On the other, customised hardware and software were essential for deploying and installing a control network according to the localized needs of the single users. Given the small size of the company, Echelon was not able to integrate this activity internally and thus launched a R&D programme called LonWorks Independent Developers (LIDs). In summary, the 'bandwagon' strategy aimed to put Echelon in a dominant position in the complemental market of network connectivity devices and to create a type of public good where many different actors could undertake independent technological trajectories.

Moreover, in order to show OEMs the technical and commercial viability of the technology Echelon developed a new type of product to be used by SIs and established alliances with some large SIs. Echelon transferred competencies to the large SIs in how to use the technology and commercialize it. A new industrial organisation emerged characterised by independent SIs, who were able to win autonomously in public tender and commission customized products based on LonWorks technology to the OEMs. This strategy could be pursued effectively only by independent SIs operating for medium-large buildings because they already had, or could develop, a sufficient level of absorptive capacity for the technology, whereas entry into this market by SIs for medium-small installations was much slower and more limited. Indeed, they had very scarce technological competencies for handling a new technology which was very different from the traditional. Finally, to reach the break-even point Echelon attempted quasi-integration downstream with a big utility. This partnership generated horizontal innovational complementaries for many other users in other markets, because Echelon could supply a more general and less expensive technology not only for the utility market but also for the home automation market.

5.7 Discussion on Factors Affecting Diffusion

As I have discussed and as we can clearly note from Figure 5.1, there are different patterns of diffusion across the main application sectors of Lon-Works. Whereas initially, building and industrial automation were the lead sectors, their importance decreased with time, and in 2005, utilities constituted the main application sector of LonWorks.

This diffusion pattern is consistent with the model suggested by Bresnahan and Gambardella (1998), according to which smaller-sized application

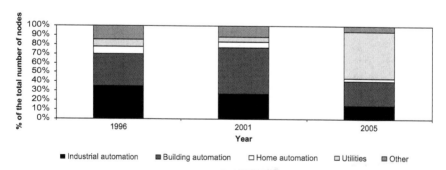

Figure 5.1 Technological diffusion by application sector

Sources: For 1996, Lonworks Resource Directory; For building automation: the estimates in 2001 were extracted from the introductory presentation of LonWorld (2001); For utilities, the estimates in 2005 were obtained from Enel s.p.a; Other estimates were computed by the author on the basis of application sector percentage in the previous period.

sectors have a higher propensity to adopt a general technology vis-à-vis larger application sectors. Indeed LonWorks experienced a relatively lower diffusion pattern in industrial automations with respect to building automations and utilities market. In the industrial automation market manufactures continued to use industry-specific control technologies, such as, for example, DeviceNet by Allen-Bradley[27]. Lonworks experienced a broader diffusion in building automation for big buildings, but the pace of adoption was much slower in the larger market for small-medium buildings. Finally, a new emerging market such as the utility market has been very attractive for LonWorks becoming the most important application sector. Furthermore, thanks to the orders coming from the utility provider Echelon has improved its technology making it attractive also for another emerging market constituted by the home automations.

In addition to size, another factor favourable to the diffusion of Lon-Works technology in utilities and home automations has been the benefits received from the new technology. The potential benefits of LonWorks for OEMs and SIs were claimed by Echelon to be very high compared to the traditional state of the art.[28] On the one hand, LonWorks would reduce the time to market of products and greatly lower the cost of installation, managing, and maintaining of a control network. On the other, LonWorks could ensure them new business opportunities through the integration of control networks on the Internet, allowing devices to be controlled remotely. In the case of integrated automations for homes and utilities, according to Enel, the degree of substitutability of LonWorks was close to zero.[29] In utilities, adoption can be articulated as a cumulative problem-solving process depending directly on the technical benefits of the technology.[30]

However, in other application sectors the learning process turned out to be very significant for new telecommunication competencies required in managing the technology, especially when it was needed to integrate different types of devices together. For this reason, Echelon launched the R&D LonWorks Independent Developers partner programme. Many of the LIDs became product manufacturers themselves, dropping out of the programme, and whereas in 1995 the LIDs programme had more than forty members located in twelve countries worldwide, in 2002 numbers had decreased to less than half, suggesting that the learning-by-doing (or—using) process had been significant in the early stage of adoption.

In addition to learning cost, on the demand side other complementary investment was required in the adoption of LonWorks by manufacturers, basically in the development of LonWorks-based products. For configuration of the network, OEMs needed to acquire the LonBuilder from Echelon that, on average, cost US $25 thousand at that time. In order to avoid this fixed sunk investment, often Echelon sponsored the acquisition of the Lon-Builder by Public Research Institutions and LIDs but SIs had to make sunk investments to acquire LonWorks installation tools.

Besides acquisition costs, users' absorptive capacity—technological and organizational—proved to be very important, especially in building automation. Of the former, handling the technology required new competencies that could be absorbed if an internal propensity to R&D already existed. Of the latter, OEM adoption decisions were characterised by a sort of myopia of learning at an early stage (because they had to be framed within the context of the costs and benefits of the entire control system) and the possibility of realizing multivendor products required important system integration capabilities. Independent SIs were scarce, mainly concentrated in the building automation market, and reconversion of integration capabilities used in other industries required internal organizational changes for developing and marketing LonWorks-based products (see Box 5.2 for a summary of the analysis of diffusion factors).[31]

Another factor that favoured the diffusion of LonWorks in building automation is the indirect network effects from economies of scale in adoption, which have been more significant than in other markets. In industrial control, for example, the size of a control network required by a single user is much larger than in the building automation. This increases the demand for more 'localized' technology in industrial control and transportation with respect to buildings (Bresnahan and Gambardella 1998). Hence, the decision to create an open standard based on the interoperability principles and the launch of LonPoints generated higher positive network effects in building automation, resulting in LonWorks being considered a de facto standard. As we saw previously, to favour the adoption of interoperability standards Echelon's management launched the LonMark programme (see section 5.5.2). In 1995, the LonMark association numbered around ninety members and, in the later years the role of the association has increased in terms of members (around five hundred by late 2005). LonMark is a coordinated and active forum in which users of LonWorks (manufacturers, end-users, and system integrators) can work together on marketing and technical problems regarding interoperability.

In addition to LonMark, Echelon launched two kinds of institutional organizations in order to advertise, coordinate, and promote various kinds of interactions among the companies that develop and use the technology: first, national and regional user organizations that publicize and promote the technology; and second, LonWorld, an annual conference and trade fair with several thousand attendees. These institutional organizations have had the aim to fill for the coordinating role traditionally played by big contractors such large firms or public procurement (see discussion in section 5.2.2.4), who were reluctant to adopt the Echelon's technology initially. The mission of LonUser Groups has been that of organizing the market for technology and initiating cooperation and complementarity between LonWorks developers and users at the national level. The LonWorld Conference and Exhibition provided an international forum for sharing information concerning LonWorks technology and applications, build alliances, meet directly the top management of Echelon, and support the LonWorks standard for control industry.

Box 5.2 Summary of the diffusion factors of LonWorks

	OEMs	System Integrators	End Users	Echelon's strategy
New technology benefits	1. Very reduced time to market 2. New business opportunities through larger product diversification	1. Easy installation, maintenance and expandability of the systems 2. New business opportunities through higher customer satisfaction	1. An increase in the proliferation of products and services 2. A redefinition of the existing control systems through higher integration 3. Economies of scale in production ensure less expensive solutions	Redefinition of the *unit of operation* in the control problems
Technology costs	1. Higher level product cannibalisation 2. Sunk costs in development tools 3. Organizational change in adopting decisions	1. Sunk costs in installation tools 2. Organizational change in developing and marketing	1. Chip costs increase unitary costs of systems 2. Reduced maintenance costs of systems	1. Free licensing part of the technology 2. Transferring competencies downstream 2. Strategies for reduction of sunk costs through economies of scope among users
Network effects	1. High in building automation, low in other application sectors			1. Creation of LonWorks Interoperability Association 2. Bandwagon creation strategies
Information and uncertainty	1. Uncertainty of FieldBus technological trajectory 2. High uncertainty in home automation and utilities	1. Uncertainty of FieldBus technological trajectory	1. Reluctance in routine changing	1. Creation of user groups 2. Annual fair

Sources: Author's elaboration from different sources (Interviews with Echelon management, LonWorks users, product catalogues, and the technical press).

5.8 Conclusions

Nathan Rosenberg (1976) made a detailed analysis of the technological convergence that took place in the US machine tools industry between 1840 and 1910. In particular, he noted that the competencies generated in the firearms industry were directly deployed in textile plants, bicycles, and automobiles. A quintessential example is the following, the *"Cadillac Company of Detroit, which was founded in 1890 as a producer of machine tools and special machinery, introduced machinery for producing bicycle gears . . . switched to gasoline engines for motor boats . . . and by 1902 had undertaken the production of automobile engines"* (Rosenberg 1976, 30).

In this study, I focused on some evolutionary changes in the control industry and discussed some of the technological and industrial convergence processes incepted by the Echelon Corporation that have taken place in the industry since the beginning of the '90s. I analysed different strategies and business models pursued by the technological provider in the commercialization phase. In this direction, this study constitutes one of the first studies to document the financial viability and sustainability of the business models of the GPT provider in the long run. Moreover I analyzed different hampering factors of licensing a GPT when there is an existing substitute technology.

Innovators always face a trade-off between a generalized versus a localized business idea. The present analysis suggests that generalization and localization need not always be considered as substitutes but sometimes as complements: The higher the number of different localized uses, the larger the business opportunities arising from scale and scope economies in different uses, hence from the existence of a generalized solution. The emergence of a generalized technology can be fuelled either by direct application of breakthrough scientific discoveries or by a unique recombination of existing capabilities. The novelty of LonWorks concerns more likely the latter aspect: the pool of engineering competencies in Echelon, inherited from ROLM, a telecommunication company, and from IBM and Apple, two computer designers, enabled a completely new framing of the control problems, potentially applicable in every context. However, the general solution that was designed required a high level of adaptation in the application sectors, both in the supply of technology and in the use of it. As in the case of the Cadillac Company, the management of Echelon propelled a broad repertoire of commercialization strategies, and the organizational capabilities of the technology provider turned out to be the crucial competitive asset.

The small size of Echelon favoured the competency recombination process, but at the same time, it was challenged by chicken-and-egg style problems in the decisions of users to undertake complementary idiosyncratic investments. Various institutional mechanisms—R&D alliances, strategic partnerships, and user consortia—fuelled the coordination of innovative efforts upstream and downstream, but at the same time, increased the tension of a balanced management across the general vis-à-vis the localized characteristics of the technological solution.

Notes

1 Other applications include aerospace and aircraft, agriculture control, computing equipment, diagnostic and monitoring, electronic testing equipment, energy management, fluid management, identification equipment, lighting and wiring devices, medical and health equipment, the military and defense industry, office equipment, robotics, security, sports and gaming, and telecommunications. By the beginning of 2000, over three thousand companies had purchased LonWorks development tools, and more than five thousand products incorporating LonWorks technology had been brought to market. According to one estimate, total revenue from the LonWorks market in 2000 was around US $1.5 billion and Echelon has been a public company listed in NASDAQ since August 1998.

2 Diffusion studies have attracted the attention of social scientists from different perspectives. For wide literature surveys, see Dosi (1991), Geroski (2000), Nelson *et al.* (2004), and Hall (2005 A).

3 On the concept of technical imbalance, see Rosenberg (1982).

4 It could be invasive and costly to install closed, centralized control systems because of the physical task of installing large amounts of wire in conduits to connect each component to one or more central controllers. On the other hand, if a system incorporates control systems from more than one OEM, the system integration process is very costly and time-consuming for connecting systems not designed to operate together.

5 Potentially, the convergence of devices in a global communication network, such as the Internet, could generate important savings and new services, because the devices could be controlled remotely by end-users and other devices programmed for that task.

6 These standards include Profibus launched in 1989 and Interbus-S in 1993 for process control, DeviceNet in 1994 for manufacturing control, BACnet in 1994 and Batibus in 1989 for building automation, Konnex in 2002 for home automation, CAN in 1989 for transportation systems, and UCA in 1999 for equipment in utilities. This information has been elaborated by the author from different Internet sources.

7 Controlling a remote device in the command-based architecture consists of sending a command message by the controller to the actuator, saying what that device has to execute. Hence, the whole system is driven by the number of commands that travel through it. When the system is made up of a large number of nodes of different types, many commands are required and problems of system management and reliability may arise, because one single tiny error can make the whole system fail.

8 On the concept of unit operation, see Rosenberg (1998).

9 At that time, commercially there were two FieldBus architecture competitors to LonWorks: CANbus and Profibus launched by two OEMs in 1989, respectively Robert Bosch in the automobile industry and Siemens in industrial applications (Batibus, later changed to EIBA, was at a very early stage).

10 In later years, Konnex Association launched in year 1999 and Zigbee Alliance in 2001 have claimed similar, but only in building automation and home automation.

11 It is worth remembering that the sum is the Herfindahl index.

12 This sampling strategy allows also to mitigate potential statistical biases in the computation of the generality index (Hall 2005 B).

13 The authors of the Echelon's business plan listed a dozen current and potential application sectors.

14 See sources as Echelon (1990), Business Week (1990), and Financial Times (1990).

15 Together with Honeywell, they controlled more than half of the market revenues in building automation at the beginning of '90s.
16 On the industrial relationship between Microsoft, IBM, and other computer producers during the '80s, see Hagedoorn *et al.* (2001).
17 Personal communication to the author by K. Oshman, CEO of Echelon (1990).
18 Author's estimates on different sources.
19 Source: www.lonmark.org
20 It is difficult to give an accurate number of the BACnet nodes installed. One possible estimate is one million, given by some technical press at that time. However, this estimate was considered very optimistic in some interviews that I did. They claimed that LonWorks nodes and Bacnet nodes were mixed in the same installation, and this could have led to this optimistic estimate.
21 Source: Energy User News (1998).
22 Source: Interview with MT, vice president of Echelon (1990).
23 Source: Interview with MT, vice president of Echelon (1990).
24 Source: Interview with MT, Manager of Business Environment Solutions, Olivetti Solutions spa, (1999).
25 Source: Interview with AP, vice-president of Enel (2001).
26 Source: Interview with AP, vice-president of Enel (2001).
27 Similarly, the transportation automation market experienced the convergence to an industry specific technology called CAN launched by Robert Bosch Gmbh.
28 Many users confirmed this during the interviews that I carried out. A comprehensive list of these interviews is available on request.
29 See footnote 25
30 In diffusion of the electric motor between 1880 and 1930, a similar pattern was argued by Goldfarb (2005).
31 A full list of sources is available on request from the author.

References

Arora A. 1996. "Contracting for Tacit Knowledge: The Provision of Technical Services in Technology Licensing Contracts." *J Dev Econ* 50(2):233–256.
Arora A., A. Fosfuri, A. Gambardella 2001. *Markets for Technology: The Economics of Innovation and Corporate Strategy.* Cambridge (MA): MIT Press.
Arora A., A. Gambardella 1994. "The Changing Technology of Technical Change: General and Abstract Knowledge and the Division of Innovative Labour." *Res Pol* 23:523–532.
Arora A., A. Gambardella 2001. "Specialized Technology Suppliers, International Spillovers and Investment: Evidence from the Chemical Industry." *J Dev Econ* 65(1):31–54.
Arrow K. J. 1962. "Economic Welfare and the Allocation of Resources for Innovation." In *The Rate and Direction of Inventive Activity*, edited by R. Nelson, 609–626, Princeton (NJ): Princeton University Press.
Arrow K. J. 1975. "Vertical Integration and Communication." *Bell J Econ* 6:173–183.
Bresnahan T. 2010. "General Purpose Technologies." In the *Handbook of the Economics of Innovation*, edited by B. H. Hall, N. Rosenberg, 1074–2091, Amsterdam: Elsevier, Kindle edition.
Bresnahan T., A. Gambardella 1998. "The Division of Inventive Labor and the Extent of the Market." In *General-Purpose Technologies and Economic Growth*, edited by E. Helpman, 253–281, Cambridge (MA): MIT Press.

Bresnahan T., S. Greenstein 1996. "Technical Progress and Co-Invention in Computing and in the Uses of Computers." *Brookings Pap Econ Act Microecon* 1996:1–83.

Bresnahan T., F. Malerba 1997. "Industrial Dynamics and the Evolution of Firms' and Nations' Competitive Capabilities in the World Computer Industry." Accessed December 10, 2014, http://www.stanford.edu/~tbres/research/ccc7.pdf

Bresnahan T., M. Trajtenberg 1995. "General Purpose Technologies. Engines of Growth?" *J Economet* 65(1):83–108.

Business Week 1990. "Is This the Chip That Will Launch a Thousand Gizmos?" December 10.

Cesaroni F. 2004. "Technological Outsourcing and Product Diversification: Do Markets for Technology Affect Firms' Strategies?" *Res Pol* 33(10):1547–1564.

David P. A. 1990. "The Dynamo and the Computer: An Historical Perspective on the Modern Productivity Paradox." *Am Econ Rev* 80(2):355–361.

Dosi G. 1991. "The Research on Innovation Diffusion: An Assessment." In *Diffusion of Technologies and Social Behaviour*, edited by N. Nakicenovic, A. Grubler, 179–208, New York: Springer-Verlag.

Echelon Corporation 1990. *The Day Everything Began to Work Together*. December 5, San Jose: Echelon's Launch Video.

Energy User News 1998. "Air Conditioning, Heating, and Refrigerating Exposition Yields Improved Building System Wares." *Energy User News* 23(3):34.

Financial Times 1990. "Talking Point for Machines." December 14.

Gambardella A. 2002. "Successes and Failures in the Markets for Technology." *Oxford Rev Econ Pol* 18(1):52–62.

Gambardella A., A. McGahan 2010. "Business-Model Innovation: General Purpose Technologies and Their Implications for Industry Structure." *Long Range Plan* 43:262–71.

Gandal N. 2006. "Network Effects Empirical Studies." In *The New Palgrave Dictionary of Economics*, 2nd edition, edited by L. Blume, S. Durlauf, Basingstoke: Palgrave Macmillan. doi:10.1057/9780230226203.1175

Geroski P. A. 2000. "Models of Technology Diffusion." *Res Pol* 29(4–5):603–625.

Giarratana M. 2004. "The Birth of a New Industry: Entry by Start-Ups and the Drivers of Firm Growth. The Case of Encryption Software." *Res Pol* 35(2):787–806.

Goldfarb B. 2005. "Diffusion of General-Purpose Technologies: Understanding Patterns in the Electrification of US Manufacturing, 1880–1930." *Ind Corp Change* 14(5):745–773.

Hagedoorn J., E. Carayannis, A. Jeffrey 2001. "Strange Bedfellows in the Personal Computer Industry: Technology Alliances between IBM and Apple." *Res Pol* 30(5):837–849.

Hall B. H. 2005 A. "Innovation and Diffusion." In *The Oxford Handbook of Innovation*, edited by J. Fagerberg, D. C. Mowery, R. R. Nelson, 459–486, New York: Oxford University Press.

Hall B. H. 2005 B. "A Note on the Bias in the Herfindahl Based on Count Data." *Rev Econ Ind* 110:149–156.

Hall B., M. Trajtenberg 2004. "Uncovering GPTs with Patent Data". NBER Working Paper No. 10901, National Bureau of Economic Research, Inc. Cambridge (MA).

Hall B., R. H. Ziedonis 2001. "The Patent Paradox Revisited: An Empirical Study of Patenting in the U.S. Semiconductor Industry, 1979–1995." *RAND J Econ* 32(1):101–128.

Katz M. L., C. Shapiro 1994. "Systems Competition and Network Effects." *J Econ Perspect* 77:93–115.

Khazam J., D. Mowery 1994. "The Commercialization of RISC: Strategies for the Creation of Dominant Designs." *Res Pol* 23(2):89–112.

LIA 1995. *Lonworks Independent Association Statute*. San Jose (CA): LonMark.

Lipsey R., C. Bekar, K. Carlaw 1998. "General Purpose Technologies: What Requires Explanation." In *General Purpose Technologies and Economic Growth*, edited by E. Helpman, 15–54, Cambridge (MA): MIT Press.

Maine E., Garsney, E. 2006. "Commercializing Generic Technology: The Case of Advanced Materials Ventures." *Res Pol* 35(3):375–393.

Nelson R. R., A. Peterhansl, B. Sampat 2004. "Why and How Innovations Get Adopted: A Tale of Four Models." *Ind Corp Change* 13(5):679–699.

Oshman K. 2005. Personal interview with the Author." San Jose (CA).

Rosenberg N. 1976. "Technological Change in the Machine Tool Industry, 1840–1910." In *Perspectives in Technology*, edited by N. Rosenberg, 9–31, Cambridge: Cambridge University Press.

Rosenberg N. 1982. *Inside the Black Box*. Cambridge: Cambridge University Press.

Rosenberg N. 1996. "Uncertainty and Technological Change." In *Technology and Economic Growth*, edited by J. Fuhrer, J. Little, 91–125, Boston (MA): Federal Reserve Bank of Boston.

Rosenberg N. 1998. "Chemical Engineering as a General Purpose Technology." In *General Purpose Technologies and Economic Growth*, edited by E. Helpman, 167–192, Cambridge (MA): MIT Press.

Rosenberg N., M. Trajtenberg 2004. "A General Purpose Technology at Work: The Corliss Steam Engine in the Late 19th Century U.S." *J Econ Hist* 64(1):61–99.

Stigler G. J. 1951. "The Division of Labour Is Limited by the Extent of the Market." *The J Pol Econ* 59(3):185–193.

Teece D. 1988. "Technological Change and the Nature of the Firms." In *Technological Change and Economic Theory*, edited by G. Dosi, C. Freeman, R. R. Nelson, G. Silverberg, L. L. G. Soete, 256–281, London: Pinter.

Part III
The Geographic Dimension of Patent Valuation

6 The Determinants of the Localization of Knowledge Spillovers

Grid Thoma

6.1 Introduction

Over the past decade or so, the regional dimension of innovation policies has propelled a growing level of attention (Bresnahan and Gambardella 2004), and notions such as cluster, learning region, *pole de compétitivité*, and industrial district have commenced to constitute a relevant geographical unit of analysis for policy interventions in most developed economies. Whereas the importance of local conditions for regional growth has been already articulated by the literature on the so-called *marshallian* economies, the recent debate has increasingly stressed the critical role for policy of the location of R&D investments, and at the same it has claimed that the geographical concentration of innovative activities is favourable to their efficiency (for a survey see Feldman and Kogler 2010).

A crucial aspect why localization matters for innovation is the existence of knowledge spillovers (Porter 1998). The production and use of knowledge often demand actors involved in the process to establish personal and repeated interactions, which are hampered by distance (Saxenian 1994). Local conditions affect the understanding and transfer of knowledge also because a relevant component of knowledge is tacit (Almeida and Kogut 1999). Knowledge generation could involve university-industry linkages, which are often triggered by the local labour market or entrepreneurship (Zucker et al. 1998; Feldman and Audretsch 1999). Furthermore, indivisibilities in the physical access to research equipment (Justman and Teubal 1995), financing of R&D projects (Sorenson and Stuart 2003), spin-offs of innovative projects (Klepper and Sleeper 2005), and demand side factors (Agrawal and Cockburn 2003) matter as well to unfolding knowledge spillovers.

Previous econometric literature has considered patent citations as a paper trail of knowledge spillovers and has brought extensive evidences regarding their localization. Jaffe et al. (1993) have shown that patent references to US-invented patents are increasingly more localized with respect to the country level, internal state border, or metropolitan area. For other countries, the localization of knowledge spillovers at the national level has been found to be more relevant in the UK and France than in the United States, Japan, or Germany (Jaffe and Trajtenberg 1999). Other scholars have extended this approach by considering the source where citations originate from: examiner-added citations vis-à-vis inventor-added ones, or self-citations by the same patentee, inventor, or examiner (Alcacer and Gittelman 2006; Thompson 2006). In particular, they have claimed that fine-grained citation based measures of knowledge spillovers are characterised by even more remarkable patterns of localization as compared to patent citations in general.

However, these studies have assimilated geographical spatial distance in the same vein of territorial units. With the exception of few works, the analysis regarding to what extent territorial borders can be expression of more general conditions than pure distance effects has been overlooked by previous literature (Singh and Marx 2013). Furthermore, the analysis of the determinants of the territorial border effect and its implications for regional policies is still in its infancy (Belenzon and Schankerman 2013). This study aims to fill this gap by analysing first how geographic spatial distance and territorial borders affect the localization of knowledge spillovers in North American and European regions, and then how the strength of the national intellectual property legislation mediates the impact of border effect on knowledge spillovers.

In this task I have developed a novel dataset by integrating and harmonizing information from various sources. First, the dataset comprehends all patent applications filed at the European Patent Office (EPO) and those granted by the United States Patent and Trademark Offices (USPTO) during the period 1990–2009 and relative priority and citation links. Second, the addresses of inventor(s) listed in a patent document have been regionalized with respect to territorial units of level two (TL2) and three (TL3). Third, I completed the dataset with information on the spatial location of borders of territorial units and neighbouring regions for every focal territorial unit. Fourth, the addresses have been linked with geographic coordinates (longitudes and latitudes), which allow to compute the spatial distance existing across two given locations.

There are several new findings associated with the study presented in this chapter. Beforehand the geographical distance exerts a negative impact on knowledge spillovers largely within 150–250 km. Territorial unit borders account for an additional significant variability of the localization of knowledge spillovers. Compared to a foreign-invented patent, the probability of citing a domestically invented one is about 6.4 percentage points higher in Europe and 2.8 points in North America. In both geographical contexts, being part of the same TL3 region increases the likelihood of citation with about one-tenth, that is 20 percent of mean citation rate. Similarly, neighbouring TL3 regions matter for citation probability with at least the same impact of being part of the same TL2 region. Last but not least, I show for the first time that the strength of the national legislation on patent protection mediates positively the country border effect, and it constitutes one-fifth of the impact of the border effect for the European regions and one-third for the North American ones. The results hold after performing several robustness checks, such as focusing on more restrictive measures of knowledge spillovers (e.g., inventor-added citations) and using multiple proxies of the strength of patent protection (Ginarte and Park 1997; Park 2008; Papageorgiadis et al. 2014).

The chapter proceeds as follows. Section 6.2 summarizes the previous literature and advances the testable hypotheses. The sampling methodology is discussed in section 6.3, and the bibliographic sources constituting the dataset are described in section 6.4. The measurement approach of the strength of national legislation on patent protection is reviewed in Section 6.5, whilst Section 6.6 presents the econometric specification and the definition of the variables. The results and final discussion section concludes the chapter.

6.2 Theoretical Background

Previous econometric studies have claimed that knowledge spillovers are geographically bounded. Jaffe et al. (1993) report that US inventors are 1.1 times more likely than the counterfactual situation to cite domestic inventors, two times more likely to cite inventors coming from the same state, and four times more likely to cite those resident in the same metropolitan area. The localization patterns of patent citations at the national level vis-à-vis foreign countries has been shown to be more severe in the UK and France then in the United States, Japan, and Germany (Jaffe and Trajtenberg 1999). Bottazzi and Peri (2003) analyse the localization of knowledge spillovers relying on R&D investments and patent counts instead of citation links. They find there is a small significant influence of distance solely with respect to a 300 km range from the focal region. Carlino et al. (2012) show that the concentration of R&D labs takes place at very small ranges (1/4 of a mile).[1] For patent citations, localization exists not solely between regions but also within a given location: doubling the distance from the core towards the periphery of a region generates a more than proportional decay in the concentration of patent citations.

The source where patent citations originate from can gauge an interesting twist with respect to localization patterns. Thompson (2006) claims that inventor-added citations—as compared to those referenced by the patent reviewer during examination—are more representative to be a true knowledge spillover, because examiners learn about prior art through internal knowledge repositories at the patent office. He finds that inventor citations are one-fifth more likely than examiner citations to match the country of origin of the citing patent and one-third more likely to show a match on the same US state or metropolitan area. By the same token, Alcacer and Gittelman (2006) show that not only examiner citations are less bounded from a geographical point of view, but examiners have a higher propensity to cite the same and more recent prior art across different citing patents. Criscuolo and Verspagen (2008) argue that inventor citations constitute the lion's share of the self-citations, that is citations to patents owned by the same patentee, and the negative effect of distance on self-citations is smaller than other patents on average. They find that large part of the effect of distance on localization of knowledge spillovers takes place within 250 km, and the additional effect of longer distances is relatively small.

According to these studies, knowledge spillovers tend to cluster in the same geographic area because the knowledge production and transfer often requires personal contacts, either of an informal, random, and repeated nature (Saxenian 1994; Moore and Davis 2004), which are typically slacked by distance. Often the outcome of the knowledge generation process is tacit, and thus it is intrinsically related to the local dimension.[2] In fact, inventors can save time on transportation and work more efficiently when they are geographically close. Ellison and Glaser (1997, 1999) devised an agglomeration index across industries to demonstrate that firms and employment are spatially concentrated at a higher degree than the random distribution. This argument applies even more remarkably to innovative activities as compared to firms and employment (Ejermo 2009), especially in industries where the fast generation of new knowledge plays an important role, such as computers, semiconductors, pharmaceuticals, and biotechnology (see also Audretsch and Feldman 2003).

Other studies have claimed the benefits of geographical agglomeration for business R&D activities with respect to university-industry linkages. Collaborations traced by scientific copublications are more likely to take place within the same regional context, country, or linguistic area (Hoekman et al. 2010). Also local labour market conditions matter to enable knowledge spillovers from universities to business firms (Jaffe 1989). In fact, Belenzon and Schankerman (2013) found that large part of the negative impact of geographical distance on knowledge spillover from university inventions is nonlinear and takes place in large extent within 150 miles. Furthermore, the location of science-based start-up firms is shown to correlate with the presence of star-scientists from a regional university (Zucker et al. 1998). Further, knowledge created in university laboratories can spill over to fuel directly the generation of commercial innovations by local firms (Feldman and Audretsch 1999).

Beyond knowledge spillovers, geographical distance also affects several factors that in turn impact the local dimension of innovative activities. First, high-skilled employment tends to settle in areas more attractive for their expertise (Almeida and Kogut 1999). Second, certain innovative activities demand physical access to specific local infrastructures (Justman and Teubal 1995). Third, geography also impacts the financing of R&D projects because the likelihood that a firm obtains funding from a venture capitalist decreases with distance (Sorenson and Stuart 2003). Furthermore, the localization of innovative activities is mediated by the types of firm present in the regional context. Klepper and Sleeper (2005) argued that spinoffs tend to colocate with their parent firms, whereas Agrawal and Cockburn (2003) showed that regions including a large and dominant firm benefit more from academic research conducted by local universities. In conclusion, it is worth mentioning that the functioning of these mechanisms is not mutually exclusive, and typically regions with the highest innovative output are characterised by a copresence of different reinforcing factors at work (Agrawal et al. 2012).

Based on these considerations, the following ceteris paribus testable hypotheses are posited:

> *Hypothesis 1(a): Geographical distance affects negatively the localization of knowledge spillovers.*
> *Hypothesis 1(b): Geographical distance exerts a nonlinear negative impact on the localization of knowledge spillovers.*

Whereas the previous literature has assimilated geographical spatial distance in the same vein of territorial units, later other studies have claimed that territorial borders can be expression of more general conditions than pure distance effects. For example, Maurseth and Verspagen (2002) have shown the negative impact of geography on citation links across European regions by analysing the spatial distance across the centroid location of TL2 units. At the same time they document that patents from inventors who are resident in the same country have a higher likelihood to cite each other. Peri (2005) adopts a similar approach based on a count data model of aggregated patterns of citation links, when he analyses a panel of regions not solely in the European context but also in the United States. This study has also the merit to take into the account spatial information on regional borders and neighbouring territorial units. Peri (2005) finds that the border effect of territorial units (i.e., same region, neighbouring region to the focal one, and same country) affect significantly the localization of knowledge spillovers above and beyond geographic distance. Both these studies report several relevant mediating factors of the negative effect of geography, such as using the same language and sharing a similar technological specialization at the regional level.[3]

In order to scrutinize more thoroughly the simultaneous effect of distance and borders on knowledge spillovers, some recent studies have adopted as a unit of analysis single inventions relying on Jaffe et al. (1993)'s methodology (see next section for further discussion). For instance, Agrawal et al. (2008) elaborate a knowledge flow production function to study not only the impact of geographic distance and territorial borders but also the mediating role of social proximity, as measured by coethnicity of inventors who are part of the same community. They confirm that both sources of proximity have a significant effect on the localization of knowledge spillovers. In particular, they show that the effect of coethnicity is smaller when a fine-grained measure of geography is considered (such as spatial distance), as compared to the case of measuring localization by the mean of territorial units. This evidence does not contradict the assumption that territorial borders and geographical distance represent different dimensions of the impact of geography on the localization of knowledge spillovers.

A simultaneous and full-fledged analysis of the impact on knowledge spillovers of both distance and territorial borders is reported by Singh and Marx (2013). In this study geographical distance is computed as geodesic spatial measure across cities, whilst the border effect is given by being part of the same country, state, and metropolitan area level with respect to the US context.[4] Singh and Marx (2013) do find that borders of the territorial units account for an additional variability of knowledge spillovers above and beyond the geographical distance effect. They demonstrate that the inclusion of geodesic spatial distance in the econometric model does not flaw the coefficients of national or state borders but only those of metropolitan areas, and hence they conclude on the importance of territorial level factors for the geography of innovation, as expression of broader linguistic, cultural, administrative, and economic differences across countries. It is noteworthy that they show the border effect of the territorial units is significantly increasing over time with respect to national borders but slacking for those borders at the level of states and metropolitan areas.

A novel attempt to analyse the determinants of the border effect at the state level in the United States is constituted by Belenzon and Schankerman (2013). This study provides an interesting advancement because it relies on very accurate measures of geographical distance based on the individual addresses of inventors.[5] Although their focus is given by knowledge spillovers solely from university-owned inventions, the results could be considered valid also from other inventions. Indeed, university patents are closer to science and more general and distant from the commercialization stage (Henderson et al. 1998); thus, hypothetically the observed localized patterns of knowledge spillovers from university patents should be statistically dominated by those generated from other patents.

Belenzon and Schankerman (2013) find that that the state border effect impacts the localization of citations with about 10 percent after having conditioned for geographical distance. As determinants of the state border effect they analyse several variables regarding the territorial local conditions—such as education in science and technology subjects of the regional employment, regulation of the local labour market, policy involvement of universities in regional development, and others. Furthermore, they find that knowledge spillovers are remarkably more localized in those states where the labour market is regulated by the mean of legislations that make more difficult to change jobs from one employer to another (the so-called noncompete agreements).[6] They conclude on the importance of the local conditions as mediators of the state border effect.

Thus, on the basis of these arguments the following ceteris paribus testable hypotheses are advanced:

Hypothesis 2 (a): Territorial borders impact positively the localization of knowledge spillovers above and beyond the effect of geographical distance.

Hypothesis 2 (b): National level conditions mediate positively the impact of territorial borders on the localization of knowledge spillovers.

6.3 Methods

The literature on the geography of innovation has commenced—with the study by Jaffe, Henderson, and Trajtenberg (JHT) (1993)—to rely on patent references for gauging potential knowledge spillovers between spatially located individuals or organizations: If patent B references patent A as previous prior art, the knowledge pool traced in the cited patent A can be assumed to have 'spilled over' to the inventor of the citing patent B. JHT's approach has been widely proposed in many economic and managerial studies, and it is essentially based on a random choice sample setting of cited-citing pairs of patents.[7]

This approach can be typically articulated in a two-stage procedure. In the first stage, the treatment group is built up of pairs of cited-citing patents where a citation actually occurred. Subsequently, a set of control pairs is chosen where the referring patent from the initial cited-citing pair has been replaced by a 'matched' non-citing set of patents. The matching of the control sample of non-citing patents is performed over the same year and technology class of the actually citing ones. By comparing the characteristics of the treatment group with the control group—such as the location of inventors and their relative geographical distance—it is possible to make inferences about whether knowledge spillovers are a localized phenomenon or not.

One of the crucial assumptions of the JHT's approach is that the matching criteria are independent of the preexisting spatial distribution of the economic and innovative activities. If this assumption is violated, then the potential localization of knowledge spillovers can be result of a spurious correlation with the uneven distribution of innovation. Building on this argument, Thompson and Fox-Keene (2005) claimed that the observed localization patterns are flawed when a more fine-grained classification of patents is taken into the account. Belenzon and Schankerman (2013) propose a generalized framework of JHT's approach controlling for several dimensions of the geographical distribution of innovative activities and technology aggregations, and they still find that knowledge spillovers are a significantly localized phenomenon.

Another drawback is given by the fact that citations show up over a very long period of time. A pharmaceutical patent receives 44.6 percent of the lifetime citations within the first decade after filing and 76.1 percent at end of the statutory term (twenty years), whereas an invention in electronics receives 59.4 percent and 86.8 percent of the lifetime citations respectively (Hall et al. 2001). Several citations could manifest many years after the lapse of the patent or the expiration of its statutory term. In order to predict the accumulation of citations over time Hall et al. (2005) propose a semistructural model to estimate the probability of the lifetime citations of patents according to different technological contexts, vintages of citations, timing of the citing patent, and the duration of the citation lag. This model takes into the account also the technological obsolescence due to the fact newer patents are more attractive and hence generate more citations. Mehta et al. (2010) propose more accurate measurements of technological vintages based on the grant publication date of the cited patent.

This study follows Belenzon and Schankerman (2013)'s approach for the construction of the control group of cited-non-citing patents, which consists on the replacement of the citing document with a patent that has been filed in the same IPC 4 digit class and in the same application or priority year as the originally citing patent. Second, the treatment and control groups consider all those citing and nonciting matched patents up to ten years from the cited document (Singh and Marx 2013). Third, the regression analysis controls for the technological match of the cited-nonciting pairs in a more detailed patent class than that used as matching criterion (i.e., IPC 6 digit class). Fourth, self-citations' pairs—that is, citations that take place among patents owned by the same patentee—have been excluded in order not to confound the localized knowledge spillovers with innovation activities internalized within the boundaries of a firm. In the same vein, a cited-citing pairs filed through the same law firm representative have been disregarded because even in this case it is plausible to assume that those references are added by the law firm and not by the inventor, and therefore they constitute solely an ex-post knowledge link across two inventions. Last, the treatment and the control groups exclude patents that do not involve a business patentee at all (i.e., they are owned by sole inventors, universities, government, hospitals, and other private nonprofit organizations) (OECD 2002).

The context is constituted by the population of the patenting regions from Europe and North America from 1990 to 2009. The European panel focuses on the citation pairs from the EPO that involve at least one inventor who is resident in one of the EU countries, Norway, or Switzerland. Symmetrically, the North American panel considers the citation pairs from the USPTO that have at least one inventor originating from Canada, Mexico, and the United States. Limiting the analysis only on these countries both on the citing and cited side does not appear to be a serious limitation of this kind. For example, about 68.9 percent of the citations to European patents involve at least one European inventor (PatStat 2015). Hence, for the European countries it could be argued that a similarly built panel captures large part of the spillovers generated from European patents. Evidences for the North American countries are even more asymmetric than for the European context.[8]

There are other two broader arguments for having separated and ad-hoc matched panels for Europe and North America. On the one hand, prior art searching and citation practices can differ across respective patent offices. At the USPTO inventors should disclose all potentially known previous prior-art when they file a patent application (so-called duty-of-candor rule), whereas at the EPO it is the examiner who typically provides the citations listed in the patent document. On the other hand, because the matching criteria of JHT's approach are typically time and technology, it is highly relevant to limit the potential spurious correlation originating from locations that are distant from a geographical point of view, but at the same time they are characterised also by a significant diversity of the preexisting spatial distribution of the economic and innovative activities (for a discussion see Thompson and Fox-Keene 2005).

6.4 Dataset

The focus of the econometric analysis is represented by all cited patents over the period 1990–2009 from the EPO and USPTO systems respectively for inventors located in Europe and North America. Because until recently the US patents were published solely in the case of grant, only granted patents have been analysed for the USPTO, whilst for the EPO the analysis has been extended also to patent applications. I combined several data repositories in order to build up the dataset. Beforehand the EPO Worldwide Patent Statistical Database (PatStat April 2015) has provided information about the filing dates, patent families, addresses of the inventors, information about the patentee name and country, and technological classes assigned to a patent during examination. The citation records extracted from PatStat have been aggregated and consolidated at the patent family level using the INPADOC family definition, which is more suitable for international comparisons.[9] Indeed, the INPADOC definition is broad enough to encompass a more homogeneous unit of invention across different offices, and within patents filed at same office it includes also variations originating from fractional applications.[10] Contrary to the other patent family definitions (e.g., DOCDB) no ad-hoc, expert knowledge is required for the identification of an INPADOC family.[11]

The inventor addresses from PatStat have been regionalized relying on city names and/or postal code numbers when available with the mean of a semiautomatic STATA procedure. The regionalisation has regarded both the secondary territorial level and also the tertiary one (namely TL2 and TL3). Furthermore, I have linked the inventor address with information on the neighbouring territorial units.[12] The neighbour regions are represented not only by those regions that are part of the same higher level of aggregation (TL2) of the focal one, but also by those TL3 regions originating from a different TL2 region of the same nation or a different country of origin at all.[13]

Appendix 6.1 depicts the structure of the territorial units by country. The TL2 regions are constituted by 12 Canadian provinces, 50 US federal states and the Columbia District, 32 states in Mexico, and 247 regions in

EU countries, Norway, and Switzerland.[14] For the UK, I relied on the primary territorial level aggregation instead of the secondary one, because information on regional characteristics on structural business statistics is not available for the latter (see below). On the other hand, the TL3 regional units are made up of 179 BEA Economic Areas in the US and 1,274 regions in Europe, such as French departments, German districts, and Italian and Spanish provinces. There are visibly more TL3 regional units for Mexico and Canada than for the US, although a large number of those regions are not relevant in terms of patenting activity.

Third, inventor addresses were supplemented with information on geographic coordinates (longitudes and latitudes) of a given location constituted by the city name or postal code number.[15] Using the geodesic algorithm, I measured the spatial distance existing between two given locations.[16] This algorithm disregards real transportation costs of travelling among those locations, which can change over time and vary from one country to another. Nevertheless, because the outcome of the geodesic algorithm is time and country invariant, I think that it is more suitable for international comparisons and more objective when the focal dataset covers long time intervals.

The fourth task has been the completion of the dataset with information on structural business statistics at the TL2 regional units from the OECD statistical database (dotstat.oecd.org), because a more complete coverage of the timeseries is available at this territorial level than for the TL3 regional units. In case of a single missing observation across consecutive years, I interpolated the time series using the geometric mean method. Further, relying on Wikipedia web searches the dataset has been extended to information on linguistic affinities at regional level.

6.5 The Strength of Patent Protection

One of the building blocks of the proposed theoretical background is constituted by the fact that the national level conditions mediate the impact of territorial borders on the local dimension of knowledge spillovers. In this context, the strength of national legislation on patent protection is likely to play a quintessential role in determining the level of innovativeness of a country (Branstetter et al. 2006). Because of the disclosing function of the patent system, a stronger patent protection could affect the localization of knowledge spillovers at the national level as well. When the national patent legislation is tightened, there is a larger incentive to patent an invention vis-à-vis the decision to protect it with other formal and informal mechanisms: the fact that the patent system publishes the patent filings largely even before grant yields a positive effect on knowledge cumulativeness at the national level of subsequent inventions. Although the knowledge disclosed by patents can be accessed anywhere independently of the location, its effective use could require additional knowledge, which is often tacit and thus it does depend on the local dimension (Almeida and Kogut 1999).

Previous empirical literature has seen the construction of indices regarding the heterogeneity of the book-law aspects of the national legislations on patent protection. The widely used index of 'patent strength' by Ginarte and Park (1997)—hereafter also GP index—is built according to five dimensions of a national legislation: extent of coverage of patentability, membership in international patent agreements, provisions for loss of protection, enforcement mechanisms, and duration of protection. This index has been employed in several studies investigating foreign direct investment, interfirm alliances, patent protection on exporting activity, economic growth, R&D internationalization, and others (for survey see Park and Lippoldt 2014). The measurement of the GP index has been broadened subsequently in terms of number of countries (Park 1999), and the time series has been extended after year 2000 (Park 2008).

More recently, this approach has been enhanced by Papageorgiadis, Cross, and Alexiou (2014)—hereafter also PCA index—who added aspects of the transaction costs theory of the firm regarding servicing, monitoring, and protection activities of patents. Servicing costs concern the replicability of the patent asset meant in the broadest sense, which can arise from internal and external activities of the firm. Firms face monitoring costs when they conduct scanning activities to limit product infringement in the market. Protection costs are related to patent enforceability and related procedural aspects of the judicial system. The PCA index is shown to correlate significantly with the GDP pro-capite of a nation at a greater extent than the GP index.

The econometric analysis in this study considers firstly the GP index, which covers the complete time frame considered from 1990 to 2009 and the large majority of the sample countries. As a robustness check I analyse the PCA index in lieu of the GP index solely for the European panel from 1998 to 2009, because of the more limited coverage of the PCA index.

6.6 Econometric Specification

The empirical approach is similar to Agrawal et al. (2008) and Belenzon and Schankerman (2013), who develop an econometric model based on the knowledge flow production function. The unit of analysis is a cited-citing patent pair ij, with a cited patent i having the priority year over the period 1990–2009, and a citing patent j observed up to ten years after i. The end of the sample of cited patents is set to year 2014, in order to have a sufficient time window for potential citations to manifest. Thus, the modified production function of the probability of a knowledge flow K_{ij} from i to j reads as the following:

$$K_{ij} = \alpha_1 D_{ij} + \alpha_2 T_{ij} + \alpha_3 N_i + \alpha_4 N_i B_{ij} + \alpha_5 R_i + \alpha_6 X_{ij} + \varepsilon_{ij} \tag{1}$$

Where D_{ij} includes measures of the relative geographic distance between the cited-citing patent pair ij; T_{ij} are co-location variables of i and j in the same territorial unit being that a region, neighbouring region, or country level (including the border effect, that is T_{ij} contains B_{ij}); N_i are national level conditions, namely the strength of patent protection that affects knowledge flow from the cited patent i and N_iB_{ij} is the interactions with the border effect B_{ij}; in turn R_i regards regional level conditions that influence knowledge flow from patent i (i.e., structural and demographic characteristics defined at the regional level and others); X_{ij} represents a set of controls which are specified at the cited patent level or cited-citing pair. The detailed list of the variables and a short description of the measurement methodology are depicted in Box 6.1., whereas Appendix 6.2 presents the sample means and the standard deviations.

Box 6.1   Variables included in the regression analysis

Variable Name	Variable Description
Geographic distance and territorial variables	
Geographic distance dummies	A set of nine binary variables that take the positive outcome if the minimal geodesic spatial distance among inventors of a cited-citing pair of patents is in the range 0–25 km, 25–50 km, 50–100 km, 100–150 km, 150–250 km, 250–500 km, 500–1000 km, 1000–1500 km, and more than 1500 km. The left-out category in the regression analysis is the range 0–25 km.
Intra—TL3 region citation	A binary variable that assumes the positive outcome when at least one inventor of a cited-citing pair is from the same TL3 region.
Neighbour TL3 citation—Same country	A binary variable that assumes the positive outcome when at least one inventor of a cited-citing pair is from a neighbouring TL3 region, and none of the other inventors originates from the focal TL3 region.
Neighbour TL3 citation— Foreign country	A binary variable that assumes the positive outcome, when at least one inventor of a cited-citing pair is from a neighbouring TL3 region of a different country, and all other inventors are from more distant regions.
Intra—TL2 region citation	A binary variable that assumes the positive outcome when at least one inventor of a cited-citing pair is from the same TL2 region.
Within country citation— Border Effect	A binary variable that assumes the positive outcome, when at least one inventor of a cited-citing pair originates from the same country.
International citation— Different country	A binary variable that assumes the positive outcome when all the inventors of a cited-citing pair are from a different country with the exception of a foreign neighbouring region (see above). This is the left-out category in the regression analysis.

National and regional level conditions

GP index	The patent protection index proposed by Ginarte and Park (1997) and Park (2008) matched at the inventor's country of residence and application or priority year of the cited patent. In case of multiple inventors average values are taken. The index has been standardized in the range 0 to 1.
PCA index	The patent protection index proposed by Papageorgiadis et al. (2014) matched at the inventor's country of residence and application or priority year of the cited patent. In case of multiple inventors, average values are taken. The index has been standardized in the range 0 to 1.
Linguistic affinity	A binary variable that assumes the positive outcome, when at least one inventor of a cited-citing pair makes usage of the same language.
GDP per capita	Annual GDP in PPP US dollars per inhabitant for a TL2 region (source the OECD stats database 2013).
Population density	Inhabitants per square kilometre for a TL2 region (source the OECD stats database 2013).
High-tech employment	Percentage of high-tech employment with respect to total annual employment for a TL2 region (source the OECD stats database 2013).

Control variables

Common inventor	A binary variable that assumes the positive outcome when there is a common coinventor in the cited and citing patent (Agrawal et al. 2006).
Nonbusiness organization	A binary variable that takes the positive outcome if the cited patent involves a copatenting with a nonbusiness organization or sole inventor(s).
Small patenting firm	A binary variable that attributes the positive outcome when all the patenting firms have less than five hundred employees. (This information is available only for the North American panel).
Match on 6 digit IPC	A binary variable that assumes the positive outcome if the patents of a cited-citing pair are classified by the examiner in the same 6 digit IPC class.
Time dummies	Binary variables (15) for every year of the cited patents (1990–2014).
Citation lag dummies	Binary variables (10) for every citing year of the focal cited patent.

The main identification assumption of the proposed econometric specification (1) is that the focal variables of interest such as geographic distance and the territorial border dummies are not correlated with the error term ε_{ij}. However, the disturbance ε_{ij} is allowed to be correlated across citing patents for the same cited document. In fact, the probability of being cited is expected to be positively mediated by the intrinsic quality of the patent, and thus the characteristics of citing patents for the same cited document are likely to be correlated. Therefore the regression standard errors are clustered using the robust estimator at the cited patent level, which can take into the account potential omitted factors.

6.7 Estimation Results

To test the proposed hypotheses, I advanced a series of linear regressions on the probability of being cited, although the dependent variable is a discrete one. In fact, the linear regression reports very similar estimates to the marginal effects of a probit regression, but at the same time it allows one to accommodate a larger number of variables from a computational point of view.

6.7.1 Evidence from the European Dataset

Table 6.1 depicts the results of the baseline regressions. All control variables enter significantly in the regressions. Having a common inventor increases the citation probability of about one-fifth, confirming the significant role played by social capital in promoting knowledge spillovers: Agrawal et al. (2006) argued that even in the case of mobility from one location to another, inventors continue to sustain social links with their former coinventors. The technology fixed effect dummy is demonstrated to be particularly important to predict citation probability: patents reporting the same IPC 6 digit class have a twice larger mean citation rate to receive a citation. This confirms anecdotal evidence that examiners first search locally for prior art, and then they extend their search more broadly to other technological fields. The negative impact of collaborating with a nonbusiness patentee or sole inventor(s) could be associated to the fact that these patents are more general and distant from commercialization, and hence their citation lifetime is longer than other patents on average (Henderson et al. 1998).

With respect to the first two hypotheses I find that knowledge spillovers from patents are a geographically localized phenomenon. As we can notice from Model 1 of Table 6.1 all the dummies on geographic distance have a negative and highly significant impact on the citation probability. This evidence is in favour of the proposition posited by Hypothesis 1(a). Further, also the Hypothesis 1(b) cannot be rejected. Indeed, the dummies on geographic distance show that distance affects the localization of knowledge spillovers in large extent within 250 km range. Beyond this threshold the additional effect of geographical distance is relatively limited. An inventor who is resident in Brussels has about 6.8 percentage points smaller probability of citing a patent invented in Paris (approximately 261 KM far) compared to an inventor who is also resident in Paris.

Table 6.1 Citation probability—European panel 1990–2009

	(1) coeff.	(1) s.e.	(2) coeff.	(2) s.e.	(3) coeff.	(3) s.e.	(4) coeff.	(4) s.e.	(5) coeff.	(5) s.e.
25<distance<50 km	-0.0296	[0.0024]***			-0.0267	[0.0024]***	-0.0153	[0.0027]***	-0.0096	[0.0033]***
50<distance<100 km	-0.0447	[0.0021]***			-0.0350	[0.0021]***	-0.0187	[0.0026]***	-0.0133	[0.0031]***
100<distance<150 km	-0.0550	[0.0022]***			-0.0393	[0.0022]***	-0.0203	[0.0027]***	-0.0150	[0.0033]***
150<distance<250 km	-0.0678	[0.0019]***			-0.0426	[0.0019]***	-0.0226	[0.0026]***	-0.0177	[0.0032]***
250<distance<500 km	-0.0901	[0.0017]***			-0.0464	[0.0018]***	-0.0263	[0.0026]***	-0.0229	[0.0031]***
500<distance<1000 km	-0.1092	[0.0017]***			-0.0503	[0.0019]***	-0.0302	[0.0026]***	-0.0292	[0.0032]***
1000<distance<1500 km	-0.1104	[0.0019]***			-0.0488	[0.0021]***	-0.0287	[0.0028]***	-0.0320	[0.0034]***
Distance>1500 km	-0.0949	[0.0021]***			-0.0331	[0.0023]***	-0.0130	[0.0029]***	-0.0243	[0.0037]***
Intra—TL3 region citation			0.1120	[0.0017]***			0.0890	[0.0027]***	0.0874	[0.0034]***
Neighbour TL3 citation—Same country			0.0833	[0.0018]***			0.0707	[0.0023]***	0.0646	[0.0029]***
Neighbour TL3 citation—Foreign country			0.0402	[0.0062]***			0.0296	[0.0063]***	0.0117	[0.0077]
Intra—TL2 region citation			0.0773	[0.0065]***			0.0686	[0.0066]***	0.0537	[0.0080]***
Within country citation—Border effect[4]			0.0673	[0.0009]***	0.0637	[0.0011]***	0.0633	[0.0011]***	0.0596	[0.0017]***
Linguistic affinity									0.0126	[0.0016]***
Population density (log)									-0.0096	[0.0004]***
GDP pro-capite (log)									0.0155	[0.0022]***
High-tech employment (%)									-0.0032	[0.0001]***
Common inventor	0.2135	[0.0021]***	0.2100	[0.0021]***	0.2115	[0.0021]***	0.2068	[0.0022]***	0.2129	[0.0026]***
Nonbusiness organization	-0.0062	[0.0020]***	-0.0063	[0.0020]***	-0.0062	[0.0020]***	-0.0061	[0.0020]***	-0.0049	[0.0021]**
Match on 6 digit IPC	0.4999	[0.0007]***	0.4989	[0.0007]***	0.4989	[0.0007]***	0.4988	[0.0007]***	0.4922	[0.0009]***
Std. error (adj. R-squared)	0.2732		0.2750		0.2751		0.2751		0.2751	
Observations	1,836,586		1,836,586		1,836,586		1,836,586		1,284,922	

Notes:
1) *** indicates statistically significant at 1 percent level, ** 5 percent level, and * 10 percent level.
2) Standard errors are clustered at the level of the cited patent.
3) All regressions include time fixed effect of the cited priority year and citation lags of the citing patents.
4) The border effect in Models 2, 4, and 5 is measured as mutually exclusive with other geographically closer citations at TL3 and TL2.

Second, the national border effect matters significantly for the probability of being cited, confirming the statement posited by Hypothesis 2(a). In particular, national inventors are 6.4 percentage points more likely than foreign inventors to cite domestic patents (Model 3 of Table 6.1), which is around 13 percent of the mean citation rate. The border effect partially correlates with the geographic distance dummies, but the correlation is small. In terms of an inventor from Brussels, the effect of spatial distance on her probability to cite a patent invented in Paris is mitigated only by 2.5 (=6.8–4.3) percentage points once I have controlled for the existence of the national border. In other words, the border effect accounts only partially for geographical distance, and more generally it can be considered as a proxy for other national and regional characteristics beyond the impact of space.

In addition to the national border effect dummy, I have analysed several other territorial level variables (Model 2 of Table 6.1). Inventors from the same TL3 unit increase the citation probability by 11.2 percentage points with respect to a foreign-invented patent. In the same vein, inventors originating from a domestic neighbouring TL3 region are 8.3 percentage points more likely to make a cite, which is similar to the citation probability (7.7 percentage points) of being part of the same focal TL2 region. Furthermore there is a statistically significant difference for inventors in foreign neighbouring regions to increasing the likelihood of receiving a citation (4.0 percentage points) with respect to any other foreign region. The results are valid even after having conditioned for the geographical distance dummies (Model 4 of Table 6.1), albeit the coefficients are reduced of about one or two percentage points, with relatively smaller changes for higher-order territorial level units. This latter finding suggests that the territory level variables—in particular the national and TL2 borders—account for a variability of the localization of knowledge spillovers which goes beyond the sole impact of geographical distance.

Other regional-level conditions enter significantly in the econometric model as well (Model 5 of Table 6.1). The usage of the same language by inventors of a citation pair has a positive elasticity with about 1.3 percent on the citation probability, confirming previous studies who have argued the importance of linguistic affinities in the diffusion of knowledge in the European context (Maurseth and Verspagen 2002; Gambardella et al. 2009). Further, regions with higher population density, lower GDP per capita, and larger share of employment in high-tech industries are corresponded with a lower number of cites per patent. Controlling for these other regional level conditions is accompanied with a smaller impact of the border effect (the difference is statistically significant at 1 percent level), corroborating the view that this effect accounts for economic differences across countries.

6.7.2 *Results with Inventor-Added Citations*

In this section inventor-added citations are analysed in order to assess the validity of the results. Previous literature has claimed that this kind of patent reference could constitute a more objective and reliable measure of knowledge spillovers (Thompson 2006). When examiners scrutinize the patentability of inventions, they conduct bibliographic searches of prior art into internal knowledge repositories at the patent office, and hence the examiner-added citations are an ex-post knowledge link across two inventions. In this direction, the inventor-added citations are a more conservative measure than those revealed by examiners in constituting a paper trail of knowledge spillovers. More generally, the analysis conducted solely on inventor citations can tackle also an endogeneity issue with respect to the uneven spatial distribution of innovation (Thompson and Fox-Keene 2005). In fact, the inventor citations are more bounded to the local regional dimension (Alcacer and Gittelman 2006; Criscuolo and Verspagen 2008), and hence they are expected to be less correlated with the preexisting spatial distribution of the economic and innovative activities across regions. On the other hand, patent reviewers are 'geographically blind' because typically they are not influenced by territorial proximity factors during the examination process, and the spatial distribution of their citations should closely mimic the geographic locations of the preexisting prior art relevant for a given invention (Singh and Marx 2013).[17]

The dataset of inventor-added citations includes about 779,176 pairs of cited-citing patents (42.4 percent of the overall EPO dataset) that have been matched to a control group of patents in the same year and technology class. Again I obtain significant and similar results to the regressions based on the overall dataset, including also examiner-added citations (see Table 6.2). These results do not falsify the testable hypotheses 1(a), 1(b), and 2(a), although some caveats are in order with respect to the size of the estimated coefficients.

The coefficients of the dummies on geographical distance are almost two times larger than the regressions with the overall dataset, including also the examiner-added citations, which suggests that inventor citations decay more rapidly with distance. Distance affects the localization of knowledge mainly within 250 km range, but the negative impact of distance continues to grow at a more rapid pace than before even beyond that threshold. The magnitudes of the national border effect and the other territorial border variables are similar to the results including also the examiner citations, with the exception of the dummy on the same TL3 region, which is about one and half times bigger than the former case. These findings support the assumption that inventor-added citations are more closely linked to the local dimension of knowledge transfers, and hence they are a less-imperfect measure of knowledge spillovers. More broadly, the results are in line with previous studies which have claimed that inventor-added citations show even more remarkable patterns of localization as compared to examiner citations (Alcacer and Gittelman 2006; Criscuolo and Verspagen 2008).

The coefficient of linguistic affinity is not significant, whilst the other regional level conditions—population density, GDP pro-capita, and the share of high-tech employment—have similar or bigger impacts than

Table 6.2 Citation probability of inventor-added citations—European panel 1990–2009

	(1) coeff.	(1) s.e.	(2) coeff.	(2) s.e.	(3) coeff.	(3) s.e.	(4) coeff.	(4) s.e.	(5) coeff.	(5) s.e.
25<distance<50 km	-0.0624	[0.0038]***			-0.0596	[0.0038]***	-0.0307	[0.0042]***	-0.0208	[0.0049]***
50<distance<100 km	-0.0799	[0.0033]***			-0.0685	[0.0033]***	-0.0280	[0.0041]***	-0.0204	[0.0048]***
100<distance<150 km	-0.0969	[0.0034]***			-0.0784	[0.0034]***	-0.0327	[0.0043]***	-0.0266	[0.0052]***
150<distance<250 km	-0.1139	[0.0030]***			-0.0845	[0.0030]***	-0.0371	[0.0042]***	-0.0320	[0.0049]***
250<distance<500 km	-0.1405	[0.0026]***			-0.0906	[0.0028]***	-0.0432	[0.0040]***	-0.0397	[0.0047]***
500<distance<1000 km	-0.1597	[0.0026]***			-0.0935	[0.0030]***	-0.0464	[0.0041]***	-0.0487	[0.0049]***
1000<distance<1500 km	-0.1648	[0.0030]***			-0.0957	[0.0034]***	-0.0486	[0.0044]***	-0.0535	[0.0053]***
Distance>1500 km	-0.1419	[0.0034]***			-0.0725	[0.0037]***	-0.0253	[0.0046]***	-0.0397	[0.0058]***
Intra—TL3 region citation			0.1682	[0.0025]***			0.1309	[0.0041]***	0.1310	[0.0051]***
Neighbour TL3 citation—Same country			0.1047	[0.0028]***			0.0851	[0.0037]***	0.0796	[0.0046]***
Neighbour TL3 citation—Foreign country			0.0500	[0.0095]***			0.0327	[0.0097]***	0.0184	[0.0120]
Intra—TL2 region citation			0.0940	[0.0105]***			0.0799	[0.0107]***	0.0578	[0.0127]***
Within country citation—Border effect[4]			0.0765	[0.0015]***	0.0718	[0.0018]***	0.0701	[0.0018]***	0.0731	[0.0028]***
Linguistic affinity									0.0030	[0.0025]
Population density (log)									-0.0112	[0.0006]***
GDP pro-capita (log)									0.0207	[0.0033]***
High-tech employment (%)									-0.0039	[0.0001]***
Common inventor	0.2024	[0.0028]***	0.1946	[0.0029]***	0.2002	[0.0028]***	0.1895	[0.0029]***	0.2020	[0.0035]***
Nonbusiness organization	-0.0085	[0.0026]***	-0.0085	[0.0026]***	-0.0086	[0.0026]***	-0.0082	[0.0026]***	-0.0058	[0.0028]**
Match on 6 digit IPC	0.4924	[0.0011]***	0.4908	[0.0011]***	0.4911	[0.0011]***	0.4907	[0.0011]***	0.4845	[0.0013]***
Std. error (adj; R-squared)	0.2826		0.2850		0.2849		0.2853		0.2811	
Observations	779,176		779,176		779,176		779,176		565,916	

Notes:
1) *** indicates statistically significant at 1 percent level, ** 5 percent level, and * 10 percent level.
2) Standard errors are clustered at the level of the cited patent.
3) All regressions include time fixed effect of the cited priority year and citation lags of the citing patents.
4) The border effect in Models 2, 4, and 5 is measured as mutually exclusive with other geographically closer citations at TL3 and TL2.

examiner-added citations. Put differently, I find that the linguistic affinities do not represent a significant mediator of the localized patterns of inventor citations, which are mainly affected by geographical distance measures and territorial unit borders.

6.7.3 The Determinants of the Border Effect

The regressions presented in Table 6.3 attempt to resolve the determinants of the border effect in order to scrutinize Hypothesis 2(b), which claims that national level conditions mediate positively this effect with respect to the localization of knowledge spillovers.

As it can be denoted from Table 6.3, there is statistically significant evidence regarding the interaction effect of the national border dummy with the strength of national patent legislation measured both as the book-law aspects of patent protection (GP index) and the transaction costs related to the patenting activities (PCA index). In particular, one standard deviation change in the GP index (S.D. = 0.1175) has a positive and significant impact on the citation probability with about 1.3 percent, which is about one-fifth of the overall national border effect (Compare Model 1 of Table 6.3 with Model 5 of Table 6.1). The estimation of the econometric model with the inventor-added citations confirms these results. On the other hand, the impact of the interaction effect with the PCA index for inventor-added citations is about twice the impact of the interaction effect for examiner-added citations.

As discussed, these findings could be explained in the light of the disclosing function of the patent system, which has the goal to increase the knowledge cumulativeness of subsequent inventions. Although the access to the knowledge disclosed by patents is not hampered by geography of innovation activities, its effective use could require operational knowledge that in turn is likely to be rather localized. The fact that the impact of the PCA index that measures also the transaction costs related to patenting activities is bigger for inventor citations than those revealed by the examiners does not contradict this view. As we argued, the inventor-added citations are a more objective and reliable measure of knowledge spillovers than the examiner-added citations, and in this direction the PCA index accounts for a larger share of their variability. Further, it is noteworthy that the main effect of the strength of patent protection is negative, but this result does not hold for the PCA index when the estimation is executed with examiner-added citations.

6.7.4 Evidence from the North American Dataset

The four posited hypotheses are also confirmed by the regression analysis with the North American panel. Both the examiner- and inventor-added citations have been analysed obtaining very similar estimated coefficients, and therefore for brevity only the latter results are presented in this section. As we can notice from Table 6.4 the citation probability is enhanced with

Table 6.3 The determinants of the country border effect

| | Examiner-added citations | | | | Inventor-added citations | | | |
| | (1) | | (2) | | (3) | | (4) | |
	coeff.	s.e.	coeff.	s.e.	coeff.	s.e.	coeff.	s.e.
25<distance<50 km	-0.0097	[0.0033]***	-0.0096	[0.0037]***	-0.0209	[0.0049]***	-0.0203	[0.0057]***
50<distance<100 km	-0.0134	[0.0031]***	-0.0137	[0.0036]***	-0.0205	[0.0048]***	-0.0184	[0.0056]***
100<distance<150 km	-0.0152	[0.0033]***	-0.0184	[0.0038]***	-0.0269	[0.0052]***	-0.0256	[0.0060]***
150<distance<250 km	-0.0179	[0.0032]***	-0.0213	[0.0036]***	-0.0321	[0.0049]***	-0.0340	[0.0056]***
250<distance<500 km	-0.0228	[0.0031]***	-0.0261	[0.0035]***	-0.0396	[0.0047]***	-0.0404	[0.0054]***
500<distance<1000 km	-0.0284	[0.0032]***	-0.0330	[0.0036]***	-0.0476	[0.0049]***	-0.0486	[0.0057]***
1000<distance<1500 km	-0.0306	[0.0034]***	-0.0377	[0.0039]***	-0.0519	[0.0053]***	-0.0569	[0.0061]***
Distance>1500 km	-0.0229	[0.0037]***	-0.0300	[0.0042]***	-0.0380	[0.0058]***	-0.0445	[0.0066]***
Intra—TL3 region citation	-0.0047	[0.0094]	0.0403	[0.0116]***	0.0289	[0.0135]**	0.0272	[0.0185]
Neighbour TL3 citation—Same country	-0.0281	[0.0094]***	0.0188	[0.0114]*	-0.0231	[0.0135]*	-0.0220	[0.0181]
Neighbour TL3 citation—Foreign country	0.0087	[0.0077]	0.0053	[0.0090]	0.0151	[0.0119]	0.0171	[0.0138]
Intra—TL2 region citation	-0.0419	[0.0122]***	0.0147	[0.0136]	-0.0481	[0.0183]***	-0.0191	[0.0216]
Within country citation—Border effect[4]	-0.0342	[0.0091]***	0.0156	[0.0111]	-0.0308	[0.0132]**	-0.0285	[0.0175]
GP index	-0.0362	[0.0034]***			-0.0448	[0.0052]***		
Border effect × GP index[5]	0.1071	[0.0102]***			0.1188	[0.0146]***		
PCA index			-0.0073	[0.0049]			-0.0363	[0.0076]***
Border effect × PCA index[5]			0.0532	[0.0134]***			0.1223	[0.0212]***
Linguistic affinity	0.0140	[0.0016]***	0.0136	[0.0019]***	0.0047	[0.0026]*	0.0095	[0.0030]***
Population density (log)	-0.0100	[0.0004]***	-0.0096	[0.0005]***	-0.0117	[0.0006]***	-0.0121	[0.0007]***
GDP pro-capita (log)	0.0169	[0.0022]***	0.0182	[0.0024]***	0.0223	[0.0033]***	0.0261	[0.0037]***
High-tech employment (%)	-0.0031	[0.0001]***	-0.0032	[0.0001]***	-0.0038	[0.0001]***	-0.0041	[0.0002]***

Common inventor	0.2124 [0.0026]***	0.2174 [0.0031]***	0.2014 [0.0035]***	0.2085 [0.0041]***
Nonbusiness organization	-0.0044 [0.0021]**	-0.0037 [0.0022]*	-0.0052 [0.0028]*	-0.0039 [0.0032]
Match on 6 digit IPC	0.4922 [0.0009]***	0.4879 [0.0010]***	0.4845 [0.0013]***	0.4802 [0.0015]***
Std. error (adj. R-squared)	0.2706	0.2665	0.2854	0.2778
Observations	1,284,922	990,960	565,916	432,040

Notes:
1) *** indicates statistically significant at 1 percent level, ** 5 percent level, and * 10 percent level.
2) Standard errors are clustered at the level of the cited patent.
3) All regressions include time fixed effect of the cited priority year and citation lags of the citing patents.
4) The border effect is measured as mutually exclusive with other geographically closer citations at TL3 and TL2.
5) The border effect includes other geographically closer citations at TL3 and TL2.

Table 6.4 Citation probability of inventor-added citations—North American panel 1990–2009

	(1)		(2)		(3)		(4)		(5)		(6)	
	coeff.	s.e.	coeff.	s.e.	coeff.	s.e.	coeff.	s.e.	coeff.	s.e.	coeff.	s.e.
25<distance<50 km	-0.0220	[0.0012]***			-0.0220	[0.0012]***	-0.0150	[0.0012]***	-0.0112	[0.0014]***	-0.0113	[0.0014]***
50<distance<100 km	-0.0275	[0.0013]***			-0.0274	[0.0013]***	-0.0184	[0.0013]***	-0.0131	[0.0014]***	-0.0132	[0.0014]***
100<distance<150 km	-0.0366	[0.0013]***			-0.0364	[0.0013]***	-0.0247	[0.0013]***	-0.0196	[0.0015]***	-0.0197	[0.0015]***
150<distance<250 km	-0.0364	[0.0011]***			-0.0361	[0.0011]***	-0.0216	[0.0011]***	-0.0179	[0.0013]***	-0.0179	[0.0013]***
250<distance<500 km	-0.0450	[0.0010]***			-0.0425	[0.0010]***	-0.0274	[0.0010]***	-0.0240	[0.0011]***	-0.0240	[0.0011]***
500<distance<1000 km	-0.0473	[0.0008]***			-0.0454	[0.0009]***	-0.0291	[0.0009]***	-0.0261	[0.0009]***	-0.0261	[0.0009]***
1000<distance<1500 km	-0.0522	[0.0010]***			-0.0506	[0.0010]***	-0.0338	[0.0010]***	-0.0323	[0.0011]***	-0.0322	[0.0011]***
Distance>1500 km	-0.0631	[0.0008]***			-0.0604	[0.0009]***	-0.0421	[0.0009]***	-0.0410	[0.0009]***	-0.0410	[0.0009]***
Intra—TL3 region citation			0.0984	[0.0012]***			0.0762	[0.0013]***	0.0918	[0.0015]***	-0.2726	[0.0342]***
Neighbour TL3 citation—Same country			0.0434	[0.0013]***			0.0310	[0.0013]***	0.0448	[0.0016]***	-0.3196	[0.0342]***
Neighbour TL3 citation—Foreign country			0.0941	[0.0409]**			0.0892	[0.0411]**	0.1166	[0.0501]**	0.1161	[0.0501]**
Intra—TL2 region citation			0.0259	[0.0017]***			0.0121	[0.0018]***	0.0239	[0.0021]***	-0.3397	[0.0341]***
Within country citation—Border effect 4)			0.0314	[0.0010]***	0.0276	[0.0010]***	0.0240	[0.0010]***	0.0318	[0.0012]***	-0.3326	[0.0342]***
GP index											-0.2269	[0.0254]***
Border effect × GP index 5)											0.3810	[0.0353]***
Linguistic affinity									0.0093	[0.0024]***	0.0086	[0.0025]***
Population density (log)									-0.0063	[0.0004]***	-0.0059	[0.0004]***
GDP pro-capita (log)									-0.0598	[0.0024]***	-0.0599	[0.0024]***
High-tech employment (%)									-0.0021	[0.0002]***	-0.0021	[0.0002]***

	Model 1		Model 2		Model 3		Model 4		Model 5		Model 6	
Common inventor	0.3059	[0.0020]***	0.2916	[0.0020]***	0.3056	[0.0020]***	0.2828	[0.0020]***	0.2835	[0.0023]***	0.2838	[0.0023]***
Nonbusiness organization	-0.0113	[0.0009]***	-0.0109	[0.0009]***	-0.0116	[0.0009]***	-0.0114	[0.0010]***	-0.0067	[0.0010]***	-0.0065	[0.0010]***
Small patenting firm	0.0135	[0.0007]***	0.0142	[0.0007]***	0.0137	[0.0007]***	0.0150	[0.0007]***	0.0138	[0.0007]***	0.0138	[0.0007]***
Match on 6 digit IPC	0.4036	[0.0005]***	0.4030	[0.0005]***	0.4035	[0.0005]***	0.4015	[0.0005]***	0.4023	[0.0005]***	0.4024	[0.0005]***
Std. error (adj.) R-squared	0.168		0.1681		0.1676		0.1688		0.1685		0.1686	
Observations	6,617,818		6,617,818		6,617,818		6,617,818		5,339,232		5,339,232	

Notes:
1) *** indicates statistically significant at 1 percent level, ** 5 percent level, and * 10 percent level. 2) Standard errors are clustered at the level of the cited patent.
3) All regressions include time fixed effect of the cited priority year and citation lags of the citing patents.
4) The border effect in Models 2, 4, 5, and 6 is measured as mutually exclusive with other geographically closer citations at TL3 and TL2.
5) The border effect includes other geographically closer citations at TL3 and TL2.

about forty percentage points by a match on the same IPC 6 digit class. This probability is smaller than the European panel because of a potential measurement error: at the USPTO examiners classify patents according to the US patent classification, and the IPC code in the US filings is attached solely for the main patent class. Conversely, the internal classification at the EPO (the so-called ECLA system) is not necessarily based on the definition of a main patent class, and it is directly harmonized with the IPC system.[18]

The other control variables are also statistically significant and have the expected signs. The coefficient of collaborating with the nonbusiness sector is negative, whilst having a common inventor is associated with about one-third higher likelihood of receiving a cite. Furthermore the regressions control for size of the patenting firm, when the patentee has less than five hundred employees.[19] It's quite interesting that being a small-sized patentee is associated with a positive and significant impact on the citation probability, which is in line with the fact that small firms have a lower patent propensity, given by number of patents for unit of R&D investment, and hence they hold on average more valuable patents than large firms (Hall and Ziedonis 2001).

The dummies on geographic distance show a negative and statistically significant impact on the citation probability, and the largest extent of the effect of distance on the localization of knowledge spillovers is traced within 150 km range, which is consistent with previous US evidence by Belenzon and Schankerman (2013).[20] Furthermore the citation probability is affected significantly by the territorial level variables. Compared to a foreign-invented patent, being part of the same TL3 region increases the likelihood of receiving a cite with about 9.8 percentage points, whereas being part of the same state increases the citation probability of 2.6 points (Model 2 of Table 6.4). In this case, the results for the United States are not directly comparable with those of Belenzon and Schankerman (2013), because the BEA economic areas partially overlap with state borders. Thus, inventors could be located in the same economic area but in different states, and vice versa. Inventors located in a domestic neighbouring TL3 region are 4.3 percentage points more likely to make a cite than foreign inventors. The citation probability is even higher for foreign inventors resident in a neighbouring region, although some caution in the interpretation of this finding is required because they are very few in number and the result did not hold when the regressions were estimated with all citation links.

Similarly to the European panel, the national border effect is found to have a significant impact on citation probability. A patent invented in the United States has 2.8 percent higher probability to be cited by another US inventor rather than an inventor located in Canada or Mexico (Model 3 of Table 6.4)—almost 6 percent of the mean citation rate. The coefficient is smaller than for the European panel (6.4 percent), but the difference is narrowed when the analysis includes also the regional characteristics such as the linguistic affinity, population density, GDP pro-capita, and intensity of high-tech employment. In turn, the linguistic affinity has a positive impact with around same size of the estimated coefficient for the European panel, that is about 1 percent on the probability of being cited.

Model 6 of Table 6.4 attempts to resolve the determinants of the national border effect. One standard deviation increase (s.d.= 0.0299) of the GP index impacts positively the citation probability of a domestic patent with about 1.1 percentage points, which is about one-third of the overall border effect (compare Model 5 and 6). It is noteworthy that the signs of the territorial level variables are reversed, which suggests that the interaction with the GP index accounts for a larger share of the variability of the border effect than the territorial-level variables.

6.8 Conclusions

This chapter has attempted to disentangle the impact of geographical spatial distance and territorial unit borders on the localization of knowledge spillovers. Overall the results are consistent with previous contributions, such as Belenzon and Schankerman (2013) and Singh and Marx (2013), who have claimed that territorial borders can be expression of more general conditions than solely the distance effect. Moreover, I have analysed how the strength of the national legislation on patent protection mediates the impact of territorial borders on knowledge spillovers.

In line with the background literature, the chapter relies on patent citations as a measure of knowledge spillovers (Jaffe et al. 1993; Thompson, 2006), and a novel dataset has been developed by drawing information from various sources. First, it encompasses the population of citation reports published with the European patent applications and US-granted patents during the period 1990–2009. Second, I have regionalized the addresses of inventor(s) to territorial units, connecting them to spatial information, such as the administrative borders and geographic coordinates (longitudes and latitudes). Third, the dataset has been extended to structural variables on the national- and regional-level conditions that could affect the pace and the direction of knowledge spillovers from patents. Last, the analysis has considered more fine-grained measures of knowledge spillovers, such as inventor-added citations.

This study reports several findings. Overall the probability of citing a patent from the same country is about one-third. At the net of distance this probability is to about 6.4 percentage points in Europe and 2.8 points in North America. Second, geographical distance exerts a negative impact on knowledge spillovers largely on the range of 150 km for North America and 250 km for Europe. Third, in North America being part of the same TL3 region (e.g., BEA Economic Area in the US) increases the likelihood of citation regardless of distance with 9.8 percentage points, whereas in Europe with about 11.2 percentage points, as compared to a foreign-invented patent. Fourth, neighbouring TL3 regions matter for citation probability with at least the same impact of being part of the same TL2 region. Fifth, regardless of distance the probability of citing a foreign region within the same linguistic area is significant for European regions to the same extent to the North American ones. Last but not least, a significant mediator of the border effect is constituted by the strength of the national legislation on patent protection, which accounts for around one-fifth of its impact in Europe and one-third in North America. The latter finding holds not only when I consider the book-law aspects of patent protection (Ginarte and Park 1997; Park 2008) but also the transaction costs related to patenting activities (Papageorgiadis et al. 2014).

Future research could advance in multiple directions. First of all, because citations are correlated to value characteristics of a patent and the portfolio of the patentee, it is relevant to condition for other patent indicators (Hall et al. 2005). Other controls could include measures of closeness to science, basicness of the invention, and generality index that proxies the technological breadth of spillovers from patents (Henderson et al. 1998). Furthermore, it could be interesting to account for differences in citation practices across examiners. Previous research has shown that the examiner's characteristics (such as experience, tenure, and others) affect the duration of lifetime citations of a patent (Cockburn et al. 2002). Thus, potential measures regarding the relative utilization of patent citations by examiners vis-à-vis inventors could constitute an additional robustness analysis of the localization patterns of knowledge spillovers from patents. Finally, future research could scrutinize how intellectual property strategies by patentees (such as renewal decisions of patent protection) affect the localization of knowledge spillovers (Marco 2012). For example this research agenda could assess how the renewal decision of a patent impacts the usage of knowledge and whether geography meant in the broadest sense has any mediating role in this process.

Appendix 6.1 The structure of territorial units of the European and North American regional dataset

Country Code	Territory level # 1 Description	Units Count Total	Territory level # 2 Description	Units Count Total	with Pats	Territory level # 3 Description	Units Count Total	with Pats
AT	Gruppen von Bundesländern	3	Bundesländer	9	9	Gruppen von politischen Bezirken	35	35
BE	Gewesten / Régions	3	Provincies / Provinces	11	4	Arrondisse-menten / Arrondissements	44	13
BG	Rajoni	2	Rajoni za planirane	6	6	Oblasti	28	24
CY	–	1	–	1	1	–	1	1
CZ	Území	1	Oblasti	8	9	Kraje	14	9
DE	Länder	16	Regierungs-bezirke	38	38	Kreise	412	108
DK	–	1	Regioner	5	5	Landsdeler	11	11
ES	Agrupacion de comunidades Autonomas	7	Comunidades y ciudades Autonomas	19	18	Provincias + islas + Ceuta, Melilla	59	59
FI	Manner-Suomi, Ahvenanmaa / Fasta Finland, Åland	2	Suuralueet / Storområden	5	5	Maakunnat / Landskap	20	20
FR	Z.E.A.T + DOM	9	Régions + DOM	26	26	Départements + DOM	100	100
GB	Government OHce Regions	12	–	12	12	Upper tier authorities or groups of lower tier authorities/unitary authorities/districts	133	133
GR	Groups of development regions	4	Periferies	13	5	Nomoi	51	14
HU	Statisztikai nagyrégiók	3	Tervezési-statisztikai régiók	7	7	Megyék + Budapest	20	20
IE	–	1	Regions	2	2	Regional Authority Regions	8	8

(Continued)

Appendix 6.1 (Continued)

Country Code	Territory level # 1 Description	Units Count Total	Territory level # 2 Description	Units Count Total	with Pats	Territory level # 3 Description	Units Count Total	with Pats
IT	Gruppi di regioni	5	Regioni	21	21	Provincie	110	108
LT	–	1	–	1	1	–	1	1
LU	–	1	–	1	1	–	1	1
MT	–	1	–	1	1	Gzejjer	2	2
NL	Landsdelen	4	Landsdelen	4	4	Provincies	12	12
PL	Regiony	6	Województwa	16	16	Podregiony	66	53
PT	Continente + Regioes autonomas	3	Comissaoes de Coordenaçao regional + Regioes autonomas	7	7	Grupos de Concelhos	30	30
RO	Macroregiuni	4	Regiuni	8	8	Judet + Bucuresti	42	37
SE	Grupper av riksomräden	3	Riksomräden	8	8	Län	21	21
SK	–	1	Oblasti	4	4	Kraje	8	8
CH	–		Grandes Regions	7	7	Cantons	26	26
NO	–		Landsdeler	7	7	Fylker	19	19
Europe		94		247	232		1274	873
CA			Provinces	12	12	Divisions	288	274
MX			Estados	32	32	Grupos de Municipios	209	89
US			States	51	51	BEA Economic Areas	179	179
Overall				342	327		1950	1415

Sources: Author's elaboration from the epp.eurostat.ec.europa.eu and stats.oecd.org.

Abbreviations: DOM Département d'outre-Mer (French overseas departments); Z.E.A.T. Zone économique d'aménagement du territoire (France).

Appendix 6.2 Descriptive statistics

| | European Panel | | | | North American Panel | |
| | All citations | | Inventor-added cites | | Inventor-added cites | |
	Mean	St.Dev.	Mean	St.Dev.	Mean	St.Dev.
Geographic distance dummies						
0<distance<25 km	0.0889	–	0.1091	–	0.1896	–
25<distance<50 km	0.0296	–	0.0307	–	0.0456	–
50<distance<100 km	0.0538	–	0.0543	–	0.0434	–
100<distance<150 km	0.0522	–	0.0525	–	0.0359	–
150<distance<250 km	0.1023	–	0.1024	–	0.0596	–
250<distance<500 km	0.2582	–	0.2518	–	0.0962	–
500<distance<1000 km	0.2695	–	0.2630	–	0.1751	–
1000<distance<1500 km	0.0929	–	0.0887	–	0.1136	–
Distance>1500 km	0.0527	–	0.0474	–	0.2410	–
Territorial units' dummies						
Intra—TL3 region citation	0.0842	–	0.1038	–	0.1498	–
Neighbour TL3 citation—Same country	0.0422	–	0.0436	–	0.0888	–
Neighbour TL3 citation—Foreign country	0.0031	–	0.0034	–	0.0000	–
Intra—TL2 region citation	0.0026	–	0.0024	–	0.0289	–
Within country citation—Border effect°	0.2207	–	0.2159	–	0.6814	–
Within country citation—Border effect	0.3527	–	0.3692	–	0.9489	–
International citation—Different country	0.6473	–	0.6308	–	0.0511	–
GP index	0.8432	0.1175	0.8447	0.1187	0.9634	0.0299
Border effect × GP index	0.2977	0.4091	0.3121	0.4143	0.9163	0.2139
PCA index	0.8070	0.0981	0.8089	0.0954		

(*Continued*)

Appendix 6.2 (Continued)

| | European Panel | | | | North American Panel | |
| | All citations | | Inventor-added cites | | Inventor-added cites | |
	Mean	St.Dev.	Mean	St.Dev.	Mean	St.Dev.
Border effect × PCA index	0.2800	0.3854	0.2956	0.3909		
Linguistic affinity (dummy)	0.3696	–	0.3763	–	0.9904	–
Population density (log)	5.7124	1.0018	5.7552	0.9939	4.3034	1.0171
GDP pro-capite (log)	10.2766	0.2326	10.2685	0.2291	10.4072	0.2426
High-tech employment (percentage)	10.2901	4.1649	10.3197	4.1609	6.5024	1.8661
Common inventor (dummy)	0.0259	–	0.0371	–	0.0040	–
Nonbusiness organization (dummy)	0.0423	–	0.0458	–	0.1277	–
Small patenting firm (dummy)					0.1665	–
Match on 6 digit IPC (dummy)	0.5482	–	0.5549	–	0.4424	–

Notes: ° It excludes other geographically closer citations at TL3 and TL2.

Notes

1 A mile is equivalent to 1.609 km.
2 Even in the case when the outcome of the knowledge generation process is highly codified, such as a scientific publication, patent, or others, a significant part of knowledge remains tacit and often difficult to replicate and transfer (Zander and Kogut 1995).
3 For a fuller discussion of the impact of linguistic affinities on regional performance see also Gambardella *et al.* (2009).
4 Measuring distance across cities allows one to accurately disentangle the bordering effect across territorial units, such as state or metropolitan area.
5 In particular using GIS information the authors have computed distances at the level of the individual addresses of inventors.
6 For a fuller discussion on noncompete agreements see Belenzon and Schankerman (2013).
7 For a fuller discussion on this methodology see Belenzon and Schankerman (2013).
8 Singh and Marx (2013) provided estimates of the share of foreign citations to US patents.
9 Typically, patent families are of three kinds (see Martinez 2011). First, strict equivalents are filings including exactly the same priorities or combination of priorities. Second, there are INPADOC families, which share any direct or indirect priority link across them, resulting in a consolidated and self-contained group of priority links. Third, DOCDB patent families, having similar sets of priorities, excluding those patents that do not add new technical knowledge. These families are manually inspected and defined by the EPO examiners for the purpose of their prior art search work.
10 These applications are typically known as continuations or divisional applications.
11 See the discussion posited in footnote 9 of this chapter.
12 For more information see the Shape Files User Documentation of the Quantum GIS project (www.qgis.org).
13 In this task I considered only geographical linkages and not transportation channels or travelling time from one region to another. In fact, it could be well assumed that two regions could be geographically separate, but they are close from a commuting time point of view. At this stage of the research, I cannot take into the account this latter aspect, but I do not think that it is serious limitation of this kind.
14 Inventors from Croatia, Estonia, Latvia, and Slovenia have been disregarded from the sample because of data incompleteness of the GP index (see section 6.5).
15 Information on geographic coordinates (longitudes and latitudes) has been drawn from the files of National Geospatial-Intelligence Agency (NGA) and the US Board on Geographic Names (USGS). Further details on the NGA and USGS databases can be found at www.nga.mil and geonames.usgs.gov, last accessed in July 2013.
16 The geodesic algorithm measures the spatial distance in kilometers as the following:

$$6371*acos((sin(Latitude_X)*sin(Latitude_Y))+(cos(Latitude_X)*cos(Latitude_Y)*cos(Longitude_X-Longitude_Y)))$$

17 Previous research has argued that patentees could consider a citation link to previous prior art as an endogenous decision, and they could strategically withhold citations (Lampe 2012). In particular, Lampe finds that patentees withhold between 21 and 32 percent of relevant citations, and withholding decisions are significantly mediated by the value of the patent asset and the portfolio size of the patentee. Whereas this hypothesis is noteworthy for future research, I do not think it is a serious limitation for a preliminary investigation of this kind. In

particular, I are not aware under which conditions the withholding decisions are directly affected by geography of knowledge spillovers.

18 In October 2010 the EPO and USPTO launched a joint initiative for a common classification scheme, namely the Cooperative Patent Classification (CPC). The scheme, which entered in force only in July 1, 2015, is fully harmonized with the IPC system and provides a more detailed classification than the IPC to facilitate prior art searching (for more information see www.cpcinfo.org).

19 Independently of their nationality, patenting firms with fewer than five hundred employees could benefit a 50 percent reduction of the maintenance fees at the USPTO (see http://www.uspto.gov/curr_fees). Similarly, sole inventors and nonbusiness organizations could obtain the same proportional fee reduction. Procedural information on fee payments is drawn from the US Patent Grant Maintenance Fee Events File, available from https://www.google.com/googlebooks/uspto-patents-maintenance-fees.html, last accessed on September 1, 2014.

20 Analyzing patenting citations from university inventions Belenzon and Schankerman (2013) claimed that geographical distance exerts a negative impact on knowledge spillovers mainly within 150 miles. Two caveats are in order when the results of this chapter are compared with those of Belenzon and Schankerman (2013). On the one hand, they considered commuting distances instead geographical spatial distances. Second, university patents are typically more general and distant from commercialization than other patents, and therefore spillovers from these patents are likely to diffuse more broadly in space.

References

Agrawal A. K., I. M. Cockburn 2003. "The Anchor Tenant Hypothesis: Exploring the Role of Large, Local, R&D-Intensive Firms in Regional Innovation Systems." *Int J Ind Organ* 21(9):1217–1433.

Agrawal A. K., I M. Cockburn, A. Galasso, A. Oettl 2012. "Why are Some Regions more Innovative than Others? The Role Of Firm Size Diversity." NBER Working Paper No. 17793, National Bureau of Economic Research, Inc. Cambridge (MA).

Agrawal A. K., I. M. Cockburn, J. McHale 2006. "Gone But Not Forgotten: Labour Flows, Knowledge Spillovers, and Enduring Social Capital." *J Econ Geography* 6(5):571–591.

Agrawal A. K., D. Kapur, J. McHale 2008. "How Do Spatial and Social Proximity Influence Knowledge Flows? Evidence from Patent Data." *J Urban Econ* 64:258–269.

Alcacer J., M. Gittelman 2006. "Patent Citations as Measure of Knowledge Flows: The Influence of Examiner Citations." *Rev Eco Stat* 88(4):774–779.

Almeida P., B. Kogut 1999. "Localization of Knowledge and the Mobility of Engineers in Regional Networks." *ManagScience* 45:905–917.

Audretsch D., M. P. Feldman 2003. "Knowledge Spillovers and the Geography of Innovation." In *Handbook of Urban and Regional Economics: Cities and Geography*, edited by J. V. Henderson, J. Thisse, 4:2713–2739, Amsterdam: North Holland.

Belenzon S., M. Schankerman 2013. "Spreading the Word: Geography, Policy and University Knowledge Diffusion." *Rev Econ Stat* 95(3):884–903.

Branstetter L. G., F. Raymond, F. C. Fritz 2006. "Do Stronger Intellectual Property Rights Increase International Technology Transfer? Empirical Evidence from U.S. Firm-Level Panel Data." *Q J Econ* 121(1):321–349.

Bresnahan T., A. Gambardella 2004. *Building High-Tech Clusters: Silicon Valley and Beyond*. Cambridge (UK): Cambridge University Press.

Bottazzi L., G. Peri 2003. "Innovation and Spillovers: Evidence from European Regions." *Eur Econ Rev* 47(4):687–710.

Carlino G. A., R. M. Hunt, J. K. Carr, T. E. Smith 2012. "The Agglomeration of R&D Labs." Federal Reserve Bank of Philadelphia Working Paper No. 12–22. Federal Reserve Bank of Philadelphia, Philadelphia, PA.

Cockburn I. M., S. Kortum, S. Stern 2002. "Are All Patent Examiners Equal? The Impact of Examiner Characteristics." NBER Working Paper No. 8980, National Bureau of Economic Research, Inc. Cambridge (MA).

Criscuolo P., B. Verspagen 2008. "Does It Matter Where Patent Citations Come from? Inventor vs. Examiner Citations in European Patents." *Res Pol* 37(10): 1892–1908.

Ejermo O. 2009. "Regional Innovation Measured by Patent Data—Does Quality Matter?" *Indust Innov* 16(2):141–165.

Ellison G., E. L. Glaeser 1997. "Geographic Concentration in U.S. Manufacturing Industries: A Dartboard Approach." *J Pol Econ* 105:889–927.

Ellison G., E. L. Glaeser 1999. "The Geographic Concentration of Industry: Does Natural Advantage Explain Agglomeration?" *Am Econ Rev* 89(2):311–316.

Feldman M., D. Audretsch 1999. "Innovation in Cities: Science-Based Diversity, Specialization, and Localized Competition." *Eur Econ Rev* 43:409–429.

Feldman M., D. Kogler 2010. "Stylized Facts in the Geography of Innovation." In *Handbook of the Economics of Innovation*, edited by B. H. Hall, N. Rosenberg, 13443–14547, Amsterdam: Elsevier, Kindle edition.

Gambardella A., M. Mariani, S. Torrisi 2009. "How 'Provincial' Is Your Region? Openness and Regional Performance in Europe." *Reg Stud* 43(7):935–947.

Ginarte, J. C., W. G. Park 1997. "Determinants of Patent Rights: A Cross-national Study." *Res Pol* 26(3):283–301.

Hall B. H., A. Jaffe, M. Trajtenberg 2001. "The NBER Patent Citations Data File: Lessons, Insights, and Methodological Tools." In *Patents, Citations and Innovations*, edited by A. Jaffe, M. Trajtenberg, Cambridge (MA): The MIT Press. Also NBER Research Working Paper No. 8498, National Bureau of Economic Research, Inc. Cambridge (MA).

Hall B. H., A. Jaffe, M. Trajtenberg 2005. "Market Value and Patent citations." *Rand J Econ* 36:16–38.

Hall B. H., R. Ziedonis 2001. "The Determinants of Patenting in the U.S. Semiconductor Industry, 1980–1994." *Rand J Econ* 32:101–128.

Henderson R., A. Jaffe, M. Trajtenberg 1998. "Universities as a Source of Commercial Technology: A Detailed Analysis of University Patenting, 1965–1988." *Rev Econ Stat* LXXX (1):119–127.

Hoekman J., K. Frenken, R. J. W. Tijssen 2010. "Research Collaboration at a Distance: Changing Spatial Patterns of Scientific Collaboration within Europe." *Res Pol* 39:662–673.

Jaffe, A. B 1989. "Real Effects of Academic Research." *Am Econ Rev* 79(5):957–970.

Jaffe A. B., M. Trajtenberg 1999. "International Knowledge Flows: Evidence from Patent Citations." *Econ Inno New Tech* 8:105–136.

Jaffe A. B., M. Trajtenberg, R. Henderson 1993. "Geographic Localization of Knowledge as Evidenced by Patent Citations." *Q J Econ* 108(3):577–598.

Justman M., M. Teubal 1995. "Technological Infrastructure Policy: Creating Capabilities and Building Markets." *Res Pol* 24(2):259–281.

Klepper S., S. Sleeper 2005. "Entry by Spinoffs." *ManagScience* 51(8):1291–1306.

Lampe R., 2012. "Strategic Citation." *Rev Econ Stat* 94(1):320–333.

Marco A. 2012. "Citations and Renewal: A Window into Public and Private Patent Value." Paper presented at the Third Asian Pacific Innovation Conference, Seoul, Republic of Korea, October 13–14.

Martinez C. 2011. "Patent Families: When Do Different Definitions Really Matter?" *Scientometrics* 86:39–63.

Maurseth, P. B., B. Verspagen 2002. "Knowledge Spillovers in Europe: A Patent Citations Analysis." *Scand J Econ* 104:531–545.

Mehta A., M. Rysman, T. Simcoe 2010. "Identifying the Age Profile of Patent Citations: New Estimates of Knowledge Diffusion." *J Appl Economet* 25(7): 1073–1222.

Moore G., K. Davis 2004. "Learning the Silicon Valley Way." In *Building High-Tech Clusters Silicon Valley and Beyond*, edited by T. Bresnahan, A. Gambardella, 2:7–39, Cambridge (UK): Cambridge University Press.

OECD 2002. *Frascati Manual.* Paris: OECD.

Papageorgiadis N. P., A. R. Cross, C. Alexiou 2014. "International Patent Systems Strength 1998–2011." *J World Bus* 49:586–597.

Park W. G. 1999. "Measuring Global Patent Protection." *Fraser Forum* 3:4–7.

Park W. G. 2008. "International Patent Protection, 1960–2005." *Res Pol* 37(4): 761–766.

Park W. G., D. Lippoldt 2014 "Technology Transfer and the Economic Implications of the Strengthening of Intellectual Property Rights in Developing Countries." In *Intellectual Property Rights for Economic Development*, edited by S. Ahn, B. Hall, K. Lee, 33–89, Northampton (MA): Edward Elgar Publishers.

PatStat 2015. *EPO Worldwide Patent Statistical Database and the EPO Patent Register*, April edition. Vienna: EPO.

Peri G. 2005. "Determinants of Knowledge Flows and Their Effects on Innovation." *Rev Econ Stat* 87(2):308–22.

Porter M. E. 1998. "Clusters and the New Economics of Competition." *Harv Bus Rev* November–December 76(6):77–90.

Saxenian A. 1994. *Regional Advantage: Culture and Competition in Silicon Valley and Route 128.* Boston (MA): Harvard University Press.

Singh J., M. Marx 2013. "Geographic Constraints on Knowledge Spillovers: Political Borders vs. Spatial Proximity." *ManagScience* 59(9):2056–2078.

Sorenson O., T. E. Stuart 2003. "The Geography of Opportunity: Spatial Heterogeneity in Founding Rates and the Performance of Biotechnology Firms." *Res Pol* 32:229–253.

Thompson P. 2006. "Patent Citations and the Geography of Knowledge Spillovers: Evidence from Inventor- and Examiner-Added Citations." *Rev Econ Stat* 88:383–388.

Thompson P., M. Fox-Keene 2005. "Patent Citations and the Geography of Knowledge Spillovers: A Reassessment." *Am Econ Rev* 95:450–460.

Zander U., B. Kogut 1995. "Knowledge and the Speed of the Transfer and Imitation of Organizational Capabilities: An Empirical Test." *Org Science* 6:76–92.

Zucker L. G., M. R. Darby, J. Armstrong 1998. "Geographically Localized Knowledge: Spillovers or Markets?" *Econ Inq* 36(1):65–86.

7 Inventor Location and the Globalization of R&D[1]

Grid Thoma and Dietmar Harhoff

7.1 Introduction

The growing importance of the globalisation of R&D activities is evident from a large number of case studies, statistics, and analyses, both at the national and corporate level.[2] Yet, it is still difficult to describe the phenomenon statistically, because systematic data which map the internationalization of R&D are still rare. Some progress has been made in using patterns of patent filings and inventor collaboration as evidence of R&D globalization, but a systematic picture of the R&D *inputs* used by firms has not materialized yet. Firm-level data capture R&D investments irrespective of location. The usually employed data sources such as Compustat or others do not contain any information on the geographic distribution of a firm's R&D activities. Conversely, most of the national R&D statistics (which are then summarized by the OECD and published via, inter alia, stats.oecd.org) capture all R&D activities within national territorial boundaries, but not the R&D performed abroad by firms headquartered in the respective national territory. In some cases the agencies collecting these data have extended their questionnaires to develop a notion of the extent of international R&D activities, but there has not been any systematic measurement over time.[3]

This chapter develops a methodology that allows us to estimate the international distribution of firms' inventive activities, and then applies it in the estimation of R&D contributions to a firm's market valuation and productivity. Towards this objective we utilize inventor location data from patent applications. From inventor addresses, we extract information on the regions in which the firm has developed inventive activities. We consolidate the inventor names in our database such as to avoid any double-counting of the personnel dedicated into the inventive activities. In this chapter, we describe succinctly our methodology and the data used. We also present descriptive statistics which allow us to document the large shifts that have occurred in the location decisions of R&D activities. In our multivariate analysis, we employ a simple accounting approach which relates total R&D to the number of inventors in different locations. Estimating linear and non-linear versions of this R&D expenditure equation provides us with highly plausible results—inventor counts have strong explanatory power, and the proposed accounting equation explains about two-thirds of the overall variation in R&D expenditures. Finally, we employ the inventor counts to estimate the impact of domestic- and foreign-located invention activities on the market value and output of the firm.

The remainder of the chapter proceeds in six sections. We first describe our conceptual approach (section 7.2) and the data used in our study (section 7.3). Section 7.4 gives details on a number of descriptive statistics characterising the development of international R&D activities and patterns of internationalization, such as the share of nondomestic inventors by country and over time. Multivariate evidence on the relationship between inventor counts and R&D expenditures is given in section 7.5. Section 7.6 contains estimates of the impact of domestic and foreign inventors on market value and sales. Section 7.7 concludes and gives an outlook to future research.

7.2 Methods and Approach

Frequently, researchers have no data available which would inform them about the geographical distribution of a firm's innovation activities. We suggest that approximations of this geographic distribution can be obtained in a systematic manner from inventor data as recorded in patent applications. Obviously, the approximation may be unsatisfactory under a number of circumstances (e.g., if the innovation output of the firm remains unpatented) so that we cannot trace it in our patent data. We therefore need some validation for the measures we use and discuss the validation results and other caveats in our final section.

The first step in our data collection approach is to identify the inventors working for a particular patentee in a given year, and to determine the overall international distribution of the inventor workforce of a particular corporation or firm. We start by defining *domestic inventors* as those inventors whose country location is the same as the location of the patentee (respectively, its headquarters). Conversely, *foreign inventors* are defined as inventors located in a country different from the location country of the patentee. Note that this definition would place nationals working at the foreign R&D location among the foreign inventors, even if they are citizens of the country of the patentee. Our definition of inventors is not related to nationality but simply to the geographic location of R&D execution.[4]

For the purpose of this study, the annual inventor counts for a given firm are based on all patent applications from the European Patent Office (EPO) and Patent Cooperation Treaty (PCT) systems with a particular priority year by the respective patentee. An inventor is recorded as active for the patentee in that year if she is named on a patent application whose priority filing was submitted *in the respective year*.[5] Consider the following example: in year 1, a firm has filed some number of priority applications, invented jointly or individually by three inventors A, B, and C. The inventor count variable for the firm in year 1 takes the value of three. Similarly in year 2, the inventor count variable is four when we have four distinct inventors A, D, E, F, irrespective of the number of patents that have been produced by them. In year 3, the inventor count variable is five if there are five distinct inventors, B, E, F, G, H, who have generated patented inventions for the patentee. But these inventor counts will not correctly reflect the number of employees active in invention processes if these processes take longer than one year, and if considerable time lags are present between the conception of the research and the filing of the patent application.[6] For a number of reasons, one might expect that a kind of moving average will provide a more reliable measure of the inventive workforce and of its development over time. Therefore, we compute as alternative measures counts over windows of three and five years to account for potential lags and delays in the invention process. For instance, applying a three-year time window in the above example, we obtain an inventor count variable of eight in year 2, because there are eight distinct inventors—A, B, C, D, E, F, G, H—who have produced patents in periods 1, 2, or 3. We will compare the different measures in our calibration exercise, and we will also use these alternatives in market value and productivity regressions.

7.3 Dataset

Our analysis will use two related datasets in which we have identified inventors and computed inventor counts. First, we apply the above approach to the population of EPO and PCT patent filings as contained in PatStat (2012). Second, we use a more precisely defined dataset containing information on 3,024 European and US publicly listed companies that have disclosed R&D data. Although firms in many European countries firms are not required to disclose R&D information, we expect that the companies included in our sample account for the lion's share of the overall domestic R&D activities in the respective countries. We can demonstrate that this assumption holds by comparing our company-level R&D to national R&D expenditures as recorded in the 'OECD, STAN database'. Similarly the US companies in our sample account for a dominant share of the R&D performed by the US business sector.

We use data on consolidated R&D expenditures at the level of the ultimate parent company holding the majority of shares. Consolidated data information is preferable to nonconsolidated data because within business groups, considerable contracting of R&D services takes place.[7] We have linked patents to the parent company level directly and indirectly through its subsidiaries firms. In particular, for European firms we have retrieved the overall list of subsidiaries using the Amadeus business directory (amadeus.bvdep.com) of the Bureau Van Dijk during the years 1998–2006. This task has generated a list of about 130 thousand subsidiaries which we relate to our 1,515 corporate groups. The consolidation of patents at the parent has relied on three levels of the hierarchy of the business group. On the other hand for 1,502 US firms included in Compustat we have employed the list of the subsidiaries from Who Owns Whom directory by Dun & Bradstreet for the years 1993–2004. We have also extracted other firm-level variables from Amadeus and Compustat database, such as sector codes, sales, labor costs, capital expenditures, and data on the financial structure of the firm, including market capitalization, assets, and debt structure.

Table 7.1 reports the geographical distribution of the R&D performers in our sample and the relative share of the invested R&D to overall business sector R&D expenditure (BERD). Only countries with more than fifty firms are explicitly tabulated. The coverage with respect to R&D expenditure as reported in the 'OECD, STAN database' has been computed for year 2000.

The R&D data at the firm level and the national (territorial) data are not directly comparable. Our firm-level data include the R&D expenditures performed by subsidiaries in countries other than the home country, whereas the country statistics are based on a territorial definition of R&D, which includes the R&D undertaken by subsidiaries of corporations headquartered in other countries. Nonetheless, we can use the comparison to make the extent of our sample somewhat transparent. Our set of R&D performers captured in our data is equal in R&D expenditures to 89.6 percent of the overall national business R&D in the European countries, and to

Table 7.1 Coverage of the sample: Top R&D Performers in Europe and United States

Country	(A) Firms with R&D data	(B) Total R&D in 2000 mln Euros	(C) National R&D by the business sector mln Euros about year 2000	(D) Coverage (B)/(C)
Finland	78	3,649	3,136	116.3%
France	203	19,182	19,348	99.1%
Germany	237	34,697	35,600	97.5%
Italy	50	1,867	6,239	29.9%
The Netherlands	66	8,582	4,458	192.5%
Sweden	126	7,364	8,118	90.7%
Switzerland	92	10,258	5,065	202.5%
United Kingdom	474	18,788	18,884	99.5%
Other E.U.@	189	4,098	42,690	9.6%
Overall Europe	1,515	108,484	121,054	89.6%
United States	1,502	157,408	216,552	72.7%
Overall	3,017	265,893	337,606	78.8%

Notes: Authors' elaboration from Amadeus, Compustat, and 'OECD, STAN database'.

@ It includes also Norway.

72.7 percent in the US context. In some countries (Finland, the Netherlands, and Switzerland) the total R&D in our sample is even higher than the R&D expenditures reported by the 'OECD, STAN database'. These are typically smaller countries in which important multinational enterprises (MNEs) have their headquarters.

Data on inventors are taken from EPO and PCT patent applications over the period from 1980 to the end of 2009. These applications are then linked with firm-level data using the patentee names (Thoma et al. 2010). We think that limiting our study to these two legislations is not a serious drawback for our investigation. In fact, EPO and PCT systems are typically used by firms to obtain international protection of their inventions, making this dataset suitable to track international knowledge flows. Further, the higher patent fee costs of these systems allow one to analyse inventions that are more comparable in economic value.[8]

To compute the inventor counts, we first implemented a cleaning of the inventor names extracted from the PatStat database.[9] Then each inventor name was tokenized and an index was created for their identification based on the following information: the two longest tokens of their name, the country given in the inventor address, the name of the patentee, and the priority year of the patent. This information was then used to identify identical inventors in order to avoid double counting of individuals active in inventive activities at the respective (consolidated) firm in a given year.[10]

In our data, we face with two kinds of truncation lags. The first one regards the publication lag. Given the eighteen-month publication delay at the EPO and PCT, there is a potential right end truncation problem in our sample affecting the priority years 2007 and 2008. The second truncation lag is generated by counting inventors over multiyear time windows—this aggravates the censoring problem. Indeed the use of three-year and five-year window inventor counts lead to additional truncation effects of one or two additional years. Thus, even years 2005 and 2006 could be affected by a right end truncation problem.

7.4 Descriptive Evidence

7.4.1. Inventor Workforce Data

We continue our empirical analysis by considering the number of active inventors for a given reference year using the count measures defined in section 7.2. The purpose of this analysis is to detect major changes in the inventor populations and to relate those to technical and economic developments. Figure 7.1 depicts inventor counts by priority year of their patent filing as share of the overall national R&D personnel from 1985 to 2005. Only the trends of the main inventor location countries are shown: Canada, France, Germany, Italy, Japan, the United Kingdom, the United States, and the OECD group of countries.[11]

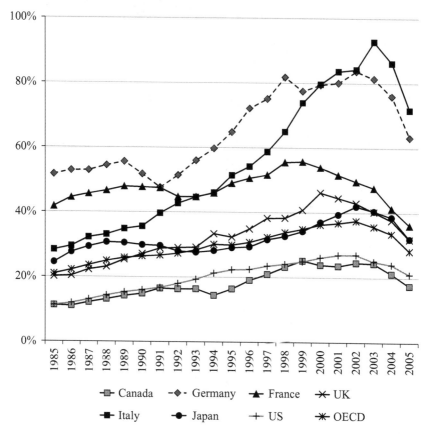

Figure 7.1 Inventor workforce in the EPO/PCT system as share of business intramural R&D personnel

There are several noteworthy trends during the two decades depicted. In the period before 1990, the number of active inventors in the dataset has grown in all the countries with an almost constant rate. On the one hand this can be associated with the increasing adoption of the EPO and PCT systems for obtaining patent protection. Indeed, we can notice from more detailed tabulations that the overall trend has been followed evenly across technical fields (see discussion below).

Japanese inventor counts are characterised by a sustained expansion of the inventor workforce in this period than that in the early '90s. This growth of inventors could be associated with the so-called the 'Japanese Miracle' after the oil crisis in the '70s when many Japanese firms outperformed the US and European companies in the manufacturing industry (Kumar 2001; Granstrand 1999). Moreover, the '80s witnessed the fast diffusion of robotics for cost reduction in manufacturing as a response to the energy crisis. Indeed, in this technological area the Japanese firms began playing a leading role in R&D at the worldwide level.

Second, after 1995 we can notice clearly the sharp increase of inventor workforce as share of the R&D personnel in all countries. This fast growth may be directly associated with the increase of patenting propensity following several pro-patent reforms in many developed and developing economies during the '90s (Hall 2005; Hall and Ziedonis 2001; Park 2008). Some these reforms include: the introduction of the World Trade Organization agreement on trade-related aspects of intellectual property rights; the extension of patenting to new subject areas such as biotechnology, software, and business methods at the USPTO, which in turn influenced directly or indirectly filings at the EPO and PCT; the inception of specialized courts to resolve legal disputes on intellectual property matters such as, for example, the US Court of Appeals of Federal Circuit.

Whereas some of these effects may simply have added to patent filings, the rise in inventors suggests that more individuals participated in the production of patents. This is in line with evidence that the national R&D expenditures grew strongly in some countries after the mid-'90s (Guellec and van Pottelsberghe de la Potterie 2001; Le Bas and Sierra 2002). Another positive factor influencing the size of inventor workforce after 1995 has been the advent and fast growth of the so-called Internet economy that required significant inventive effort both on the hardware and software technologies— including computing, memories, telecommunication, remote management, and new business models conveyed through the Internet (Patel and Vega 1999). This phenomenon has been particular marked in the US context and may have reinforced the effects from the mentioned pro-patenting reforms.

Last but not least, a final factor sustaining the growth of the inventor workforce active in the EPO and PCT systems has been the globalization of the R&D activities. Several scholars have pointed that during the '90s the internationalization of R&D activities increased significantly (Howells 1990; Archibugi and Iammarino 1999). Previous research have claimed that the channels of the globalisation of R&D has been threefold: (i) the exploitation of technology through international trade flows undertaken by both multinational and national firms; (ii) collaborations in the business and academic sectors through international joint ventures; (iii) generation of technology by multinational corporations undertaken through their foreign direct investment activities in foreign countries.

Figure 7.2 reports the foreign-employed inventor counts by reference year for the overall EPO and PCT dataset. As we notice the share of inventors employed by a foreign patentee or a patentee owned by a foreign company has been very high and increasing during the '90s. This is particularly relevant for the European countries but has also been clearly increasing for the United States and the OECD countries. However, the absolute share is not directly comparable. Indeed, the share of foreign-employed inventors is higher for

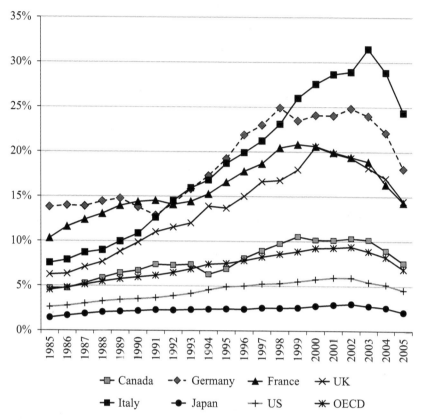

Figure 7.2 Foreign-employed inventors in the EPO/PCT system as share of business intramural R&D personnel

European countries because Figure 7.2 considers a foreign patentee also an intra-European company. In synthesis, at the OECD level about 10 percent of the inventors have been directly or indirectly employed with a foreign company. This evidence points to the important role of the access to scientific and technical human capital as driver for globalization of R&D activities (Florida 1997; Granstrand 1999; Von Zedtwitz and Gassmann 2002).

7.4.2 Country and Technology Trends in the Process of R&D Globalization

In this section we explore how the geographical distribution of inventor locations by the national origin of the patentee has evolved over time in the overall dataset and in our sample of patentee firms whose ownership structures have been codified.

First, we can notice from Table 7.2 that there is considerable variation in terms of the extent to which inventive activity is located in a foreign country. For example, even after year 2000 Japanese patentees had concentrated four out five of their inventors in their home country, followed by US and Canadian patentees with about three-quarters of them. Conversely, even as early as between 1986 and 1990, patentees in Switzerland and Netherlands had located more than three-quarters of their inventors in foreign countries. In France and the UK domestic inventors have accounted for about 40 percent of the R&D workforce, whereas in Germany and Italy this share is around two-thirds.

Second, in some countries there is a clear tendency towards internationalization of R&D activities over time. Comparing the period 1996–2000 to the first time period (1986–1990), the share of domestic inventors has decreased from 43.4 percent to 40.0 percent for French firms, 35.0 percent to 28.2 percent in the UK, 29.2 percent to 24.4 percent in Switzerland, and 46.1 percent to 38.1 percent in Sweden. The evidence documented in Table 7.2 is therefore consistent with the view that the globalisation of R&D activities is increasing over the period 1986–2000.

Third, we can notice that the United States has gained most strongly in this process, followed by Germany and France. For example, within two decades the countries that have directed more inventors toward the US are Canada and Switzerland, whereas Germany and France have attracted relative more patentees respectively from Sweden and United Kingdom.

For a number of reasons, these estimates are likely to underreport the true extent of globalization. Much larger measures of R&D internationalization can be expected once the full-fledged identity of the parent companies is taken into account. To do so, we have followed the principle of allocating firms in our patentee sample to the country where the owner with the dominant ownership share resides. Table 7.3 reports the geographical distribution of inventors by the country of the top R&D-performing patentees in Europe. The results confirm many of the previous findings. First, the Swiss and Dutch firms are the most globalized in terms of the location of their inventors. A more differentiated picture emerges for the time trend— the share of nondomestic inventors has been almost stable for patentees from Germany and France, whereas inventive activities have become more global over time for the UK and US patentees. Third, the United States and France have attracted a large part of the inventive activities in our sample.[12]

Table 7.4 attempts to provide a dynamic view of the development in various technological areas. For simplicity, we have reported the one-digit aggregated technological areas (for further details see OST 2008).

For (1) Electrical and Electronic technologies we can notice a very fast process of locating inventive activities outside the domestic borders of Germany, France, Sweden, Switzerland, the UK, and the United States. In the same countries a similar trend, although less marked, can be encountered also for (2) Instruments and (5) Process Engineering. In (3) Chemicals

Table 7.2 Distribution of inventors by patentee and inventor country

Overall Dataset—Business Applicants—Row Percent

Priority Years 1986–1990

Patentee country code	Inventor country code												
	CA	CH	DE	FR	GB	IT	JP	KR	NL	other EU	RoW	SE	US
CA	76.4	0.2	1.2	1.1	6.7	0.1	2.7	0.0	0.1	1.3	1.2	0.1	9.0
CH	1.8	29.2	22.8	4.8	5.1	2.4	4.0	0.0	0.9	3.4	1.5	2.7	21.4
DE	0.2	1.1	62.6	4.1	2.1	0.8	4.5	0.1	0.6	2.6	1.3	0.6	19.4
FR	1.0	0.6	19.6	43.4	4.0	2.4	5.8	1.5	1.1	3.0	0.7	0.8	16.1
GB	1.8	2.1	10.3	5.4	35.0	1.1	8.4	0.5	2.8	2.2	1.1	1.4	27.9
IT	0.4	0.9	5.8	6.5	3.9	62.7	1.6	0.0	0.4	2.4	1.0	0.5	13.8
JP	0.4	0.1	0.9	0.1	0.4	0.0	90.6	0.7	0.4	0.1	0.5	0.0	5.8
KR	0.0	0.0	0.2	7.6	0.4	0.0	40.3	49.3	0.0	0.1	0.4	0.0	1.6
NL	0.9	1.6	25.1	5.5	7.8	3.9	12.4	0.0	18.6	3.6	0.9	1.5	18.1
other EU	1.0	2.0	12.2	7.8	4.1	0.9	7.3	0.0	1.4	39.7	2.7	2.0	19.0
RoW	2.8	0.4	2.9	0.9	1.6	0.4	39.4	3.9	0.2	1.2	31.8	0.3	14.3
SE	0.4	4.1	13.5	5.8	4.1	2.6	0.6	0.0	1.0	5.2	1.2	46.1	15.3
US	1.2	0.3	5.3	1.4	2.3	0.4	6.1	0.4	1.8	0.9	1.0	0.2	78.8

Priority Years 1991–1995

Patentee country code	Inventor country code												
	CA	CH	DE	FR	GB	IT	JP	KR	NL	other EU	RoW	SE	US
CA	73.3	0.3	2.1	1.0	5.2	0.2	0.7	0.0	0.1	0.9	2.7	0.1	13.5
CH	1.2	24.2	22.8	5.5	5.3	2.7	3.3	0.0	1.1	4.2	3.1	3.0	23.5
DE	0.5	1.3	57.9	5.2	2.2	1.1	4.5	0.7	0.7	3.3	1.4	0.5	21.0

Patentee country code	CA	CH	DE	FR	GB	IT	JP	KR	NL	other EU	RoW	SE	US
FR	1.2	0.8	17.8	41.7	4.0	2.4	4.6	4.3	1.2	3.2	1.2	0.9	16.9
GB	1.8	1.0	11.2	6.3	28.3	1.3	11.2	1.3	2.4	2.8	2.2	1.5	28.8
IT	0.4	1.0	5.5	8.4	3.3	59.8	1.7	0.0	0.3	2.8	1.4	0.3	15.0
JP	0.4	0.0	1.3	0.1	0.5	0.0	87.4	2.0	0.3	0.3	1.3	0.0	6.3
KR	0.1	0.0	0.1	1.6	0.3	0.0	18.3	74.9	0.1	0.2	2.1	0.0	2.2
NL	0.7	1.8	23.0	5.9	6.4	4.7	12.8	0.1	15.5	4.3	2.2	2.0	20.4
other EU	0.8	1.9	11.9	8.0	4.0	1.4	6.9	0.1	1.3	38.1	4.4	2.1	19.2
RoW	2.3	0.3	4.0	0.9	1.5	0.5	29.9	9.0	0.2	1.0	33.9	0.2	16.3
SE	0.7	4.1	16.4	4.1	4.5	2.3	0.7	0.2	1.2	5.9	1.5	42.5	15.8
US	1.2	0.3	4.6	1.4	2.4	0.5	5.7	0.9	1.6	1.1	2.0	0.2	78.2

Priority Years 1996–2000

Patentee country code	Inventor country code												
	CA	CH	DE	FR	GB	IT	JP	KR	NL	other EU	RoW	SE	US
CA	64.2	0.7	2.7	1.2	5.2	0.2	0.7	0.0	0.3	0.8	4.6	0.2	19.2
CH	1.2	22.6	21.1	6.0	4.2	2.7	3.2	0.1	1.0	4.7	6.0	3.2	24.0
DE	0.7	1.4	59.6	5.3	2.5	1.0	2.8	1.1	1.0	3.7	2.1	0.6	18.3
FR	2.7	0.9	17.2	37.2	3.3	2.6	4.3	4.9	1.3	3.4	1.7	0.9	20.0
GB	2.8	1.0	11.2	6.3	26.7	1.0	11.4	2.3	2.0	3.2	3.3	1.6	27.3
IT	0.6	1.0	5.1	8.5	2.3	58.8	1.9	0.0	0.6	3.0	2.4	0.5	15.3
JP	0.4	0.1	1.9	0.2	0.6	0.1	84.7	2.5	0.3	0.2	2.3	0.1	6.7
KR	0.2	0.0	0.5	0.1	0.3	0.0	12.3	74.3	0.2	0.6	6.5	0.1	4.8
NL	0.7	1.2	24.0	6.1	5.5	3.7	9.4	0.6	16.4	4.3	3.5	2.0	22.6
other EU	1.2	1.4	10.7	6.9	4.3	1.4	5.2	0.1	1.3	40.3	5.7	2.0	19.5
RoW	1.8	0.4	3.2	0.9	1.3	0.5	22.6	7.2	0.3	0.9	42.2	0.2	18.6
SE	1.2	3.2	18.5	3.5	5.0	1.9	1.1	0.1	1.0	8.0	2.5	38.6	15.3
US	1.4	0.3	4.7	1.4	2.6	0.5	4.8	1.1	1.7	1.4	3.4	0.3	76.5

(Continued)

Table 7.2 (Continued)

Patentee country code	Priority Years 2001–2005 Inventor country code												
	CA	CH	DE	FR	GB	IT	JP	KR	NL	other EU	RoW	SE	US
CA	69.0	0.7	2.4	1.3	4.6	0.2	0.4	0.2	0.3	1.0	4.1	0.1	15.8
CH	1.1	24.4	20.1	7.6	4.0	3.3	2.3	0.1	0.9	5.4	5.0	1.9	23.8
DE	0.7	1.4	62.3	6.1	2.3	1.3	2.5	0.4	1.0	4.2	2.2	0.6	14.9
FR	1.9	1.1	16.9	40.0	3.1	3.3	4.4	4.2	0.8	4.3	2.3	0.9	16.9
GB	1.6	1.3	10.3	7.2	28.2	1.2	7.3	6.4	1.9	3.9	4.2	1.8	24.6
IT	0.4	0.9	3.9	6.8	1.9	68.7	1.8	0.0	0.4	3.1	2.4	0.4	9.1
JP	0.4	0.1	1.5	0.3	0.6	0.1	86.2	2.1	0.4	0.4	2.2	0.2	5.6
KR	0.2	0.0	0.5	0.1	0.2	0.2	5.5	86.6	0.4	0.3	3.2	0.0	2.7
NL	0.6	1.4	25.1	7.7	6.3	4.0	6.9	0.7	18.4	5.4	4.3	1.8	17.4
other EU	0.9	1.1	10.2	7.2	3.8	1.7	5.0	0.1	1.3	46.5	6.3	1.7	14.1
RoW	1.0	0.4	2.2	0.9	1.5	0.5	13.9	5.6	0.4	1.0	56.9	0.1	15.7
SE	1.2	4.0	17.5	3.3	5.9	2.4	1.4	0.1	1.4	8.4	2.4	38.1	13.7
US	1.4	0.3	5.1	1.6	2.8	0.6	3.3	1.0	1.9	1.8	4.3	0.3	75.6

Notes: Country codes are based on the ISO 2-digit classification. RoW is the acronym for 'Rest of World'.

Table 7.3 Distribution of inventors by patentee and inventor country—Top European and US R&D Performers

Top European and US R&D Performers—Row Percent

1986–1990

Patentee country code	Inventor country code												
	CA	CH	DE	FR	GB	IT	JP	KR	NL	other EU	RoW	SE	US
CH	0.5	26.5	22.3	6.0	7.0	1.1	1.6	0.0	0.9	2.6	1.2	3.6	26.6
DE	0.3	0.9	55.5	5.9	2.9	0.8	2.4	0.2	0.6	2.4	0.8	0.7	26.6
FR	1.1	0.7	26.0	35.9	4.3	2.2	4.1	0.0	1.4	3.9	0.8	1.1	18.5
GB	0.6	0.3	9.8	5.5	33.2	0.8	8.6	0.0	3.6	1.6	1.0	1.9	33.0
IT	0.6	0.4	8.6	8.6	11.4	53.7	0.1	0.0	0.1	3.4	0.4	0.1	12.5
NL	0.3	0.9	38.2	7.7	6.8	2.2	3.8	0.0	22.8	2.3	0.5	1.0	13.5
other EU	0.5	0.8	11.4	10.8	4.9	1.0	5.6	0.0	2.6	40.3	0.7	4.1	17.3
SE	0.5	5.9	15.7	8.2	4.9	2.7	0.6	0.0	1.5	6.9	1.3	37.8	14.0
US	0.9	0.4	7.0	2.3	2.7	0.5	2.7	0.0	2.7	1.2	0.7	0.4	78.5

1991–1995

Patentee country code	Inventor country code												
	CA	CH	DE	FR	GB	IT	JP	KR	NL	other EU	RoW	SE	US
CH	0.4	20.7	23.1	7.2	7.6	1.6	1.7	0.0	1.1	4.2	1.5	3.9	27.0
DE	0.6	1.3	50.1	7.2	2.7	1.1	3.2	1.1	0.7	3.4	1.4	0.6	26.4
FR	1.3	0.9	23.0	37.0	3.5	2.6	3.4	0.4	1.6	4.0	1.1	1.1	20.0
GB	0.9	0.5	9.7	6.4	25.4	1.1	13.1	0.1	2.7	2.5	1.7	2.1	33.7
IT	0.6	0.3	7.8	11.1	8.1	52.7	0.4	0.1	0.3	4.1	0.6	0.3	13.7
NL	0.3	1.5	35.2	8.8	6.6	3.1	2.7	0.0	18.8	3.0	2.2	1.3	16.4
other EU	0.3	0.8	11.3	11.7	4.8	1.3	4.4	0.1	2.0	41.5	1.2	3.5	17.1
SE	1.0	4.9	15.9	4.8	5.0	2.2	0.9	0.3	1.8	5.8	1.2	40.3	15.8
US	1.0	0.4	5.7	2.0	2.7	0.6	3.1	0.1	1.6	1.4	1.5	0.3	79.5

(Continued)

Table 7.3 (Continued)

Patentee country code	1996–2000 Inventor country code												
	CA	CH	DE	FR	GB	IT	JP	KR	NL	other EU	RoW	SE	US
CH	0.7	20.5	21.7	8.5	5.7	2.3	1.8	0.1	0.9	5.3	2.4	4.8	25.2
DE	0.8	1.2	53.1	7.1	3.2	1.4	2.3	1.7	0.9	3.7	2.1	0.8	21.6
FR	1.6	1.1	22.1	35.2	2.9	3.1	3.3	0.5	1.6	4.1	1.6	1.2	21.9
GB	1.4	1.2	9.8	7.8	23.2	1.7	14.6	0.1	2.4	2.9	2.0	2.5	30.4
IT	0.9	0.8	8.1	14.4	4.9	45.4	2.4	0.0	0.8	4.2	1.5	0.6	15.9
NL	0.4	1.0	33.4	8.3	4.9	3.6	2.0	1.0	19.1	3.5	4.2	1.1	17.6
other EU	0.8	0.8	11.0	8.8	5.4	1.3	3.0	0.1	1.8	42.2	1.9	3.5	19.4
SE	1.7	2.8	13.9	3.3	5.8	1.8	1.4	0.1	1.7	9.1	2.9	40.2	15.3
US	1.3	0.4	6.4	2.1	3.4	0.7	2.6	0.1	2.5	1.8	2.8	0.3	75.7

Patentee country code	2001–2006 Inventor country code												
	CA	CH	DE	FR	GB	IT	JP	KR	NL	other EU	RoW	SE	US
CH	0.7	21.2	19.9	10.9	4.9	2.6	1.6	0.2	0.7	6.5	2.4	3.2	25.1
DE	0.9	1.1	55.2	8.5	3.0	1.5	2.5	0.6	0.7	4.3	2.5	0.8	18.4
FR	2.0	1.4	20.6	36.7	2.7	3.7	4.0	0.6	0.9	4.6	2.1	1.2	19.6
GB	1.5	1.9	9.4	11.4	22.8	1.9	7.3	0.1	2.6	3.4	3.4	3.0	31.3
IT	0.7	0.5	6.1	15.1	4.1	53.4	1.8	0.1	0.5	5.4	1.7	0.6	10.0
NL	0.3	1.0	32.5	10.2	5.3	4.2	1.5	1.1	19.3	4.7	4.8	0.7	14.4
other EU	0.8	0.7	11.0	10.7	4.2	1.8	3.2	0.1	1.5	44.1	2.9	3.0	15.9
SE	1.5	3.1	15.0	2.9	7.0	3.4	1.5	0.2	2.0	9.3	2.8	37.5	14.0
US	1.3	0.4	7.7	2.4	3.6	0.9	2.0	0.2	3.1	2.3	3.5	0.4	72.0

Notes: Country codes are based on the ISO 2-digit classification. RoW is the acronym for 'Rest of World'.

Table 7.4 Share of foreign inventors by technological class and patentee country

Overall Dataset—Business Applicants

1 Electricity—Electronics

year	CA	CH	DE	ES	FR	GB	IT	JP	KR	NL	RoW	SE	US
1986–1990	41.6	29.8	19.0	16.2	26.7	16.8	36.5	6.8	77.9	48.5	80.2	10.7	14.3
1991–1995	42.0	38.2	28.4	11.8	35.3	21.1	36.0	14.9	74.9	48.0	76.9	21.1	16.4
1996–2000	46.4	51.9	31.4	6.5	40.0	29.6	33.7	20.6	68.9	41.0	64.7	33.1	16.6
2001–2005	31.9	54.1	26.0	3.7	35.1	24.2	38.2	15.8	31.3	49.3	43.0	39.1	17.4

2 Instruments

year	CA	CH	DE	ES	FR	GB	IT	JP	KR	NL	RoW	SE	US
1986–1990	27.5	36.5	13.2	9.8	15.3	17.0	28.9	6.1	89.3	45.2	62.7	15.7	10.7
1991–1995	27.5	39.6	15.2	15.2	17.5	23.1	24.9	8.9	75.1	39.9	63.9	15.7	12.2
1996–2000	29.4	45.1	17.6	11.6	22.8	24.9	22.1	11.5	62.1	36.7	55.7	22.9	14.0
2001–2005	25.7	50.6	16.0	5.7	17.9	20.4	17.7	9.4	30.9	41.5	41.9	23.5	13.9

3 Chemicals

year	CA	CH	DE	ES	FR	GB	IT	JP	KR	NL	RoW	SE	US
1986–1990	28.4	46.5	13.6	13.2	16.8	26.5	25.2	3.2	55.1	51.1	36.1	24.6	11.3
1991–1995	31.3	56.0	17.8	28.2	18.5	28.8	22.9	5.0	34.7	53.6	42.4	31.3	15.0
1996–2000	31.4	61.5	21.5	18.9	22.7	34.9	21.3	6.3	28.7	53.2	38.9	42.8	18.1
2001–2005	23.6	63.0	21.0	7.3	21.8	33.4	13.6	5.8	10.8	54.7	24.3	46.2	17.5

(Continued)

Table 7.4 (Continued)

4 Pharmaceuticals—Biotech

year	CA	CH	DE	ES	FR	GB	IT	JP	KR	NL	RoW	SE	US
1986–1990	19.7	61.1	20.5	16.5	14.8	22.8	11.7	4.9	17.5	39.8	27.0	26.8	9.0
1991–1995	22.1	62.0	22.1	18.0	15.6	31.1	11.5	6.7	10.6	47.0	35.6	37.2	11.9
1996–2000	20.4	65.9	25.5	14.0	18.0	34.7	15.9	6.7	19.6	46.2	31.5	41.6	13.1
2001–2005	20.5	69.6	24.5	9.3	18.8	28.5	8.9	5.0	6.0	45.7	20.8	43.7	13.8

5 Process engineering

year	CA	CH	DE	ES	FR	GB	IT	JP	KR	NL	RoW	SE	US
1986–1990	19.9	34.7	8.6	16.1	11.5	18.1	12.1	3.3	75.3	31.5	35.3	15.2	9.7
1991–1995	21.8	42.0	10.5	19.6	13.6	23.1	10.4	4.9	55.6	32.3	37.0	19.2	11.6
1996–2000	29.1	50.0	12.7	7.9	14.6	24.3	10.0	6.1	46.4	30.5	35.4	22.7	13.7
2001–2005	19.0	54.5	12.0	5.5	14.0	20.4	6.4	4.3	14.7	31.1	26.2	20.9	15.1

6 Mechanical engineering

year	CA	CH	DE	ES	FR	GB	IT	JP	KR	NL	RoW	SE	US
1986–1990	24.4	27.8	7.5	10.9	11.7	30.8	7.5	4.8	86.0	28.7	48.6	12.3	9.9
1991–1995	27.7	32.5	8.0	15.7	12.7	38.9	8.5	7.2	59.4	32.2	50.6	15.1	10.5
1996–2000	28.6	39.0	9.7	5.0	12.0	33.0	7.8	7.4	48.9	26.4	49.0	22.4	13.3
2001–2005	24.3	41.2	11.1	7.1	10.7	24.7	7.8	5.7	16.6	26.4	36.1	33.8	15.8

7 Other

year	CA	CH	DE	ES	FR	GB	IT	JP	KR	NL	RoW	SE	US
1986–1990	9.8	31.9	7.5	4.8	8.5	16.1	8.2	3.8	52.8	30.2	29.0	8.8	7.5
1991–1995	10.7	32.5	9.2	5.2	10.3	19.2	7.8	6.5	33.8	32.7	30.7	11.7	8.7
1996–2000	15.6	33.2	9.4	4.2	11.8	23.9	7.5	6.8	27.5	30.3	28.9	17.5	10.9
2001–2005	13.6	40.4	10.6	4.1	12.8	21.8	7.1	5.6	8.6	40.3	24.0	20.6	12.7

Notes: Country codes are based on the ISO 2-digit classification. RoW is the acronym for 'Rest of World'.

and (4) Pharmaceuticals the share of foreign inventors has been relatively high compared to the other technological areas. Moreover, this share has been increasing visibly in France, Sweden, Switzerland, the UK, and the United States. It also appears that areas in which the respective countries may have some comparative advantage (e.g., mechanical engineering in Germany and Japan) show relatively low tendencies to locate inventors in other countries.

7.5 Calibrating Inventor Count Data

In this section we discuss the econometric specification and the results of the R&D accounting model. We start by showing the descriptive statistics of the variables used in the multivariate analysis, and then we present estimates from the proposed econometric specification.

7.5.1 Accounting for R&D and Inventors

In the following we advance a simple accounting model linking the R&D investments of a firm with its domestic and foreign R&D employment. In line with the Frascati Manual definitions (OECD 2002), we assume that R&D expenditures R_{it} of a firm i in year t can consist of labour costs L_{it}, expenditures for materials M_{it}, and capital investment C_{it}. From the survey data collected in OECD countries, it is well know that R&D labour costs account for roughly 60 percent of overall R&D budgets. Materials make up roughly 30 percent, and capital goods approximately one-tenth of R&D expenditures.[13] The exact composition differs by industry, technology, and possibly other factors, but it appears to be relatively stable over time.

Hence our initial accounting equation is given by:

$$R_{it} = L_{it} + M_{it} + C_{it} \tag{1}$$

We proceed by setting labour expenditures equal to the wages incurred in the various countries in which the firm is active. We assume that there are K countries in which firms are actively pursuing inventions:

$$L_{it} = \left(\sum_{k=1}^{K} W_{ikt} I_{ikt} \right) \tag{2}$$

where I_{ikt} is the inventor workforce of firm i in country k at time t and W_{ikt} is the relative wage level in that country. We model total R&D expenditures R_{it} of firm i in year t then in the following simple accounting manner:

$$R_{it} = \left(\sum_{k=1}^{K} W_{ikt} I_{ikt} \right) \cdot m_{it} \cdot c_{it} \tag{3}$$

Where the materials and capital components are modelled as time- and firm-specific mark-ups m_{it} and c_{it}. Taking the logarithm of equation (3) we have the expression:

$$\log R_{it} = r_{it} = \log\left(\sum_{k=1}^{K} W_{ikt} I_{ikt}\right) + \log m_{it} + \log c_{it} \tag{4}$$

We do not observe inventor wages in our data, but (4) can in principle be estimated as a nonlinear equation in which wages are treated as unknown coefficients. To simplify (4) further, we assume that the time trends are homogeneous across countries and that wage levels are the same across firms within a given country. Let $W_{ikt} = W_{0k} * f(t)$ where $f(t)$ is a time-dependent markup describing the wage behaviour across countries. Then we can estimate for each country a base wage W_{0k} whereas the time development would be subsumed in time dummy variables. The base wage may also be industry-specific if we assume a multiplicative form as for the time impact.

Our nonlinear regression equation is then given by:

$$\log R_{it} = \alpha + \log\left(\sum_{k=1}^{K} \beta_k I_{ikt}\right) + \sum_{j=1}^{J} \delta_j D_j + \sum_{t=1}^{T} \gamma_t D_t + \varepsilon_{it} \tag{5}$$

Where the D_j dummies reflect industries, and the time effects are contained in the D_t variables. The error term is supposed to satisfy the usual *i.i.d.* assumptions. It is important to note that equation (5) would not be identified if we treat the β parameters in the logarithmic function as coefficients of the regression. One of the coefficients needs to be set to an arbitrary level in order to identify the other coefficients up to scale.

An approximation to equation (5) would be to estimate the linear equation

$$\log R_{it} = \alpha + \beta_0 \log I_{it} + \sum_{k=1}^{K} \beta_k \left(\frac{I_{ikt}}{I_{it}}\right) + \sum_{j=1}^{J} \delta_j D_j + \sum_{t=1}^{T} \gamma_t D_t + \varepsilon_{it} \tag{6}$$

using the logarithm of the total number of inventors and country shares as a approximation to the non-linear term in equation (5).[14]

If we can estimate the above equations with reasonable precision, then the estimated coefficients would allow us to derive the total R&D expenditures of a firm from inventor count data. More importantly, we can estimate the R&D expenditures in the respective countries in which a firm is active and thus generate information about the extent to which the firm has internationalized its R&D activities and about the distribution of those R&D activities.

7.5.2 Descriptive statistics

The firm sample is an unbalanced panel of European and US companies who have filed at least one patent application in the EPO or PCT system. In particular, we have 1,515 firms and 10,480 observations for Europe from one to fifteen years per firm over the period 1991–2005, whereas for the United States the sample is made up of 1,502 firms and 14,285 observations over the same period. For these firms we have complete information contemporaneously regarding annual sales, R&D expenditures, cost of employees, capital expenditures, inventor counts, and sector activity code. For a smaller subset we have retrieved tangible assets, debt structure, and market capitalization (see below section 7.6).

As we can notice from Table 7.5 the EU firms in the sample are relatively large with median sales of 319 million euro, whereas operative turnover of the median US firm is only 128 million euro. Conversely, the median R&D intensity of US firms is over two times bigger than the European companies. This evidence points to the larger presence in the US of specialized R&D firms as compared to Europe. These firms are typically young and originate from sectors like pharmaceuticals and biotechnology, software,

Table 7.5 Descriptive statistics

	European firms @			US firms #		
	Mean	S.D.	Median	Mean	S.D.	Median
R&D expenditures^	118	452	9	113	474	12
Sales^	3,551	11,817	319	2,461	10,616	128
Cost of Employees^	657	1,888	62	2,828	5,061	1,036
Capital Expenditures^	301	864	17	135	694	6
R&D/Sales (in percentage)	98.5	2,149.0	3.0	416.8	6,251.0	8.0
Tobin's q*	3.956	6.539	1.753	2.462	3.625	1.447
Assets ^*	3,015	10,555	158	3,388	20,117	177
R&D stock/assets*	0.856	1.652	0.293	0.681	1.182	0.289
Inventors at the home country	49.3	203.3	2	33.4	117.9	0
Inventors at the home country (3 years mav)°	118.9	474.4	7	85.4	290.2	4
Inventors at the home country (5 years mav)°	209.6	837.8	12	147.1	493.9	7
Inventors in the foreign countries	53.7	234.3	1	10.7	89.1	0
Inventors in the foreign countries (3 years mav)°	135.7	573.0	4	27.5	216.4	0
Inventors in the foreign countries (5 years mav)°	236.8	1,003.5	8	47.5	376.6	0

Notes: @10,480 useful observations for 1,515 firms in eighteen countries during 1991–2005.
\# 14,285 useful observations for 1,502 firms during 1991–2005.
^ Milion € deflated with a price index of 2000
* For these variables, there are 7,410 useful observations for 1,103 European firms in eighteen countries during 1991–2005.
° Year moving average (yrs mav) measures.

and other business services. Both in Europe and the United States, a strong skewness of the R&D to sales ratio denotes the presence a few observations of younger firms having very low sales.[15]

Table 7.5 also reports some statistics on the inventor annual counts and stocks according to their geographical location—that is, the home country vis-à-vis other foreign countries. Taking as a benchmark the five-year moving average measures, a typical EU firm has employed about 209.6 inventors in the home country, whereas there a few more in the foreign countries. On the other hand US firms have employed relatively a smaller number of inventors abroad. This evidence can be linked again with the previous discussion on the prominent importance of the United States as locus of inventive activities at the worldwide level.

A first analysis of the relationship between R&D expenditures and the number of inventors is contained in Table 7.6, which depicts the Pearson product-moment correlations for levels and growth rates.

For the European firms, the correlation coefficients in levels of uncorrected annual inventor counts range between 0.754 and 0.792. Using three-year or five-year moving averages leads to an increase in the correlation—for five-year moving averages, the correlation between inventor counts and R&D ranges between 0.760 and 0.811. Growth rates are also correlated rather strongly, but as expected less so than levels. Here the correlation coefficients range between 0.183 and 0.718 for uncorrected annual inventor counts,

Table 7.6 Correlation of inventor counts and R&D expenditures

European firms

Year	log of annual counts			growth rates		
	annual	*3 yrs mav°*	*5 yrs mav°*	*annual*	*3 yrs mav°*	*5 yrs mav°*
1991	0.776	0.778	0.787	–	–	–
1992	0.773	0.795	0.795	0.718	0.719	0.711
1993	0.789	0.800	0.806	0.597	0.659	0.655
1994	0.792	0.809	0.811	0.570	0.673	0.694
1995	0.783	0.794	0.798	0.664	0.712	0.743
1996	0.760	0.779	0.778	0.487	0.583	0.586
1997	0.770	0.774	0.772	0.496	0.592	0.608
1998	0.772	0.781	0.781	0.603	0.631	0.645
1999	0.768	0.769	0.773	0.510	0.648	0.655
2000	0.754	0.760	0.760	0.515	0.631	0.654
2001	0.765	0.773	0.774	0.494	0.574	0.575
2002	0.771	0.777	0.773	0.545	0.652	0.660
2003	0.780	0.788	0.787	0.383	0.514	0.532
2004	0.764	0.771	0.770	0.183	0.290	0.268
2005	0.767	0.779	0.775	0.251	0.356	0.404
Total	0.771	0.780	0.780	0.556	0.628	0.635

US firms

Year	log of annual counts			growth rates		
	annual	*3 yrs mav°*	*5 yrs mav°*	*annual*	*3 yrs mav°*	*5 yrs mav°*
1991	0.542	0.572	0.574	–	–	–
1992	0.568	0.585	0.598	0.573	0.583	0.601
1993	0.568	0.591	0.613	0.494	0.596	0.632
1994	0.554	0.588	0.605	0.450	0.552	0.596
1995	0.586	0.599	0.601	0.161	0.249	0.274
1996	0.570	0.588	0.586	0.485	0.551	0.570
1997	0.573	0.591	0.604	0.254	0.367	0.384
1998	0.574	0.584	0.596	0.493	0.595	0.601
1999	0.589	0.603	0.602	0.337	0.453	0.469
2000	0.577	0.596	0.600	0.237	0.353	0.436
2001	0.574	0.581	0.592	0.289	0.461	0.468
2002	0.582	0.600	0.607	0.299	0.442	0.438
2003	0.565	0.591	0.598	0.388	0.539	0.532
2004	0.573	0.578	0.585	0.165	0.297	0.348
2005	0.555	0.574	0.573	0.172	0.400	0.452
Total	0.574	0.592	0.599	0.417	0.506	0.528

Notes: All coefficients are statistically significant at 1 percent level.

° Year moving average (yrs mav) measures.

and between 0.268 and 0.711 for the five-year moving averages. For US firms we find similar range of correlation coefficients, although their variability across years is bigger. These results are promising—they suggest that there is a strong bivariate relationship between the number of active inventors and overall R&D expenditures. In the following section we explore if the information on inventor location decisions can be utilized to gain further insights into this relationship.

7.5.3 Multivariate Results

In the regression analysis we clustered inventors in five macro regional areas according to their relative levels of pro-capita GDP: i) European Union, fifteen countries (EU15), including also Island, Norway, and Switzerland; ii) other Europe, which groups all the remaining European countries; iii) North America group with the United States and Canada; iv) Far East countries, including Australia, Hong Kong, Indonesia, Japan, Republic of Korea, Malaysia, New Zealand, Singapore, and Taiwan; v) a residual group of countries not considered in subcategories i)–iv).

Panel A of Table 7.7 reports the results of linear estimates of equation (6) with the logarithm of the total number of inventors and the regional shares of inventors as the main variables. The dependent variable is R&D

Table 7.7 R&D accounting regressions based on inventor counts

Dependent Variable: Annual R&D expenditure deflated with a price index of year 2000

Panel A: Log linear regressions@					Panel B: NLLS regressions#		
	European firms		US firms			European firms	US firms
	(1)	(2)	(3)	(4)		(5)	(6)
Total number of inventors (log)	0.728*** [0.007]	0.791*** [0.008]	0.539*** [0.007]	0.603*** [0.009]			
Share of inventors in EU15^		-0.923*** [0.055]		-0.227*** [0.064]	Inventors in EU15*	0.260*** [0.013]	0.460*** [0.040]
Share of inventors in other Europe		-1.425*** [0.482]		-2.044*** [0.264]	Inventors in other Europe	0.085*** [0.030]	0.165*** [0.063]
Share of inventors in Far East§		-1.003*** [0.170]		-1.147*** [0.184]	Inventors in Far East**	0.144*** [0.036]	0.207*** [0.078]
Share of inventors in other countries		-1.138** [0.453]		-1.866*** [0.358]	Inventors in other countries	0.094 [0.101]	-0.060 [0.054]
Share of inventors in the US and Canada		-0.906*** [0.081]		-0.535*** [0.045]	Inventors in USA and Canada	1.000	1.000
Std. error (adj. R-squared)	0.676	0.678	0.436	0.445	Std. error (adj. R-squared)	0.655	0.411

Notes: Consistent estimates are computed with heteroskedasticity robust standard errors. All the regressions include the constant, twenty-four industry dummies, fifteen annual dummies, and only for the European panel fifteen country group dummies and annual-country interaction effect dummies.
^It includes also Island, Norway, and Switzerland.
§It includes AU, HK, ID, JP, KR, MY, NZ, SG, and TW.
@ 10,480 useful observations, 1,515 firms, 20 countries, during 1991–2005
# 14,285 useful observations, 1,502 firms, during 1991–2005
*** indicates statistically significant at 1 percent level, ** 5 percent level, and *10 percent level.

expenditure in deflated prices with price levels of year 2000. Other control variables include dummies for sector of activity, fiscal year, country of incorporation, and annual-country interaction dummies. Second, Panel B of Table 7.7 presents the nonlinear estimations, including similarly built control variables. We used the TSP International Econometric Toolbox (TSP 2005) in order to estimate the specification in absolute terms given by equation (5), which requires the assumption of at least one restriction on the wage coefficients. In particular we set the coefficient of the US and Canada region equal to unity.

As we can notice, inventor counts have considerable explanatory power in these regressions. When we experiment with different count measures, we find that the moving averages perform much better than the simple inventor count variable computed on an annual basis.[16] Therefore for brevity in Table 7.7 we present only the five-year moving average counts. The overall goodness of the linear model as measured by the adjusted R squared index is between 0.728 for the European firms and 0.539 for the US ones. This finding attests to the high correlation of inventor counts to the (consolidated) R&D expenditures at the firm level.

In terms of the elasticity of R&D with respect to the number of inventors, doubling the total number of inventors leads to about a 70 percent increase in total R&D expenditures. This is an expected result, and it is consistent with the previous statement that labour costs are the lion's share of reported R&D expenditures.

The coefficients of the share variables suggest that on average inventive activities for US and European companies in foreign countries are undertaken because they are typically labour cost saving compared to the home country. Two main arguments can be invoked in order to explain this finding. On the one hand, there are cost-reduction drivers in the R&D outsourcing, such as lower cost of labour, government incentives, sponsored university or other research organization research activities, availability of scientists and engineers, smaller turnover rates, more relaxed regulations of the labour markets, and other offset requirements (De Fontenay and Carmel 2004). These drivers could be associated with different types of the outsourced R&D activities: technology augmenting in the developed countries, whereas technology adaptation in the developed ones (Hall 2010). Also the strength of patent protection legislation in the host country could be assimilated to cost opportunity factors, because it directly affects the economic return from R&D activities (Hall 2014).

On the other hand, home country R&D activities could be relatively more expensive than the outsourced ones because they include also some management and coordinating tasks of production with marketing; these tasks are typically difficult to outsource and on average more costly, in particular when the product-development phase requires multiple and continuous interactions with the lead customers from the home country. Furthermore, when a firm operates R&D investments in multiple locations, the R&D management costs typically arise because additional coordination activities are required, and plausibly these activities are also expected to be performed in the home country.

For both the European and US firms in our sample we find that R&D sourcing in the United States and Canada is the most expensive strategy, whereas the converse is true for the other European countries and the Far East. In particular the evidence depicted in Panel B of Table 7.7 suggests that the average labour cost per inventor in the regional grouping of the other European countries is about half of the costs in the EU15 countries. This evidence is fully consistent with the distribution of the income pro-capita. In addition, we can notice that R&D outsourcing in the EU15 countries by US firms is relatively more expensive than for European firms. This finding points to a potential regional advantage by European R&D doers, but it could be also symptom of a lower attractiveness of the EU15 countries for US firms in conducting R&D activities.

7.6 Market Valuation and Productivity Analysis

In this section we attempt to disentangle to what extent R&D activities in foreign countries influence the firm's performance such as market valuation and output. In advancing this task we first rely on the estimation of Tobin's q market value equation. In addition, to corroborate the consistency of the market value approach that markets are efficient in performing the assessment of R&D effects, we estimate several production function regressions combining both static and dynamic panel data frameworks.

7.6.1 Market Value Equation

As discussed in chapter 1 (this volume) the market value approach is forward looking and the goal is to estimate a shadow price return of a given knowledge asset given the market valuation of the firm. The main assumption of this approach regards the fact that markets are featured by a significant level of efficiency in order to have the assets' shadow price equals the discounting factor that allow convergence to the equilibrium where the shadow price of knowledge is equal to unity. From an econometric point of view we simply assume the value of the firm is stylized as a bundle two assets, A_{it} as tangible assets and K_{it} knowledge assets:

$$logV_{it} = f(A_{it}, K_{it}) \qquad (7)$$

In order to have the coefficients measured as elasticities a first-order logarithmic expansion can be performed obtaining the following estimating equation:

$$logQ_{it} = logV_{it}/A_{it} = logq_t + \sigma log(A_{it}) + \gamma_t \, log(K_{it}/A_{it}) \qquad (8)$$

Where γ_t is marginal or shadow value of K/A and σ a scaling factor. We implemented the estimation of equation *(8)* with ordinary least squares, including dummies for the firm's country of origin, industry of activity, year, and year-industry interaction effects.

Implementing the estimation of (8) demands the construction of knowledge capital K. We relied on the perpetual inventory method, assuming a declining balance formula of this kind:

$$K_{it} = (1 - \delta)K_{i,t-1} + R_{it} \tag{9}$$

Where—for a lack of more precise information—δ is usually set to 15 percent (see discussion in chapter 1, this volume).

7.6.2 Production Function Approach

This approach uses the usual Cobb-Douglas production function augmented with an additional input called 'knowledge' capital:

$$Y = \mathring{A}\, L^\alpha\, C^\beta\, K^\delta\, e^u \tag{10}$$

Where L is a measure of labour input, C is tangible capital, K is knowledge asset, $\mathring{A}$ is an efficiency parameter, and u is a disturbance.[17] After taking the logarithms we have:

$$y_{it} = \eta + \lambda_t + \alpha l_{it} + \beta c_{it} + \lambda k_{it} + u_{it} \tag{11}$$

Where the η is the log of the technical efficiency $(\mathring{A})$ and λ_t is a time effect.

Typically, the estimation of (11) can done by ordinary least squares controlling for time invariant fixed effects. In this case suitable price deflators are required. Because firm-specific deflators are not available, we follow the usual practice to use deflators at the industry (2–3 digit) level.

However, if the impact on the productivity adjusts with a lag, then even panel data regressions are obsolete and the productivity literature has suggested alternative estimations by the mean of the generalized method of moments (GMM) (Hall and Mairesse 1996). The GMM is particularly suitable for the estimation of production functions because it is robust to heteroskedasticity across firms and correlation of the disturbances within units over time. Moreover, the efficiency can be achieved under fewer assumptions on the disturbances given that the cross-section dimension is sufficiently large.[18] A possible specification could be that of estimating (11) in log levels accounting also for the autoregressive structure of exogenous and endogenous variables. In this case we have that:

$$y_{it} = y_{it-1} + \eta_i + \lambda_t + \sum_{k=0}^{n} \alpha l_{i(t-k)} + \beta c_{i(t-k)} + \gamma k_{i(t-k)} + u_{it} \tag{11}$$

The approaches of GMM estimations are twofold. First, the GMM-DIF estimator adopts first-differenced panel data approach and exploits all possible lags of the regressors as instruments (Arellano and Bond 1991). This transformation allows one to eliminate any time-invariant unobserved firm-specific effect. On the other hand, GMM-SYS estimator uses lagged differences as instruments for a system of equation in differences and levels (Arellano and Bower 1995). This system approach is more efficient than the GMM-DIF in case of highly persistent time series, which are characterised by a weak correlation between the variable in first differences and its past levels. Whereas the size of the coefficients of the GMM-SYS estimator are comparable to the fixed effects context, the GMM-DIF offers different insights on the regressors' elasticities.

7.6.3 Results

The results of the market value approach are reported in Table 7.8, with productivity estimates in Table 7.9 and Table 7.10. For brevity we estimated the market valuation and productivity analysis only for European firms.

The stock variables based on inventor workforce perform well in the market value approach. In Table 7.8(a) these variables have coefficients of comparable size as the R&D stock, and R squared goodness of fit index scores higher than the models with R&D stock. One possible explanation is that the ex-ante valuation could be different from ex-post, and plausibly the inventor count variables could be a stronger signal for financial markets than an input variable such as R&D. The inventor count variables have a marginal impact on market value of around two-thirds of the impact of R&D stock, which mimics the ratio of R&D labour costs to the overall R&D investment (see footnote 14). Furthermore, the share of inventors in the foreign countries brings further significance in the Models 5–8 in Table 7.8(a). A significant stability of the log tangible asset variable can be denoted pointing to the fact that the inventor counts variables—in particular those based on moving averages—capture almost all the variability explained by the R&D stock (Compare Models 5–7–8). The point elasticity of tangible assets is statistically significant but close to zero, suggesting the existence of a relatively small scaling factor.

Table 7.8(b) presents a detailed decomposition of the yield in firm's market valuation of inventor location by region. On the one hand, the impact of the stock variable of foreign inventors is one-third smaller than the domestic ones (Model 3). On the other hand, the inventor workforce in the EU15 countries show on average a larger impact on firm's market valuation than inventors located in the United States, whereas it is negative or insignificant for the other regions albeit the impact is small. These results are in line with the assumption that, because the market value approach is intrinsically forward looking and overcomes problems related to the timing of costs and revenues, it encompasses also the option value of the R&D investments. In

Table 7.8(a) Market value regressions based on inventor counts: dependent variable—log Tobin's q

(7,410 useful observations, 1,103 European firms, 18 countries, 1991–2005)

	(1)	(2)	(3)	(4)	(5)	(6)	(7)	(8)
Log Assets	-0.043*** [0.006]	-0.043*** [0.006]	-0.040*** [0.006]	-0.038*** [0.006]	-0.065*** [0.006]	-0.058*** [0.007]	-0.053*** [0.006]	-0.050*** [0.006]
Log stock of R&D/Assets§	0.231*** [0.013]				0.227*** [0.013]			
Log stock of inventors/ Assets—yearly counts		0.165*** [0.008]				0.155*** [0.009]		
Log stock of inventors/ Assets—3 yrs mav°			0.179*** [0.009]				0.170*** [0.009]	
Log stock of inventors/ Assets—5 yrs mav°				0.189*** [0.009]				0.180*** [0.009]
Share of foreign inventors					0.362*** [0.036]	0.214*** [0.037]	0.182*** [0.037]	0.154*** [0.037]
Std. error (adj. R-squared)	0.351	0.353	0.358	0.365	0.362	0.357	0.361	0.367

Notes: Consistent estimates are computed with heteroskedasticity robust standard errors. All the regressions include the constant, nineteen country group dummies, twenty-four industry dummies, fifteen annual dummies, and annual-industry interaction effect dummies.
§ The R&D stock and assets are computed in current values.
*** indicates statistically significant at 1 percent level, **5 percent level, and *10 percent level.
° Year moving average (yrs mav) measures.

Table 7.8(b) Market value regressions based on inventor counts: dependent variable—log Tobin's q

(7,410 useful observations, 1,103 European firms, 18 countries, 1991–2005)

	(1) yearly counts	(2) 3 yrs mav°	(3) 5 yrs mav°	(4) yearly counts	(5) 3 yrs mav°	(6) 5 yrs mav°
Log Assets	-0.030*** [0.006]	-0.025*** [0.006]	-0.024*** [0.006]	-0.092*** [0.010]	-0.074*** [0.010]	-0.064*** [0.009]
Log stock of inventors in the home country/Assets	0.110*** [0.008]	0.118*** [0.008]	0.121*** [0.009]			
Log stock of inventors in the foreign country/Assets	0.043*** [0.006]	0.065*** [0.007]	0.078*** [0.007]			
Log stock of inventors in EU15/Assets^				0.118*** [0.009]	0.135*** [0.009]	0.146*** [0.009]
Log stock of inventors in other Europe/Assets				-0.021*** [0.004]	-0.021*** [0.004]	-0.019*** [0.004]
Log stock of inventors in Far East/Assets§				-0.025*** [0.004]	-0.022*** [0.005]	-0.020*** [0.005]
Log stock of inventors in other countries/Assets				-0.013*** [0.003]	-0.012*** [0.004]	-0.011** [0.005]
Log stock of inventors in the US and Canada/Assets				-0.008 [0.005]	0.006 [0.006]	0.018*** [0.006]
Std. error (adj. R-squared)	0.332	0.341	0.350	0.345	0.347	0.353

Notes: Consistent estimates are computed with heteroskedasticity robust standard errors. All the regressions include the constant, fifteen country group dummies, twenty-four industry dummies, fifteen annual dummies, and annual-industry interaction effect dummies.

^It includes also Island, Norway, and Switzerland.

§It includes AU, HK, ID, JP, KR, MY, NZ, SG, and TW.

*** indicates statistically significant at 1 percent level, **5 percent level, and *10 percent level.

° Year moving average (yrs mav) measures.

fact, when a firm incepts its R&D activity across multiple locations, it could well be that the communication and coordination costs arise, and hence the option value of distant-from-headquarters R&D investments could be lower than those in proximity. This effect is typically exacerbated when distant R&D investments are irreversible and the evolution of market needs is unpredictable before their inception (Bloom and Van Reenen 2002).

With respect to the production function approach the size of the coefficients of inventor stocks are large and very significant across all the specifications. Models 1–4 in Table 7.9(a) reveal that the size of the coefficients of inventor stocks are about half of the R&D stock, which is again not distant from the percentage of the R&D labour costs compared to the overall R&D investments. The share of inventors in the foreign countries is confirmed to add further explanatory power in the Models 5–8. The magnitude of the R-squared index of the models with inventor stocks approximate closely the case of the R&D stock: this evidence suggests that not only inventor count measures can be informative on the relative geographical distribution of inventive activities, but also that the absolute statistical loss is relatively limited as compared to the model encompassing the R&D stock.

Nevertheless, it is worth mentioning that in models with inventor counts the impact of capital expenditure is pushed up with about 30 percent. One possible speculation could be that the capital expenditure proxies part of the variability of the R&D stock variable that is not related to labour costs, such as other capital for R&D and potentially materials for R&D, if these costs are positively correlated with capital expenditures—and presumably they are.[19]

A more accurate decomposition of the return to R&D investments by region is advanced in Table 7.9(b). As we can notice one-third of the overall productivity propelled by the inventors' workforce is made by the home country inventors, whereas foreign inventors are responsible for two-thirds of it. Inventors located in the EU15 countries account for the lion's share of the overall productivity, whereas those resident in the United States matter for two-thirds of the impact of the EU15 ones. We find a positive and significant effect also for the other locations, although the relative impact is much smaller. This latter evidence does not necessarily contradict the results of Table 7.8(b) because the variables in the productivity analysis are absolute measures of depreciated stocks, whereas for market value they are normalized by assets.

Table 7.10 presents the dynamic panel estimations, which are supported both by Arellano-Bond test for the second-order serial correlation and the Sargan test on the overidentifying restrictions. With respect to the GMM-DIFF estimator, the impact of R&D stock has a twice larger effect than the stock of the inventor workforce, which is plausible with the fact that the latter variable is more persistent over time than the former one (compare Model 1 with Model 2), and therefore the GMM-SYS would provide more efficient estimates. Second, when we separate the effect of the stock variable

Table 7.9(a) Productivity regressions based on inventor counts. Dependent variable: log sales deflated with a price index of year 2000

(10,480 useful observations, 1,515 European firms, 18 countries, 1991–2005)

	(1)	(2)	(3)	(4)	(5)	(6)	(7)	(8)
Log cost of employees	0.163*** [0.007]	0.222*** [0.009]	0.222*** [0.009]	0.222*** [0.009]	0.162*** [0.007]	0.222*** [0.009]	0.222*** [0.009]	0.222*** [0.009]
Log depreciation of the capital	0.339*** [0.014]	0.452*** [0.014]	0.452*** [0.014]	0.453*** [0.014]	0.336*** [0.014]	0.451*** [0.014]	0.451*** [0.014]	0.452*** [0.014]
Log stock of R&D	0.473*** [0.013]				0.460*** [0.013]			
Log stock of inventors—yearly counts		0.231*** [0.010]				0.217*** [0.010]		
Log stock of inventors—3 yrs mav°			0.233*** [0.010]				0.222*** [0.010]	
Log stock of inventors—5 yrs mav°				0.229*** [0.009]				0.217*** [0.010]
Share of foreign inventors					0.238*** [0.035]	0.190*** [0.041]	0.158*** [0.041]	0.195*** [0.042]
Std. error (adj. R-squared)	0.804	0.767	0.767	0.767	0.804	0.767	0.767	0.767

Notes: Consistent estimates are computed with heteroskedasticity robust standard errors. All the regressions include the constant, fifteen country group dummies, twenty-four industry dummies, fifteen annual dummies, and annual-industry interaction effect dummies.
*** indicates statistically significant at 1 percent level, **5 percent level, and *10 percent level.
° Year moving average (yrs mav) measures.

Table 7.9(b) Productivity regressions based on inventor counts. Dependent variable: log sales deflated with a price index of year 2000

(10,480 useful observations, 1,515 European firms, 18 countries, 1991–2005)

	(1)	(2)	(3)	(4)	(5)	(6)
	yearly counts	*3 yrs mov avg°*	*5 yrs mov avg°*	*yearly counts*	*3 yrs mov avg°*	*5 yrs mov avg°*
Log cost of employees	0.211*** [0.008]	0.211*** [0.008]	0.213*** [0.009]	0.217*** [0.008]	0.213*** [0.008]	0.213*** [0.008]
Log depreciation of the capital	0.437*** [0.014]	0.438*** [0.014]	0.440*** [0.014]	0.446*** [0.014]	0.441*** [0.014]	0.441*** [0.014]
Log stock of inventors in the home country	0.080*** [0.009]	0.076*** [0.009]	0.071*** [0.009]			
Log stock of inventors in the foreign country	0.190*** [0.009]	0.178*** [0.009]	0.168*** [0.008]			
Log stock of inventors in EU15^				0.169*** [0.010]	0.158*** [0.010]	0.147*** [0.010]
Log stock of inventors in other Europe				-0.012 [0.021]	-0.004 [0.017]	0.000 [0.015]
Log stock of inventors in Far East§				0.010 [0.012]	0.020* [0.012]	0.023** [0.011]
Log stock of inventors in other countries				0.044** [0.021]	0.036** [0.018]	0.037** [0.016]
Log stock of inventors in the US and Canada				0.098*** [0.009]	0.095*** [0.009]	0.091*** [0.009]
Std. error (adj. R-squared)	0.771	0.771	0.770	0.769	0.770	0.770

Notes: Consistent estimates are computed with heteroskedasticity robust standard errors. All the regressions include the constant, fifteen country group dummies, twenty-four industry dummies, fifteen annual dummies, and annual-industry interaction effect dummies.
^It includes also Island, Norway, and Switzerland.
§It includes AU, HK, ID, JP, KR, MY, NZ, SG, and TW.
*** indicates statistically significant at 1 percent level, **5 percent level, and *10 percent level.
° Year moving average (yrs mav) measures.

Table 7.10 GMM productivity regressions based on inventor counts

| | GMM-DIFF Estimator | | | GMM-SYS Estimator | | | | |
| | (N=7,487; 1,184 firms) | | | (N=8,860; 1,320 firms) | | | | |
	(1)	(2)	(3)	(4)	(5)	(6)	(7)	(8)
Log Sales—Lag 1	0.495*** [0.067]	0.544*** [0.058]	0.548*** [0.059]	0.735*** [0.042]	0.766*** [0.029]	0.733*** [0.043]	0.766*** [0.029]	0.760*** [0.030]
Log cost of employees	0.030*** [0.005]	0.031*** [0.005]	0.031*** [0.005]	0.034*** [0.006]	0.035*** [0.007]	0.034*** [0.006]	0.036*** [0.007]	0.034*** [0.006]
Log depreciation of the capital	0.033*** [0.009]	0.035*** [0.009]	0.034*** [0.009]	0.044*** [0.010]	0.046*** [0.011]	0.044*** [0.010]	0.046*** [0.011]	0.044*** [0.011]
Log stock of R&D	0.190*** [0.055]			0.114*** [0.043]		0.114*** [0.044]		
Log stock of inventors		0.093*** [0.024]			0.087*** [0.024]		0.089*** [0.025]	
Share of foreign inventors						0.198*** [0.042]	0.098** [0.048]	
Log stock of inventors in the home country			0.047* [0.024]					0.026*** [0.008]
Log stock of inventors in the foreign country			0.053** [0.024]					0.072*** [0.013]
Hansen test (DF)+	99.1 (90)	101.5 (90)	102.1 (90)	391.5 (401)	405.4 (401)	384.5 (401)	402.5 (401)	391.1 (401)
AR(1) test	-4.8*** [0.000]	-5.0*** [0.000]	-5.0*** [0.000]	-5.7*** [0.000]	-5.381*** [0.000]	-5.693*** [0.000]	-5.381*** [0.000]	-5.361*** [0.000]
AR(2) test	0.500 [0.638]	0.500 [0.620]	0.500 [0.613]	0.500 [0.611]	0.507 [0.612]	0.509 [0.611]	0.508 [0.611]	0.515 [0.629]

Notes: Consistent estimates are computed with heteroskedasticity robust standard errors. The PDP-SYS estimator regressions include the constant, fifteen country group dummies, twenty-four industry dummies, fifteen annual dummies, and annual and industry interaction effect dummies. The PDP-DIFF estimator regressions include the constant, fifteen annual dummies, and annual-industry interaction effect dummies.
+ The Hansen test is reported for the two-step estimations.
*** indicates statistically significant at 1 percent level, **5 percent level, and *10 percent level.

of foreign inventors from the domestic ones, the coefficients are of a similar order of magnitude (Model 3).

The GMM-SYS estimator, which is comparable to the pooled linear estimator, reveals the size of the marginal impact of the inventor workforce stock variable is not far distant from the impact of the R&D investment variable. These results hold even when the share of inventors in the foreign countries is included in the regressions. Moreover, we find that the stock variable of foreign inventors has twice as much of an impact than the stock of the domestic ones, and these two coefficients almost round the impact of the overall inventor workforce stock variable (compare Model 5 with 8). As we expected for the inconsistency of the static analysis, the system estimator also shows that the coefficients of the linear regressions are twice upward biased.

In conclusion, the productivity analysis suggests that the impact of the foreign inventor workforce has a bigger impact than the domestic one, whereas in the market value analysis such a result is not confirmed. Two caveats are in order to explain these differential results. On the one hand, productivity estimates are an ex-post analysis based on the historical cost values, and typically it does not take into account the prospect profitability of knowledge. In this context, the foreign inventor workforce is featured by a bigger impact than the domestic ones because a crucial driver of the outsourcing decisions is given by the fact that firms generally multilocate R&D when the foreign countries are lower cost as represented by wages for inventors (see section 7.5).

On the other hand, in the market value analysis the domestic inventor workforce could be a stronger signal for financial markets of the firm's future profitability than the foreign inventors, given that the ex-ante valuation could be different from ex-post. Further, the market value analysis, being unhampered by problems of timing of costs and revenues, takes into account also the option value of a knowledge asset, which is not considered in the case of the productivity analysis.[20] Various supply and demand side factors slack the option value of distant-from-headquarters R&D independently of the wage costs of the foreign inventor workforce (Bloom and Van Reenen 2002).

7.7 Concluding Remarks

In this study, we have reported first results of a new measurement approach seeking to relate total R&D expenditures as well as firm market value and output to inventor count variables. One objective is to obtain robust relationships between the number of inventors and R&D expenditures. Whereas some previous studies have used inventor location data in order to measure regional spillovers or even the distribution of inventors for narrowly defined technical fields, we are not aware of any systematic and large-scale attempt to generate estimates of the distribution and size of the inventive workforce of corporations or countries. We hope that further steps towards this objective may help to trace the globalization of R&D more systematically and that the estimates described here will be helpful in analysing the impact of globalization, including the analysis of the impact of R&D on profitability and productivity.

Our results are quite encouraging. We find that there is a strong relationship between our inventor measures and R&D expenditures. Using inventor counts and various fixed effects for technical fields and countries, we can explain about two-thirds of the variation in the growth of firm level R&D expenditures. Moreover, the time trends we find using our measure of R&D globalization allow us to derive interesting implications for R&D and innovation policies. The relationship between R&D and inventors is stable. However, our exercise would profit considerably from having access to reliable wage data for inventors. The regional distribution of inventors matters, with some locations (Far East, the United States, Canada) adding considerably to R&D expenditures. This effect is expected because firms presumably undertake sourcing of R&D in foreign locations in order to tap into valuable knowledge pools which are not available and/not affordable at the home location.

As to our market valuation and productivity analysis, we obtain interesting results which confirm the view that foreign R&D activities are extremely important from a business perspective. First, the size of the coefficients of inventor stocks are large and very significant across all the specifications. Second, in terms of goodness of fit the absolute statistical loss of using inventor counts instead of R&D accounting information is limited. Third, the share of inventors in the foreign countries add further explanatory power, and its impact is comparable to the share of domestic inventors. Fourth, the detailed decomposition of inventor workforce by regions allows one to analyse more succinctly the impact to market values and sales of different R&D sourcing strategies.

Future work will use a more comprehensive set of patents and inventors, including filings in the USPTO and other national systems, in order to detect more accurately changes in the international distribution of inventive activity within and across firms. Moreover, we hope that our data will allow us to cast more light on the extent of international knowledge flows within MNEs. Because these have not been measured satisfactorily in the past, there is an open question how estimates of international R&D spillovers will fare once within-MNE flows are accounted for.

Notes

1 This chapter has been written in collaboration with Dietmar Harhoff (Max Planck Institute for Innovation and Competition and Ludwig-Maximilians-Universität in Munich and CEPR and ZEW).
2 For comprehensive surveys see Keller (2002, 2004, 2010), Narula and Zanfei (2005), and Carlsson (2006).

3 For example, Wissenschaftsstatistik GmbH in Germany estimates R&D expenditures of German firms in foreign countries. The annual report (Wissenschaftsstatistik 2008) shows that corporations in German ownership expended €38.3 billion on R&D, of which 11.4 billion was spent in foreign countries. Thus the share of foreign-conducted R&D was 29.7 percent. An amount of about equal size was expended by non-German firms on German territory. Unfortunately, these data have not been available for further studies at the firm level.

4 To be precise, our allocation simply rests on the country information contained in the patent document. We assumed that at the country level, this corresponds to the country of R&D execution. For smaller countries and regions close to national borders (e.g., between Belgium and the Netherlands), the validity of this assumption will have to be checked later on in market value and productivity regressions.

5 Research on invention processes (see Harhoff and Wagner 2009) has shown that the duration of R&D projects is on the order of ten months. Hence, if the patent is filed immediately at the conclusion of the typical project, this date is reasonably close to the midpoint of an average project.

6 There are many other circumstances under which these counts would be biased (e.g., if the average work time for which inventors are active in invention processes would differ across industries or time periods). We think that this aspect is not serious limitation for a preliminary investigation of this kind.

7 The business group is the typical form of organization of large-firm industrial activities in the European context. In the United States the role of business groups is less important within national boundaries because of a different fiscal regulatory framework. However, many US firms hold foreign subsidiaries for which they are required to report a consolidated account.

8 See chapter 8 (this volume) for a detailed comparison of patenting costs across several offices, including estimates in PPP currency.

9 The name of each inventor were transformed to the ASCII standard codepage using the twenty-six letters of the English alphabet.

10 Obviously, this approach invokes several caveats. For example, we assume implicitly that there is no migration of inventors within a given priority year from one applicant to another.

11 In this study we consider the thirty signatory countries of the OECD convention as resulting by the end of year 2009. Since then four more countries have become OECD members. For further details see www.oecd.org.

12 Unfortunately, as of yet we cannot identify in our data if this is due to acquisitions, mergers, or the establishment of new subsidiary activities.

13 In Germany, the 2007 data indicate a composition of 61 percent, 31 percent, and 8 percent for labour, materials, and capital investments respectively. See http://www.stifterverband.org/statistik_und_analysen/publikationen/fue_datenreport/fue_datenreport_2008.pdf (Last accessed May 12 2009).

14 A particularly simple variant of (6) would be to aggregate all nondomestic inventors in one pooled share variable.

15 These variables have been truncated at the top 1 percent of the distribution to mitigate the presence of outlier observations.

16 We also computed inventor stock variables with different forms of 'depreciation'. It is worth mentioning that the size of the coefficients of the domestic inventor counts and of R squared ratio are larger for the stocks than the flows. This finding is not surprising, and typically it might suggest some lags in the inventive process by an inventor since his employment in a firm.

17 For a recent and comprehensive survey on this kind of studies see Hall et al. (2010).

18 For further discussion on the rationales of GMM estimation for production functions see Hall and Mairesse (1996).

19 Because of severely reduced data availability—our dataset includes information on material costs for only one-third of the observations—we opted to disregard material costs in the productivity estimations in order to avoid potential selection bias effects.

20 Even an analysis based solely on the net present value approach cannot fully take into the account the option value of an asset. See discussion in chapter 1 (this volume).

References

Archibugi D., S. Iammarino 1999. "The Policy Implication of the Globalisation of Innovation." *Res Pol* 28:317–336.

Arellano M., S. Bond 1991. "Some Tests of Specification for Panel Data: Monte Carlo Evidence and an Application to Employment Equations." *Rev Econ Stud* 58:277–297.

Arellano, M., O. Bover 1995. "Another Look at the Instrumental Variable Estimation of Error-Components Models." *J Economet* 68:29–51.

Bloom N., J. Van Reenen 2002. "Patents, Real Options and Firm Performance." *Econ J* 112:C97–C116.

Carlsson B. 2006. "Internationalization of Innovation Systems: A Survey of the Literature." *Res Pol* 35(1):56–67.

De Fontenay C., E. Carmel 2004. "Israeli's Silicon Wadi: The Forces Behind the Cluster." In *Building High-Tech Clusters: Silicon Valley and Beyond*, edited by T. Bresnahan, A. Gambardella, 40–77, Cambridge (UK): Cambridge University Press.

Florida R. 1997. "The Globalization of R&D: Results of a Survey of Foreign-Affiliated R&D Laboratories in the USA." *Res Pol* 26(1):85–103.

Granstrand O. 1999. "Internationalisation of Corporate R&D: A Study of Japanese and Swedish Corporations." *Res Pol* 28:275–302.

Guellec D., B. van Pottelsberghe de la Potterie 2001. "The Internationalisation of Technology Analysed with Patent Data." *Res Pol* 30(8):1253–1266.

Hall B. H. 2005. "Exploring the Patent Explosion." *J Technol Transfer* 30:35–48.

Hall B. H. 2010. "The Internationalization of R&D." In *Global Value Chains: Impacts and Implications*, edited by A. Sydor, Ottawa: Foreign Affairs and International Trade Canada, Government of Canada, Ebook last accessed October 30 http://www.international.gc.ca/economist-economiste/analysis-analyse/policy-politique/TPR_2011_GVC_ToC.aspx?lang=eng

Hall B. H. 2014. "Does Patent Protection Help or Hinder Technology Transfer." In *Intellectual Property Rights for Economic Development*, edited by S. Ahn, B. Hall, K. Lee, 11–32, Northampton(MA): Edward Elgar Publishers.

Hall B. H., J. Mairesse 1996. "Estimating the Productivity of Research and Development: An Exploration of GMM Methods Using Data on French & United States Manufacturing Firms." NBER Working Paper No. 5501, National Bureau of Economic Research Inc., Cambridge (MA).

Hall B. H., J. Mairesse, P. Mohnen 2010. "Measuring the Returns to R&D." In *Handbook of the Economics of Innovation*, edited by B. H. Hall and N. Rosenberg, 9520–10972, Amsterdam: Elsevier, Kindle edition.

Hall B. H., R. Ziedonis 2001. "The Determinants of Patenting in the U.S. Semiconductor Industry 1980–1994." *Rand J Econ* 32:101–128.

Harhoff D., S. Wagner 2009. "Modelling the Duration of Patent Examination at the European Patent Office." *Manag Science* 55(12):1969–1984.

Howells J., 1990. "The Internationalization of R&D and the Development of Global Research Networks." *Res Pol* 20:472–476.

Keller W. 2002. "Geographic Localization of International Technology Diffusion." *Am Econ Rev* 92(1):120–142.

Keller W. 2004. "International Technology Diffusion." *J Econ Lit* 42(3):752–782.

Keller W. 2010. "International Trade, Foreign Direct Investment, and Technology Spillovers." In *The Handbook of the Economics of Innovation*, edited by B. H. Hall, N. Rosenberg, 2092–3258, Amsterdam: Elsevier, Kindle edition.

Kumar N. 2001. "Determinants of Location of Overseas R&D Activity of Multinational Enterprises: The Case of US and Japanese Corporations." *Res Pol* 30:159–174.

Le Bas C., C. Sierra 2002. "Location Versus Home Country Advantages' in R&D Activities: Some Further Results on Multinationals Locational Strategies." *Res Pol* 31:589–609.

Narula R., A. Zanfei 2005. "Globalization of Innovation: The Role of Multinational Enterprises." In *The Oxford Handbook of Innovation*, edited by J. Fagerberg, R. Nelson, D. Mowery, 318–345, Oxford: Oxford University Press.

OECD 2002. *Frascati Manual*. Paris: OECD.

OST 2008. *Science and Technology Indicators*. Paris, France: Observatoire des Sciences et des Techniques.

Park W. G. 2008. "International Patent Protection, 1960–2005." *Res Pol* 37(4): 761–766.

Patel P., M. Vega 1999. "Patterns of Internationalisation of Corporate Technology: Location vs Home Country Advantages." *Res Pol* 28:145–155.

PatStat 2012. *EPO Worldwide Patent Statistical Database and the EPO Patent Register*, April edition. Vienna: EPO.

Thoma G., S. Torrisi, A. Gambardella, D. Guellec, B. H. Hall, D. Harhoff 2010. "Harmonizing and Combining Large Datasets—An Application to Firm-Level Patent and Accounting Data." NBER Working Paper No. 15851, National Bureau of Economic Research Inc., Cambridge (MA).

TSP 2005. *TSP 5.0. User's Guide* edited by B. H. Hall, C. Cummins. Palo Alto: TSP International.

Von Zedtwitz M., O. Gassmann 2002. "Market Versus Technology Drive in R&D Internationalization: Four Different Patterns of Managing Research and Development." *Res Pol* 31:569–588.

Wissenschaftsstatistik 2008. *FuE- Datenreport 2008—Analysen und Vergleiche*. Last accessed August 1, 2014. http://www.stifterverband.org/statistik_und_analysen/publikationen/fue_datenreport/fue_datenreport_2008.pdf

8   The Value of Chinese Patenting

Grid Thoma

8.1 Introduction

In the last decade, Chinese patenting has grown impressively, and in 2011 the State Intellectual Property Office (SIPO) of China outperformed all other offices in terms of patent applications published (The Economist, October 14, 2010). However, little is known about trends in Chinese patenting outside national borders, with the exception of the study by Eberhardt et al. (2011). This study attempts to fill this gap with focus on international patenting according to the European Patent Office (EPO) and the Patent Cooperation Treaty (PCT) systems.

The growth of international patenting has paralleled internal reforms by the Chinese government. It is noteworthy that adoption of a modern patent system is a relatively new legislative change in China. Indeed, until the beginning of the '80s, the development of intellectual property in China was limited, and the first patent law dates to 1985. Subsequently, the Chinese government promoted three reforms to harmonize Chinese patent law with international treaties, increase statutory protection for the private sector, and extend patentability in novel subject areas. The first revision of 1992 introduced some administrative changes in the regulation of the legal services sector. In 2001, China entered the WTO, and its patent law was fully harmonized with the Patent Cooperation Treaty of the International Patent Cooperation Union and the World Trade Organization agreement on trade-related aspects of intellectual property rights (TRIPS). In 2008, the Chinese government launched the 'National Intellectual Property Strategy' to reduce bureaucratic costs, increase transparency in the patent system, and enhance incentives for inventors who intend to carry out R&D in China.

According to the Joint Experts Group for Patent Examination of the trilateral cooperation commission among SIPO, Japan Patent Office (JPO), and Korean Intellectual Property Office (KIPO), there are no significant differences between China's patent authority and other major patent offices regarding the examination process and the criteria for the patentability of an invention (JEGPE, December 2, 2010). In the Chinese patent law, article 22, paragraph 3 defines the criteria as novelty, inventiveness, and practical applicability. For the Chinese patent office, as for the JPO and EPO, the patent application is published eighteen months from filing, and novelty is established according to a 'first-to-file' principle. Instead, the Chinese system differs from the Japanese one regarding when the validity of a patent can be challenged: in China, it can be opposed up to nine months from the date the patent was granted in the same vein as for the EPO (OECD 2009).

Notwithstanding efforts to harmonize the patent-granting process internationally,[1] patentees face substantial differences in fees for the process, according to the entity to whom they present their application. In 2003 the average cost for obtaining a standard patent was estimated at €46,700 for a EURO-PCT, €30,530 for the EPO, €10,250 for the US Patent and Trademark Office (USPTO), €14,018 for Germany, and €5,460 for the JPO.[2] In China, the full cost of a patent from filing to renewal with up to twenty years validity has been estimated at about €2,505 EUR. These significant differences persist even when PPP exchange rates are taken into account. In particular—according to statistics of the United Nations Industrial Development Organization (www.unido.org, December 2012), which take US price levels as a benchmark—the PPP patent fees can be estimated at PPP €13,393 for Germany, €10,250 for USPTO, € 4,213 for the JPO, and €5,047 for the SIPO. Furthermore, it is worth remembering that since July 1, 2010, China's SIPO can function as an International Search Authority (ISA) under the PCT agreement,[3] and here again, its fees differ substantially from those of other ISAs for patent searches and examination of inventions. The overall fee for patent search and preliminary examination of a Chinese-PCT is about 3,600 Chinese Yuan (RMB), which is about €424.[4]

These institutional and economic considerations and the spectacular growth of Chinese patenting at the domestic and international level prompt a number of questions. For example, what are the macro trends of Chinese patenting in the EPO/PCT systems compared to those of other countries? How do Chinese patents compare to patents from other countries in terms of quality and value? Do the characteristics of the patentee determine the quality and value of Chinese patenting,[5] and if so, which characteristics are most important? How do Chinese companies benefit domestically and internationally from patenting?

Previous studies have conducted extensive analyses at the country, regional, or industry level, and a few have scrutinized the determinants of the growth of Chinese patenting at the firm level. These studies have found a significant strengthening of patent protection in China and noted that pro-patent reforms were followed by a burst of patenting activities, which in turn accelerated when China joined the WTO (see Hu and Mathews (2008) and Park (2008) respectively). In addition, the vast majority of patent applications originate from a small number of regions (Crescenzi et al. 2012), notably the Guangdong region, which accounts for two-thirds of all such applications, and certain industries tend to have a very high propensity to patent their inventions (Eberhardt et al. 2011). Many studies have posited a 'strategic patenting' hypothesis, suggesting that both domestic and foreign firms file patents not only to protect real products in the market but also for strategic reasons (Hu 2010).

A few authors (Hu and Jefferson 2009; Liang and Xue 2010; Eberhardt et al. 2011) have begun to scrutinize the 'strategic patenting' hypothesis at the firm level, along the lines of Hall and Ziedonis (2001). All these studies agree that R&D investment can only partially explain the surge in propensity to apply for patents. It has been shown that patenting takes place in industries which are more international and that the growth of patenting in China's SIPO has also been accompanied by an increase in that done in other offices (e.g., the USPTO). However, none of these studies has analyzed Chinese patenting at the international level (for example, according to EPO and PCT systems) and the determinants of the quality and value of Chinese patents, which is a key topic of the 'strategic patenting' literature.[6] This study aims to fill this gap and attempts to identify how the institutional context of the patent owner[7] and its experience with patenting and portfolio size impact patent quality and value.

To this end, I used a novel dataset including the whole population of EPO and PCT patents and introduced a new taxonomy of Chinese patenting to take into account both the location of residence of the patent inventor(s) and the national origin of the patent owner(s) (Goldberg et al. 2008), thus making it possible to track cross-country knowledge flow and differentiate the investigation based on the twofold geographical dimension of the patenting activities: indigenous patenting by Chinese firms relying on the domestic inventor workforce and foreign multinational enterprises (hereafter also MNEs) employing Chinese inventors. Next, on the basis of this taxonomy an econometric model has been used to analyze prior-art searching, granting, opposition, and renewal decisions, which can allow one to test some testable hypotheses on patent quality and value, which are drawn from the 'strategic patenting' literature.

The chapter is structured as follows. Section 8.1 summarizes the literature and advances the testable hypotheses, and section 8.2 presents the dataset and the variables included in the econometric analysis. The descriptive trends are reported in section 8.3, and the econometric model is developed and fully discussed in section 8.4. The final remarks propose directions for further inquiry.

8.2 Literature Background

With only a few exceptions, patenting by businesses in China is an almost unexplored topic. Most of the studies present aggregate data at the country, regional, or industry level.

To analyze patenting on the country level, numerous researchers have devised indices that rank and compare the patent legislation of many nations, including China.[8] The GP index (Ginarte and Park 1997; Park

2008) indicates a remarkable strengthening of patent protection in China, which doubled during the decade of 1995–2005, reaching the same level as that of member countries of the Organisation for Economic Co-Operation and Development (OECD). Whereas this index is based on book-law aspects of patent protection, Papageorgiadis et al. (2014) claim the China's patent protection status is closer to that of the Central and East European countries and the other member countries of BRICS (Brazil, Russia, India, and South Africa) when factors of servicing costs, property rights protection costs, and monitoring costs are taken into account as well.

The growth of Chinese patenting has been found to be unevenly distributed geographically. The Guandong region accounts for about one-tenth of R&D investment in China and two-thirds of the overall patenting (OECD 2010), making it one of the top regions in the world for cumulative R&D spending in recent years; in 2008 the per capita R&D investment relative to GDP is 1.41 percent, not far from the average ratio for the OECD regions (1.59 percent). In terms of growth rates, R&D spending in Guangdong increased fivefold from 2000 to 2008. According to Crescenzi et al. (2012), the strong polarization of R&D in China is a typical symptom of the increasing return to scale in R&D, where regions better endowed with 'knowledge capital' have become even more R&D intensive over time. However, they claim that the new geography of innovation in China cannot be considered as a failure of government intervention in favour of less-developed regions, but the outcome of a top-down policy in which patent reforms and attraction of foreign direct investment (FDI) have played a key role via the mechanism of labour mobility.[9]

The impact of FDI on patenting was thoroughly analyzed by Hu (2010) at the industry level. He compiled a dataset of 1.37 million patents from China's SIPO at the two-digit industry level over the period 1985–2004 and categorized them on the basis of the field of technology they concern, using the International Patent Classification (IPC) list of fields, organizing the patent counts in a fixed concordance table.[10] Hu found that the growth of domestic patenting in China was highly correlated with foreign patenting in China in the same industries in which the foreign firm specialized in its home country. Moreover, the foreign patenting in China from a given focal country has been found to be significantly and negatively affected by foreign patenting done by other nations in competition with China. According to Hu (2010), this evidence strongly supports the competitive threat hypothesis, according to which the increase in the propensity to patent is caused by the fact that companies file patents not only to protect real products in the market but also for strategic reasons, such as barriers to market competition, for reducing the risk of being held up by other patent owners, and to gain stronger contractual power towards competitors in cross-licensing settings (Hall and Ziedonis 2001). Hence, the sustained patenting in China by foreign firms has ballooned the propensity to patent even for domestic innovators. On the one hand, the value of patent protection has increased in China with the advancement of internal reforms, whereas on the other hand, foreign firms have conveyed new business practices in China where intellectual property strategies play a key role.

One of the first studies at the firm level was by Liang and Xue (2010), who scrutinized the strategic patenting hypothesis with a dataset of one thousand companies. In particular, they analyzed the patenting activities of Fortune 500 firms and a similarly sized control sample of the biggest Chinese companies. They showed that patenting by domestic firms essentially grew only after the year 2000, and it is highly concentrated in the hands of a small group of firms. The growth of patenting by foreign firms in China began in 1996, well before that of domestic companies. On the basis of their investigation of the patent priorities of foreign companies, they concluded that the majority of the R&D investments that led to these patents was spent elsewhere and not in China. However, this study is limited by the fact that it that does not take into account the location of the inventors involved in the patents, which is far more indicative proxy regarding the geography of the R&D activities (See discussion on Chapter 6 and 7, this volume).

At the firm level, other hypotheses have been proposed to better understand the factors spurring the growth of patenting. Hu and Jefferson (2009) advanced two hypotheses in addition to the strategic patenting hypothesis. First, they pointed to the numerous central government reforms to favour pro-patent legislation, including initiatives undertaken after the China's entrance into the WTO to harmonize Chinese regulations with those of important international standards. Second, they noted the acceleration of R&D investment in China from 0.5 percent of GDP in the mid-'90s to 1 percent in 2000, continuing to 1.3 percent in 2004.[11] To test these hypotheses, Hu and Jefferson analyzed a unique survey dataset from the National Bureau of Statistics of China for the seven-year period 1995–2001, comprising over 29,525 firms that account for 38 percent of Chinese R&D spending and 8.5 percent of domestic patent applications. The main drawback of this dataset is that it does not distinguish whether the filings regarded invention patents, utility models, or designs. In fact, for utility models or designs no substantive examination is required, and hence the inventive steps can be more limited (Wright et al. 2011).

Econometric evidence suggests that the R&D push hypothesis can only explain 24 percent of the surge of Chinese patenting. The cross-industry variation in the value added by the foreign firms (a proxy for foreign direct investments) in China accounts for another 20 percent of patenting growth. Quite interestingly, Hu and Jefferson found that FDI impact is significantly different for domestic firms than it is for foreign-owned ones. They interpreted these results, on the one hand, as a strategic response by domestic firms to the entrance of new innovators from abroad, and on the other, they claim that foreign firms in China typically perform only low-potential R&D which can yield on average more incremental innovations and thus less patenting. They also found that the dummy years 2000 and 2001 had a strong impact on patent propensity, explained by the anticipation of reforms in patent legislation related to China's entrance in the WTO. However, the limited time coverage of the sample does not allow for a full-fledged analysis of the impact of this latter hypothesis.

Another way institutional reforms can affect patent propensity is through public subsidies to compensate application fees.[12] In China, since the introduction of the first compensation program in the Shanghai area in 1999, these policies have been typically managed by the local government. Wright and Lei (2011) quantified the impact of a policy change at the provincial level in 2005 using a matched dataset of 2,634 firms from six provinces. They found that doubling the fee compensation encouraged an impact of about 28 percent in the patent propensity for firms participating in the program. It is noteworthy that they did not find a statistically significant effect for utility models, which does not contradict the anecdotal claim that the major stakes are in the utility patents.

Eberhardt et al. (2011) provided the first evidence on patenting strategies of Chinese firms outside the domestic market, in particular in the USPTO. For this task, they developed a novel dataset of companies with a portfolio of Chinese and US patents. They matched company records with patents using a compressive dataset of 19,956 Chinese firms over the period 1999–2006 and found that a small number of industries and patentees accounted for the bulk of patenting in the SIPO and USPTO. The lion's share of patenting was done in the 'Instruments and Office Machinery' sector; 75.1 percent of the matched patents were with the SIPO and 88.9 percent with the USPTO. On the other hand, in the same period the top ten patent owners accounted for 86.7 percent of patenting in the US and 75.0 percent of patenting in the SIPO.

They then analyzed the determinants of patent productivity and the decision to apply for a patent abroad (i.e., filing in the USPTO) using an econometric model. Export intensity, firm size, and experience are particularly relevant in understanding the variability in the patent portfolio size in the United States and China. Put differently, firms that patent in the United States are larger, younger, and more export-oriented than firms that seek protection for their inventions solely in the domestic market. Last, R&D investment does not have a large differential impact on US patent counts compared to those filed with the SIPO; however, R&D investment matters positively in the decision to file patents in the USPTO, although the effect is relatively small.

Based on these considerations in the literature on the growth of strategic patenting, the following ceteris paribus testable hypothesis can be posited:

Hypothesis 1: Chinese patents are of lower economic value than other patents on average.

When patent quality is taken into the account, it is worth recalling several factors related to the fact that the legal services market in China is still in its infancy (China IP, March 6, 2011).[13] The exceptional growth of patenting has meant a squeeze in the supply of patent agents. According to one estimate, because of heavy workload, a patent agent only devotes about 2.3 days of work to drafting a patent application, which is considered too little to produce a good patent filing.[14] In the same vein, firms generally chose legal services mainly on the basis of cost, and thus patent agents have little incentive to invest in drafting skills and tools in order to produce high-quality patents.

Second, this boom in patent applications and the squeeze in the supply of examiners has also created problems for the Chinese patent office (The Economist, October 14, 2010). Hiring a large number of high-quality examiners in a short period of time is a serious challenge for any patent office. Given this dearth of qualified examiners, the large number of applications can lead to bureaucratic and managerial bottlenecks for the patent office, generating a large backlog of applications which demand examination. Thus, the following ceteris paribus testable hypothesis can be put forward:

> *Hypothesis 2: Chinese patent are of lower quality than other patents on average, because they lack suitable prior–art research.*

8.3 Dataset and Measures

This study used a novel dataset based on EPO and PCT patent applications. The unit of analysis is the patent family as defined by the INPADOC, with at least one patent application under the EPO and PCT systems. Typically, these patent families are also known as international patent families (Martinez 2010).

The main source of data is the EPO Worldwide Patent Database (PatStat, April 2012) and the related Patent Register Data regarding procedural information. From PatStat bibliometric information has been extracted regarding claims, references, patent classifications, inventors, opposition received, and renewal decisions.

PatStat was also used to extract full information on the addresses of inventors and patentees, which served to identify the geographic origin of inventions. For the purposes of this study, both types of addresses could reveal different aspects of the geography of invention processes in China. On the one hand, the addresses of inventors, which are most often the address of their workplace, or more rarely, their personal address, reflect the place where the research leading to the patent was done. On the other hand, the country of origin of the patentee indicates the location where the R&D investor of the patent comes from, and hence if properly combined with information on the location of inventors, it can document the existence of any cross-country and cross-regional dimension of the invention process.[15]

In this direction, to identify Chinese patents, the study advances a threefold taxonomy (Goldberg et al. 2008). First, indigenous inventions (Set 1) are those patents that have at least one inventor and at least one patentee originating in China. Second, Set 2 is made up of those patents that have at least one Chinese patentee, but none of the inventors are located in China (i.e., it includes inventions from Chinese patentees hiring foreign inventors working outside China). Last, Set 3 considers multinational enterprises performing R&D in China, when at least one inventor in the patent is from China. In other words, Sets 2 and 3 could be considered respectively a proxy for the outward and inward R&D foreign direct investments (FDIs) in China whose innovation output has been patented at the international level.

Box 8.1 depicts Chinese patenting by types along the two geographical dimensions, that of the location of the patentee and that of the inventor. It identifies about 48,207 INPADOC families relating to Chinese patenting activities with EPO and PCT systems. Slightly more than half of the patents can be considered indigenous inventions involving both Chinese inventors and patentees, whereas patents from MNEs performing R&D in China constitute about 44.2 percent. The outward FDIs (Set 2) matter only for about 3.5 percent of all Chinese patents.

Due to data availability, in the econometric analysis the sample was limited to patent families with at least an EPO equivalent. In fact, for this dataset I have complete procedural information on applications, grants, oppositions, and renewals. Limiting the sample to one single patent office allows more homogeneity and precision in the definitions and computations of the variables. In this direction, focusing the econometric analysis on the EPO dataset alone is not a serious drawback of this kind.

Box 8.1   Defining Chinese patents

(48,207 INPADOC patent families)

		Chinese patentee	
		YES	NO
Chinese inventor	YES	Set 1—Indigenous R&D 25,210 (52.3%)	Set 3—Inward FDIs 21,327 (44.2%)
	NO	Set 2—Outward FDIs 1,670 (3.5%)	----

Sources: PatStat database (April 2012)

Notes: Set 1 relies on the indigenous inventions when both the inventors and patentees originate from China. Set 2 is made up of outward R&D FDIs when Chinese firms employ foreign inventors. Set 3 is based on inward R&D FDIs when MNEs employ Chinese inventors.

The final sample is made up of 2,192,793 patent families with EPO equivalent during the period 1978–2007, which is the whole population of patent applications published by the EPO.[16] According to the combined definition of Box 8.1, there are 30,738 Chinese patents, which constitute a sufficient number of positive outcomes in the dataset to allow analysis of the whole population of INPADOC patent families with EPO equivalents.

In the econometric analysis, I divided the sample into two subsets, taking as the reference year 2001, when China entered the WTO. As discussed in the literature section, several studies found that the acceleration of Chinese patenting took place in this year. In addition, Hu and Jefferson (2009) claimed that China's entrance into the WTO was anticipated in the patenting decisions of one year because the negotiations had started and were active long before that date. In this direction, the timeline of the analyzed subsets are the periods 1978–1999 and 2000–2007 corresponding to 1,215,987 and 976,806 patents respectively.

The analysis integrated the patent dataset with additional information. First, in order to explore the technological specialization of China during the two time periods considered, I assigned patents to the thirty groups of the categorization proposed by OST (2008). Indeed, this categorization allows for a more accurate definition of technological fields compared to the international patent classification (IPC) system.

Due to the lack of data, our analysis cannot account for the R&D investment done by the owner and other financial information originating from company books. Previous studies have shown that R&D investment can only partially explain the growth of patenting by Chinese firms. Moreover, extending the investigation beyond the companies that report R&D expenditures avoids potential selection biases in the analysis, such as patentees that perform R&D but do not report it in the company books, patentees that do not perform R&D in a formalized and systematic matter, and business patentees compared to the nonbusiness ones.

To account for the characteristics of the patent owner, the patentees are fully indexed according to their institutional context, namely whether they are businesses, individuals, nonbusiness organizations (hereafter also NBOs) including universities, hospitals, governments, and other private-nonprofit sectors (Thoma et al. 2010). Considering also individual inventors and the nonbusiness sector affords a more complete picture of different incentives to patenting in China. The nonbusiness sector can be considered a proxy for government intervention in the Chinese innovation system (Eun et al. 2006).

In conclusion, Box 8.2 presents the definition of the main variables computed at the patent owner level, whereas the means and standard deviations of those variables by groups of patents are depicted in Table 8.1. Furthermore, the multivariate econometric analysis controls for several patent indicators, whose measurement approach is discussed in chapter 2 (this volume).

Box 8.2   Main variables included in the multivariate analysis

Variable Name	Variable Description
Dependent variables on patent quality and value	
Supplementary search report	A binary variable if the patent was accompanied by a supplementary search report by the examiner. In the EPO the examiner can optionally choose to elaborate an additional prior art search when she thinks the patent application still lacks relevant prior art in the matter.
Granted	A binary variable that assumes the positive outcome if the patent application has been granted by the EPO, zero otherwise. It measures the complexity and uncertainty of the examination process (Harhoff and Wagner 2009).
Opposition	A binary variable that takes the positive outcome if a patent was opposed at the EPO, zero otherwise. Oppositions can be filed at the EPO within nine months from the granting date, and they are proxy of economic potential of a patent (Harhoff and Reitzig 2004).
Renewal decisions	The family maintenance value index as defined in section 2.3.3. This index is a weighted sum of the normalized GDP (the US GDP set to unity) of the countries where the patent protection is sought and renewed over its years of validity.[17]
Independent variables at the patent owner	
Patentee is an individual	A binary variable that attributes the positive outcome if the patent is owned by a sole inventor, zero otherwise.
Patentee is an NBO	A binary variable that attributes the positive outcome if the patent is owned by a nonbusiness organization (NBO), zero otherwise.
Chinese indigenous inventions	A binary variable that attributes the positive outcome if at least one inventor and at least one patentee originate from China (Set 1), zero otherwise.
Outward FDIs from China	A binary variable that attributes the positive outcome if at least one patentee and none of the inventors originate from China (Set 2), zero otherwise.
Inward FDIs in China	A binary variable that attributes the positive outcome if at least one inventor and none of the patentees originate from China (Set 3), zero otherwise.
Patentee's portfolio size	Number of patents owned by the patentee in the previous five years before the reference year. The variable is in logs.
Age of the patentee	Year of the first patent by the patentee. The variable is in logs of the difference from year 2010.

Table 8.1 Descriptive statistics by groups of patents

	Overall dataset excluding Chinese patents		Chinese patents					
			Set 1 Indigenous R&D		Set 2 Outward FDI		Set 3 Inward FDI	
Observations	2,162,055		7,573		1,089		22,076	
	mean	s.d.	mean	s.d.	mean	s.d.	mean	s.d.
D (Granted patent)	0.506	–	0.264	–	0.352	–	0.274	–
D (Supplementary search report)	0.114	–	0.565	–	0.174	–	0.189	–
D (Patent opposed)	0.029	–	0.010	–	0.006	–	0.011	–
Family maintanance value index	0.184	0.078	0.153	0.076	0.193	0.074	0.200	0.085
D (Patentee being an individual)	0.061	–	0.169	–	0.028	–	0.027	–
D (Patentee being NBO)	0.039	–	0.059	–	0.037	–	0.049	–
Log (Patentee's portfolio size)	4.720	2.831	4.141	3.538	3.404	2.793	5.481	2.722
Log (Patentee's age)	3.192	0.508	2.238	0.523	2.616	0.727	3.129	0.576

Notes: 1) Set 1 relies on the indigenous inventions when both the inventors and patentees originate from China. Set 2 is made up of outward R&D FDIs when Chinese firms employ foreign inventors. Set 3 is based on inward R&D FDIs when MNEs employ Chinese inventors.
2) The dataset is made up of INPADOC patent families with at least an EPO equivalent. Patent indicators have been aggregated at the patent family level. Citation and family links are consolidated both on the citing and cited side. The other indicators—with the exception of the binary variables—are at the median value levels. For size and experience variables I included the patentee with the largest value.

8.4 Descriptive Trends

As in the case of the SIPO, there is a strong growth of Chinese patents obtained in the international context. Figure 8.1 depicts the share of Chinese patents as share of the overall patenting from all countries. As can be seen in the figure, there is a continuous growth of Chinese patents from about 0.5 percent in 1995 to about 2 percent in the year 2000, and then to 5 percent in 2007. The growth is even more spectacular if one considers that this period is characterized by a sharp increase in patenting worldwide. The fast growth of patenting has been directly associated with the increase of patenting propensity following several pro-patent reforms in many developed and developing economies during the 1990s (Hall and Ziedonis 2001; Hall 2005; Park 2008).[18]

The growth of Chinese patenting was initially propelled by the globalization of R&D activities—that is, multinational enterprises off-shoring R&D activities in China. Up to 1997, patenting by inward FDIs in China constituted two-thirds of all Chinese patents, although a decade later this share decreased to only one-third. In our dataset (Set 3), the MNEs with inward FDIs in China originate to a large extent in the United States (52.7 percent), the EU27 (24.0 percent), and less dramatically, in Taiwan (7.8 percent), Japan (6.25 percent), and Korea (2.35 percent).

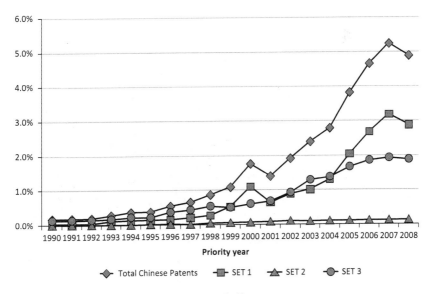

Figure 8.1 Chinese patents as percentage of all patents

Notes: Set 1 relies on the indigenous inventions when both the inventors and patentees originate from China. Set 2 is made up of outward R&D FDIs when Chinese firms employ foreign inventors. Set 3 is based on inward R&D FDIs when MNEs employ Chinese inventors.

Since year 2000 patenting by MNEs has undergone a deceleration and has been outperformed by the so-called indigenous R&D processes—that is, patenting by Chinese firms employing national inventors. In the five years after 2002, indigenous patenting accelerated compared to patenting by foreign inventors, shifting from 1 to 3 percent of the overall patenting in the EPO and PCT systems. In particular, indigenous patenting reached 478.5 in 2007, considering 2002 as base year with value equal to 100. In terms of the compound annual growth rate, it means 97.3 percent, and this trend has well outperformed that of other BRICS and Central and East European countries (Goldberg et al. 2008; Crescenzi et al. 2012).

Quite interestingly, we can notice that a sharp decrease of indigenous patenting occurred in 2001. This can be explained by the collapse of the dotcom bubble of 2001, which further tightened the financial constraints on innovative firms. Put differently, the decrease of patenting during the financial crisis confirms the fact that patenting activities are highly procyclical (Von Graevenitz 2009). Figure 8.2 reveals that the decrease of patenting in 2001 was essentially caused by business patentees and not by the other institutional sectors of the economy. Overall, patenting by nonbusiness organizations in China has remained quite stable over the last two decades, whereas patenting by individual inventors has shrunken from 25.4 percent to 15.7 percent of Chinese patents, which nonetheless is still double the rate of patenting by individuals in developed economies (Thoma et al. 2010).

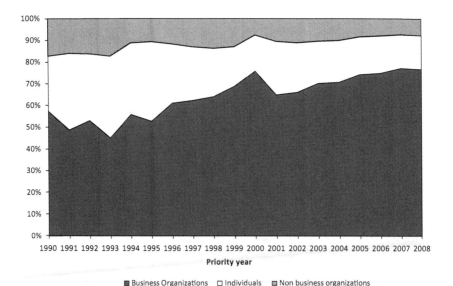

Figure 8.2 Chinese patents according to institutional sector

These trends are consistent with the model of technology catch-up by the Chinese economy discussed in Amighini et al. (2010). They claim that Chinese firms benefit from technology acquisition from more advanced economies through imports of final goods and inward FDIs, which can then propel the production of market-oriented products with lower costs. In particular, inward FDIs have played a crucial role by allowing foreign MNEs to establish joint-ventures with domestic firms, which in turn can have access to more advanced technology suppliers.

Second, in some key high-technology fields—mainly telecommunication and electronics—Chinese firms have increasingly enlarged their knowledge assets via outward FDIs by establishing international technology alliances and merger and acquisitions (M&A) with firms in developed economies. Typically, the target of the outward FDIs by the Chinese MNEs has been the acquisition of strategic knowledge assets, such as technology and know-how. However, in some consumer industries, Chinese MNEs have extended to the acquisition of recognized brands and reputation in sophisticated markets to access unique managerial and marketing competences.

In our sample, the outward FDIs from China account for about 3.5 percent of all Chinese patents. From Figure 8.1 we can notice that whereas in the 1990s the outward FDIs from China were practically nonexistent, after year 2000 they have grown steadily. In particular, Chinese MNEs have invested relatively more in the European Union (26.8 percent), United States (16.5 percent), Australia (16.1 percent), Hong Kong (12.9 percent), and Japan (8.6 percent) than in other nations. It is noteworthy that the level of international openness of Chinese patentees—ratio SET2/SET1 is about 6.7 percent—lags well behind that of many developed economies, but it is similar to the case of Japan during the 1980s, when the level of international openness was about 9.4 percent (Chapter 7, this volume).

At the level of technological specialization,[19] Chinese patents have a positive technological advantage in a small group of fields (see Figure 8.3)—media, telecommunications and communications, and consumer goods, chemicals, and pharmaceuticals and biotechnology—whereas it is following more distantly in a larger group of technologies such as environment, mechanics, transport, space technology, medical devices, instruments, materials, construction, etc.[20] The dynamic perspective of Figure 8.3 suggests that in recent years, Chinese patents have shifted from previous technological specializations and accelerated in an even narrower set of areas with very high patenting propensity, namely media, telecommunications, and communications and consumer goods. These technology fields are typically characterized by strategic patenting behaviour of firms and are responsible for the lion's share of the growth of patenting recorded in major offices (Hall and Ziedonis 2001; Hall 2005).

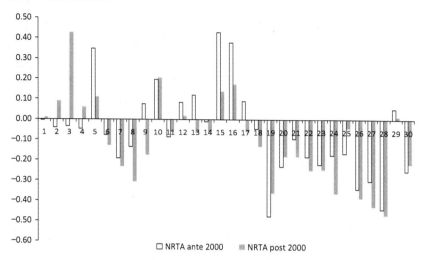

Figure 8.3 Technological specialization of Chinese patenting over time: Normalized Revealed Technological Advantage (NRTA) index

Notes: The technology aggregations are articulated in 30 categories: 1 Electrical devices—electrical engineering; 2 Audiovisual technology; 3 Telecommunications; 4 Information technology; 5 Semiconductors; 6 Optics; 7 Analysis, measurement, control; 8 Medical engineering; 9 Nuclear engineering; 10 Organic fine chemicals; 11 Macromolecular chemistry, polymers; 12 Basic chemical processing, petrol; 13 Surfaces, coatings; 14 Materials, metallurgy; 15 Biotechnology; 16 Pharmaceuticals, cosmetics; 17 Agriculture, food; 18 General processes; 19 Handling, printing; 20 Material processing; 21 Agriculture & food machinery; 22 Environment, pollution; 23 Mechanical tools; 24 Engines, pumps, turbines; 25 Thermal techniques; 26 Mechanical elements; 27 Transport; 28 Space technology, weapons; 29 Consumer goods & equipment; 30 Civil engineering, building, mining.

8.5 The Determinants of Patent Value and Quality

In order to test our hypotheses, I regressed a series of probit equations for the probability of a grant conditional on application (Table 8.2), a supplementary search report conditional on the PCT route (Table 8.3), and opposition conditional on grant (Table 8.4). For the renewal decisions in the patent lifecycle, given by the patent family maintenance value index measured by the patent family size weighted by the GDP where protection is sought and renewed, I estimated a linear regression (Table 8.5).

Indeed, as previously mentioned, these outcome variables are a valid indicator of the quality and value of the patent filing and of the speed with which the patentee pursues the application. For example, after having checked for time and technology effects, a grant decision is a direct indicator telling us whether the patent application fulfils the criteria of subject matter and inventive steps. Second, if the examiners call for a supplementary search report, this indicates that they think the original search report of the PCT filing lacks relevant prior art. Third, opposition has been

Table 8.2 Probability of granting decision

	1978–1999		2000–2007	
	(1)	(2)	(3)	(4)
D (Indigenous R&D)	-0.107*** [0.020]	-0.344* [0.167]	0.005 [0.006]	-0.017 [0.031]
D (Inward FDI)	-0.306*** [0.007]	-0.306*** [0.007]	-0.081*** [0.004]	-0.081*** [0.004]
D (Outward FDI)	-0.039 [0.036]	-0.039 [0.036]	-0.010 [0.016]	-0.010 [0.016]
D (Individual patentee)	-0.051*** [0.002]	-0.051*** [0.002]	-0.053*** [0.002]	-0.053*** [0.002]
D (Individual patentee) * D (Indigenous R&D)		0.018 [0.042]		0.040* [0.021]
D (NBO Patentee)	0.002 [0.002]	0.002 [0.002]	-0.014*** [0.003]	-0.014*** [0.003]
D (NBO Patentee) * D (Indigenous R&D)		0.001 [0.059]		0.045 [0.031]
Log (Patentee's portfolio size)	0.012*** [0.000]	0.012*** [0.000]	0.001*** [0.000]	0.001*** [0.000]
Log (Patentee's portfolio size) * D (Indigenous R&D)		0.023 [0.016]		0.030*** [0.002]
Log (Patentee's age)	-0.023*** [0.002]	-0.023*** [0.002]	0.038*** [0.001]	0.040*** [0.001]
Log (Patentee's age) * D (Indigenous R&D)		0.070 [0.062]		-0.054*** [0.015]
Chi-squared (3) geographic origin	1760.7***	1734.9***	445.8***	441.0***
Chi-squared (2) institutional type	689.2***	688.0***	487.6***	467.7***
Chi-squared (2) size and age	2458.5***	2456.4***	2222.6***	2195.0***
Chi-squared all patentee characteristics	6083.6***	6089.0***	4025.6***	4229.3***
Pseudo R-squared	0.138	0.138	0.107	0.107
Number of observations (number=1)	1,215,987 (775,888)		976,806 (325,684)	

Notes: 1) Marginal effects and their robust standard errors are shown. 2) Significance at 1 percent ***, 5 percent **, and 10 percent *. 3) The equations control for a complete set of patent indicators in logs: family size, family value, forward citations after five years, technological classes, nonpatent literature references, number of claims, inventors, XY type backward citations, backward citations, PCT route (dummy), and divisional (dummy). See chapter 2 (this volume) for the measurement methodology of the controls based on patent indicators. In addition, the equations include priority year and technology dummies. 4) The variables' definitions are reported in Box 8.1 and Box 2.1.

Table 8.3 Probability of supplementary search report (non EURO PCTs) Chinese patents vs. all sample

	(1)	*(2)*
D (Indigenous R&D)	0.411***	0.222***
	[0.005]	[0.045]
D (Inward FDI)	−0.040***	−0.040***
	[0.005]	[0.005]
D (Outward FDI)	0.030	0.031
	[0.031]	[0.031]
D (Individual patentee)	−0.021***	−0.018***
	[0.004]	[0.004]
D (Individual patentee) * D (Indigenous R&D)		0.045
		[0.028]
D (NBO patentee)	0.091***	0.092***
	[0.003]	[0.003]
D (NBO patentee) * D (Indigenous R&D)		−0.027
		[0.045]
Log (Patentee's portfolio size)	−0.044***	−0.046***
	[0.000]	[0.000]
Log (Patentee's portfolio size) * D (Indigenous R&D)		0.092***
		[0.004]
Log (Patentee's age)	0.037***	0.041***
	[0.002]	[0.002]
Log (Patentee's age) * D (Indigenous R&D)		−0.053**
		[0.023]
Chi-squared (3) geographic origin	2464.1***	74.3***
Chi-squared (2) institutional type	800.8***	798.6***
Chi-squared (2) size and age	1549.4***	1598.3***
Chi-squared all patentee characteristics	1947.7***	2001.9***
Pseudo R-squared	0.107	0.109
Number of observations (number=1)	485,436 [229,005]	485,436 [229,005]

Notes: 1) Marginal effects and their robust standard errors are shown. 2) Significance at 1 percent ***, 5 percent **, and 10 percent *. 3) The equations control for a complete set of patent indicators in logs: family size, family value, forward citations after five years, technological classes, nonpatent literature references, number of claims, inventors, XY type backward citations, backward citations, PCT route (dummy), and divisional (dummy). See chapter 2 (this volume) for the measurement methodology of the controls based on patent indicators. In addition, the equations include priority year and technology dummies.
4) The variables' definitions are reported in Box 8.1 and Box 2.1.

Table 8.4 Probability of opposition conditional on grant Chinese patents vs. all sample

	1978–1999		2000–2007	
	(1)	(2)	(3)	(4)
D (Indigenous R&D)	-0.029**	-0.050	0.041***	0.046
	[0.010]	[0.016]	[0.008]	[0.070]
D (Inward FDI)	-0.036***	-0.036***	-0.007***	-0.006**
	[0.002]	[0.003]	[0.002]	[0.002]
D (Outward FDI)	-0.036	-0.036	-0.015	-0.015
	[0.014]	[0.014]	[0.007]	[0.007]
D (Individual patentee)	-0.022***	-0.022***	-0.014***	-0.014***
	[0.001]	[0.001]	[0.001]	[0.001]
D (NBO Patentee)	-0.002***	-0.002***	-0.001***	-0.001***
	[0.000]	[0.000]	[0.000]	[0.000]
Log (Patentee's portfolio size)		0.010		0.014***
		[0.007]		[0.002]
Log (Patentee's portfolio size) * D (Indigenous R&D)	0.003***	0.004***	0.004***	0.005***
	[0.001]	[0.001]	[0.001]	[0.001]
Log (Patentee's age)		0.020		-0.036**
		[0.043]		[0.016]
Log (Patentee's age) * D (Indigenous R&D)	-0.086***	-0.086***	-0.010***	-0.011***
	[0.003]	[0.003]	[0.003]	[0.003]

(Continued)

Table 8.4 (Continued)

| | 1978–1999 | | 2000–2007 | |
	(1)	(2)	(3)	(4)
Chi-squared (3) geographic origin	111.6***	81.4***	60.4**	9.3**
Chi-squared (2) institutional type	762.8***	758.6***	139.5***	133.0***
Chi-squared (2) size and age	257.3***	257.9***	39.3***	55.2***
Chi-squared all patentee characteristics	985.1***	963.9***	230.0***	383.1***
Pseudo R-squared	0.056	0.098	0.068	0.069
Number of observations (number=1)	775,888 (50,078)	775,888 (50,078)	325,684 (11,935)	325,684 (11,935)

Notes: 1) Marginal effects and their robust standard errors are shown. 2) Significance at 1 percent ***, 5 percent **, and 10 percent *. 3) The equations control for a complete set of patent indicators in logs: family size, family value, forward citations after five years, technological classes, nonpatent literature references, number of claims, inventors, XY type backward citations, backward citations, PCT route (dummy), and divisional (dummy). See chapter 2 (this volume) for the measurement methodology of the controls based on patent indicators. In addition, the equations include priority year and technology dummies. 4) The variables' definitions are reported in Box 8.1 and Box 2.1.

Table 8.5 Probability of renewal conditional on grant Chinese patents vs. all sample

	1980–1990		1991–1995		1996–2000	
	(1)	(2)	(3)	(4)	(5)	(6)
D (Indigenous R&D)	-0.036***	-0.033	-0.020**	-0.047	-0.023***	-0.131***
	[0.011]	[0.298]	[0.009]	[0.229]	[0.005]	[0.044]
D (Inward FDI)	-0.057***	-0.057***	-0.050***	-0.050***	-0.013***	-0.013***
	[0.004]	[0.004]	[0.003]	[0.003]	[0.002]	[0.002]
D (Outward FDI)	0.045	0.045	0.044**	0.044**	0.014	0.014
	[0.035]	[0.035]	[0.022]	[0.022]	[0.008]	[0.008]
D (Individual patentee)	-0.010***	-0.010***	-0.006***	-0.007***	-0.008***	-0.008***
	[0.001]	[0.001]	[0.001]	[0.001]	[0.001]	[0.001]
D (Individual patentee) * D (Indigenous R&D)		-0.026		0.055***		0.026**
		[0.029]		[0.021]		[0.013]
D (NBO patentee)	-0.002**	-0.002**	-0.002**	-0.002**	0.000	0.000
	[0.001]	[0.001]	[0.001]	[0.001]	[0.001]	[0.001]
D (NBO patentee) * D (Indigenous R&D)		0.002		0.075***		-0.007
		[0.035]		[0.029]		[0.016]
Log (Patentee's portfolio size)	0.000**	0.000**	0.001***	0.001***	0.000***	0.000***
	[0.000]	[0.000]	[0.000]	[0.000]	[0.000]	[0.000]
Log (Patentee's portfolio size) * D (Indigenous R&D)		-0.001		0.007		-0.005**
		[0.010]		[0.014]		[0.002]
Log (Patentee's age)	0.003***	0.003***	0.001	0.001	0.005***	0.005***
	[0.001]	[0.001]	[0.001]	[0.001]	[0.001]	[0.001]
Log (Patentee's age) * D (Indigenous R&D)		0.003		-0.006		0.042**
		[0.095]		[0.081]		[0.016]
Chi-squared (3) geographic origin	5.0***	29.4***	47.3***	45.1***	16.6***	12.9***
Chi-squared (2) institutional type	72.6***	72.0***	32.3***	33.0***	40.7***	41.8***
Chi-squared (2) size and age	16.9***	17.0***	97.9***	97.6***	40.1***	39.1***
Chi-squared all patentee characteristics	50.7***	33.2***	71.1***	49.0***	35.8***	26.5***
Std. error (adj. R-squared)	0.133	0.133	0.126	0.127	0.135	0.135
Number of observations	175,591	175,591	204,529	204,529	244,868	244,868

Notes: 1) Elasticities and their robust standard errors are shown. 2) Significance at 1 percent ***, 5 percent **, and 10 percent *. 3) The equations control for a complete set of patent indicators in logs: family size, family value, forward citations after five years, technological classes, nonpatent literature references, number of claims, inventors, XY type backward citations, backward citations, PCT route (dummy), and divisional (dummy). See chapter 2 (this volume) for the measurement methodology of the controls based on patent indicators. In addition, the equations include priority year and technology dummies. 4) The variables' definitions are reported in Box 8.1 and Box 2.1.

shown repeatedly to correlate with the economic value and importance of the patented invention.[21] Last, renewal decisions have been considered an objective and reliable measure of the central moments of the patent value distribution.[22]

The main explanatory variables for these equations are shown in Box 8.2, plus three dummies for Chinese patenting for each of the definitions adopted: indigenous inventions (Set 1), outward FDIs (Set 2), and inward FDIs (Set 3). I included two binary variables to identify whether the patentee is an individual or nonbusiness organization, considering business patentees as the excluded category. Then, the equations control for a complete set of patent indicators with respect to patent breadth and technology potential, prior art and background of the invention, and filing and procedural aspects of the patent (see discussion chapter 2, this volume).

For individuals or NBOs there is a negative probability of grant, opposition, and renewal decision. To interpret this evidence, it is worth recalling that these kind of patentees lack complementary assets in the market and hence their inventions are more abstract and general compared to the business patents (Henderson et al. 1998). Put differently, these inventions require further adaptations to become commercially viable, and compared to business patents, their time to market is much longer. Typically, the economic exploitation of these inventions takes place through technology licensing programs and/or technology acquisitions by business firms.

Experience and the size of the patentee's portfolio have a positive impact on granting and a negative one on supplementary search report. In this case, I think that the experience of these patentees makes them better at selection and drafting than inexperienced patentees and enables them to recognize which inventions can be successfully patented and which cannot. For renewals, patentee experience and patent portfolio size have a positive impact, a finding consistent with the claim that large firms have better access to other appropriability mechanisms—such as lead time, complementary assets, and secrecy—increasing the premium value of patents (see discussion in chapter 3, this volume). In terms of oppositions, size and experience produce an interesting twist, because the size of the patentee's portfolio has a negative impact, whereas its experience has a positive one. This is seen in the skewness of the patent value distribution: large patentees who file many patents have higher patent propensity (i.e., ratio of patents to R&D) and hence the average value of a given patent is lower (Hall and Ziedonis 2001). On the other hand, patents with higher commercial potential are those filed by serial innovators who also have more experience with the patent system (Hicks and Hedge 2005).

The findings on Chinese patenting depict a broader picture of the 'strategic patenting' hypothesis, and it would be well to take into consideration a few caveats. First, when foreign MNEs employ Chinese inventors (Inward FDIs), a negative impact on granting decisions can be noted. Before the year 2000, this category of patent applications had 30.6 percent less probability of being granted the patent than other categories whereas the granting probability dropped to about minus 8.1 percent after that year. Being a foreign MNE in China has a positive impact on the opposition decision and a negative one on renewals—although the effects are quite small (on the order of 1 percent). The impact on renewal decisions before the year 2000 was about 5 percent. These finding are consistent with previous studies that claimed that foreign firms in China perform lower potential R&D, which can yield on average more incremental innovations (Hu and Jefferson 2009) and thus less valuable patenting. However, this conclusion needs to be interpreted with caution. First, the patents by MNEs in China are relatively strong regarding the prior art, which counters the statement of hypothesis 2; in fact, on average, they receive fewer supplementary search reports from examiners. Second, the effects are relatively small (except for a grant decision), which might underline not only lower value of the underlying invention but also less valuable patent premium for foreign MNEs in China, particularly before the year 2000. Last, it is possible that some applicants deliberately seek a delay in processing their patent application because in this way they postpone payment of the associated fees and gain more time to understand the commercial potential of the technology they seek to patent. In some technological fields, it could be beneficial to delay the granting decision by several months in order to assess the commercial viability of their invention and monitor the evolution of the market and competition (Grodal and Thoma 2011). In summary, keeping in mind these caveats, hypothesis 1 on 'strategic patenting' for foreign MNEs employing Chinese inventors cannot be rejected.

For Chinese indigenous inventions, two different scenarios are in act regarding granting decisions before and after the year 2000. In the first period, there is a negative impact which is mediated neither by the institutional sector of the patentee nor by its size and patenting experience. After the year 2000, there was negative probability of grant for indigenous Chinese patent applications by individuals and NBOs. Put differently, the probability of grant is positive for business patentees, the excluded category; this observation is also corroborated by the positive impact of experience and size of the patentee. Thus, hypothesis 1 with respect to the granting decision is rejected for business patentees, whereas it is accepted for individuals and NBOs.

Regarding hypothesis 2 about the examiner's prior art search, indigenous Chinese patents have 41.1 percent probability of getting a supplementary search report, which can be associated to the lack of suitable research into prior art rather than to patentability issues related to subject matter. Indeed, the Chinese SIPO has been quite conservative on the patentability of software and business methods, and even chemical, pharmaceutical, and food and beverage inventions only became patentable in 1992 (Liang and Xue 2010). The lack of relevant prior art research is associated with individuals and business patentees, but not with NBOs. Also, the size and younger age of the patentee positively mediate the probability of getting a supplementary search report. Thus, hypothesis 2 is substantially confirmed.

There is also support for hypothesis 1 regarding opposition. In particular there was about 4.1 percent higher probability during the period 2001–2007 that a third party would request a post-grant review in the case of a Chinese indigenous patent. This is not a small percentage considering that an opposition action is costly for a third party (about €25 thousand (Graham and Harhoff 2006)). I cannot trace the effect of the patentee's institutional sector because no oppositions were received by NBOs and only one by individuals. However, the mediating effects of patentee size and patenting experience can be estimated, revealing that large and young patentees are targets for a higher number of oppositions. This is in line with the claim by Eberhardt et al. (2011) that the bulk of Chinese patenting is filed by recently founded firms in a few industries with very high patent propensity.

We think that the higher opposition rates for Chinese indigenous patenting is not related to higher patent value but to the opposite: lower patent quality. Third parties consider them more controversial because they lack suitable prior art research (that is, they receive more supplementary search reports by examiners). This claim is also corroborated by the renewal rates decisions. During priority years 1996–2000, Chinese indigenous patents had a shorter life cycle compared to other Chinese patents and patenting in general. Being a large and less experienced patentee has a negative impact on patent renewal decisions. Quite surprisingly, individuals and the non-business sector renew for a longer time period, a result that prompts the desire for further investigation into how these patents are exploited economically. To sum up, there is confirming evidence for hypothesis 1 with respect to renewal decisions for larger and younger patentees, but not for individuals and NBOs. In conclusion, regarding our two testable hypotheses, there seems to be no differential effect for the outward FDIs of Chinese MNEs inventing abroad.

8.6 Conclusions

This study has offered one of the first analyses in the literature of the determinants of the quality and value of Chinese patenting at the international level. It has discussed the implications of the 'strategic patenting' hypothesis, according to which companies file patents not to protect real products in the market but also for strategic reasons (Hall and Ziedonis 2001), and has drawn upon the related literature to develop two testable implications and then examined them using econometric analysis.

I developed a novel dataset based on the population of EPO and PCT filings, in such a way as to avoid potential selection issues, and propose a new taxonomy to account for the geographical location where the R&D invention process takes place and where R&D innovators come from. Two main groups of owners have been defined regarding Chinese inventions:

indigenous patenting by Chinese patentees relying on domestic inventors, and foreign MNEs off-shoring R&D in China, and therefore employing local inventors.

The econometric model has been used to attempt to trace how patentee geographic origin, institutional sector, and characteristics such as size and experience impact patent quality and value. The results obtained are generally consistent the 'strategic patenting' hypothesis for the two groups of patentees, with some caveats. On the one hand, except in granting decisions the effects for foreign MNEs are relatively small, particularly after the year 2000, and thus it would be wise to examine more carefully not only the estimation of the patent value of the invention but also of the premium value obtained from patent protection. These patents are also robust from the prior art point of view (less probability of getting a supplementary search report). Conversely, ample evidence confirms that Chinese indigenous patents are considered more controversial, and are targets of more oppositions, probably because of the lack of prior art research (obtaining a supplementary search report) rather than because it has a higher value. Indeed, a shorter renewal life cycle characterizes Chinese indigenous patents compared to other Chinese patents and patenting in general (the finding is particularly remarkable for the cohort 1996–2000). These effects are positively mediated by the patentee's size and experience, in this case, larger and younger patentees that are concentrated in a few industries with high patent propensity, which adds further evidence in favour of the 'strategic patenting' hypothesis.

Future research could advance in several directions. First of all, it is of high interest to understand how patents are used by firms, individual inventors, and NBOs. For firms, analyses of the impact on performance, in terms of total factor productivity, the firm's growth and profitability, and other factors could shed light on the returns of investing in R&D in China compared to other countries. On the other hand, the large share of patenting (and renewals) by individuals and NBOs demands further investigation into how these patents are exploited in licensing, commercialization, launching a new technology venture, etc.

A second direction of research regards the impact of regional dimension on patent value and quality. As discussed above, patenting is highly concentrated in a few Chinese regions. On the one hand, this depends on the preexistent industrial specialization of regions, which has given rise to industries with high R&D intensity and high patent propensity. On the other hand, local governments have implemented active policies to promote patenting at various levels, including financial and nonfinancial incentives. In this regard, it would be interesting to evaluate the impact of policy changes in patent fee compensation programs on patent quality and value.

Third, the finding that Chinese patents owned by businesses have shorter renewal life cycles calls for a careful analysis to distinguish the patent asset value from the patent premium one. In this direction, one could study how the different patterns of renewals of the same invention change in the different patenting systems—including China's SIPO—as a base for devising an indicator for patent premium value in China.

Notes

1 Recently, China's SIPO has announced initiatives under the aegis of the JEGPE to scrutinize and harmonize with the JPO and KIPO the procedures to be taken by patent examiners for the evaluation of the inventive steps in determining whether to grant a patent application. For more information see: https://www.jpo.go.jp/torikumi_e/kokusai_e/comparative_study.htm, last accessed January 2016.
2 My elaboration from OECD (2009) and other sources.
3 See for example http://www.wipo.int/export/sites/www/pct/en/texts/agreements/ag_cn.pdf last visited September 2012.
4 The reference date for the exchange rate RMB-EUR is July 1, 2010.
5 See chapter 4 (this volume) for an articulation of the meaning of patent quality vis-à-vis patent value.
6 See chapter 4 (this volume) for a detailed discussion on the topic.
7 Such as businesses, individuals, and nonbusiness organizations including universities, hospitals, government, and other private-nonprofit sectors.
8 For a wider presentation of these kind of indices see chapter 6 (this volume).
9 There are significant incentives for individual inventors who file patents (Economist, October 14, 2010). Patents are used in public and private companies as evaluation indicators deciding on promotions and career enhancements. Also, the education system in China takes into the account patenting during the admission and grading process of students. Patents allow individuals to obtain fiscal bonuses from the government and ease some bureaucratic obligations, for example in obtaining a resident permit in a large and more modern urban area.
10 See for example http://www.oecd-ilibrary.org/science-and-technology/the-oecd-technology-concordance-otc_521138670407, last visited September, 2012.
11 The Chinese R&D effort is quite comparable even with some developed economies and puts the Chinese economy as the R&D leader among the low-income countries (OECD 2010).
12 In addition large patenting companies could obtain significant discounts on the profit tax and improve their likelihood to be selected in public procurement tenders.
13 In developing the hypothesis on patent quality, this study also draws upon anecdotal information about the development of the labour market for patent agents and examiners, from primary sources. Indeed, to the best of our knowledge, no previous studies have scrutinized the determinants of patent quality with respect to Chinese patenting.
14 Estimates from China IP (March 6, 2011) that elaborates on statistics from China Patent Agent Association (http://www.acpaa.cn/englishnew/content.asp?id=181) document that in 2009 there were active about 6,022 patent agents in China and about 976 thousand applications were filed at SIPO. This means that each agent took about 162.1 documents on an annual basis and had to draft one patent every 2.3 days.
15 See the analysis advanced in chapter 6 (this volume).
16 In conclusion, it is worth mentioning that in this study, the comparison group used for scrutinizing the testable hypotheses is not limited to a specific subset of patents, originating from some countries, technology fields, time periods, or other criteria for two reasons. First, I sought to avoid any selection bias that could be present in a reduced sample dataset, even for a random choice sample

setting. Second, comparison of our focal group of patents to an average benchmark should help us draw some conclusions on the patenting strategies of the patent owners, in terms of their institutional characteristics (whether they are businesses, individuals, or nonbusiness organizations, including universities, hospitals, government, and other private-nonprofit sectors), their size, and their previous experience in patenting.

17 I relied on the Penn Tables dataset to obtain data on a GDP of a covered country (see http://pwt.econ.upenn.edu, last accessed September 9, 2012).

18 See discussion on these reforms presented in chapter 7 (this volume).

19 To explore the technological specialization of Chinese patenting, I rely on the (Normalized) Revealed Technological Advantage Index (RTA). The RTA index was originally defined as: $RTA_{ij} = (n_{ij}/\sum_i n_{ij})/(\sum_j n_{ij}/\sum_i \sum_j n_{ij})$ where n_{ij} is the count number of the patents of the country i in the technological field j. This definition generates an index that takes the values between zero and infinity with an average of one. As has been shown, the scaling of this index can be improved by taking the normalized formulation (Grupp 1994). In particular I have: *Normalised RTA = (RTA–1)/(RTA+1)*. This formulation makes the *RTA* change in the unitary interval and has the advantage of attributing to negative variations the same weight as the positive ones.

20 This finding should be interpreted attentively, and at least two caveats are called for. First of all, in this study I am considering only international patenting and not domestic filings. Patenting in some technological fields could be less internationalized because of the presence of a large internal market, such as in agriculture, food industry, and construction. On the other hand, in some fields internationalization could be limited because of government regulations, as in space and military technologies. Thus, it could be expected that an analysis based on domestic filings could reveal a different picture.

21 See discussion in chapter 2 (this volume).

22 See discussion in chapter 3 (this volume).

References

Amighini A., R. Rabellotti, M. Sanfilippo 2010. "Outward FDI from Developing Country MNEs as a Channel for Technological Catch-Up." *Seoul J Econ* 23(2):239–261.

China IP 2011. "Who Is Making Junk Patents?" March 6.

Crescenzi R., A. Rodríguez-Pose, M. Storper 2012. "The Territorial Dynamics of Innovation in China and India." IMDEA Working Papers Series 2012/09. Instituto Madrileño de Estudios Avanzados (IMDEA) Ciencias Sociales, Madrid.

Eberhardt M., C. Helmers, Z. Yu 2011. "Is the Dragon Learning to Fly? An Analysis of the Chinese Patent Explosion." University of Oxford CSAE Working Paper 2011/15. Department of Economics, University of Oxford, Oxford.

The Economist 2010. "Patents, Yes; Ideas, Maybe. Chinese Firms Are Filing Lots of Patents. How Many Represent Good Ideas?" October 14.

Eun J.-H., K. Lee, G. Wu 2006. "Explaining the 'University-run enterprises' in China: A Theoretical Framework for University-Industry Relationship in Developing Countries and its Application to China." *Res Pol* 35(9):1329–1346.

Ginarte J. C., W. G. Park 1997. "Determinants of Patent Rights: A Cross-national Study." *Res Pol* 26(3):283–301.

Goldberg I., L. Branstetter, J. G. Goddard, S. Kuriakos 2008. "Globalization and Technology Absorption in Europe and Central Asia the Role of Trade, FDI, and Cross-border Knowledge Flow." World Bank Working Paper No. 150. The World Bank Publishing, Washington DC.

Graham S. J. H., D. Harhoff 2006. "Can Post-Grant Reviews Improve Patent System Design? A Twin Study of US and European Patents." CEPR Discussion Papers No. 5680. Center for Economic and Policy Research, London.

Grodal S., G. Thoma 2011. "Institutional Logics and Status: Strategic Patenting in the Legal Service Sector." Paper presented at the DRUID Conference, Copenhagen, Denmark, June 15–17.

Grupp H. 1994. "The Measurement of Technical Performance of Innovations by Technometrics and Its Impact on Established Technology Indicators." *Res Pol* 23:175–193.

Hall B. H. 2005. "Exploring the Patent Explosion." *J Techno Transfer* 30:35–48.

Hall B. H., R. Ziedonis 2001. "The Determinants of Patenting in the U.S. Semiconductor Industry, 1980–1994." *Rand J Econ* 32:101–128.

Harhoff D., M. Reitzig 2004. "Determinants of Oppositions Against EPO Patent Grants: The Case of Biotechnology and Pharmaceuticals." *Int J Ind Organ* 22(4):443–480.

Harhoff D., S. Wagner 2009. "Modelling the Duration of Patent Examination at the European Patent Office." *Manag Science* 55(12):1969–1984.

Henderson R., A. Jaffe, M. Trajtenberg 1998. "Universities as a Source of Commercial Technology: A Detailed Analysis of University Patenting, 1965–1988." *Rev Econ Stat* LXXX(1):119–127.

Hicks D. M., D. Hegde 2005. "Highly Innovative Small Firms in the Markets for Technology." *Res Pol* 34(5):703–716.

Hu G. A. 2010. "Propensity to Patent, Competition and China's Foreign Patenting Surge." *Res Pol* 39:985–993.

Hu G. A., G. Jefferson 2009. "A Great Wall of Patents: What Is Behind China's Recent Patent Explosion?" *J Dev Econ* 90(1):57–68.

Hu M. C., J. A. Mathews 2008. "China's National Innovative Capacity." *Res Pol* 37(9):1465–1479.

Jegpe 2010. "Comparative Study Report on Inventive Step, published by the Joint Experts Group for Patent Examination between JPO, KIPO, and SIPO." Accessed July 30, 2012, http://www.jpo.go.jp/torikumi/kokusai/kokusai3/pdf/nicyukan_hikakuken/jegpe_comparative_study.pdf

Liang Z., L. Xue 2010. "The Evolution of China's IPR System and Its Impact on the Patenting Behaviors and Strategies of Multinationals in China." *Int J Techno Manag* 51(2–4):469–496.

Martinez C. 2010. "Insight into Different Types of Patent Families." OECD Science, Technology and Industry Working Papers 2010/2, OECD, Paris.

OECD 2009. *OECD Patent Statistics Manual.* Paris: OECD.

OECD 2010. *Territorial Reviews: Guangdong, China 2010.* Paris: OECD.

OST 2008. *Science and Technology Indicators.* Paris, France: Observatoire des Sciences et des Techniques.

Papageorgiadis N. P., A. R. Cross, C. Alexiou 2014. "International Patent Systems Strength, 1998–2011." *J World Bus* 49:586–597.

Park W. G. 2008. "International Patent Protection, 1960–2005." *Res Pol* 37(4): 761–766.

PatStat 2012. *EPO Worldwide Patent Statistical Database and the EPO Patent Register,* April edition. Vienna: EPO.

Thoma G., S. Torrisi, A. Gambardella, D. Guellec, B. H. Hall, D. Harhoff 2010. "Harmonizing and Combining Large Datasets—An Application to Firm-Level Patent and Accounting Data." NBER Working Paper No. 15851, National Bureau of Economic Research, Inc., Cambridge (MA).

Von Graevenitz G. 2009. "The Impact of Recessions on the Utilization of Intellectual Property, Paper presented at the OECD Workshop on Trademarks and Trademark Data," OECD, Paris, July 17.

Wright B., S. Cao, Z. Lei 2011. "Utility Models vs Invention Patents: Why File Utility Models for Good Inventions in China?" Working Paper, University of California, Berkeley.

Wright B., Z. Lei 2011. "Patenting Subsidy and Patent Filing's in China." Working Paper, University of California, Berkeley.

Conclusion

Patent Valuation from the Decision Maker's Perspective

Grid Thoma

The present section articulates some implications for the decision-making process spurring from the valuation approaches analysed in this book. Beforehand, it is worth mentioning that the analysis has regarded two main valuation approaches according to the type of results generated, monetary versus nonmonetary. Chapter 1 introduced three traditional approaches for the monetary valuation of patent assets: cost-based approaches concerning the appraisal of the investments required to obtain an asset, market-based approaches relying on value benchmarks obtained from direct or similar market transactions of the asset, and revenue-based approaches consisting on the estimation of future cash-flows generated by the asset.

Each of these approaches has its own merits and drawbacks, and several critical factors have been discussed regarding their practical implementation. The very unique and intrinsic characteristics of intellectual property posit challenges regarding the comparability of the valuation attempts across different patent assets and for the same asset in relation to the time when the valuation is made. Second, there is the complementarity in use because technologies covered by patents yield positive effects when they are used together with other technologies, which could question the objectivity of the valuation of a single patent asset. Third, decision makers face several issues related to patent asset obsolescence because rarely is the valuation performed for an existing brand-new asset. The obsolescence could manifest from different points of view (technical, functional, and economic), and hence the chosen valuation approach has to take into the account also specific characteristics of the technologies covered by the patents (e.g., complex versus discrete technologies). Further, the implementation of the valuation approach could be hampered by the lack of information and uncertainty about salient aspects on which the valuation is based.

Some of these drawbacks are less severe when the decision maker proceeds with the stock market valuation of patent assets based on the Tobin's q equation, which builds upon a particular combination of the revenue and market-based approaches. Assuming that capital markets are efficient in taking into the account all the relevant information needed to assess firm's market prices, the estimated impact of R&D and patents on the firm's market value incorporates the discounted future cash flows obtainable by the firm's assets. The Tobin's q model yields indirect estimates—typically known as shadow value—of the impact of R&D and patents on the market value of the firm, because it relies on the pricing of the firm's component assets by the mean of the market prices for its stock shares.

Recently scholars have proposed the real option approach for patent valuation, which can be seen as an advancement of the traditional methods. The goal of patent real options is to establish the additional value arising when complementary investment for the successful exploitation of the patent can be delayed. Typically the direct implementation of this approach is more information demanding because it requires the completion of the other approaches as well. The potential benefits of the patent are assessed with the revenue approach, whilst the investment needed for the patent exploitation is appraised with the cost approach. The real option approach for patent valuation has the merit that it can be reconciled with the market value model based on the Tobin's q equation, which is forward looking and is not hampered by problems of the timing of costs and revenues.

Chapter 1 and chapter 7 presented extensive empirical evidences about the market value of R&D and patents with respect to several geographical contexts and multiple patent issuing authorities. Chapter 1 introduced a new methodology to disentangle the market valuation of the stocks of granted patents versus patent applications, whereas chapter 7's market value regressions have taken into the account the geographical distribution of a firm's inventive activities. The econometric analyses confirmed the validity of the measurement approaches across various datasets, and the productivity estimates based on the production function framework supported the results of the Tobin's q model. Furthermore, chapter 1 showed that the real option capability of the firm with respect to the patent activities impacts significantly the market valuation above and beyond the effects of R&D investment and the private value of inventive activities.

Whereas the stock market value approach constitutes an indirect or implicit valuation of innovation activities, a direct valuation of patents can be advanced by the means of direct survey information or patent renewal decisions. In spite of the high cost of data collection, surveys can provide more precise estimates of the patent asset value as compared to the market value approaches. Chapter 2 discussed how survey information could be combined with bibliographic patent information to obtain value estimates allowing to draw inferences on the validity of patent indicators with respect to the overall population of patents. One of the drawbacks of this approach is represented by the limited replicability of the survey information for different patent cohorts and patents with different number of years remaining before the expiration.

Chapter 3 presented estimates of the patent premium value relying on the renewal fee decisions of patent maintenance: to keep a patent alive, a patentee needs to pay fees, and typically not all patents are brought till the end of their statutory life. Then, the fee cost structure could be considered as lower bound revenue that the patent can ensure to the owner. Nevertheless, the valuations based on patent renewal decisions generate estimates about the central moments of the patent value distribution and not its upper tail, which is of particular interest given the high skewness of the successful outcomes of the inventive activities. Another limitation is represented by the fact that the renewal fee decisions can be adopted in large extent for prospective historical patent valuations.

When the implementation of monetary approaches is limited or not applicable at all, the decision maker could rely on patent bibliographic information to generate timely indicators for the valuation of the innovation activities. The analysis advanced in this book has distinguished two main groups of patent indicators according to their dimensionality. On the one hand, there are the one-dimensional indicators regarding filing and procedural aspects of a patent, such as the probability of grant, refusal, supplementary search report, fractional patent application, opposition of a patent, and others. Generally these indicators are available not far distant after the filing date of a patent application, and they can deal also with the uncertainty related to the patented technology.

The supplementary search report is significantly correlated with the patent asset value, and its impact is comparable to other indicators more frequently used in the literature (chapter 2). Chapter 3 showed that the premium protection value of patents is significantly higher for divisional patents and when the patent has been targeted by an opposition action, which in turn affects also the patent asset value. The probability of grant, supplementary search report, and opposition have been fully analysed in chapter 4 and chapter 8, revealing that demographic characteristics of the patentee do affect significantly the positive outcomes of these indicators. The citation probability has been scrutinized in chapter 6 in function of several characteristics of patentee and the team of inventors who are involved in the R&D process. Furthermore, mediating effects defined at the macro level—such as the strength of the national legislation on patent protection and other national and regional level conditions—have been found to play a significant role as determinants of the probability of being cited.

The second group of patent indicators is defined according to their multidimensionality. Chapter 1 analysed the impact on firm's Tobin's q of the patent family value index that looks at the breadth of the patent family—that is, the extent of countries where the patent protection has been sought. This index gauges the potential market size of an invention, and it is constructed by summing up the real GDP of the countries covered by the patent family, normalized to that of the United States, with the US GDP set to unity.

The patent family maintenance value index enhances this index along a secondary dimension—that is, the time of maintenance of a patent in the countries where the patent has been granted. In particular this index is computed by taking into the account the renewal fee decisions for the jurisdiction(s) where the patent entered in force. Then, the years of maintenance of a patent are weighted by the GDP of the country of protection, which in turn varies as well over time in addition to the cross-section geographical dimension. The family maintenance value index can be more indicative of the expected future profitability of the patent than the former index, because it is characterized by a higher statistical power due to the bigger dispersion. Chapter 2 showed that the family maintenance value index is significantly correlated with the patent asset value above and beyond the family size and family value index.

Patent citations can be used to build up multidimensional indicators such as the generality index, which is a quadratic dispersion measure (the inverse of the Herfindhal index) of the received citations from other patents over their technology classes. This index is particularly suitable to assess patent valuation according to the different uses that a patented technology could encounter during its life cycle. Chapter 3 demonstrated that the generality index is significantly correlated with the premium protection value of patents above and beyond the total number of forward citations and other indicators, although its first-order statistical term does not have an additional impact on patent asset value (chapter 2). The analysis presented in chapter 5 regarding the historical evolution of a quintessential example of a General Purpose Technology (GPT) revealed that the generality index based on patent citations is highly predictive of the ubiquitous use of the underlying technology in various industries. Nevertheless, the financial analysis of the specialized GPT provider showed that the break-even point of the innovator is reached only in the long run, a finding that corroborates the evidences of chapter 2 regarding patent asset valuations.

The statistical power of the patent indicators can be substantially increased by aggregating several indicators and analyzing their correlation structure. Chapter 2 deviced a novel composite value index, combining twenty different uni-dimensional indicators according to several features of a patent with respect to patent breadth and technology potential, prior art and background of the invention, and filing and procedural aspects of a patent. A novel selection approach of patent indicators and their validation with market value of patents has been advanced, whereas the computation of the composite value index was done with the factor analysis. The econometric analysis showed that the proposed composite value index can effectively summarize the information conveyed by every single indicator, because the reduction of the goodness-of-fit of the market value model is very limited as compared to the case of the indicators taken separately.

Finally, the structure of patent indicators is greatly improved by taking into the account other IP strategies pursued by the innovator beyond patenting. Chapter 3 elaborates a novel method to gauge combinations of IP strategies regarding the same innovative project, when the patentee pairs the patenting strategy with trademarks and design patents. This method is based on the joint analysis of the content of legal documents using textual matching algorithms. The econometric evidences revealed that a pairing strategy based on the combination of patents and trademarks doubles the premium value of patent protection, whereas design patents do not further increase patent valuations. The results hold after controlling for several patentee demographic characteristics and patent indicators, such as those used in chapter 2. These findings are consistent with the assumption that combined IP strategies based patent and trademark pairs constitute a signaling device in the hands of the innovator regarding the future profitability of the underlying patent asset from a commercial point of view.

Index

Note: Page numbers in *italics* indicate figures and tables.

adoption of new technology: benefits and costs of 153–4, 171–2; information, uncertainty, and 155; network effects 154–5, 172
Allen-Bradley 163–4
Apple iPhone 65–6

backward citations 43, 95n15, 107; *see also* examiner citations; inventor citations; XY type backward citations
Bacnet 164–5
'bandwagon' strategy 169
Bilski, Bernard 146n2
Black and Scholes method 18
building automation and LonWorks 162–3, 165–6
business groups 249n7, *21*, *218*
business methods, patenting of 100–1, 103; *see also* financial patents

call options, patent real options modeled as 18–19
capital market efficiency and market value approach 11–12
Chinese innovation system 260
Chinese patenting: dataset and measures 258–61; descriptive statistics *262*; determinants of value and quality of 266, 272–4; overview 252–5, 274–6; previous literature and hypotheses 255–8; technological specialization of 266; trends in *263*, 263–5, *264*; types of patentees 258–60, 272
citations: accumulation of, over time 187–8; backward 43, 95n15, 107 (*see also* examiner citations; inventor citations; XY type backward

citations); financial patents and 117, 122; forward 19–20; inventor-added 196–7; localization patterns of 183–4, 186; as patent indicators 4, 9–10, 45, 78–83; 283; patent valuation and 19–20, 49, 52, 84; return on value of 43; *see also* knowledge spillovers
combined IP strategies: case study 69–71; data and variables 73–6; descriptive statistics of trademark dataset *94*; determinants of patent premium value 76–7, 78–83, 84–6, *86*; limitations of study 90–1; overview 63–5, 90–1, 283–4; patent premium value 71–2; robustness analysis 86–7; theoretical background 65–9
composite value index of patent indicators: aggregation of 52–3, *54*, *55*; data and variables 44–7; overview 42–3, 48–9, 55–7, 283; robustness analysis 53, *55*, *56*; selection and validation of indicators 49, *50–1*, *52*
control industry, emergence of technological paradigm in 155–8
Cooperative Patent Classification 212n18
cost-based patent valuation approaches 14–15, 280
costs: of adoption of new technology 154; of obtaining standard patents 24, 253; replacement and reproduction 14–15; social, of patent system 103
Courts of Appeals for the Federal Circuit (CAFC) and financial patents 100, 116

decision lags for financial patents 105–6, 125, 127
decision trees 18–19
design patents 75, 85
diffusion: factors affecting *170*, 170–3; of GPT 153–5; Schumpeterian distinction between invention, innovation, and 152
direct survey estimates 43
discounted cash flow method 17
divisional applications 95n16–96n16
DOCDB patent families 211n9
domestic inventors 216
downstream integration and technology commercialization 167–9, 172

Echelon Corporation 151, 156, 157, 160; *see also* LonWorks control technology
Enel 167–9
enforceability of financial patents, uncertainty of 105
entrepreneurial finance literature 66–7
EPO *see* European Patent Office
EURO-PCT procedure 23, 24
Europe: knowledge spillovers in 194, *195*, 196; market value approach results in 28, *29*, 30, *31–3*, 34–5; R&D expenditures in 12–14; *see also* European Patent Office
European Patent Convention (EPC) 68; *see also* European Patent Office
European Patent Office (EPO): applications 20, 23; cost of patents 24; examination process for financial patents 106–7, 122–3; financial patent grant rate *123*; financial patent opposition rate *124*; financial patents *112*, *144*, *145*; opposition system 106; selection of financial patents 109–10, 134–7, *135*, *136*, *137*; software, business methods, and 100; unitary patents 38n15; validity challenges and 100–1; Worldwide Patent Database 44
examination process for financial patents 106–7, 122–3, *123*, *124*
examiner citations 183–4, 84, 95n5, 95n15, 20, 57n2, 78–83
external financing, patents used for 63, 66

factor models 52–3
family of patents: definition 189; kinds of 211n9; size of 4–5, 20–1, 34

FieldBus 156, 161
financial patents: aggregate trends by priority year at EPO and USPTO *112*; background and hypotheses 103–9; challenges to 107–9; characteristics of patentees 132; comparison to other patents 117, *120–1*, 122, 131–2; by country and sector of patentee *114–15*; data and variables 109–11; determinants of outcomes for 124–5, 127, 130–1; ECLA classes with *138–41*; EPO *112*, *144*, *145*; identification of 109; IPC classes and 122; opposition to 106, 107–9, 123–4, *124*, 130–1, 132; overview 100–3, 131–3; probability of granting 105–6, 124–5, *126*, 127, *128–9*, 130, 132; selection of, at EPO 109–10, 134–7, *135*, *136*, *137*; time evolution of *142*, *143*, *145*; top patentees and portfolio composition *118–19*; trends and descriptive statistics 111, 113, 115–17, 122–6; USPTO *112*
financial systems, innovation in 99, 103–4
firm characteristics: controls for 75–6, *94*, *110–11*, *261–2*; for Chinese patenting 256–7
foreign direct investment (FDI) in China 255–6, 265
foreign inventors 216
forward citations 19–20, 45, 49, 77, 86, 107, *120–1*, *126*, 160, 187
Frascati Manual definitions 231

generality index 160, 283, 45–6, 81–3
generalized method of moments (GMM) 239–40, 243, *246*, 247
General Purpose Technology (GPT): defined 99; factors affecting diffusion of 153–5; financial viability and sustainability of 174; profitability and 169; *see also* commercialization of GPT; financial patents
geographical spatial distance and knowledge spillovers: in Europe 194; inventor-added citations 197; localization of knowledge spillovers and 182; measurement of 190; in North America 204; overview 205–6; R&D and 184–5; theoretical background 183–7
Giesecke & Devrient 131

globalization of R&D *see* inventor location and globalization of R&D
GMM (generalized method of moments) 239–40, 243, *246*, 247
GPT *see* General Purpose Technology

home automation and LonWorks 162, 167

incremental revenue analysis 17
industrial automation and LonWorks 163–4
innovation, distinction between invention, diffusion, and 152
innovative activities: geographical concentration of 181; localization of 184–5; novel timely indicators of 55–6; valuation of 6–14
INPADOC patent families 189
in re Bilski 100
intangible assets 3–4, *4*, 11
intellectual property legislation: in China 252–3; knowledge spillovers and 182; strength of patent protection in 186, 190–1, 199, 206
internationalization of R&D *see* inventor location and globalization of R&D
Internet economy and growth of inventor workforce 221
invention, distinction between innovation, diffusion, and 152
inventor citations 20, 57n2, 183–4, 196–7, *198*, 199, *202–3*
inventor counts and R&D growth 75–6, 234–5
inventor location and globalization of R&D: correlation of inventor counts and R&D expenditures *234–5*; country and technology trends 222–3, *224–6*, *227–8*, *229–30*, 231; dataset 217–19; descriptive statistics 232–5, *233*; inventor workforce data 219–22, *220*, *222*; market valuation 238–9, 243, 247; methods and approach 216–17; overview 215–16, 247–8; production function approach 239–40, 243, 247; results 231–5, *236*, 237–8

Japan: inventor workforce in *220*, 220–1; market value approach results in 28, *29*, 30, *31–3*, 34–5

Japanese Patent Office (JPO) 20, 23, 24, 252–3

knowledge flow production function 185–6, 191–2
knowledge production function 6–7, 239–40; *see also* production function estimations
knowledge spillovers: border effect 199, *200–1*; citations as measure of 181–2, 205; dataset 189–90; descriptive statistics *209–10*; econometric specification 191–4; in Europe *195*, 196; inventor-added citations 196–7, *198*, 199, *202–3*; localization of 181–3, 205–6; methods 187–9; in North America 199, *202–3*, 204–5; results 194, 196–7, 199, 204–5; strength of patent protection 190–1; territorial border effect 199, *207–9*; theories and hypotheses 183–7
Korean Intellectual Property Office (KIPO) 253

legal protection of financial innovations 103–4
legal services market in China 257–8
licensing technology 164–5, 169, 174
linear models of market valuation and Tobin's q 10–14
localization of knowledge spillovers *see* knowledge spillovers
LonBus 156, 158; *see also* LonWorks control technology
LonWorks control technology: commercialization strategies 161–8; discussion of commercialization strategies 168–70; early adopters 161–2; factors affecting diffusion *170*, 170–2; overview 151, 157, 174; patenting strategies *159*, 159–60
L'Oreal Corporation, AMINEXIL product 70–1

market-based patent valuation approaches 15–16, 280
markets for technology 152–3
market value approach: baseline model 8–9; econometric specification and variables 24–8; empirical studies 9–14; linear models 10–14; nonlinear models 9–10; overview 7–8, 35–6; patent strategies 23–4; R&D and 3–6; R&D location 238–9, 240,

241, 242, 243, 247, 248; results 28, 29, 30, 34–5; sample 21–3; setting and variables 21, 22–8; Tobin's *q* as dependent variable *31–3*
Markkula, Mike 156, 158, 163
multinational enterprises (MNEs), and Chinese patenting 254, 259, 263–4, 265, 272–3
multiple indicators model 53

network externalities and financial services 104
networking effects 154–5, 172
nonlinear models of valuation 9–10

obsolescence of patent assets 15; *see also* perpetual inventory method
OEM (original equipment manufacturer) firms 155
open standard and LonWorks 164–5, 169, 172
opposition: in China 272, 274; EPO and 106; to financial patents 106, 107–9, 123–4, *124*, 130–1, 132; to patents 42–3, 45–6, 55, 56–7
original equipment manufacturer (OEM) firms 155
Oshman, Kenneth 158
outsourcing R&D activities 237–8

patent and trademark pairs (PTPs): case study 69–71; computation method 64; data and variables 73–6; findings 64–5; IP strategies articulated through 67; overview 63; signaling strategy and 84–5; strength of signaling of 68–9, 70–1, 85–6; textual similarity index 92
patent applications: divisional 95n16–96n16; outcomes of 147n21; at patent offices 20, 23; public subsidies for fees 257; *see also* PCT applications
patent asset value 43–4, 47–8
patent citations *see* citations
Patent Cooperation Treaty (PCT) 6, 23, 24, 68, 252; *see also* PCT applications
patent coverage, strengthening of 99–100
patent family maintenance value index 47, 56, 266, 282–3
patent family value index 30, 34, 282
patent indicators: detrending, for time and technology effects 47–8; dimensionality of 282; patent

asset value and 43–4; statistical power of 283; structure of 283–4; unidimensional 45–6, 53; valuation with 19–21; *see also* citations; composite value index of patent indicators
patent premium value: determinants of 76–7, *78–9, 80, 81–3, 86*; overview 71–2, 281–2
patent quality: in China 257–8, 261, 266, 272, 274, 275; economic value and 49, *45–6*, 84, 102–7; measures of 107
patent real options 17–19, 34–5, 247
patent stocks 26, 34–5; *see also* perpetual inventory method
patent system, social benefits and costs of 103
patent valuation approaches: in China 266, 267, 268, *269–70*, 271, 272–4; cost-based 14–15; decision-making process and 280–4; with indicators 19–21; market-based 15–16; real options 17–19, 281; revenue-based 16–17
payment systems, innovation in 99
PCT (Patent Cooperation Treaty) 6, 23, 24, 68, 252
PCT applications 24, 26–8, 34–5, 52
perpetual inventory method 26, 239
principal component analysis 53
prior art: in Chinese patenting 258–9, 273–4; on financial methods 20, *45–6*, 49, 84, 105, 107, 117
probability of granting financial patents 105–6, 124–5, *126*, 127, *128–9*, 130, 132
production function estimations: globalization of R&D 239–40, 248; R&D location 243, *244–5, 246*, 247
productivity: patenting 30; total factor productivity 6–7
promotion activity for LonWorks 165
protection of patents, strength of 186, 190–1, 199, 206
PTPs *see* patent and trademark pairs
public subsidies for application fees 257

R&D *see* research and development
R&D accounting regressions 236
R&D push hypothesis 256
R&D stocks 6, 26, 240, 243; *see also* perpetual inventory method
real options 17–19, 34–5, 247; *see also* patent real options

renewal decisions: in China 273, 274; optimal patent maintenance 71; patents 42–3, 46–7, 55, 56–7, 272; trademarks 86–7, *88–9*

renewal fees 71, 72

replacement costs 14–15

reproduction costs 14–15

research and development (R&D): in China 255; expenditures on 12–14, 22–3, 217–19; market value of 3–6; profitability and 169; top performers *218*; *see also* inventor location and globalization of R&D

residual value analysis 17

revenue-based patent valuation approaches 16–17

ROLM 158

Schumpeterian distinction between invention, innovation, and diffusion 152

signaling strategy 64–5, 70–1, 84–5

signaling strength 68–9, 85–6

SIPO (State Intellectual Property Office) of China 252–3, 258

SIs (system integrators) 155, 163, 165, 166, 170

social benefits and costs of patent system 103

software, patenting of 100–1, 103

specialized technological firms 152–3

standardization, demands for, and financial services 104

State Intellectual Property Office (SIPO) of China 252–3, 258

State Street v. Signature Financial 100, 105, 111, 116

strength of patent protection 186, 190–1, 199, 206

strict equivalent patent families 211n9

substitution, principle of 14

survey information 47

system integrators (SIs) 155, 163, 165, 166, 170

technical imbalances 156

technological effects and patent asset value 47–8

technology catch-up model 265

territorial borders and knowledge spillovers: in Europe 196; localization of knowledge spillovers and 182, 185–6, 199, *200–1*; in North America 204–5; overview 205–6; structure of territorial units *207–8*; TL2 regions 189–90; TL3 regions 190

textual similarity index 92

time effects and patent asset value 47–8

titles of patents, words of 74

Tobin's *q*: in decision-making process 280–1; defined 8; as dependent variable 25, *31–3*; market value approach to R&D location *241, 242*; of patent family value index 282; stock market valuation and 16

total factor productivity 6–7, 239–40, 243–7

trademark indicators 65, 93

trademarks: data on 73–4; patent valuation and 85; renewal decisions 86–7, *88–9*; valuation of 65–6

trade secrets 103

TSP International Econometric Toolbox 237

United States, market value approach results in 28, *29, 30, 31–3*, 34–5; inventor counts and R&D expenditures correlations 234–5; knowledge spillover analysis 199–205; R&D accounting regressions 236

US Patent and Trademark Office (USPTO): applications 20, 23; Business Patent Initiative 113; CASE file of trademark procedural information 73; cost of patent 24; financial patents in 101, *112*; Manual of Acceptable Identifications of Goods and Services 74; SGML files of the Cassis trademark database 73; validity challenges and 100

utility services and LonWorks 167–8

validity challenges, post-grant 100–1

venture capital and trademarks 66

weighted average cost of capital 17

wordmarks 74, 87

WTO (World Trade Organization), and China 252, 260

XY type backward citations *45*, 49–50, 53–5, 57n2, 79, 82, 84, 86, 95n5, 95n15, 107–9, 111, 117, 120, 125, 126, 127, 130, 132